Simplified Swahili

ACKNOWLEDGEMENTS

I would like to express my thanks to: ——
Mr Horace Mason, O.B.E. *who was my original Swahili tutor in
1958 and also to Professor Whiteley, University of London,
Professor E. Polomé, Department of Linguistics, University of
Texas, Dr W. A. A. Wilson, Translations Consultant for the United
Bible Societies, and the Hon. Hussein O. Mongi, for their valued
advice, suggestions and assistance in draft reading, without whose
help it would not have been possible to complete this book.*

P.M.W.

Simplified Swahili

Peter Wilson

LONGMAN

Pearson Education Limited
Edinburgh Gate, Harlow,
Essex CM20 2JE, England
and Associated Companies throughout the world.

First published 1970
New edition 1985
20 19 18 17 16 15 14 13 12
IMP 36 35 34 33 32 31 30 29 28 27
Set in Sabon

Printed in Malaysia, KHL

ISBN 978-0-582-62358-3

Contents

Introduction   vii

1   Pronunciation   1
2   Greetings   3
3   Verbs—1: The Infinitive   6
4   Verbs—2: Imperatives (Direct, Negative and Polite)   8
5   Nouns—1: M- WA- Class   14
6   Subject Prefixes   17
7   Present Verb Tense (-NA-)   18
8   Nouns—2: M- MI- Class   20
9   Adjectives—1 (Consonant stem)   23
10 Demonstratives   25
11 Locations (Where?) and Responses   28
12 Past Simple Tense (-LI-)   33
13 Nouns—3: KI- VI- Class   35
14 Adjectives—2 (Vowel stem)   40
15 Adjectives—3 (Arabic)   43
16 Adverbs—1   45
17 Verbs—3: Passive Verbs (-W-)   46
18 Personal Pronouns   49
19 'To Be'—Present Tense   51
20 'To Have'—1 (and 'There is' etc.)   53
21 Numerals—1 (1–20)   56
22 Future Tense (-TA-)   57
23 Days of the Week   59
24 Indeclinable Words—1 (Prepositions and Conjunctions)   60
25 Verbs—4: Stative verbs (-K-)   63
26 Past Perfect Tense (-ME-)   66
27 'To Have'—2 (Other tenses)   70
28 Adverbs—2   72
29 Possessives   74
30 Questions   77
31 Verbs—5: The Causative (-SH/Z-)   80
32 Negative Tenses (Prefixes, present, future and past)   84
33 Nouns—4: N Class   91
34 Useful Expressions   96
35 Numerals—2: (20 and over, fractions, etc.)   101
36 Time   104
37 The -JA- Tense   107
38 Object Infixes   110
39 Weights and Measures   116
40 The Subjunctive   118
41 Position (up, down, etc.)   126
42 Adjectives—4: -ote, -enye-, etc.   129

43	Verbs—6: Prepositional Form (-i/e-)	131
44	Adjectives—5: Compound Adjectives	134
45	Months and Dates	137
46	Nouns—5: MA- Class	139
47	The -KI- Tense (Conditional and Present Participle)	145
48	Indeclinable Words—2 (Prepositions, Adverbs and Conjunctions)	153
49	The Relatives—1 (Amba- and infixes, etc.)	158
50	Verbs—7: (Additional verbs)	171
51	Relatives—2 (General Relative, etc.)	172
52	Relatives—3 (Manner and Time)	183
53	Nouns—6: U- Class	185
54	Present Indefinite Tense (-A-)	192
55	Verbs—8: Reciprocal Verbs (-NA-)	194
56	Nouns—7: 'Mahali' (locative) Class	196
57	Comparison of Adjectives	205
58	The -KA- Verb Tense (Narrative, etc.)	207
59	More Conditional Tenses (-NGE-, -NGALI-)	211
60	Demonstratives of Reference	217
61	Emphatics	220
62	The HU- Verb Tense (Habitual)	221
63	Which? (-PI?)	224
64	Nouns—8: KU- Class (Gerunds)	225
65	Compound Tenses	227
66	Summary of Verb Derivatives	229
	Additional Exercises in Prose	231
	Appendices	
1	Summary of Verb Tenses	235
2	Use of Kupiga	237
3	Agricultural Crops and Produce	238
4	Summary of Grammar for Noun Classes	240
5	Simplified Glossary of Grammatical Terms	243
6	Writing Letters in Swahili	244
	Answers to Exercises	246
	Vocabulary: Swahili—English	288
	Vocabulary: English—Swahili	300

Introduction

You may have often heard it said that Swahili is an easy language to learn. When you first see that in fact there are seven or eight noun classes, each of which must take its correct agreements, this may make you somewhat sceptical. But, nevertheless, Swahili *is* an easy language, for there are few languages with so few exceptions to contend with. Furthermore, although the vocabulary has little or no similarity to that of European languages, there is often a close similarity between various Swahili words relating to a particular subject, and many words can, by following typical patterns, be made into nouns, adjectives or verbs with a common root.

This course has been written for the person wishing to achieve a quick working general knowledge of the language. Grammar is, therefore, kept moderately simple, and is introduced stage by stage, in order of relative importance. Approximately one thousand words are introduced throughout the course, which is considered adequate for general working topics. For those who find the vocabulary difficult to learn, it is strongly recommended that a number of squares of paper be prepared (say 5 cms square), and a Swahili word written on one side, with the English on the reverse. These can then be shuffled and thus learnt in differing sequence. As a word becomes known, so its card can be placed to one side, thus gradually reducing the cards of unknown words. It is guaranteed that this method will greatly speed up vocabulary retention.

Each chapter has a set of exercises designed to 'work in' the particular new point of grammar, and answers to these exercises will be found at the back of the book. It is suggested that as a form of revision, the student may wish to translate these answers back again, and thus compare his retranslations with the actual exercise.

For the student who wishes to make a serious study of this language, it is estimated that within a 2–3 month period (i.e. about a chapter per day), the contents of this book may be mastered, provided a concentrated study is made for some 2 hours daily. Do not be afraid of practising spoken Swahili, making use of every opportunity, however short, whenever you meet a Swahili speaker.

The Swahili language is spoken throughout East Africa (that is to say Tanzania, Kenya and Uganda), and also in areas a little on the Eastern side of Zaïre and Burundi. The purest Swahili is to be found on the island of Zanzibar and along the mainland coastline closest to it. But as you get farther away, both north and south as well as inland, so the standard of the language lowers. Therefore, in northern Kenya, the extreme west of Tanzania and its southern borders, the language may be little known or extremely ungrammatical. In Uganda, the language is fairly commonly used except in the south-west. In eastern Zaïre and

Burundi, the Swahili language has a strong French flavour which is perfectly understandable to someone conversant with both languages.

I hope that this book will therefore enable the reader to use this fine Bantu language to advantage within East Africa.

P. M. Wilson, C.D.A., Cert. Ed.,

To my wife Dorothy in gratitude for her encouragement without which this book would not have been completed.

1 Pronunciation

One of the easiest aspects of the Swahili language is that each letter of the alphabet always represents the same sound, the only slight exception being where two letters occur together to represent one specific sound. But this is again always the same, unlike the letters 'gh' in English which correspond to many different pronunciations. Generally speaking, the intonation is not unlike that of the French language.

There are only 24 letters in the Swahili alphabet, Q and X being absent.

The vowels

The vowels are the most important sounds to pronounce correctly, since mis-pronunciation of these gives rise to an obvious 'foreign' accent.

All vowel sounds are short, thus:

A as in 'far' but cut short   e.g. bata (a duck)
E as in 'bed'   e.g. embe (a mango)
I as the 'ee' in 'feel'   e.g. kiti (a chair)
O as in 'off'   e.g. jambo (hello)
U as the 'oo' in 'fool'   e.g. tundu (a hole)

N.B. Be very careful with the 'o' since this is the most commonly mispronounced of the Swahili vowels. It must never be pronounced long as in 'go', or as in 'do'.

Stress

Before progressing, it is as well to give the correct stress on words. This is again very easy in Swahili, since stress never changes from word to word, and is *always* found on the penultimate (last but one) syllable of a word.

For example, we may break up any word into its syllables, thus:

bata—ba ta. Therefore stress the ba, thus *ba*ta
or Tanzania—Tan za ni a, stressing the *ni*, thus Tanza*ni*a
or mtu—m tu. Here the syllable is a consonant, but this does not alter the position of stress, thus *m*tu.

Consonants

Remember these never vary in sound, thus we get:

B as in 'bad'   e.g. baba (father)
C is only found together with H as CH, and is pronounced as in 'each' e.g. chache (a few)
D as in 'do'   e.g. dada (a sister)

F as in 'far'   e.g. futa (wipe)
G as in 'gone'   e.g. gogo (a log) It is never soft as in 'germ'.
H as in 'hat'   e.g. hali (condition)
J as in 'John'   e.g. jambo (hello) In practice it is slightly different, not having the 'DJ' sound but rather a 'DY' sound.
K as in 'kid'   e.g. kaka (a brother)
L as in 'log'   e.g. lala (sleep). See also 'R' below.
M as in 'man'   e.g. mama (a mother)

N.B. If a consonant occurs without a vowel at the beginning of a word it is generally given a syllable of its own,
   e.g. m*toto* (m-to-to) (a child) Take care not to say 'me-to-to'.

N as in 'nut'   e.g. nani? (who?)

N.B. This may also occur as a separate syllable,
   e.g. *n*cha (a point). Take care not to say 'ne-cha'.

P as in 'pot'   e.g. papa (a shark)
R as in 'rat'   e.g. roho (soul)

N.B. You may often hear 'L's interchanged since in practice there is very little difference in sound between the two,
   e.g. You may hear either 'filimbi' or 'firimbi' (a whistle).

S as in 'soap'   e.g. sisi (we/us). See also 'SH' below.
T as in 'tame'   e.g. tatu (three)
V as in 'very'   e.g. vita (war)
W as in 'wide'   e.g. watu (people)
Y as in 'you'   e.g. yaya (a nanny) Never as in 'very'.
Z as in 'zoo'   e.g. zamu (a turn, bout)

Combinations
CH   is as in 'each' e.g. chache (few);
DH   is as 'TH' in 'that' e.g. fedha (silver). Never as in 'thin';
GH   is a voiced gutteral sound not generally encountered in English, e.g. ghali (expensive);
KH   is found in Arabic words only, and is a voiceless gutteral sound. It is similar to the Scottish 'CH' as in 'loch' e.g. Sabalkheri (Good morning);

N.B. The relationship between GH and KH might be compared to that of V and F, Z and S, and DH and TH, the first of each pair being voiced, the second being voiceless.

NG'   Where the apostrophe occurs a specialised sound is made such as in the word 'singer'. It is rather difficult to produce this sound separately.
   e.g. ng'ombe (a cow/ox);
NG   Without the apostrophe, each consonant is given its almost normal pronunciation.
   e.g. ngano (wheat) as in 'sunglory';

2

NY as in 'lanyard' e.g. nyanya (a tomato; grand-mother);
SH is as in 'shop' e.g. shida (a difficulty);
TH is as in 'thin' e.g. thamani (value).

Definitions

Throughout this course the following terminology will be used to describe certain parts of the word:

Concord—This is the name given to agreements common to nouns and adjectives which occur at the beginning of the word;

Stem—This is the part of a word which remains virtually unchanged in the various derivations of words, which may be adjectives, nouns, or verbs;

Prefix—This is a letter, or syllable, which is added to the front of a word. Thus a concord is a type of prefix;

Infix—This is a letter or syllable added into the middle of a word, generally between a prefix and the stem of verbs;

Suffix—Is a letter or syllable added onto the end of a word. Because these come at the end of a word, and thus add a syllable, they affect the stress of a word. The stressed syllable therefore moves up one, to keep its penultimate place.

e.g. In the English word 'disafforestation'
'dis-' is the prefix
'-af-' is an infix
'-forest-' is the stem, and
'-ation' is the suffix.
Or in this Swahili word 'Niliwaambieni' (I told you (pl.))
'Ni-' is the prefix
'-li-' is an infix
'-wa-' is an infix
'-ambi-' is the stem, and
'-eni' is the suffix.

N.B. Hyphens will be used to denote that a particle must be used in conjunction with another.

2 Greetings

Before progressing with the grammar, it is as well to introduce some of the Swahili greetings. Unlike the British, who are rather lax with regard to greetings, the Swahili speaking people make a very strong use of them. Particularly after prolonged absence, several minutes may be taken up with greetings, before the subject for discussion is broached. To fail to reply to a greeting can cause great offence, and English greetings given in reply will not always be understood, or accepted. It is therefore important to learn *and use* these greetings.

The most common greeting used between two persons is:

Jambo!　　Reply:　　Jambo!

As in English, however, it is more polite, and therefore more usual to give the other person some sort of title.

The usual titles used are:

Bwana　　for a male

Mama　　for a female } either may be followed by a proper name, e.g. Bwana Ali.

mtoto　　for a child

and Memsabu where Madam would be used in English,

Thus we find:

Jambo Bwana!　　Reply: Jambo Bwana!

or Jambo Mama!　　Reply: Jambo Bwana!

or whatever combination is appropriate.

N.B. Contrary to popular belief, Bwana does not necessarily mean 'Sir' or 'Master', but is a title used between any persons when addressing a male, and has no implication of rank or superiority. It is almost a direct equivalent of the French 'Monsieur'.

These greetings will then often be followed by a fuller form of greeting, which actually is asking the question in the negative.

Hujambo? (to one person) Reply: Sijambo!

(lit. Is nothing the matter with you? Nothing!)

Hamjambo? (to several people) Reply: Hatujambo!

Recently in Tanzania the age-old common greeting Jambo! has seemingly totally dropped from common usage. Its place has been taken by Vipi?, used in exactly the same context as the former Jambo! but with a variety of replies. The most common ones are: nimesha poa asante! or salama tu!, or a variety of similar alternatives.

These greetings revert to questions asked about almost anything topical. This takes the form of

Habari ya ....?　　if specific news is expected,

or Habari ya ....?　　if general news is anticipated.

This means loosely, 'What is the news of ....?'

The reply is always 'Good' which can be either 'Nzuri' or 'Njema'. (For the learner, it is suggested that you keep on to 'Nzuri' as being the more common.) Thus, if you fail to catch the question and simply hear 'Habari ya ....' (something), your reply should always be 'Nzuri' regardless. (A third alternative one may hear is 'Salama' which means 'Peaceful'.)

The form of Habari ya ....?' may be any of the following:

'Habari ya nyumbani?'　　What is the news of home?'

'Habari za siku nyingi?'　　What is the news of many days?'

'Habari za watoto?' 'What is the news of the children?'
'Habari ya safari?' 'What is the news of the journey?'
'Habari ya kazi?' 'What is the news of work?'
or many dozens of others.

The reply, then, will always be 'Nzuri', or 'Nzuri Bwana!'
Other greetings one will hear:

(a) Arabic greetings, used especially on the coast:
    Sabalkheri! (Good morning!) Reply: Sabalkheri!
    Masalkheri! (Good evening!) Reply: Masalkheri!

(b) To a superior:
    Shikamuu! (lit. I hold your feet!) Reply: Marahaba! (delightful)
    Plural: Shikamuuni! Reply: Marahaba!

N.B. If this greeting is offered to you, it would be most impolite to ignore it, or to fail to reply correctly.

Other conversational gambits are:

U hali gani?   How are you?   Reply: Nzuri! or Mzima!
                                   or Sijambo!
U mzima?   Are you well?   Reply: Mzima!
Habari gani?   What news?   Reply: Nzuri!
Umelalaje?   How have you slept?   (Used mainly to a
    sick person) Reply: Salama! (peacefully)
Asante!   Thank you.

N.B. It is the custom in many areas for Africans not to say 'Asante' as liberally as Europeans are used to, and therefore one should not be offended if no thanks are received for any service rendered.

Kwa heri! Good-bye! (Used only if it is known to be the last parting of the day.)
Kwa herini! (plural 'Good-bye'). The reply is the same using singular or plural as appropriate.
When only parting temporarily, one says:
Nakwenda sasa! (I'm off now) Reply: Haya, or Vema, Bwana! (Right!).

Hodi?

When approaching a house, or sometimes a river along a footpath, the custom is to call 'Hodi?' (In some areas, the custom is to make this call three times, each of which should receive an answer before proceeding.) The word has no equivalent meaning in English, but vaguely means 'Hello, is anyone about, please may I enter?' The reply, if in the affirmative, is 'Karibu' (Draw near). On entering either party might then say 'Starehe' (Be at ease) if they see the other is not at ease. If the

5

answer is to 'wait', as opposed to 'Come in', then one can say 'Ngoja' or 'Ngoja kidogo' (wait a little).

Pole!

This is a word of condolence often used to a person who shows signs of fatigue or illness, or in times of bereavement or distress. It can, however, also be used when one has been successful in such things as childbirth or examinations.

In all these cases, the reply to 'Pole!' can just be 'Asante!', or after illness more appropriately 'Asante, nimekwisha poa'. (Thanks, I have already cooled down (from fever).)

One may even encounter 'Poleni!' when offered to several people, or such phrases as 'Pole ya safari!' (Condolences of the journey!) the reply still being 'Asante!'.

3 Verbs — 1

The Infinitive

Throughout this course, verbs will always be presented in the 'infinitive' form, such as is the tendency in English grammars. Strictly speaking there is no Verb Infinitive in Swahili, since they use a verb-noun in its stead. But the use of this verb-noun is identical to the English Infinitive equivalent so that for easy comprehension throughout this book, the term 'Infinitive' will be used when referring to the English equivalent usage. This 'infinitive' is also the present participle. Thus the verb 'kufanya' can also mean 'doing' or 'making. (See Ch. 64.)

In English, the infinitive is made up of adding the word 'to' before the verb itself. In Swahili the same is achieved by adding the prefix 'ku-' in front of the verb stem.

In addition, all Swahili verbs must end with a suffix, even in the infinitive. For normal use, i.e. for the simple action of 'doing' a verb (active) (as opposed to a verb 'being done' for example), all Swahili verbs of Bantu origin have the suffix '-a';

e.g. kufanya (to do)   ku-   'infinitive' prefix
                      -fany- verb stem
                      -a   active affirmative suffix.

The following are verbs in common use:
ku-anguka   to fall   ku-ngoja   to wait, wait for

ku-fanya	to do, make	ku-nunua	to buy, purchase
ku-fika	to arrive	ku-penda	to like, love
ku-fuata	to follow	ku-piga	to beat, hit

N.B. The verb 'ku-piga' has a very wide usage, such as for applying things, using certain tools, etc., etc. (See Appendix 2 p 237)

ku-funga	to shut, close, to fasten	ku-pika	to cook
ku-fungua	to open, undo	ku-safisha	to clean
ku-jua	to know	ku-sema	to speak, say
ku-kaa	to stay, dwell, sit	ku-simama	to stand, halt
ku-kamata	to seize, hold	ku-tafuta	to search, look for
ku-kata	to cut, reduce	ku-taka	to want
		ku-uza	to sell
ku-leta	to bring, fetch	ku-weka	to put, place
		ku-weza	to be able

There are also many verbs in Swahili of Arabic origin. In these cases they do not take the suffix '-a', but end in either '-e', '-i' or '-u', these being part of their stems. Thus we get:

ku-samehe	to forgive, sacrifice
ku-baki	to remain, be left over
ku-fikiri	to think, consider
ku-furahi	to rejoice, be happy
ku-keti	to sit
ku-safiri	to travel
ku-rudi	to return
ku-faulu	to succeed
ku-haribu	to destroy, spoil
ku-jaribu	to try
ku-jibu	to answer, reply

There are also some verbs with monosyllabic stems which will be frequently referred to since they create their own set of exceptions. The common ones are:

ku-fa	to die	ku-la	to eat
ku-ja	to come	ku-nywa	to drink
ku-wa	to be, to become		(-nywa is one syllable)

Also included, though not strictly monosyllabic are:

kwenda (ku-enda) to go   kwisha (ku-isha) to be finished

4 Verbs—2

Imperatives

I The Direct Imperative

The following is an abrupt form of the imperative, and since it is abrupt, should not be used indiscriminately. It is, however, perfectly usable with one's subordinates.

The procedure in making this imperative from the infinitive is exactly the same as in English, for the singular, i.e. if we take the infinitive 'to do', we remove the infinitive 'to' and we are left with the imperative 'do!'. Thus in Swahili we remove the 'infinitive' 'ku-' and we are left with the singular imperative. 'Kufanya'—'Fanya!'

Similarly, verbs listed on the previous page will have the following imperatives:

Fanya!	Do!	Nunua!	Buy!
Fika!	Arrive!	Piga!	Hit!
Fuata!	Follow!	Pika!	Cook!
Funga!	Shut!	Safisha!	Clean!
Fungua!	Open!	Sema!	Speak!
Kaa!	Stay!	Simama!	Halt! (or Stand!)
Kamata!	Seize!	Tafuta!	Search!
Kata!	Cut!	Uza!	Sell!
Ngoja!	Wait!	Weka!	Put!

The same will apply to verbs of Arabic origin:

Samehe!	Forgive!	Jaribu!	Try!
Fikiri!	Think!	Jibu!	Answer!
Rudi!	Return!		

Monosyllabic verbs, however, are treated differently, and they retain their 'infinitive' 'ku-' even for the imperative. The tone of voice used emphasises the imperative.

Kula!	Eat!	Kunywa!	Drink!

Exceptions

There are only three exceptions:

Kuleta has the imperative 'Lete!' (instead of 'Leta!') Bring!
Kwenda has the imperative 'Nenda!' (instead of 'Kwenda!') Go!
Kuja has the imperative 'Njoo!' (instead of 'Kuja!') Come!

Imperative—plural

To make the plural imperative, the 'infinitive' 'ku-' is again dropped, but the suffix '-a' is replaced by the suffix '-eni'. Thus we get:

Fanyeni!	Do!	Nunueni!	Buy!
Fikeni!	Arrive!	Pigeni!	Hit!
Fuateni!	Follow!	Pikeni!	Cook!
Fungeni!	Shut!	Safisheni!	Clean!
Fungueni!	Open!	Semeni!	Speak!
Kamateni!	Seize!	Simameni!	Stand!
Kateni!	Cut!	Tafuteni!	Search!
Kaeni!	Stay!	Uzeni!	Sell!
Ngojeni!	Wait!	Wekeni!	Put!

With verbs of Arabic origin, however, the suffix '-ni' is merely added to the original final vowel, thus:

Sameheni!	Forgive!	Jaribuni!	Try!
Fikirini!	Think!	Jibuni!	Answer!
Rudini!	Return!		

Monosyllabic verbs still retain their 'infinitive' 'ku-' in spite of the fact that by adding another syllable they become di-syllabic. The suffix '-a', however, is again replaced by the suffix '-eni'.

Kuleni!	Eat!	Kunyweni!	Drink!

Exceptions
In the plural, there are only two exceptions, since the verb 'kuleta' follows the normal ruling:

Leteni!	Bring!	('-a' changed to '-eni')

The other two are similar exceptions to the singular:

Nendeni!	Go!	(final '-a' to '-eni')
Njooni!	Come!	('-ni' simply added)

Exercise 1
(Try to complete this exercise without looking at the grammar.)
(a) *Translate:* Rejoice! (pl.); Bring!; Sit!; Stand! (pl.); Go!; Come! (pl.); Remain!; Eat!; Answer!; Do!; Open!; Sell! (pl.); Search! (pl.); Answer! (pl.); Try!; Drink!; Come!; Eat! (pl.); Beat! (pl.); Buy!; Arrive! (pl.); Speak! (pl.); Follow! (pl.); Halt! (pl.); Put!; Stay! (pl.); Cook!; Wait!; Clean!; Forgive! (pl.); Reduce!; Bring! (pl.); Come back! (pl.); Answer!; Try to answer!; Go to buy!; Sit, Mr Juma!; Come to fetch!; Wait to try!; Sit! (pl.); Try to consider! (pl.); Drink! (pl.); Open! (pl.); Wait to go!; Arrive!; Stay!; Try to forgive!
(b) *Translate into English:* Fuateni!; Fungua!; Pigeni!; Njoo!; Kunyweni!; Kaa!; Nendeni!; Semeni!; Ngojeni!; Rudini!; Kamateni!; Kula!; Tafuteni!; Wekeni!; Baki!; Nunua!; Jaribuni!; Jibu!; Fikirini!; Fungueni!; Ngoja!; Funga!; Jaribu kuuza!; Keti kungoja!; Njooni!; Pika!; Lete!; Nenda kununua!; Fuata!

II The Negative Imperative
There is no abrupt negative imperative, instead the negative subjunctive has to be used, and being subjunctive, this imperative is automatically polite, having a sense of 'would you not————'

The negative subjunctive is made up as follows:

The prefix 'ku-' is removed from the verb 'infinitive' (all verbs);
The prefix 'u-' is used for the singular, 2nd person;
The infix '-si-' is used to denote the negative;
The suffix '-a' is replaced by the suffix '-e' to denote subjunctive.

Thus if we take the verb 'ku-fany-a', we get

U- -si- -fany- -e (Usifanye) Do not do! (sing.)

Note that there are no exceptions to this rule, and even the mono-syllabic verbs are regular here.

Thus we get:

Usifanye!	Don't do!	Usinunue!	Don't buy!
Usifike!	Don't arrive!	Usipige!	Don't hit!
Usifuate!	Don't follow!	Usipike!	Don't cook!
Usifunge!	Don't shut!	Usisafishe!	Don't clean!
Usifungue!	Don't open!	Usiseme!	Don't speak!
Usikamate!	Don't seize!	Usisimame!	Don't stand!
Usikate!	Don't cut!	Usitafute!	Don't search!
Usikae!	Don't stay!	Usiuze!	Don't sell!
Usingoje!	Don't wait!	Usiweke!	Don't put!

With Arabic verbs, the only difference is that the final letter never changes, since this is not a suffix, but part of the original stem (See ch. 2).

Usisamehe!	Don't forgive!	Usijaribu!	Don't try!
Usifikiri!	Don't think!	Usijibu!	Don't reply!
Usirudi!	Don't return!		

Monosyllabics:

Usile!	Don't eat!	Usinywe!	Don't drink!
Usije!	Don't come!	Usiende!	Don't go!
Usiwe!	Don't be! Don't become		

N.B. 'Usiwe' must be followed by a noun or adjective.

To obtain the plural negative imperative, all that is done is to change the prefix 'u-' to 'm-' which denotes second person plural, thus:— M- -si- -fany- -e (Msifanye) Don't do!

Msifanye!	Don't do!	Misinunue!	Don't buy!
Msifike!	Don't arrive!	Msipige!	Don't hit!
Msifuate!	Don't follow!	Msipike!	Don't cook!
Msifunge!	Don't shut!	Msisafishe!	Don't clean!
Msifungue!	Don't open!	Msiseme!	Don't speak!
Msisamehe!	Don't forgive!	Msijaribu!	Don't try
Msifikiri!	Don't think!	Msijibu!	Don't reply

Msirudi!	Don't return!	Msile!	Don't eat!
Msinywe!	Don't drink!	Msije!	Don't come!
Msiende!	Don't go!	Msiwe!*	Don't be!
			Don't become!

Use of Imperative with 'Infinitive'

The imperative in English is often followed by another verb in infinitive form such as 'Try to sell'. In every day English, this is more usually expressed as 'Try *and* sell'. In either case, this translates into Swahili as 'Jaribu kuuza', where it will be seen that the second verb is simply expressed as an 'infinitive'.

Exercise 2

(a) *Translate:* Don't stay!; Don't put! (pl.); Don't die! (pl.); Don't sell! (pl.); Don't destroy!; Stand! (pl.); Don't cut!; Don't bring! (pl.); Wait!; Don't wait! (pl.); Don't do!; Don't try!; Don't open!; Don't stay! (pl.); Don't sell!; Don't arrive!; Don't search!; Don't wait to go!; Don't answer!; Don't open! (pl.); Don't try! (pl.); Don't drink! (pl.); Don't speak! (pl.); Don't remain! (pl.); Don't come!; Don't sit! (pl.); Don't eat! (pl.); Don't wait to try!; Don't beat! (pl.); Don't come to fetch!; Don't buy!; Don't become!;* Don't arrive! (pl.); Don't go to buy!; Don't follow! (pl.); Don't try to answer!; Don't fall!; Don't answer! (pl.); Don't stop!; Don't come back! (pl.); Don't put!; Don't bring!; Don't stay! (pl.); Don't cut!; Don't cook!; Don't clean!; Don't be!* (pl.); Don't travel!; Don't undo!; Don't come! (pl.)

(b) *Translate into English:* Usifuate!; Usiende kununua!; Usifungue!; Usilete!; Msipige!; Usipike!; Usije!; Msifuate!; Msije!; Msinywe!; Usiketi!; Usikae!; Usijaribu kuuza!; Msiende!; Usifunge!; Msiseme!; Usiwe!*; Usingoje!; Usipende!; Msifungue!; Msingoje!; Msifikiri!; Msirudi!; Usijibu!; Msikamate!; Usinunue!; Usile!; Usibaki!; Msitafute!; Msiweke!;

III The Polite Imperative

When addressing 'the man in the street', it is as well to use the polite form of imperative, rather than the abrupt imperative already mentioned. This is achieved, as in the negative imperative, by using the subjunctive, which gives a sense of, 'Would you . . . . .

It is made up as follows:

The prefix 'ku-' is removed from the verb 'infinitive'.
The prefix 'u-' is again used to denote the second person singular.
No infix is required.
The suffix '-a' is again replaced by '-e' to denote subjunctive.

Thus, using 'kufanya', we get:
U- -fany- -e (Ufanye!) Would you do! (sing.)

Ufanye!	Would you do!	Ununue!	Would you buy!

---

* Remember that these *must* normally be used with a noun or adjective.

11

Ufike!	Would you arrive!	Upige!	Would you hit!
Ufuate!	Would you follow!	Upike!	Would you cook!
Ufunge!	Would you shut!	Usafishe!	Would you clean!
Ufungue!	Would you open!	Useme!	Would you speak!

With Arabic verbs, again the final vowel remains unchanged:

Usamehe!	Would you forgive!	Ujaribu!	Would you try!
Ufikiri!	Would you think!	Ujibu!	Would you reply!
Urudi!	Would you return!		

Monosyllabics also drop their 'infinitive' 'ku-'

Ule!	Would you eat!	Unywe!	Would you drink!
Uje!	Would you come!	Uende!	Would you go!
Uwe!	Would you be!		

N.B. 'Uwe' must always be followed by a noun or adjective.

Similarly, the plural polite imperative is obtained by using the 2nd person plural prefix 'm-' (if 'm-' precedes a vowel a '-w-' must also be inserted). Thus:

Mfanye!	Would you do!	Mnunue!	Would you buy!
Mfike!	Would you arrive!	Mpige!	Would you hit!
Mfuate!	Would you follow!	Mpike!	Would you cook!
Mfunge!	Would you close!	Msafishe!	Would you clean!
Mfungue!	Would you open!	Mseme!	Would you speak!

And Arabic verbs:

Msamehe!	Would you forgive!	Mjaribu!	Would you try!
Mfikiri!	Would you think!	Mjibu	Would you reply!
Mrudi!	Would you return!		

Monosyllabics:

Mle!	Would you eat!	Mnywe!	Would you drink!
Mje!	Would you come!	Mwende!	Would you go!
Mwe!	Would you be!		

N.B. (1) 'Mwe, must always be followed by a noun or adjective. (2) 'm-' in front of a vowel takes a '-w-'.

There is a word for 'Please'—'Tafadhali' which may be used in conjunction with this form of imperative. It is not essential, however, and would only be used when one wanted to be especially polite.

e.g. Ufanye!   Would you do!
     Tafadhali ufanye!   Would you please do!

Exercise 3
(a) *Translate:* Would you be! (pl.); Would you sit! Would you go! (pl.); Would you eat! Would you please bring! Would you stand! (pl.); Would you please come! (pl.); Would you answer! (pl.); Would you do! (pl.); Would you please open! Would you sell! (pl.); Would you please search! (pl.); Would you answer! Would you please try! (pl.); Would you drink! Would you come! Would you eat! (pl.); Would you beat! (pl.); Would you please buy! Would you arrive! (pl.); Would you please speak! (pl.); Would you please follow! (pl.); Would you fall! Would you halt! Would you put! Would you stay! (pl.); Would you cook! Would you please wait! Would you clean! Would you forgive! (pl.); Would you cut! Would you bring! Would you come back! (pl.); Would you answer! Would you try to answer! Would you go to buy! Would you sit, Mr Juma! Would you please come to fetch! Would you wait to try! Would you sit! (pl.); Would you please try to consider! Would you drink (pl.); Would you open! (pl.); Would you please wait to go! Would you arrive! Would you please stay! Would you try to forgive!
(b) *Translate:* Mfuate! Ufungue! Mpige! Uje! Mnywe! Ukae! Mwende! Mseme! Mngoje! Mrudi! Mkamate! Ule! Tafadhali mtafute! Mweke! Ubaki! Tafadhali ununue! Mjaribu! Ujibu! Mfikiri! Tafadhali mfungue! Ungoje! Ufunge! Ujaribu kuuza! Uketi kungoja! Mje! Upike! Tafadhali ulete! Uende kununua! Ufuate!

13

5 Nouns — 1

There are 7 noun classes in Swahili. Sometimes verb 'infinitives' are used as nouns and thus constitute an eighth noun class. (See ch. 64.) The nouns are grouped into classes according to their initial concord or prefix. Adjectives are generally given the same agreement. In all but two of these seven classes, there is a different concord for singular and plural nouns. This means that in Swahili, nouns change at the beginning, or as we say, its concord changes to denote singular or plural.

A further point to remember is that in Swahili there is no definite or indefinite article ('the', 'a' or sometimes in the English 'some'). Thus one cannot differentiate, at this stage at any rate, between 'the thing', 'a thing' and 'some thing'.

M-WA- Class

This is one of the few noun classes in which the nouns almost all refer to one particular type of thing. In this case, all nouns refer to people (except for two common nouns), but on the other hand, not *all* nouns referring to people are contained in this class. A further point to note is that one cannot differentiate, as in French for example, the genders masculine and feminine. This has to be done with adjectives if necessary.

Typical of the class is the word 'mtu' a person. (N.B. It does not mean 'a man' unless one is talking of 'man' as opposed to 'beast'). This particular noun has a monosyllabic stem and therefore the stress falls on the concord prefix:

> *m*tu   a person   *wa*tu   people

Note that the concord prefix has changed from 'm-' to 'wa-' to denote the plural.

Commonly in use in this noun class are the following:

Singular	Plural	
mganga	waganga	a doctor, a witchdoctor
mgeni	wageni	a visitor, guest, stranger, newcomer
mgonjwa	wagonjwa	a sick person, patient
mpishi	wapishi	a cook
mtoto	watoto	a child (either sex)
mtumishi	watumishi	a servant
mzee	wazee	an old person, elder (term of respect)
Mzungu	Wazungu	A 'European' (in fact any white person)

And the only two nouns not referring to humans:

Singular	Plural	
mdudu	wadudu	an 'insect' (any 'creepy-crawly')
mnyama	wanyama	an animal

N.B. Remember one cannot express the definite or indefinite article in Swahili, so that 'mtu' could mean either 'a person' or 'the person'.

Where 'm-' occurs in front of a vowel, a '-w-' is inserted. ('m-' was originally 'mu-' c.f. kwenda from kuenda).
The following are common vowel stem nouns:

Singular	Plural	
mwana	wana	a son/daughter
mwanafunzi	wanafunzi	a pupil/student
mwalimu	walimu	a teacher
mwenyeji	wenyeji	an inhabitant, householder
mwizi	wezi	a thief

It will be seen that the plurals appear inconsistent. They are derived as follows:

1. There is frequently a merging of vowels when two occur together by addition of prefixes and infixes. The following is common:
   - a + a goes to a
   - a + e goes to e
   - a + i goes to e

Thus mw-ana goes in the plural to wa-ana = wana;
mw-enyeji goes in the plural to wa-enyeji = wenyeji
and mw-izi goes in the plural to wa-izi = wezi

2. The following, however, need special mention with regard to their plurals:

Singular		Plural
mwanamke	a woman	wanawake
mwanamume	a man	wanaume
mwindaji	a hunter	wawindaji

Mwanamke is really made up of two words:

mwana + mke   (mke denoting female)

When the combined word is put in the plural, both halves change:
wa-ana + wa-ke = wanawake (women)

Mwanamume, similarly is made up of two words:

mwana + mume   (mume denoting male)

15

But here, in the plural, the concord is removed from the second half, so we get:

wa-ana + (wa)-ume = wanaume (wana-ume)

Mwindaji is a word made up from the verb 'kuwinda' to hunt. Therefore the stem is -winda which shows that the 'w' is not the insert on account of a vowel, but part of the stem. It is therefore not removed when making up the plural, but the noun is treated as a normal consonant-stem noun, thus:

m-windaji   wa-windaji = wawindaji

Nationalities also are often exceptions in the plural, since the merging of vowels might lead to a loss of identity of the orignal word. For example:

Mwislamu, a Muslim, goes to Waislamu
(Not Weslamu which is more like Wesleyan than Islam)

Thus the following are used:

Mwafrika	An African	Waafrika (sometimes Wafrika)
Mwamerika	An American	Waamerika
Mwarabu	An Arab	Waarabu (sometimes Warabu)
Mwingereza	A Britisher	Waingereza
Mwitalia	An Italian	Waitalia

Consonant-stem nationalities present no problem, e.g.

Mfaransa	A Frenchman	Wafaransa
Mdachi	A German	Wadachi
Mholanzi	A Dutchman	Waholanzi (Not Mdachi to avoid confusion with above).
Mgiriki	A Greek	Wagiriki

N.B In spoken Swahili it is important, even with nationalities to keep the word stress in its proper position, on the penultimate syllable of every word, regardless of where it might be found in spoken English.

Exercise 4

(a) *Translate:* Europeans; students; an insect; new-comers; women; a patient; children; a man; teachers; thieves; men; Africans; a person; servants; an animal; an inhabitant; a Britisher; hunters; a son; American children.

(b) *Translate:* Seize the thief! Bring the children! Don't beat the teacher! Don't (pl.) destroy! Follow (pl.) the animal! Look for the doctor! Would you be the cook! Beat the child! Would you wait (for) the guest! Don't eat the insects! Sell the animals! Don't bring the guests! Don't follow the old man! Try to look for the children! Bring (pl.) the patients!

(c) *Translate:* Wadudu; mwenyeji; wezi; mpishi; Mdachi; watoto Wazungu; mpishi mzee; walimu; mwanamke; mgonjwa; wenyeji Waafrika; mwalimu; mwindaji; wanyama; Waislamu; Mgiriki; mgeni; mwanamume; mtumishi; wanafunzi.

6 Subject Prefixes

In Swahili, the subject of a verb is always added onto the verb as a prefix. These subject prefixes, however, are quite different from the concords used on nouns.

In order to use good Swahili, it is *essential* to be thoroughly acquainted with these subject prefixes, since they are used constantly, both in verbs and in many other constructions.

The subject prefixes for the M- WA- class are as follows:

Sing. {
1st. Ni- I
2nd. U- You (sing.)
3rd. A- He/She (*Never* 'it')

Plur. {
1st. Tu- We
2nd. M- You (pl.)
3rd. Wa- They

(We are already familiar with the 2nd person singular and plural from the negative imperative, and polite imperative.)

If the subject noun is stated in a sentence, the subject prefix must still be used. Thus, literally translating, one would have to say:

> 'The cook, he is cooking', not 'The cook is cooking'.
> or 'The guest, she is staying', not 'The guest is staying'.
> or 'The children, they are playing', not 'The children are playing'.

N.B. One cannot differentiate between 'he' and 'she' in the subject prefix.

More verbs

Ku-amka	to wake up.	Ku-lima	to cultivate, plough.
Ku-anza	to start, begin.	Ku-lipa	to pay.
Ku-chukua	to carry, take.	Ku-nusa	to smell something, sniff.
Ku-fagia	to sweep.	Ku-ona	to see, feel, think.
Ku-futa	to wipe.	Ku-panda	to climb, sow.
Ku-hitaji	to need, require.	Ku-pata	to get, obtain.
Ku-ingia	to enter in, go in.	Ku-sahau	to forget.
Ku-jifunza	to learn.	Ku-soma	to read, study.
Ku-kauka	to dry, to get dry (active).	Ku-tumia	to use.
Ku-lala	to sleep, lie down.	Ku-tunza	to tend, to take care of.
		Ku-winda	to hunt.

7 Present Verb Tense

-NA- present definite

In Swahili, verbs are used as follows:
    Subject prefix + Tense marker + Verb stem.
      I   am   wanting.

As in English, we have to remove the 'infinitive' marker from a verb before using it in other tenses. This does not always apply, however, to the monosyllabic verbs.

The tense marker for this tense is -NA-

Thus 'I am wanting' is made up as follows:

    Ni- -na- -taka.
    I   am wanting.

but it is all written as one word—'Ninataka'.

Similarly the verb declines as follows:

Ni-na-taka	Ninataka	I am wanting.
U-na-taka	Unataka	You are wanting.
A-na-taka	Anataka	He/she is wanting.
Tu-na-taka	Tunataka	We are wanting.
M-na-taka	Mnataka	You are wanting.
Wa-na-taka	Wanataka	They are wanting.

Verbs of Arabic origin are treated in the same way:

Ku-jaribu—to try		
Ni-na-jaribu	Ninajaribu	I am trying.
U-na-jaribu	Unajaribu	You are trying.
A-na-jaribu	Anajaribu	He/she is trying.
Tu-na-jaribu	Tunajaribu	We are trying.
M-na-jaribu	Mnajaribu	You are trying.
Wa-na-jaribu	Wanajaribu	They are trying.

But monosyllabic verbs with this tense retain their 'infinitive' 'ku-', thus:

Kuja—to come		
Ni-na-kuja	Ninakuja	I am coming.
U-na-kuja	Unakuja	You are coming.
A-na-kuja	Anakuja	He/she is coming.
Tu-na-kuja	Tunakuja	We are coming.
M-na-kuja	Mnakuja	You are coming.
Wa-na-kuja	Wanakuja	They are coming.

This tense is only used when the action is definitely being done at the moment. It must never be used when the implication is future, such as when we say in English, 'I am going on leave next year'. Such a statement should take the future tense in Swahili, 'I *shall* go on leave next year'.

N.B. This tense, when used with the verb 'kuwa' (to be) has only the meaning of 'I am becoming'. On account of its meaning, it is rarely heard. A special form of the present tense occurs for 'I am (being)', 'You are', 'He is' etc. (See ch. 19.)

Examples

Watoto wanaamka	The children are waking up.
Mtumishi anafagia	The servant is sweeping.
Mzee analala	The old man is lying down.
Ninatafuta mganga	I am looking for the doctor.
Tunakaa Arusha	We are staying in Arusha.

N.B. Proper nouns do not take a preposition.

Anataka kusoma	He/she is wanting to read.
Mnahitaji mpishi	You (pl.) are needing a cook.
Mwalimu anapiga watoto	The teacher is beating the children.
Wageni wanaanza kufika	The guests are starting to arrive.
Ninafuata mnyama	I am following an animal.

Vocabulary
The following vocabulary will be found useful at this stage:

Kabisa	Completely, extremely.
Sana	Very, a lot, very much.

These follow the word they qualify:

Anajaribu sana	He is trying hard (very much).
Fungeni kabisa!	Shut (pl.) completely!

The next four words are placed as in the English:

Na	And, with.
Leo	To-day
Sasa	Now
Tena	Again

	Leo ninafurahi	To-day I am (being) happy.
or	Ninafurahi leo	I am (being) happy to-day.
	Anangoja sasa	He is waiting now.
or	Sasa anangoja	Now he is waiting.
	Jaribu tena!	Try again!

Exercise 5

(a) *Translate:* Begin! Sweep! Don't wipe! Enter! (pl.) Pay! (pl.). Don't forget! (pl.). Read! (pl.). Climb! Don't start! Don't take! Don't use! (pl.) Don't lie down! Don't sweep now! Don't pay to-day! Read again! Get completely! Wake up and start! Wipe a lot! Don't start to read now! (pl.). Take care of the children!

(b) *Translate:* He is doing; we are trying; they are buying; you are searching; she is thinking; I am needing; you (pl.) are carrying; we are reading; he is hunting; he is paying; they are using; she is lying down; we are starting; I am staying; you are bringing; he is eating; they are coming; she is going; he is becoming; you (pl.) are remaining.

(c) *Translate:* The European is hunting; I like (am liking) a lot to read; they are extremely happy; the cook is cooking to-day; don't wait now; now I am needing a servant; pay now; the guest is staying to-day; try a lot to learn; you (pl.) are able to go now; the women and children are lying down; the doctor is coming to-day; we are shutting completely; the hunters are following the animals; the American is bringing teachers; we are learning a lot to-day; the patient is speaking again; you are selling (pl.) the animal; the child is becoming a thief; the visitors are trying to come to-day.

(d) *Translate:* Amka! Chukueni! Upate! Mwanze! Pandeni! Utunze! Fagia! Mwingie! Msipige! Usipate! Usome! Usiingie! Usianze sasa! Laleni! Msitumie! Futa! Ujifunze! Mchukue! Someni! Rudini sasa!

(e) *Translate:* Anakuja; tunaanza; unasoma; wanawinda; ninalima; mnachukua; anapata; wanafagia; tunaingia; analala; unapanda; ninachukua; tunahitaji; ninafikiri; anangoja; unajaribu; mnakula; ninakuwa; wanapika; ninanunua.

(f) *Translate:* Mzungu anakuja sasa; mwanamke anatunza watoto; wanaume wanalima leo; watumishi wanafagia na wanasafisha; wanafunzi wanasoma sana; wageni wanarudi Nairobi leo; wanyama wanakula sana sasa; wanawake wanachukua watoto; mgonjwa anaamka sasa; wanakaa Dar es Salaam.

8 Nouns — 2

M- MI- Noun Class

This class has not any specific content such as the previous one, but one thing we can say is that there are no nouns in common use descriptive of humans or animals in this class. Most trees and plants, however, are found in this class, but there are many other nouns which do not appear to have any general classification. Since most trees are contained in this class, we shall take as typical of the class the word

mti   a tree

Being a monosyllabic stem, the stress falls on the concord M-. This concord changes to MI- in the plural:

*m*ti   *mi*ti

The following are commonly used in this class:

Singular	*Plural*	
mbuyu	mibuyu	a Baobab tree (a very common, large, grotesque tree found in dry areas in East Africa) *adansonia digitata*
mchezo	michezo	a game (not animals), a toy
mfereji	mifereji	a ditch, furrow, channel
mfuko	mifuko	a bag, pocket
mguu	miguu	a leg, foot
mji	miji	a town, city
mkate	mikate	a loaf, bread
mkono	mikono	an arm, hand
mlango	milango	a door, opening, gate
mlima	milima	a mountain
mmea	mimea	a plant, crop
mshahara	mishahara	a salary, wages (used mainly in singular)
msumari	misumari	a nail (carpenter's)
mti	miti	a tree, post, tree trunk
mtihani	mitihani	an examination, test (scholastic)
mto	mito	a pillow, cushion, river
mzigo	mizigo	a load, luggage (pl.), burden

Unlike the other vowel stem nouns, those beginning with an 'o' do not take the 'w' after the concord 'M-':

moshi	mioshi	smoke (rarely used in plural)
moto	mioto	fire, heat (rarely used in plural)
moyo	mioyo	a heart

The other vowels, however, take the 'w' as in the previous class, but not in the plural:

mwaka	miaka	a year
mwembe	miembc	a mango tree
mwendo	miendo	speed, a journey
mwezi	miezi	a month, moon
mwiba	miiba	a thorn tree, thorn, prickle
mwili	miili	a body (living)
mwisho	miisho	an end, conclusion

It will be noted that there is no difference in appearance between the singular nouns of either this class or the M- WA- class. Thus, in order to know which plural concord should be given to a noun beginning

21

with 'm-', the meaning must be known, i.e. if the meaning is descriptive of a human being or animal, then the plural will be 'wa-'. If not human or animal, then it will be 'mi-'.

Subject prefixes

Each noun class has its own set of subject prefixes. Only the M- WA-class has six. The remaining classes have only one for singular and one for plural. For this class they are:

'u-' for the singular   (it)
'i-' for the plural   (they)

They are used in the same way as the other subject prefixes, being followed by a verb tense and verb stem. Before being able to use them, we need some more verbs:

ku-faa	to be suitable, of use (of quality)	ku-ota	to grow, bask, dream
ku-ficha	to hide	ku-poa	to get cool
ku-iva	to be ripe, cooked, to be ready for eating	ku-saidia	to help, assist
		ku-sitawi	to flourish, prosper
ku-legea	to be loose, slack	ku-toa	to give/put out
ku-nuka	to stink, smell bad	ku-tosha	to be sufficient (of quantity)
ku-nukia	to smell sweet		

Examples

Mimea inasitawi	The crops are flourishing.
Mkate unapoa	The bread is cooling.
Moshi unaficha mji	The smoke is hiding the town.
Msumari unalegea	The nail is loose.
Mpishi anapika mkate	The cook is cooking bread.
Wazungu wanapanda mlima	The Europeans are climbing the mountain.
Mzee anapanda mimea	The old man is planting crops.
Mkate unatosha	The bread is enough.
Miti inanukia	The trees are smelling nice.

Exercise 6

(a) *Translate:* Ditch; nails; a river; luggage; mountains; legs; smoke; a year; fire; pillows; trees; a door; crops; salary; hands; a Baobab tree; a thorn; games; bread; the end.

(b) *Translate:* The Baobab tree is flourishing; the bread is sufficient; the fire is cooling; the tree is smelling sweet; the crops are ripening; the ditch is suitable; the salary is sufficient; the mountains are hiding; the river is stinking; the year is starting.

(c) *Translate:* The child is shutting the door; the ditch is suitable; the crops are growing; the mountain is hiding the town; the mango trees are flourishing; open the door now! Bring bread to-day! Don't (pl.) shut the door!; the nails are sufficient; the child is climbing the tree now; the child is smelling the plant.

(d) *Give plurals of, and translate:* Mti; mtu; mto; msumari; mtoto; mlima; mwezi; mwili; mwizi; mganga; mfereji; mmea; mguu; mwanamke; mshahara; mwaka; mwalimu; mwanamume; moshi; mdudu.

(e) *Translate:* Ninanunua mkate; mtoto anaficha mikono; tunaleta mifuko; tunaweza kuona mwezi; anasaidia watoto kupanda mlima; funga mlango! Mzungu analipa mishahara leo; mti unaanguka sasa; toeni mikono; mtihani unaanza leo; watumishi wanachukua mizigo; mbuyu unasitawi sana; watu wanatosha; mnahitaji mkate; mimea inakauka; mwisho unakuja; moto unaleta moshi; tunapanda mimea sasa; usitumie mguu kufunga mlango!; mtoto ananunua mkate; mnyama ananusa mgeni.

9 Adjectives — 1

Consonant stem adjectives

Adjectives in Swahili are best divided into three groups:
(i) those which take agreements with the nouns they qualify;
(ii) those which take agreements, but have a vowel stem; and
(iii) those which are of Arabic origin, and do not take agreements.

The following take agreements, and have consonant stems:

-baya	bad	-nene	fat, thick
-bovu	rotten	-ngapi?	how many?
-chache	few (takes pl. only)		(takes pl. only)
-chafu	dirty	-pana	wide, broad, flat
-dogo	small, little	-pya	new
-fupi	short, low	-refu	long, deep, high, tall
-geni	strange, foreign, new (of people)	-tamu	sweet (sugary)
-gumu	hard, difficult	-tupu	empty, bare, pure ('nothing but')
-kali	fierce, sharp, steep, strict		
		-vivu	lazy, idle
-kavu	dry	-zima	whole
-kubwa	big, large	-zito	heavy

23

| -kuu | great, main, important | -zuri | good, nice, pleasant, beautiful, lovely |
| -kuukuu | old (of things) | -zee | old (of people) |

N.B. 'Ngapi?', *though not a true adjective, may be regarded as one.*

The Prefixes they take are almost always identical to the concord on the noun they describe. The agreements so far, then, will either be 'm-' or 'wa-', or for the other class, 'm-' or 'mi-'. (It will be seen in ch. 13 that exceptions do occur when dealing with humans and animals in other noun classes.)

Word order
Adjectives directly follow the noun they describe. They *never* precede it as in English. Thus we say:

| Mtu mzuri | A nice person | Watu wazuri | Nice people |
| Mti mdogo | A small tree | Miti midogo | Small trees |

We can also add the words 'sana' and 'kabisa' to an adjective to stress it.

e.g. Mwalimu mkali sana — A very strict teacher
Mzigo mzito kabisa — An extremely heavy load

Adjectives can follow one another in any order, except that adjectives descriptive of *quantity* usually come at the end of the list. In the above list '-chache' and '-ngapi?' are quantitative,

e.g. Mtoto mchafu mfupi — A dirty, short child
(these adjectives could be in any order)
Mikate mitamu michache — A few sweet loaves.
(here '-chache' must come at the end of the list)
Mizigo mizito mingapi? — How many heavy loads?
(again '-ngapi?' must come at the end)
(i.e. They are in exact reversal of order from the English)

N.B. It is fairly unlikely that three adjectives would be used all together, but the same principles would apply should it be necessary.

Sentence examples
Watoto wangapi wanasoma? — How many children are reading?
Anaficha mikono michafu — He is hiding dirty hands.
Mwanafunzi mnene mrefu anachukua mfuko mdogo mtupu — The tall fat pupil is carrying a small empty bag.
Mpishi mpya anapika mikate michache — The new cook is cooking a few loaves.

Exercise 7

(a) *Translate, adding the hyphen:* Empty; fat; a few; dirty; large; hard; bad; sweet; good; lazy; strict; small; rotten; sharp; long; great; wide; how many? deep; short.

(b) *Translate:* A bad door; a few loaves; a tall person; a lazy cook; a whole loaf; an empty bag; high mountains; a strange teacher; a fat woman; a new game; a large town; long legs; a small salary; heavy loads; sweet bread; a steep mountain; dirty hands; sharp thorns; fierce fires; how many inhabitants?

(c) *Translate:* A small bad loaf; a very good salary; a few long nails; a big fierce fire; long arms and short legs; a few small fierce insects; lazy old men; a whole big loaf; how many fat women? strange European hunters; I am planting good new crops; he is trying a difficult examination; shut the big doors! the small children are buying a good game; how many people are coming to-day? the long nails are loose; we are looking for a dry river; the small heavy doors are suitable; would you bring a few loads now! don't cook with dirty hands!

(d) *Translate:* -kavu; -chafu; -zima; -ngapi?; -pya; -baya; -chache; -bovu; -tamu; -zito; -dogo; -geni; -kubwa; -nene; -gumu; -fupi; -kuu; -tupu; -vivu; -refu.

(e) *Translate:* Mwanamume mfupi; mito mipana; mkate mkavu; mchezo mzuri; watoto wangapi?; mbuyu mkubwa; mganga mkuu; misumari michache; mimea mirefu; mwezi mzima.

(f) *Translate:* Tunaingia mji mkubwa; lete mfuko mtupu! mimea mipya inasitawi; mtoto mnene anachukua mzigo mdogo; mikate michache inatosha; wageni wangapi wanakuja leo? mtumishi anasafisha mlango mchafu; mkate mbovu unanuka; ninahitaji mto mdogo; unajaribu mwendo mkali.

10   Demonstratives

There are two demonstratives. The demonstrative of proximity, 'this', and the demonstrative of distance, 'that'. Both have plurals, namely 'these' and 'those'.

In Swahili, the demonstrative must agree with the noun it qualifies. The agreements, however, are not concord agreements as on nouns, but are taken from the *subject prefix* agreements, though not necessarily placed as a prefix.

Demonstratives of proximity: this, these

All these demonstratives begin with the letter 'h-'. They all end with the appropriate subject prefix, then between the two, the same vowel occurring in the subject prefix is repeated. Thus in the M- MI- class, we get

Singular: 'h-?-u' The vowel is a 'u' so we get 'huu';
Plural: 'h-?-i' The vowel is an 'i' so we get 'hii'.

For the M- WA- class, we get the only exception found throughout the demonstratives. It occurs in the singular form. We would expect the demonstrative to end with '-a', but instead we find '-yu' which is derived from an old Bantu form. So we get:

Singular: 'h-?-yu' The vowel is a 'u', so we get 'huyu';
Plural: 'h-?- wa' The vowel is an 'a', so we get 'hawa'.

Demonstratives of distance: that, those
All these demonstratives this time *begin* with their appropriate subject prefixes (again getting 'yu' for the M- WA- class singular) and this time they *all* end with '-le'. So we get:

m- wa- class Singular: yu + le = yule
           Plural: wa + le = wale
m- mi- class Singular: u + le = ule
          Plural: i + le = ile

Summary

	This	These	That	Those
M- WA- class	huyu	hawa	yule	wale
M- MI- class	huu	hii	ule	ile

N.B. The demonstrative is only used with the 3rd person so that it has only one form for singular, and one for plural.

Word order
It is now necessary to summarize word order.

Basically, Swahili sentences follow the trend of the English as far as subject—verb—object is concerned. The complete reversal is found, however, in the description of the subject or object.

e.g. In English we say, 'These few good little children' whereas in Swahili we have to say, 'Children little good, few, these'.

As in English, the adjectives 'good' and 'little' can be interchanged, but 'few' in English must come first of the adjectives, and in Swahili, must come last of the adjectives. The demonstrative, note, comes at the very end in Swahili. So in Swahili we get:

noun—adjectives—quantity—demonstrative

e.g. Watoto wadogo wazuri wachache hawa—
       These few small good children.

N.B. Though this is not a strict rule, the learner is advised to stick to this order initially. Alternative positions of the demonstrative are encountered due to stress. (See ch. 60.)

Examples

Wazungu hawa	These Europeans
Mpishi mzuri yule	That good cook
Miti mirefu hii	These tall trees
Mkate mbovu huu	This rotten bread
Watoto wadogo wale	Those small children
Misumari mifupi ile	Those short nails

Exercise 8

(a) *Translate:* These people; that child; this bread; those trees; this month; that leg; those nails; this year; that doctor; those women; this heart; these thorns; that fire; this luggage; that door; that salary; those Europeans; that teacher; those thieves; those mountains.

(b) *Translate:* That high mountain; these few loaves; those dirty hands; these good crops; this new year; that fierce speed; that fat body; that large town; those small insects; that dry ditch; that empty bag; those long legs; that large Baobab tree; this small Britisher; that fierce fire; this difficult examination; those sharp nails; these small children; these new pupils; that large animal.

(c) *Translate:* Bring (pl.) that heavy load! That teacher is waiting for these children. Seize that thief! That bad bread is smelling very bad. These tall trees give out (are giving out) a very nice smell. Those small loaves are enough. This small test is very suitable! That child is trying hard this year. Don't hide those hands! Would you shut that door!

(d) *Translate:* Mzee yule; mpishi huyu; Wagiriki wale; mlima huu; mtu yule; mmea huu; miaka ile; mkate ule; michezo ile; mfuko huu; wenyeji wale; mgonjwa huyu; mti huu; wageni hawa; moshi ule; wanaume hawa; wadudu wale; mishahara ile; mnyama huyu; mkono huu.

(e) *Translate:* Mlango mdogo ule; mkate mrefu huu; mlima mdogo ule; mpishi mgeni yule; mwaka mpya huu; wenyeji wachache wale; mchezo mzuri ule; mto mpana ule; mti mrefu huu; mwalimu mkali yule; mganga mdachi huyu; mshahara mkubwa huu; moyo mzuri ule; mtumishi mvivu huyu; mwembe mdogo huu; miguu michafu ile; wageni Wazungu hawa; miiba mikali hii; mwili mnene huu; mzigo mzito ule.

(f) *Translate:* Wanakamata mwizi mbaya yule; watu wazuri hawa wanafaa sana; watoto wachache wale wanakwenda Nairobi; usije na mikono mitupu; miti midogo ile inasitawi sana; ninapenda mkate mtamu huu; wageni wale wanapanda mlima mkubwa ule; misumari michache hii inatosha; mtumishi huyu anasaidia sana; wadudu wakali hawa wanatafuta wanyama wale.

11 Location (Where?) and Responses

Locational suffix

There is a very useful suffix which can be added to almost any common noun (except human or animal) to denote the meaning of 'in, on, at, near, by' etc. This suffix is '-ni'

e.g.
mfereji	—a ditch	mferejini	—in the ditch
mfuko	—a pocket	mfukoni	—in the pocket
mguu	—a leg	mguuni	—on the leg
mkono	—a hand	mkononi	—in the hand
mlima	—a mountain	mlimani	—on the mountain
mwisho	—the end	mwishoni	—at the end
mto	—a river	mtoni	—at/in/by the river

N.B. *The same can also be used with their plurals.*

We can also, for this purpose, add a few other useful nouns from other classes:

jiko	—a kitchen	jikoni	—in the kitchen
kikapu	—a basket	kikapuni	—in the basket
meza	—a table	mezani	—on the table
nyumba	—a house	nyumbani	—in the house/at home
soko	—a market	sokoni	—on/at the market

(The context of the sentence usually makes it clear which preposition is meant.)

Proper nouns, however, do not take this suffix. The preposition is left as understood. Thus

'to Nairobi' in Swahili would simply be 'Nairobi'
or 'in Nairobi' in Swahili would simply be 'Nairobi'
e.g. Mzee yule anakaa Nairobi—That old man lives in Nairobi,
but Mzee yule anakaa mjini—That old man lives in the town.

N.B. *If this prepositional suffix is used, we cannot at this stage qualify the noun bearing the suffix with any other word such as an adjective or demonstrative.*

We cannot, for example, say, 'Mfukoni ule' for 'in that bag'. We shall, at this stage, only be able to say 'in the/a bag' with no other qualification. The reason for this will be seen in chapter 56, since the addition of this suffix in fact renders the word one of location which must therefore be given locative agreements.

Where?

If we ask the question 'Where?' we automatically refer to location. Location in Swahili takes three types of agreements depending on the type of location.

The letter 'P' denotes definite location;
The letter 'K' denotes indefinite location, or area;
The letter 'M' denotes inside location.

In the question, 'Where is the bread?' we have the word 'Where?', the verb 'to be' and finally the noun. In Swahili the verb 'to be' (in this case in the present tense) is replaced by a construction which always ends in -O which is preceded by either -P-, -K-, or -M- according to the location as shown above. Note that this construction only applies to the present tense. If the past or future tense is needed, the verb 'to be' is used in its regular form. (See chapters 12 and 22.) Thus we get '-po', '-ko', and '-mo'. We now have to place the subject prefix agreeing with the noun in question on the front.

N.B. The third person singular of the M- WA- class is again 'yu-' and not 'a-' in this form.

Thus to return again to our question, 'Where is the bread?', in Swahili we have to reverse the question, 'The bread is where?' The word for 'Where?' is 'Wapi?'. So we get:

Mkate uko wapi?

Notice that the '-ko' agreement has been used. This is logical because if we are asking where something is, it is because the location is unknown and therefore indefinitive, hence '-ko'. The reply, however, could be either of the locative agreements, depending on where it is to be found.

Thus the reply could be:

Mkate upo mezani	The bread is on the table (definite)
Mkate uko jikoni	The bread is in the kitchen (somewhere)
Mkate umo kikapuni	The bread is in the basket (inside)

Similarly we might ask:

Misumari iko wapi?   Where are the nails?

Reply: Misumari imo mfukoni. The nails are in the bag; or we might simply get 'Imo mfukoni' with the noun omitted.

With the M- WA- class, the same would apply:

Watoto wako wapi?   Where are the children?

Reply: Watoto wapo nyumbani The children are *at* the house

29

Watoto wako nyumbani	The children are at home (somewhere)
Watoto wamo nyumbani	The children are *in* the house
or we might get	
Watoto wanakula jikoni	The children are eating in the kitchen.

(There is no reference to location here, and this time the verb 'to be' is not used.)

N.B. Remember that this construction is a form of the verb 'to be' so should never be used when another verb exists in the same sentence.

Singular:	Mwalimu *yu*ko wapi? (NOT ako wapi?)	Where is the teacher?
reply:	Mwalimu *yu*ko nyumbani	The teacher is at home.
or:	Mwalimu analala	The teacher is sleeping.

Summary

	Definite	*Indefinite*	*Inside*
M- WA-	yupo	yuko	yumo (sing.)
	wapo	wako	wamo (plu.)
M- MI-	upo	uko	umo (sing.)
	ipo	iko	imo (plu.)

Interesting note: Many East Africans, when pointing, do so with their chin.

Demonstratives of location: here; there.

Using the same P and K for definite and indefinite location, we can make up the demonstratives of location. We need the subject prefix for both which is
  'pa-' and 'ku-' respectively.
Thus we get

Hapa —Here (definite)	Pale —There (definite)
(*Lit.* this place)	(*Lit.* that place)
Huku —Hereabouts	Kule Thereabouts

Note the Swahili idiom for the expression: 'Here and there'

In Swahili they say—'Hereabouts and hereabouts'
                     'Huku na huku' (not 'Huku na kule')

IMPORTANT: In Swahili, you should never mix up locative 'P's with locative 'K's in the same phrase, since this would be contradictory.

For example, you must *not* say
    'Yuko hapa' for 'He is here'.
It must either be 'Yupo hapa' (He is here) or
                 'Yuko huku' (He is hereabouts)

Examples

Mlango mkubwa uko wapi?	Where is the big door?
Upo pale	It is right there
Watoto wako wapi?	Where are the children
Wanasimama kule	They are standing over there
Mpishi yuko wapi?	Where is the cook?
Yuko jikoni	He is somewhere in the kitchen
Mgeni yupo?	Is the guest here?
Yupo	He is here

N.B. In the last example, the question was not 'Where?' but simply 'Is he here?', therefore definite location can be used.

Negative location

The construction of the negative form of this specialised use of the verb 'to be' is very easy. We simply add the negative prefix 'ha-' to each agreement, thus:

M- WA- class

Hayupo	He is not here	Hawapo	They are not here
Hayuko	He is not about	Hawako	They are not about
Hayumo	He is not in	Hawamo	They are not in

M- MI- class

Haupo	It is not here	Haipo	They are not here
Hauko	It is not about	Haiko	They are not about
Haumo	It is not inside	Haimo	They are not inside

Examples:

Mganga yupo hapa?	Is the doctor here?
Hayupo hapa, yuko mjini	He is not here, he is in town
Moto uko wapi?	Where is the fire?
Hauko huku, uko mlimani	It is not around here, it is on the mountain.
Wanyama hawako?	Aren't the animals about?
Hawako	They aren't.
Mgonjwa hayupo?	Isn't the sick person here?
Yupo	He is here.
Bwana yuko?	Is the Bwana about?
Yuko sokoni.	He is at the market.

Exercise 9

(a) *Give the '-po' agreement to the following to convey the meaning—is here.* e.g. *Mganga yupo—The doctor is here:* Bread; the nails; the children; the bag; the European; the river; the trees; the end; the guests; the luggage.

(b) *Translate:* Where is the patient? Where are the nails? Where is the pillow? Where is the teacher? Where are the children? Where are the salaries? Where is the cook? Where is the moon? Where is the German? Where are the women? The game is here; the doors are there; the animals are thereabouts; the guest is hereabouts; the men are here; the servant is thereabouts; the luggage is there; the plants are thereabouts; the mountain is there; the old man is here; the end is here.

(c) *Translate:* At the door; in the hands; in the year; on the tree; at the game; on the leg; in the Baobab tree; in the ditch; on the mountain; in town; on the table; at the end; in the pockets; in the basket; in the kitchen; at home; at the river; in the fire; in the smoke; on the foot; at the market.

(d) *Translate:* The toys are not here; the children are not about; the end is not here; the doctor is not about here; the insects are not here; the mango tree is not thereabouts; the loaves are not here; the students are not about here; that woman is not here; that luggage is not there.

(e) *Translate:* Where is the river? It is over there. Where are the new games? They are on the table. Where are the animals? They are not here, they are among the Baobab trees. Where is the servant? He is sweeping in the house. Where are those bad insects? They are not about here, they are by the river. Where is the old man? He is buying bread in town. Where are those servants? They are helping to bring the luggage here. Is the European here? He is not here, he is on the mountain. Are the animals not about? They are not about here. Is the luggage not here? It is not here, it is in the house. The women are at the market.

(f) *Translate:* Mwembe upo pale; miiba iko kule; mchezo upo mezani; mgeni yupo mlangoni; watoto wako kule; mwizi yuko; mlango upo pale; mkate upo jikoni; mshahara umo mfukoni; mto haupo hapa.

(g) *Translate:* Mkate uko wapi? Pale mezani; Wanyama wakubwa wale wako wapi? Wako mitini; Misumari mirefu ile iko wapi? Imo mfukoni; Wanafunzi wachache wale wapo? Hawapo. Wanasoma mjini; Mwiba mbaya ule uko wapi. Upo hapa mkononi; Mtoto mgonjwa yuko wapi? Yumo nyumbani; Mzigo mzito ule uko wapi? Upo pale; Mtumishi yupo? Hayupo; Mgeni yuko? Analala; Mji uko wapi? Upo pale.

Responses

No. The Swahili for 'no' is 'la!' 'siyo' or 'sivyo!' ('Siyo' and 'Sivyo' are also used to translate 'not' in the sense of 'not so' or 'not thus'; e.g. mti mkubwa siyo mdogo—a large tree not a small (one).)

But one will often hear 'Hapana!' used instead. This is more or less accepted now, but literally means 'There is not here', therefore it is better (and easier) to use the proper words.

Yes. There is no word in Swahili for 'Yes'.

Instead, one has to use an emphatic which really means 'Indeed', or 'That is so'. The word used is 'Ndiyo!' This means that you have to remember that 'Ndiyo' given in reply to a negative question will in fact mean 'no', but to an affirmative question 'Yes'.

e.g. Watoto wanakula?	Are the children eating?
Ndiyo!	Yes (indeed they are)
Bwana hayupo?	Is the Bwana not here?
Ndiyo!	No. (indeed he isn't)
Bwana yupo?	Is the Bwana here?
La!	No, he isn't.

Bwana yupo?   Is the Bwana here?
Ndiyo, yupo   Yes, he is here.

N.B. You will have noticed that there is no reversal of words when asking a question without an interrogatory word as there is in English. In speech, intonation stresses the question by raising the voice slightly at the end of the question. In statements, the voice is slightly lowered at the end.

12 Past Simple Tense

The past simple tense in English is the tense we use to express 'I did go', or 'I went'. (This is *not* the same as 'I have been'.) In Swahili, the tense sign used is -LI-. It is used in exactly the same way as the -NA-present tense. Thus if we take the verb 'Kutaka' again, we get:

Ni-li-taka	Nilitaka	I wanted, or I did want
U-li-taka	Ulitaka	You wanted, or you did want
A-li-taka	Alitaka	He/she wanted, or he/she did want
Tu-li-taka	Tulitaka	We wanted, or we did want
M-li-taka	Mlitaka	You wanted, or you did want
Wa-li-taka	Walitaka	They wanted, or they did want

Verbs of Arabic origin are treated the same way:

Kujibu—to reply

Ni-li-jibu	Nilijibu	I replied, or I did reply
U-li-jibu	Ulijibu	You replied, or you did reply
A-li-jibu	Alijibu	He/she replied, or he/she did reply
Tu-li-jibu	Tulijibu	We replied, or we did reply
M-li-jibu	Mlijibu	You replied, or you did reply
Wa-li-jibu	Walijibu	They replied, or they did reply

Monosyllabic verbs again retain their infinitive 'ku-':

Kuwa—to be

Ni-li-kuwa	Nilikuwa	I was, I became
U-li-kuwa	Ulikuwa	You were, you became
A-li-kuwa	Alikuwa	He/she was, he/she became
Tu-li-kuwa	Tulikuwa	We were, we became
M-li-kuwa	Mlikuwa	You were, you became
Wa-li-kuwa	Walikuwa	They were, they became

33

Examples

Mti ule ulianguka.	That tree fell.
Ulikuwa wapi?	Where were you?
Nilikuwa pale.	I was there.
Misumari ilikuwa mezani.	The nails were on the table.
Mimea ilisitawi sana.	The crops flourished much.
Mzigo ulitosha.	The load was sufficient.
Mliweza kununua mkate?	Were you (pl.) able to buy bread?

More verbs

ku-andika	to write	ku-inua	to lift, raise
ku-angalia	to watch out, pay attention, to look at, to be careful of	ku-jaza	to fill (causative)
		ku-kimbia	to run
ku-chagua	to choose	ku-ongeza	to increase, to add to
		ku-panga	to arrange, hire
ku-cheza	to play	ku-pumzika	to rest, stop working
ku-endelea	to continue, progress	ku-tazama	to look at, gaze
ku-funika	to cover	ku-tembea	to walk
ku-fyeka	to slash, cut with a panga, to clear the bush	ku-toka	to come out of, come from, go out
ku-kohoa	to cough	ku-uliza	to question, ask (a question)
ku-kubali	to agree		
ku-kumbuka	to remember		
ku-maliza	to finish, end	ku-zoea	to get used to, become accustomed
ku-nawa	to wash hands and face	ku-zungumza	to converse (with purpose)
ku-omba	to beg, pray, to ask (a favour)		

Exercise 10

(a) *Translate:* I wrote; he remembered; we increased; you covered; they raised; you (pl.) became accustomed to; I asked; he got; we filled; you (pl.) coughed; she ran; we ate; they went; he played; I slashed; you brought; they went out; we conversed; he agreed; they paid attention; I chose; we continued; we thought; you finished; he washed hands; they begged; he answered; you arranged; you (pl.) rested; she looked at; they walked; we tried; I asked; he forgot; he slept; I dreamt; they did start; you read; she did see; they paid.

(b) *Translate:* Would you write; he is taking care; get out!; don't cough; would you (pl.) raise; don't (pl.) fill; he is washing hands; ask! (pl.); they are playing.

(c) *Translate:* The animal ate the insects; I bought a few small loaves (of bread); the small child fell into the ditch; that salary was sufficient; he loved that woman; those hunters hunted fierce animals; we climbed that tall mountain; did you (pl.) see those tall trees? Those trees smelt very nice; was he able to sell that load in town? I paid those people; those children continued to play; the cook put out that bread on the table; those students went to the town; these children wanted to try to play that new game; we agreed to try again to-day; the old man stayed here a whole year; did you remember to cover that bread? We are becoming accustomed to living here; that pupil finished that examination to-day.

(d) *Translate:* Tulilala; walitumia; aliwinda; anauliza; walizungumza; aliandika; anatembea; ukimbie; msicheze; walipata; nilipenda; tulikuwa; kumbukeni; tunaomba; alifika; endelea!; pumzikeni; nilihitaji; waliingia; tunakubali.

(e) *Translate:* Msicheze nyumbani; mtoto yule anamaliza kuandika mtihani sasa; mnyama huyu alipanda mbuyu ule; mzee yule alikuwa mpishi mzuri; mfereji mkavu ule ulinuka sana; watu wale walitosha kusaidia; mimea michache ilisitawi mwaka huu; tunapenda sana kucheza mchezo ule; aliweka mkate pale mezani; alifagia nyumbani na sasa anapumzika.

13 Nouns—3

KI- VI- Noun Class

This class is one of the easiest classes to use as far as agreements are concerned.

The following have the concords KI- in the singular. VI- in the plural

Singular	*Plural*	
kiatu	viatu	a shoe (or any footwear)
kiazi	viazi	a potato
kiberiti	viberiti	a box of matches, lighter
kichwa	vichwa	a head
kidole	vidole	a finger, toe
kidonda	vidonda	a sore, ulcer
kidonge	vidonge	a pill, tablet
kijiji	vijiji	a village (cf. Mji a town)
kijiko	vijiko	a spoon, teaspoon (cf. Mwiko a ladle)
kikapu	vikapu	a basket
kiko	viko	a pipe (smoker's)
kikombe	vikombe	a cup
kilima	vilima	a hill (cf. Mlima a mountain)

kilimo		agriculture (not used in plural)
kioo	vioo	a mirror, sheet of glass
kipande	vipande	a piece, portion, stint, slice
kipimo	vipimo	a measuring device of any sort
kisahani	visahani	a saucer (cf. Sahani, a plate)
kisima	visima	a well, water hole
kisu	visu	a knife
kitabu	vitabu	a book
kitanda	vitanda	a bed
kitambaa	vitambaa	a cloth, material
kiti	viti	a chair, stool, seat
kitu	vitu	a thing

But many nouns of vowel stem, instead of having the concords KI-, and VI-, have CH- and VY- instead. However, as it will be seen from the above list, this does not apply to *all* vowel stem nouns.

chakula	vyakula	food
chandalua	vyandalua	mosquito net, tarpaulin (sometimes chanda*r*ua)
cheti	vyeti	note, chit, certificate, reference of work, etc.
chombo	vyombo	tool, container, vessel of any kind —also used for furniture.
choo	vyoo	lavatory, latrine, faeces (contrast kioo, vioo)
chuma	vyuma	piece of iron, metal (unspecific)
chumba	vyumba	room (cf. nyumba, a house)

Besides all these nouns referring to things, a few nouns are found referring to animals, the most common being:

kiboko	viboko	a hippopotamus (or a whip, since in days of slavery, hippo hide was used for whips)
kifaru	vifaru	a rhinoceros

And the following persons are also included, either because of incapacity, or subordinate status:

kibarua	vibarua	a labourer, daily-paid worker
kijana	vijana	a youth
kipofu	vipofu	a blind person
kiwete	viwete	a lame person, cripple
kiziwi	viziwi	a deaf person

N.B. *The prefixes KI- and VI- (together with the infix -JI- before a vowel or monosyllabic stem) are often used to denote a diminutive form when the stem is taken from another noun class as is seen from some words in the above list. (However, a JI- prefix on its own may suggest augmentation. See Ch. 46.)*

Adjectival agreements
With the consonant-stem adjectives already given, the concord agreements follow similarly to the other classes, taking the same concord prefixes as the noun described, namely KI- in the singular, and VI- in the plural.

e.g.		
Viazi vidogo		Small potatoes
Kijiji kidogo		A small village
Vikombe vichafu		Dirty cups
Kisu kikali sana		A very sharp knife
Viko virefu vipya vingapi?		How many long new pipes?

Note also that though a vowel-stem noun may have a CH- concord, the adjective, if consonant stem, will still have the KI- concord.

Cheti kichafu	A dirty note
Chumba kikubwa	A large room
Chuma kizito sana	A very heavy piece of iron

Subject prefixes
These are easily remembered in this class, since they are the same as the concords, namely KI- in the singular, and VI- in the plural. Thus:

Chakula kinanuka	The food smells bad
Kitambaa kidogo kinafaa	A small cloth is suitable
Vidonge vidogo vilitosha	The small pills were sufficient
Vyeti vilikuwa virefu	The references were long

The verb 'to be' with the locative
The forms are:

Kipo	Vipo	(definite place)
Kiko	Viko	(indefinite place)
Kimo	Vimo	(inside place)

Examples:

Kisu kiko wapi?	Where is the knife?
Kipo pale mezani	It is there on the table.
Viazi viko wapi?	Where are the potatoes?
Vimo kikapuni	They are in the basket.
Chakula kipo mezani?	Is the food on the table?
Ndiyo, Bwana, kipo.	Indeed, Bwana, it is.

Demonstratives
From the subject prefixes, we can also make up the demonstratives:

THIS	Beginning with 'h', ending with 'ki', then 'i' in between — 'hiki'
THESE	Beginning with 'h', ending with 'vi', then 'i' in between — 'hivi'

37

THAT	Beginning with 'ki', ending with 'le' — 'kile'
THOSE	Beginning with 'vi', ending with 'le' — 'vile'

Thus:

Kitabu hiki	This book
Chakula kile	That food
Visu hivi	These knives
Vyumba vile	Those rooms
Kidonda kibaya kile	That bad sore
Vyombo vipya hivi	This new furniture (These new furnishings)

Languages
Most languages are also placed in this class, and are given, therefore, normal KI- VI- agreements, but are not used in the plural.

Kiswahili	Swahili
Kiingereza	English
Kifaransa	French
Kidachi	German
Kigiriki	Greek
Kilatini	Latin
Kilugha (can have plural Vilugha)	Local tribal language (unspecified), dialect

Examples

Safisha vitu vichafu vile	Clean those dirty things
Funika chakula hiki	Cover this food
Tunajifunza Kiswahili	We are learning Swahili
Kiko kiko wapi?	Where is the pipe?
Kipo mezani	It (the pipe) is on the table.
Kitambaa kipya hiki kilikuwa kichafu sana.	This new cloth was very dirty.
Tulipanda kilima kidogo kile.	We climbed that small hill.
Ninasoma kitabu kizuri kabisa.	I am reading an extremely good book.
Mpishi anaomba cheti.	The cook is asking for a chit.
Choo kiko wapi? Kipo pale.	Where is the lavatory? It is there.

Person and animal agreements
Special mention must be made of agreements given to nouns referring to persons and animals which are not classified in the M- WA- class, such as we have just seen in the KI- VI- class.

The rule is that regardless of noun class, a word describing an animal or person is given M- WA- agreements, both in concords, and subject prefixes.

Thus we should say:

Vibarua wachache wale walikuja—Those few labourers came (and NOT 'Vibarua vichache vile vilikuja.')

Similarly, we should say:

Kifaru mkubwa yule alikuwa mkali sana—That large rhino was very fierce (and NOT 'Kifaru kikubwa kile kilikuwa kikali sana.')

N.B. The same applies to 'Bwana', e.g.
Bwana yule anakuja   That gentleman is coming.

Exercise 11

(a) *Translate:* Fingers; a lighter; agriculture; Latin; a sheet of glass; saucers; pills; a spoon; shoes; potatoes; a knife; baskets; a labourer; a head; youths; Swahili; a water hole; a village; English; a rhinoceros; a pipe; a W.C.; a mirror; a room; food; a whip; a measuring device; a note; a well; a hill.

(b) *Translate:* This village; those rooms; this bed; these labourers; this cup; that basket; those hippos; this chit; this agriculture; this Swahili; that pipe; those pieces; these hills; this thing; that chair; this food; this knife; that lighter; this cloth; these potatoes.

(c) *Translate:* That small spoon; this bad sore; that difficult dialect; these empty baskets; this small chair; those dirty shoes; that large empty room; this long new pipe; how many good books? that heavy iron.

(d) *Translate:* That room was very small; Do the washing up (lit. Wash the vessels); be careful of this sharp knife; that old man is speaking a tribal language; would you arrange this room; don't forget to go to the village to buy potatoes; the women bought new shoes in Arusha; fill this basket with potatoes at the market; that sore on the finger was very bad; put out those new cups and saucers; Where is the sore? It is there on the leg; These large potatoes are very suitable; those labourers came to clean that room; the doctor brought these pills; we saw a very fierce rhinoceros in Manyara; that bed needs a new pillow; put these things in the basket; where is the W.C.? It is over there; how many pieces are you wanting? A few; those tall youths went to bring a few chairs.

(e) *Translate and give plurals to:* Kidole; kitu; chombo; kioo; kidonda; kikapu; kisahani; choo; kifaru; kijiji; chandalua; kibarua; kiatu; kiazi; kilima; kiko; cheti; kiberiti; chumba; kichwa; kiboko; kidonge; kijana; kijiko; kikombe; kipofu; kipande; kiziwi; chuma; kipimo; kitabu; kisu; kiwete; kitambaa; kisima; kiti; kitanda; chakula; kilugha.

(f) *Translate:* Cheti kizuri kabisa; kitabu kikubwa kile; chakula kitamu hiki; viti vizuri vingapi? vyumba vidogo vile; mzee kipofu yule; kisima kirefu kile; vijiko vichafu hivi; vikapu vitupu vichache; chombo kikubwa kile.

(g) *Translate:* Nilipata kitambaa kipya mjini leo; vibarua wazuri wale walifaulu kuinua chuma kizito hiki; chandalua kikubwa kile kinafaa kufunika vitu hivi; mtoto yule anapenda kutazama kiooni; usisahau kula vidonge vile; kibarua huyu anaomba cheti; wenyeji wale wanazoea kilimo hiki; chakula kizuri hiki kinatosha sana; kisu kikali hiki kinafaa sana kukata mkate; kiko kiko wapi? kipo pale kitini.

14 Adjectives—2

Vowel stem adjectives

The following are vowel stem adjectives commonly in use:

-aminifu	honest, trustworthy, faithful
-ema	good (character), used mainly of people instead of -zuri.
-embamba	thin, narrow, slender
-ekundu	red
-epesi	light, easy
-erevu	cunning, crafty
-eupe	white, light coloured.
-eusi	black, dark coloured.
-ingi	many, much
-ingine	some (when referring to part of the whole), another, other(s)

N.B. (1) Since '-ingi' and '-ingine' refer to quantity, they will come last in order of adjectives.

(2) In a sentence such as 'Give me some bread', the word 'some' is a form of indefinite article, and is therefore not translated into Swahili. Being an indefinite article, it is not in fact translated at all. A fairly accurate guide as to when to use '-ingine' in Swahili, is to test the phrase to see if you could go on by saying, '..... others .....' i.e. 'some people like mangoes'. You could go on with 'others don't', whereas you could not make sense with 'Give me some bread, others .....' The former will therefore use 'ingine', the latter will not.

Agreements

These being vowel stems, care must be taken to cater for a few changes which result:

M- WA- class. The changes are similar to those which occurred in vowel stem nouns, such as Mwana, where the stem was -ana, and the concord M- took a -W- on account of the vowel. (M- before a vowel takes a -W-) Thus—Mwaminifu.

e.g. Mtumishi mwaminifu—a trustworthy servant.

In the plural we get WA- plus -A giving WA-, since the two A's merge. Thus—Waminifu.

e.g. Watumishi waminifu—trustworthy servants.

N.B. By virtue of its meaning, this adjective is never used with nouns denoting things, therefore other agreements do not exist.

Similarly, with the other adjectives we can use the following guide:

```
M plus a vowel  = MW
A plus A        = A
I plus E        = YE
I plus I        = I
A plus E        = E
A plus I        = E
```

Thus we get:

M- WA- class. *Singular*

M-w-ema	=Mwema.	e.g. Mtu mwema—a good person.
M-w-eusi	=Mweusi.	e.g. Mzee mweusi—a dark old man.
M-w-ingine	=Mwingine.	e.g. Mtoto mwingine—another child.

N.B. The adjective '-ingi' is never used with singular agreements in this class, although frequently used in the singular in other classes.

Plurals

wa-ema	=wema.	e.g. Watu wema—good people.
wa-eusi	=weusi.	e.g. Wazee weusi—dark old men.
wa-ingi	=wengi.	e.g. Wazungu wengi—many Europeans.
wa-ingine	=wengine.	e.g. Watoto wengine—other children.

M- MI- class. *Singular*

m-w-eusi	=mweusi.	e.g. Mti mweusi—a dark tree.
m-w-ekundu	=mwekundu.	e.g. Mlango mwekundu—a red door.
m-w-ingi-	=mwingi.	e.g. Mkate mwingi—much bread.
m-w-ingine	=mwingine.	e.g. Mto mwingine—another river.

Plurals

mi-eusi	=myeusi.	e.g. Miti myeusi—dark trees
mi-ekundu	=myekundu.	e.g. Milango myekundu—red doors.
mi-ingi	=mingi.	e.g. Mikate mingi—many loaves
mi-ingine	=mingine	e.g. Mito mingine—other rivers.

The KI- VI- class, however, is not constant. The vowel -E takes CH-singular, and VY- plural, whereas the vowel -I takes KI- singular and VI- plural, thus:

Singular

ki-epesi	=chepesi	e.g. Kiti chepesi—a light chair.
ki-eupe	=cheupe.	e.g. Kiatu cheupe—a white shoe.

| ki-ingi | =kingi. | e.g. Kitambaa kingi—much cloth. |
| ki-ingine | =kingine. | e.g. Kitabu kingine—another book. |

Plural

vi-epesi	=vyepesi.	e.g. Viti vyepesi—light chairs.
vi-eupe	=vyeupe.	e.g. Viatu vyeupe—white shoes.
vi-ingi	=vingi.	e.g. Vitambaa vingi—many cloths.
vi-ingine	=vingine.	e.g. Vitabu vingine—other books.

Adjectives describing 'people'

Where any adjective taking agreements is used to describe a 'person' or 'people' as translated by 'Mtu' or 'Watu', the actual words 'Mtu' and 'Watu' are often omitted as being understood. This has the effect of making the adjective into a noun. For example:

'A good person' could be translated as 'Mtu mwema' or just 'Mwema'.

'A few people' could be translated as 'Watu wachache' or just 'wachache'.

'How many people?' could be translated as 'Watu wangapi?' or just 'Wangapi?'

'Some people are going, others are coming', could be 'Watu wengine wanakwenda, watu wengine wanakuja', or just simply 'Wengine wanakwenda, wengine wanakuja.'

In practice, the words 'Mtu' and 'Watu' will always be omitted where the context is perfectly obvious. Other words such as 'Mpishi' and 'Mtoto' etc., will always be left in, since they are essential to describe the person.

Examples:

Mwizi mrefu mwerevu.	A tall, cunning thief.
Watoto Wazungu wengi.	Many European children.
Watoto waminifu wachache.	A few trustworthy children.
Mlango mwembamba mwekundu.	A narrow red door.
Mkate mweusi mwingine.	Another brown loaf.
Miti mirefu myembamba mingi.	Many tall, slender trees.
Lete kiti kizuri kingine.	Bring another good chair.
Mfupi yule anangoja.	That short person is waiting.
Wangapi wanataka kwenda?	How many (people) want to go?
Ninataka wengine.	I want some other people.

Exercise 12

(a) *Translate, inserting the hyphens:* Much; cunning; dark; another; trustworthy; light coloured; thin; good (character); light (weight); many; red.

(b) *Translate:* Faithful servants; white bread; a good woman; red shoes;

42

another month; many people; a slender tree; a light load; a black book; an honest African; much cloth; many things; a thin book; a cunning thief; thin bodies; dark materials; many rooms; easy Swahili; another rhinoceros; crafty labourers.

(c) *Translate:* This long narrow river. That old man knows much good husbandry (agriculture). Bring another large red cup. How many small white mosquito nets? That big fire is putting out much black smoke. That examination was very easy. That cunning animal is eating those red plants. I need other efficient labourers. We saw a fierce black rhinoceros in Serengeti. I am trying to learn this Swahili. Some children are playing a game. He went to town to buy some potatoes. Many guests are coming to eat here to-day. We need other youths to help to catch that cunning animal. He got a very thin nail in the foot. That old man was a very good person. We put some red cloth in the room. He needs a faithful animal to stay in the house. I need a few brown (dark) loaves. Some inhabitants lived there many years.

(d) *Translate:* Kidonda chekundu; vitanda vyembamba; mlango mwingine; moshi mweusi; mikono myeupe; kijana mwerevu; mimea mingi; kitu kingine; weusi; milima myeusi.

(e) *Translate:* Nilinunua kitabu kingine kile. Vitu vingine vilikuwa vyekundu, vingine vilikuwa vyeusi. Wanawake wengi walikuwa mjini; wengine walikaa nyumbani. Unaweza kuchukua mizigo myepesi hii; ile inaweza kubaki hapa. Mtumishi mwaminifu anaweza kupata mshahara mkubwa. Wadudu weupe wale wanakula miti mibovu. Wageni wengi walifika Tanzania mwaka ule. Mti mrefu mwembamba ulianguka pale. Lete chakula kingine hapa. Usafishe viatu vyeusi vingine vile.

15 Adjectives—3

Arabic adjectives

Many adjectives are derived from the Arabic language in Swahili and these are grouped together in this Course, since not being of Bantu origin, they do not take any agreements with the nouns they qualify. The only difficulty they present is remembering that they do *not* take agreements!

bora	best, better, excellent
bure	useless (see also compound adjectives page 135)
ghali	expensive
hodari	efficient, able, energetic, strong, clever
kamili	complete, exact
kila	every, each
laini	soft, smooth

maridadi	fancy, adorned fancifully (sometimes malidadi)
maskini	poor (financially), miserable.
rahisi	easy, cheap
safi	clean, pure, (cf. ku-safisha, to clean).
sawa	alike, equal
tayari	ready
tele	plenty of, many, much
wazi	open, plain (clear)

N.B. *'Tele', since it refers to quantity, will come last in a list of adjectives, as previously explained.*

All the above adjectives are treated in the same way as all other adjectives, as far as word order is concerned, i.e. they follow the noun, EXCEPT the word 'kila' (every), which *always* precedes it. e.g.—

Kila mwaka	Every year	Kila chumba	Every room
Kila mtu	Everybody	Kila kisu kikali	Every sharp knife

Note also that it only takes nouns in the Singular.

But the remainder are normal:

Vyombo safi hivi.	These clean vessels. (This clean furniture).
Kitambaa ghali chekundu.	Expensive red cloth.
Mito mipana tele.	Plenty of wide rivers.
Watu bora wale.	Those best people.
Vitu rahisi bure vile.	Those cheap useless things.

Exercise 13

(a) *Translate:* Soft; equal; open; best; expensive; fancy; every; poor; useless; able; exact; plenty; clean; smooth; cheap; ready; efficient; excellent; complete; miserable.

(b) *Translate:* A clean cloth; every month; fancy food; an able cook; a cheap book; a useless container; soft pillows; the best people; plenty of labourers; an open door; equal pupils; a poor cripple; every body (every person); a useless game; the best chairs; clean cups; soft shoes; plenty of potatoes; clever children; better agriculture.

(c) *Translate:* Every clever child; those fancy sweet loaves; the complete meal (food) was ready; those poor small children; these open doors; these small equal loads; many strong labourers; this useless nail; every tree was tall; every empty vessel.

(d) *Translate:* Kisahani safi sana; vitu rahisi vile vilikuwa bora; kila mwanafunzi alikuwa tayari; angalia mlango wazi ule!; vitabu vingine vilikuwa ghali, vingine vilikuwa rahisi; nilipata chandalua kingine, hiki kilikuwa bure; viatu safi viko wapi?; anataka kitu maridadi; mwaka ule alikuwa maskini sana; usilete vitu bure vile hapa.

16 Adverbs — 1

Some adverbs, as is the tendency in English, are made up from adjectives. The adjectival stems remain unchanged, and an adverbial prefix is merely added to them. The adverbial prefix is identical to the KI- VI- class concord agreements, and is sometimes singular, and sometimes plural. There is no guide as to whether the prefix should be KI- or VI-, but whichever it is, it never changes, no matter in what context the adverb may be found. This may lead to a little confusion at first, but in practice, the context invariably shows when an adverb is intended, since nouns and adverbs behave quite differently in the sentence.

vibaya	badly
kidogo	a little, slightly, rather, quite, fairly
vigumu	hardy, toughly, difficult
vizuri	well, nicely, properly, O.K.!

A different construction is used to form other adverbs. This will be dealt with later, in chapter 28.

Word order
As in English, adverbs invariably follow the verb they qualify, but also can follow an object noun.

Alianguka vibaya	He fell badly.
Tunafurahi kidogo.	We are rather happy.
Jibu vizuri.	Answer properly.
Mti ule uliota vibaya.	That tree grew badly.
Mtoto alifanya vizuri mtihanini.	The child did well in the examination.
Nunua mkate kidogo!	Buy a little (bit of) bread!
Vizuri!	O.K.!

Exercise 14
Translate: The month started very badly. The European is increasing salaries a little. You (pl.) are using those knives very badly. That examination was a little difficult. These plants are drying up very well. You put that mirror badly. The servant cleaned this room well. That child cut the finger a little. That journey was quite (a little) difficult. Would you bring the bread? O.K.!

17 Verbs—3

Passive verbs (the -W- infix)

The verbs which have been introduced up to this point have mostly been 'active' verbs, such as 'ku-piga'—to hit, and 'ku-fanya'—to make. In English these verbs are made passive, by the addition of the word 'be' as a kind of infix. i.e. 'to *be* hit' and 'to *be* made'. In Swahili, the same result is achieved by the addition of an infix -W- just before the final -A of verbs of Bantu origin. So in our two examples we get:

ku-pigwa	to be hit
ku-fanywa	to be made

From the verbs already given, we can therefore use the following forms of the Passive.

ku-andikwa	to be written
ku-anzwa	to be begun, started
ku-chezwa	to be played
ku-endelewa	to be continued
ku-fanywa	to be done, made
ku-fichwa	to be hidden
ku-fuatwa	to be followed
ku-fungwa	to be closed/shut up, to be imprisoned
ku-funikwa	to be covered
ku-futwa	to be wiped
ku-fyekwa	to be slashed
ku-kamatwa	to be seized
ku-katwa	to be cut
ku-kumbukwa	to be remembered
ku-letwa	to be brought
ku-limwa	to be cultivated
ku-lipwa	to be paid
ku-ombwa	to be asked/begged
ku-onwa	to be seen
ku-ongezwa	to be increased
ku-pandwa	to be climbed/planted
ku-pangwa	to be arranged/hired
ku-patwa	to be got/obtained
ku-pendwa	to be liked/loved
ku-pigwa	to be hit/struck
ku-pikwa	to be cooked (though not necessarily ready for eating)
ku-safishwa	to be cleaned
ku-semwa	to be spoken, to be said

ku-somwa	to be read
ku-tafutwa	to be looked for
ku-takiwa	to be wanted

N.B. Although 'ku-takwa' is regular and can occur, 'ku-takiwa' is in fact always used instead. It is actually the passive of the prepositional form. (See ch. 43.)

ku-tumiwa	to be used
ku-tunzwa	to be cared for
ku-ulizwa	to be asked
ku-wekwa	to be put/placed
ku-windwa	to be hunted

There are unfortunately certain exceptions, but these are mainly so because the verbs in question are easier to pronounce or distinguish in the form of their exception, than they would be if they followed the normal rule.

Exception 1
Verbs ending in the double vowels '-oa' and '-ua'. If the normal -W-were put in '-owa' and 'uwa', you will notice, if you say it aloud, that the W is quite inaudible. For this reason, verbs ending in '-oa' become '-olewa', and verbs ending in '-ua' become '-ulewa'.

N.B. A rule applies here which will apply to most derivative formations. Where the previous vowel in the verb stem is an A, I or U, then the extra vowel added in the derived form will always be I. But when the previous vowel is an E or O then E will be extra vowel. Thus we get:

ku-chagua	ku-chaguliwa	to be chosen
ku-chukua	ku-chukuliwa	to be carried
ku-fungua	ku-funguliwa	to be opened
ku-jua	ku-juliwa	to be known
ku-nunua	ku-nunuliwa	to be bought/purchased
ku-toa	ku-tolewa	to be put out
ku-oa	ku-olewa	to be married (woman only)

N.B. (1) The double-vowel endings '-ia' and '-ea' are normal since the W is quite audible, if inserted. e.g. Ku-endelewa. (from Kuendelea).
(2) Ku-oa——to marry (man only), i.e. the man marries, the woman is married.

Verbs ending in a double 'aa' take '-liw-' in between the two.

ku-zaa	to bear, give birth, beget	ku-zaliwa	to be born
ku-kataa	to refuse	ku-kataliwa	to be refused

47

Exception 2
Verbs of Arabic origin ending in 'i' and 'u' become '-iwa', thus:

ku-fikiriwa	to be considered
ku-hitajiwa	to be needed
ku-jaribiwa	to be tried
ku-jibiwa	to be answered
ku-kubaliwa	to be agreed

(Previous vowels 'i' or 'a', hence '-iwa')

Exception 3
Arabic verbs ending in '-e' become '-ewa' thus:

ku-samehewa   to be forgiven
(Previous vowel 'e', hence '-ewa')

Exception 4
Arabic verbs ending in '-au', the suffix '-liwa' is added, thus:

ku-sahauliwa   to be forgotten
(Previous vowel 'u', hence '-liwa')

Exception 5
Monosyllabic verbs have each their own version 'kula' goes to 'ku-liwa'—to be eaten; 'kunywa' goes to 'ku-nywewa'—to be drunk (NOT intoxicated). These derivatives are now no longer monosyllabic and are therefore treated as normal verbs in this form.

N.B. Not all verbs have a passive form, since, by virtue of their meanings, such a form is not possible.

Furthermore, do not confuse this with the Stative derivation which suggests resultant state, such as 'to be broken'. The Stative form will be dealt with in chapter 25.

Using the passive verb

Unlike the Stative verb, the Passive verb is generally followed by a preposition such as 'by' or 'with', i.e. 'The child was cut *with* a knife.' 'The food was cooked *by* that woman.' In Swahili either of these conjunctions is translated by one word, but that word is not always the same, depending on its context. The words used for either 'by' or 'with' are 'na' or 'kwa'.

If the conjunction refers to humans, the word used is 'na'. If the conjunction refers to things, the word used is 'kwa'.

e.g. Kitabu kililetwa *na* mtoto yule.
     The book was brought *by* that child.
     Chakula kilipikwa *na* mwanamke yule.
     The food was cooked *by* that woman.
     Mtoto alikatwa *kwa* kisu.
     The child was cut *with* a knife.

Kiti kilifunikwa *kwa* kitambaa.

The chair was covered *by* a cloth.

It may be, of course, that no conjunction or noun follows even a passive verb. e.g. Mlango ulifungwa.—The door was closed.

Exercise 15

(a) *Translate:* To be cut; to be paid; to be married; to be answered; to be eaten; to be written; to be hit; to be used; to be seized; to be loved; to be hunted; to be forgotten; to be thought; to be opened; to be closed; to be forgiven; to be bought; to be started; to be brought; to be finished.

(b) *Translate:* To be cut with a knife; to be cut by another person; to be known by the teachers; he was answered by the child; they were born that year; the mountain was climbed on foot *(lit.* with feet); the food was covered with a cloth; the food was cooked by that able cook; to be spoken in (with) Swahili; the animals were hunted.

(c) *Translate:* Those new potatoes were brought by that youth. This fierce animal was caught by the legs. That game is being played by children. This chit was written by the European doctor. That good book is read a lot. Efficient teachers are wanted in Tanzania. These large rooms are cleaned every month. That tree fell and this child was hit by that piece. These cups were put out by the servant. I was asked to go to Dar es Salaam.

(d) *Translate and write active forms where appropriate:* Kukataliwa; kupangwa; kupatwa; kusafishwa; kuanzwa; kufuatwa; kunywewa; kuhitajiwa; kufutwa; kununuliwa; kuzaa; kulimwa; kuombwa; kusomwa; kuliwa; kuoa; kukumbukwa; kutolewa; kusahauliwa.

(e) *Translate:* Watoto wadogo wale wanatafutwa. Mishahara iliongezwa na Wagiriki. Vibarua wale walipangwa na Mzungu yule. Michezo hii ilianzwa mwezi huu. Vikombe hivi vilisafishwa kwa kitambaa kichafu hiki. Mwizi mwerevu yule alikamatwa na watu wale. Mwanamke mwema yule anapendwa sana na watoto. Chakula hiki kinaliwa sana na Waafrika. Mlango ule ulifunguliwa vibaya. Mizigo mizito ile inachukuliwa na vibarua wale.

18 Personal Pronouns

In addition to the Subject prefixes used with the M- WA- class, there are the following Personal Pronouns:

mimi	I, me
wewe	you
yeye	he, him, she, her. (But NEVER 'it' unless referring to animals.)
sisi	we, us
ninyi	you (pl.)
wao	they, them (of persons only)

49

N.B. Thère is no word for 'it' in Swahili. As an alternative they either use appropriate object infixes, or the relative construction, as will be explained later.

These pronouns must only be used *in addition* to the Subject prefix or Object infix, but *never instead of them*. They serve to emphasise the subject or object, or to clarify it in the case of the verb 'to be' which is often omitted in the present tense.

e.g. Mimi nilikwenda Dar es Salaam—As for me, I went to Dar es Salaam.

It is quite incorrect to say—Mimi kwenda Dar es Salaam,
or —Mimi likwenda Dar es Salaam.

Contractions
It often happens that one needs to say 'with me' or 'and you' etc. In Swahili, the word required here for 'and' and 'with', is 'na', but instead of saying 'na mimi' and 'na ninyi', they use the following contractions:

na mimi	=nami	—with me, and me
na wewe	=nawe	—with you, and you
na yeye	=naye	—with him/her, and him/her
na sisi	=nasi	—with us, and us
na ninyi	=nanyi	—with you, and you
na wao	=nao	—with them, and them

In other words, the first part of the pronoun is omitted, but it would not be wrong not to use the contraction.

Exercise 16
(a) *Add the appropriate personal pronoun in translating the following:* I went; he came; she is reading; would you enter; don't come back (pl.); they are trying; we followed; don't wait; I am drinking; he died; you (pl.) spoke; we are doing; you used; he climbed with me; we entered with him; I am hunting with you (pl.); they are staying with us; he spoke with her; I studied with them; we are remaining with you.

(b) *Translate:* As for you (pl.), you get good salaries. He and I (we) went to the Serengeti. They came with me. As for them, they read a lot. Those children came with us. As for him, he studied at Makerere. Did you come with her? Yes, I came with her. *He* went to Nairobi, *I* stayed here. Would you come with me?

19 'To Be'

Present tense

As has already been mentioned in chapter 7 the verb 'kuwa'—to be, or to become, when used with the present tense -NA- is only used for the meaning of 'to become'.

A special tense exists for the Present of 'to be', which has fairly recently become completely modified. In books etc. printed a few years ago, this present tense will be seen as being almost identical to the Subject Prefix on its own, with the exception of the third person singular, thus—Ni; U; *Yu*; Tu; M; Wa; U; I; Ki; Vi. But in modern Swahili you can get by in all instances with 'ni' with no matter what subject, in this tense, although in certain cases the second and third persons singular are also still heard. The remainder have all disappeared from common use. Thus 'ni' can mean 'I am, you are, he/she is, we are, you are, they are, it is, they are.'

It is clear therefore, that the actual subject invariably needs clarification, otherwise the phrase 'ni mzuri' could be 'I am good, you (sing.) are good, he/she is good, *or* it is good'. To clarify the subject, if a person the personal pronouns are used:

Mimi ni mzuri	can now only mean	I am good.
Wewe ni mzuri	can now only mean	You are good
Yeye ni mzuri	can now only mean	He/she is good.

Similarly:

Sisi ni wazuri	can now only mean	We are good.
Ninyi ni wazuri	can now only mean	You (pl.) are good.
Wao ni wazuri	can now only mean	They are good.

Alternatively, for the second person singular, one can simply say—'U mzuri',—'you are good', but you would not normally say 'Wewe u mzuri'. For the third person singular you can say 'Yu mzuri'—'He is good,' but you would not normally say 'Yeye yu mzuri'. The words 'U' and 'Yu' are now only used where no other introduction to the subject is mentioned.

If a subject noun (Proper or Common) is used, then 'Ni' would be correct, not 'Yu'.

> e.g. Mtoto ni mzuri—The child is good.
> (not—Mtoto yu mzuri).
> Hamisi ni mzuri—Hamisi is good.
> (Not—Hamisi yu mzuri).

Where you want to say 'It is .....', there is no word for 'it', and the verb is, of course 'Ni'. The only thing that can be done to clarify the 'it' is to use the appropriate demonstrative and say 'This is . . . . .' or 'That is . . . . .'. The demonstrative must of course agree with the object referred to.

Huu ni mzuri.	This is good.	(something in the M- MI- class)
Hiki ni kizuri.	This is good.	(something in the KI- VI- class)
Ule ni mzuri.	That is good.	(something in the M- MI- class)
Kile ni kizuri.	That is good.	(something in the KI- VI- class)

Similarly, the actual noun may be used instead,

Mti ni mzuri.	The tree is good.
Kiti ni kizuri.	The chair is good.

Although when learning this language it is as well always to insert the verb in a sentence, in practice there is often a tendency to omit the verb altogether where the sense obviously infers that the verb 'to be' is understood. This especially applies when demonstratives are being used. (A similar tendency occurs in English, e.g. 'Nice tree, this'— meaning—'This is a nice tree'.) e.g. Mti huu mzuri. This tree is nice. (If the verb were included, it would be 'Mti huu ni mzuri.') In this case, the apparent reversal of word order between the demonstrative and the adjective draws attention to the missing verb.

N.B. In all other tenses of the verb 'to be', the full form of the monosyllabic verb 'kuwa' will be used in the appropriate tense, and will never be omitted. Remember, where this verb tense refers to location, it will take the form of 'Yupo yuko, yumo', etc. (See ch. 11.)

Negative present tense

The negative present of this verb has been modified even further than its equivalent affirmative tense. For many years it has been reduced to only 'Si' for all subjects. No other form exists. 'Si' can therefore mean 'I am not, you are not, he/she is not, we are not, you are not, they are not, it is not and they are not (of things). Thus, as with 'Ni', a personal pronoun, noun or demonstrative must be used to clarify the subject. e.g.:

Mimi si mzuri.	I am not good.
Wewe si mzuri.	You are not good.
Yeye si mzuri.	He/she is not good.
Sisi si wazuri.	We are not good.
Ninyi si wazuri.	You are not good.
Wao si wazuri.	They are not good.
Mtoto si mzuri.	The child is not good.
Watoto si wazuri.	The children are not good.
Hamisi si mzuri.	Hamisi is not good.
Huu si mzuri.	This one is not good.
Hii si mizuri.	These ones are not good.

Hiki si kizuri.	This one is not good.
Hivi si vizuri.	These ones are not good.
Ule si mzuri.	That one is not good.
Ile si mizuri.	Those ones are not good.
Kile si kizuri.	That one is not good.
Vile si vizuri.	Those ones are not good.
Mti si mzuri.	The tree is not good.
Miti si mizuri	The trees are not good.
Kiti si kizuri.	The chair is not good.
Viti si vizuri.	The chairs are not good.

Obviously, this tense is never omitted, since only the verb carries the negative and no other word would convey it. (Other negative tenses of 'to be' will be dealt with together with other verbs, as they are normal.)

N.B. Where this negative refers to location, it will take the form of 'hayupo, hayuko, hayumo', etc. (See ch. 11.)

Exercise 17

(a) *Translate:* Hamisi is a cook; we are students; they are labourers; she is not bad; that tree is a baobab; we are not Americans; you are a teacher; that is a chair; this basket is empty; are you David?; he is a hunter; this book is not cheap; I am a stranger; you are not efficient; I am not English; this examination is not difficult; this food is sweet; that is not sweet; the cook is in the house; the children are not here; we are coming.

(b) *Translate:* Those animals are fierce; this knife is not sharp; this bread is hard; that basket is empty; Swahili is very easy; that is Hamisi; these are not good potatoes; that sore was very bad; the salary was good; these loads are not heavy.

20 'To Have' — 1

Present tense

There is no actual verb for 'to have' in Swahili, so instead one has to say, 'to be with' which is 'kuwa na'. Note that the 'infinitive' comprises two separate words. In all but the present tense, this verb always stays as two words. These other tenses will be dealt with in a later chapter.

In the present tense, however, the two words merge together, the verb 'to be' in fact reverting to a simple form identical to the subject prefix, *including* the third person Singular (unlike the verb 'to be' on its own). Thus, the present tense conjugates:

nina	I have (I am with)
una	You have (you are with)
ana	He/she has (he/she is with)
tuna	we have (we are with)
mna	you have (you are with)
wana	they have (they are with)

Similarly,

una	it has (M- Mi- class)
ina	they have (Mi- Vi- class)
kina	it has (Ki- Vi- class)
vina	they have (Ki- Vi- class)

Examples:

Nina watoto watatu.	I have three children.
Wana vitabu vingi.	They have many books.
Kiti hiki kina miguu mitatu.	This chair has three legs.
Mti ule una mizizi mikubwa.	That tree has big roots.
Tuna mpishi mwema.	We have a good cook.
Mtoto ana kidonda kibaya.	The child has a bad sore.

Exercise 18

(a) *Translate:* You have; she has; they have; we have; I have; you (pl.) have; he has.

(b) *Translate:* He has a good cook; this room has many beds; have you a book?; that leg has a bad sore; those mountains have many trees; I have a few pieces; that cup has a useless saucer; the doctor has many pills; that bed has a mosquito net; that youth has a knife; he has a book, it is good; this is a chair, it has short legs; that child has a big head; the old man has a good heart; this room has a mirror; we have many animals; the women have many children; those children have a good teacher; have you (pl.) some potatoes?; Juma has dirty shoes; I have a cup here; that village has many inhabitants; this animal has many insects; you (pl.) have dirty hands; these beds have pillows; this fire has much smoke; that tree has sharp thorns; the labourers have references; we have an exam today; have you a lighter?

(c) *Translate:* Nina kiko kizuri; ana mizigo pale; chumba kina milango midogo; watoto wana mchezo mpya; mganga ana wagonjwa wengi; mna vitabu vingi; kilima kile kina miiba mikali sana; kijana yule ana mwili mwembamba; nina mtihani leo; una mfuko?

There is, there are, etc.

If in Swahili you wish to say 'There is . . . . .' or 'There are . . . . .' and so on, you have to say literally, 'the place has . . . . .' We need to use the subject prefixes referring to 'place' in order to use this construction. These will be remembered (from the demonstratives) as being

pa — for definite place
ku — for indefinite place
m — for inside place

Thus, using the verb 'to have' as just shown, we get:

pana   there is/are.
kuna   there is/are.
mna   there is/are inside

It will be seen that there are no singular or plural differences. The particular agreement given will depend on context, relating to definite or indefinite location etc. This construction will invariably be followed by a suitable demonstrative for 'here' or 'there', but this MUST agree with the prefix used on the verb.

e.g. Pana miti mirefu hapa.   There are tall trees here.
     Pana miti mirefu pale.   There are tall trees there.
     Kuna wanyama huku.   There are animals about here.
     Kuna wanyama kule.   There are animals thereabouts.

or a noun with '-ni'

     Mna mkate jikoni.   There is bread in the oven.

but one should not say—(although it is often heard)

     *Pa*na wanyama hu*ku*.   OR   *Ku*na miti ha*pa*.

since the agreements are contradictory. (The phrases 'there were
.....' and 'there will be .....' follow the same pattern as above, but use appropriate tenses and will be dealt with in chapter 27.)

Exercise 19
Translate: There is a big baobab tree over there (definite); there are some high mountains in Tanzania; there are some potatoes in the basket; there is a knife on the table; there is a stranger at the door; there are large baobabs in Kenya; is there any bread in the kitchen?; Is there a doctor here?; here, there are many clever pupils; there are a few Europeans in Tanzania.

Revision exercise 20
(a) *Translate:* Don't come today; bring the food; go to town; think hard; come again; would you be ready?; clean this room well; look for (pl.) the children; come! (pl.); eat!; I am reading; the women are cultivating; the men are hunting; this nail is loose; those loaves are enough; many people came; we went to Nairobi; the tall tree fell into the river.
(b) *Translate:* These spoons; those rivers; this room; that door; this luggage; these good beds; how many Europeans?; those inhabitants; that black smoke; this new game; that year; this month; that poor old man; these mountains; that furniture; those able labourers; this fierce rhinoceros; that easy examination; some good books and a good pipe; red shoes.
(c) *Translate:* I am a teacher; we are English; they are becoming efficient; Hamisi is a good cook; there is a fire thereabouts; he has many children; he is in the room; we are progressing; you are a sick person; this tree is a Baobab; that smoke is black; that nail is not sharp; he is not a doctor; he was a big child; those animals are not hippopotami; mind out, there is a nail here; the leg was cut here; the sore was quite bad; that is a good chair; there are many insects hereabouts.

(d) *Translate:* Funga mlango; leteni mizigo; usirudi hapa tena; chukua kitabu hiki; usimame pale; msiharibu mimea ile; njoo hapa!; kunywa tena; mngoje kidogo!; mwingie!; msianguke!; andika cheti!; msijaze vikapu vingine; uongeze mshahara!; usiwe mwizi!; tokeni hapa!; kaeni!; anapika; tulitaka; wengine walikufa.

(e) *Translate:* Una watoto wangapi?; mizigo iko wapi?; mlango ule si wazi; mkate huu mpya; mzungu yule ana kiko kirefu; kilima kile kina wanyama wengi; chumba kile kina kitanda; vijana wale wana miili mirefu; kiboko yumo mtoni; mzee yule ana mifuko mitupu.

21 Numerals—1

Numbers 1–20

Numbers in Swahili are treated just like other adjectives and being of course concerned with quantity, will come at the end of the adjectives, but before the demonstrative. Only the units 1, 2, 3, 4, 5, and 8 take agreements with the noun they describe, the remainder take no agreements. The numbers are:

-moja	1	kumi na -moja	11
-wili	2	kumi na -wili	12
-tatu	3	kumi na -tatu	13
-nne	4	kumi na -nne	14
-tano	5	kumi na -tano	15
sita	6	kumi na sita	16
saba	7	kumi na saba	17
-nane	8	kumi na -nane	18
tisa	9	kumi na tisa	19
kumi	10	ishirini	20

N.B. The word '-moja' will only ever take singular agreements and similarly '-wili' and upwards will only take plural agreements.

You may hear 'mbili' for '2', but this is only used when either counting abstractly, or when agreeing with the 'N' class.

Examples

Mikate miwili.	Two loaves.
Miezi sita.	Six months.
Wanyama wakubwa wanne.	Four large animals.
Mpishi hodari mmoja.	One able cook.

Viti kumi na kimoja.	Eleven chairs. (lit. 'Ten chairs and one chair', hence the singular agreement on '-moja')
Watoto wadogo kumi na wanane hawa.	These 18 small children.
Miaka mitano hii.	These five years.
Vikombe ishirini vinatosha.	Twenty cups are enough.
Nilinunua vitabu vipya vinne hivi.	I bought these four new books.

Exercise 21

(a) *Translate:* One person; two trees; three rooms; four children; six nails; eight books; ten months; twelve disciples (learners); eleven loads; twenty years; eighteen spoons; ten fingers; two arms; five mountains; seven pieces; thirteen baskets; fifteen cups; a dozen knives; eleven Europeans; one loaf; twelve youths; nineteen beds; one mirror; fifteen hippopotami; two white loaves and three brown (dark); five heavy loads and three light ones; four beds and eight mosquito nets; eleven children and one teacher; seven men and one woman; one cripple.

(b) *Translate:* Six white cups and two saucers; those two red shoes are not clean; each hand has five fingers; they stayed here twelve months; this room has one small door; she read nine books this month; one African has eleven labourers; bring two other loaves; I need a dozen small spoons; did you see those ten youths?

(c) *Translate:* Waganga wawili na wagonjwa ishirini; watoto kumi; mikate mitatu; miaka mitano; mto mmoja; wageni kumi na mmoja; mpishi mmoja na watumishi wanne; vibarua wavivu wanane; vyumba sita; vitabu tisa; Wazungu kumi na watatu na Waafrika kumi na wanane; wanyama kumi na wawili; lete mikate miwili mingine; alisahau vitu vitatu; wenyeji hawa wana visima vitatu; alifunga milango mitano; miti mirefu minane ili-anguka; kuna mito mingapi kule? minne; kibarua yule ana vyeti saba; pana mgeni mmoja mlangoni.

22 Future Tense

This has the tense sign -TA-. It is used in the same way as the previous tense signs such as the -LI- and -NA- tenses. Thus if we use the verb 'kufika' —to arrive, we get:

Ni-ta-fika.	Nitafika.	I shall arrive.
U-ta-fika.	Utafika.	You will arrive.
A-ta-fika.	Atafika.	He/she will arrive.
Tu-ta-fika	Tutafika.	We shall arrive.

| M-ta-fika. | Mtafika. | You will arrive. |
| Wa-ta-fika | Watafika. | They will arrive. |

M- MI- class
| U-ta-fika. | Utafika. | It will arrive. |
| I-ta-fika. | Itafika. | They will arrive. |

KI- VI- class
| Ki-ta-fika. | Kitafika. | It will arrive. |
| Vi-ta-fika. | Vitafika. | They will arrive. |

Arabic verbs are treated in the same way—

| Ni-ta-jaribu. | Nitajaribu. | I shall try, etc. |

and Monosyllabic verbs again retain their 'infinitive' 'ku'—

	Ni-ta-kuja.	Nitakuja.	I shall come.
or	A-ta-kula.	Atakula.	He/she will eat.
or	Wa-ta-kuwa.	Watakuwa.	They will be, etc.

N.B. This tense will always be used in Swahili where the future is implied, even though the actual future tense may not be used in the English equivalent,
> e.g. —'I am going to Europe in a year.' We should say—I *shall* go to Europe in a year, which in Swahili is—Nitakwenda Ulaya mwakani.

Exercise 22

(a) *Translate:* I shall wake up; we shall need; he will plant; I shall beat; you will sell; will you wait?; we shall stay; the tree will fall; these knives will do; those loaves will be sufficient; we shall die; he will become a cook; you will forget; you (pl.) will say; will she come back?; we shall come today; they will go; the food will be brought; the game will be played; salaries will be increased.

(b) *Translate:* That tree will fall there; I shall need a cook and two other servants; Those cups will be suitable; Those loads will be very heavy; Don't cook the food, I shall eat in town; They are going to Nairobi again this month; How many visitors will come here?; One youth will try to climb that mountain; This well will be quite deep; Those potatoes will be enough.

(c) *Translate:* Utakumbuka?; tutaandika cheti; cheti kitaandikwa; nitanunua mkate; mkate utanunuliwa; chakula kitaletwa na Ali; chumba kitafagiliwa; tutaweza kwenda leo; atakunywa; watamaliza leo; mlango utafungwa; watataka kusafiri leo; viti hivi vitahitajiwa; tutapata chakula mjini; viatu vitakauka vizuri hapa; mtihani utaanzwa leo; watapanda mlima ule; mtafurahi; kijana huyu atakuwa mganga; mtajaribu kurudi tena?

23 Days of the Week

In Swahili, the days of the week are taken from the Mohammedan calendar in which Friday is the important day. Thus the week revolves about it.

			Abbreviated
Ijumaa	Friday		Ij.
Jumamosi	Saturday	(1st day after)	J1.
Jumapili	Sunday	(2nd day after)	J2.
Jumatatu	Monday	(3rd day after)	J3.
Jumanne	Tuesday	(4th day after)	J4.
Jumatano	Wednesday	(5th day after)	J5.
Alhamisi	Thursday	(Day for preparation)	Al.

Being proper nouns, they never take a preposition. The position in a sentence is as in English, either before the subject, or at the end.

Jumamosi, nitakwenda Nairobi.   On Saturday, I shall go to Nairobi.

or   Nitakwenda Nairobi Jumamosi.   I shall go to Nairobi on Saturday.

It is sometimes the habit to precede the days of the week by 'siku ya .....' 'the day of .....' e.g. 'Siku ya Alhamisi'.

Other days, etc.

kesho kutwa	the day after tomorrow
kesho	tomorrow
leo	today
jana	yesterday
juzi	the day before yesterday
juzijuzi	the other day
zamani	some time ago, long time ago, etc.

These again do not take prepositions, and whilst generally are used at the end of a phrase, may lead it. (They are all 'N' class nouns in their own right).

N.B. *Remember that the first two listed above will always go with a future tense; 'leo' could be past, present or future, and the remainder will take a past tense.*

Examples:

Mgeni yule alifika jana.   That stranger arrived yesterday.
Mpishi atapika mkate kesho.   The cook is cooking bread tomorrow.

Mzungu yule alikwenda zamani kidogo.	That European went quite a while ago.
Tutasoma kitabu hiki leo.	We shall read this book today.

Exercise 23

(a) *Translate:* Monday; Thursday; yesterday; Wednesday; the day after tomorrow; Friday; the day before yesterday; Saturday; tomorrow; Tuesday; some time ago; Sunday; the other day.

(b) *Translate:* He came yesterday; we shall go on Tuesday; the doctor is coming on Sunday; I am going the day after tomorrow; they will try again on Thursday; I came yesterday, I am staying today, I shall return tomorrow; you will return on Wednesday; the game will be played tomorrow; I conversed with him the other day; this bread was cooked on Monday.

(c) *Translate:* They climbed that tall mountain on Thursday; We arrived in Tanzania the day before yesterday; The thief was caught yesterday; There is much smoke on the mountain today; The examination will start tomorrow; Those shoes were bought on Wednesday; The game will be played the day after tomorrow; Salaries are paid every Saturday; The old man died some time ago; That child was brought yesterday.

(d) *Translate:* Mpishi alileta chakula zamani kidogo; watalipwa Jumamosi; usisahau kuja Jumanne; cheti hiki kiliandikwa juzijuzi; watasafiri kesho kutwa; mgeni atafika Ijumaa; tunakwenda mjini kila Jumatatu; zamani, nilikaa Nairobi; rudi kesho!; vyumba hivi vinasafishwa kila Jumatano.

24   Indeclinable Words — 1

Prepositions and conjunctions

Prepositions
The following are commonly used Prepositions which can now be introduced to make more interesting sentences:

toka, kutoka	from, out of
mpaka	up to, as far as, until. (This is really a M- Mi-class noun meaning a boundary).
hata	even, up to (of time), not even (if used with a negative tense)
bila	without, not having. (*must* be followed by noun or 'infinitive')
kwa	for, towards, in the direction of, to someone, by means of (see Passive verbs, page 48). It is also used with nouns etc., to make adverbs. (See page 72). (A very important word of wide usage).

| katika | in, on, near, to, towards, from, amongst, into, out of, etc. (It has an identical meaning to the '-ni' suffix on nouns, vide page 28) |
| na | and, with (already dealt with on page 19) |

N.B. The -NI suffix can be used on a noun only when it is not supported by any other qualifying word such as an adjective or demonstrative. Where such an adjective or demonstrative needs to be used, then the word 'katika' has to be used in front of the noun in place of the suffix '-ni',

e.g. Aliingia chumbani.—He entered the room.
or Aliingia katika chumba.—He entered the room.
but only Aliingia katika chumba kikubwa kile.—He entered that large room.
never Aliingia chumba*ni* kikubwa kile.

Further examples

	Alipata mkate toka mjini.	He got bread from (in) town.
or	Alipata mkate kutoka mjini.	He got bread from (in) town.
	Atakaa hapa toka leo mpaka kesho.	He will stay here from today until tomorrow.
	Nilisafiri mpaka Nairobi.	I travelled as far as Nairobi.
	Tulikwenda Tanzania bila kuona Dar es Salaam.	We went to Tanzania without seeing Dar es Salaam.
	Tuliona wanyama wengi, hata wanyama wakali.	We saw many animals, even fierce ones.
	Atakaa hata kesho.	He will stay till tomorrow.
	Yeye si mpishi, hata kidogo.	He is no cook, not the slightest.
	Mtoto alifika bila vitabu.	The child came without books.
	Nenda kwa Bwana Smith.	Go to Mr Smith's.
	Nilikata hiki kwa kisu.	I cut this with a knife.
	Alileta kitu hiki kwa Bwana Smith.	He brought this for Mr Smith.
	Tulikuja kwa miguu.	We came on foot (by means of feet).

Conjunctions

The following are also commonly used conjunctions:

kwa sababu	because, the reason being
sababu	because, the reason being
ila	except
basi (bas)	and so, well then (introducing a paragraph in a narrative), enough! no more! cease! oh well! right!
Basi? (Bas?)	Is that all? (the tone of voice will convey which of the above meanings is intended)

kama	if, like, approximately
kwamba	that (in the sense of 'he said *that* .....)
au	or
au ..... au	either ...... or
lakini	but, however, nevertheless
ingawa	although, though

All of the above are used in the same way, in the same position as the English equivalent.

Examples:

Tulifika Tanzania kwa sababu tulitaka kuona Serengeti.	We came to Tanzania because we wanted to see Serengeti.
Vibarua hawa, ila yule, ni hodari sana.	These labourers, except that one, are very efficient.
Nilitaka sana kuja hapa, basi nilifika.	I wanted very much to come here, and so I came.
'Utakaa hapa miezi mingapi?'	'How many months will you stay here?'
'Kama miezi sita,'	'About six months.'
'Basi?'	'Is that all?'
'Ndiyo'.	'Yes'.
Ninahitaji kisu kama hiki.	I need a knife like this one.
Kama atakuja, nitangoja.	If he will come, I shall wait.
Mtumishi yule alisema kwamba mgeni alifika jana.	That servant said that the visitor came yesterday.
Ninaweza kuona kwamba wanyama wale ni wakali.	I can see that those animals are fierce.
Lete mkate mweusi au mweupe.	Bring brown bread, or white.
Mimi ninajifunza Kiswahili lakini yeye anajifunza Kiingereza.	I am learning Swahili but he is learning English.

Exercise 24

(a) *Translate:* Approximately; because; from; without; or; until; in; even; although; but; except; for; enough!; either; well then!; if.

(b) *Translate:* He said that .....; either bread or potatoes; about two years; from here to Dar es Salaam; in that book; even you!; until that year; these cups, except this one, are dirty; I know because I went; the guests are ready, so bring the food; bring about three loaves; this book or that; he is not good, not the slightest; from now until Tuesday; the guest will stay up to the day after tomorrow; if you (will) go on Wednesday, take these things; they went but they forgot; the bag is heavy because it has many potatoes; the examination is easy although it is long.

(c) *Translate:* She came without the children because they were sick; We travelled from London as far as Nairobi; you can see that he is not about, so go (pl.)!; those students will study for about one year; they want to see either Mombasa or Dar es Salaam; the doctor put about ten pills in that small container; he likes to eat many potatoes, even sweet potatoes; that tall tree fell into that wide river; they succeeded in the examination without trying much; Swahili is not difficult (hard), not the slightest!

(d) *Translate:* Alikuja kwa miguu; usije bila cheti; hata mimi nilikwenda; weka mto huu katika kitanda kile; wanyama toka kijiji kile ni wazuri kabisa; nitakula kama viazi viwili. Basi? Ndiyo!; ninaona kwamba milima ile ni mirefu sana; yeye anakwenda leo, lakini sisi tutakwenda Alhamisi; kama atafika kesho, usisahau kusema naye; mti ulianguka kwa sababu ulikuwa mbovu.

25 Verbs—4

Stative verbs

A stative verb is rather similar to the Passive verb, except that it does not refer to by what, or whom, the action was done, and invariably implies a resultant state.

> e.g. The window was broken (ambiguous).
> The window was broken for a whole month (stative).
> The window was broken just as I left the room (passive).
> The window was broken by that boy (or stone) (passive).

Some verbs have a stative meaning even in their basic stem, though others can be derived from their basic stems to produce the stative.

The derivation of a stative verb is generally made by the addition of a K either on its own or with accompanying vowels in the form of '-ika' or '-eka'.

> e.g. 'Ku-kata' goes to 'Ku-katika' (previous stem vowel—A)
> 'Ku-samehe' goes to 'ku-sameheka' (previous stem vowel—E)
> 'Ku-jibu' goes to 'ku-jibika' (previous stem vowel—I)
> 'Ku-choma' goes to 'ku-chomeka' (previous stem vowel—O)
> 'Ku-funga' goes to 'ku-fungika' (previous stem vowel—U)

(It will be seen from the above examples that Arabic verbs change their final vowel as do the Bantu verbs in this construction.)

Exceptions
1. Where Bantu verbs end with double vowels, then just '-k-' is inserted between the two:
> e.g. ku-fungua goes to ku-fungu*k*a

2. Where Bantu verbs end with double A, then '-lik-' is inserted between the two:

e.g. ku-kaa goes to ku-ka*lik*a

3. Arabic verbs ending in double vowels take the suffix '-lika' after them both:

e.g. ku-sahau goes to ku-sahau*lika*

Thus of the verbs previously introduced we get:

ku-badili	to alter, change	ku-badilika	to be altered, changed
ku-choma	to burn, roast, toast, pierce	ku-chomeka	to be burnt, toasted, pierced, etc.
ku-funga	to close, shut	ku-fungika	to be closed, shut
ku-fungua	to-open, undo	ku-funguka	to be opened, undone
ku-haribu	to destroy, damage	ku-haribika	to be destroyed, damaged to go rotten
ku-jibu	to answer, reply	ku-jibika	answered, replied
ku-kata	to cut	ku-katika	to be cut, come apart
ku-kubali	to agree	ku-kubalika	to be agreed
ku-mwaga	to pour out, waste	ku-mwagika	to be poured out, wasted
ku-pasua	to saw, split, tear	ku-pasuka	to be sawn, split, torn
ku-pindua	to turn over	ku-pinduka	to be turned over
ku-sahau	to forget	ku-sahaulika	to be forgotten
ku-tosha	to be enough	ku-tosheka	to be satisfied with
ku-vunja	to break	ku-vunjika	to be broken

In addition, the following verbs have stative meanings without necessarily being derived from simpler terms:

ku-chelewa	to be late	ku-kosa	to be wrong, mistaken, be without, fail
ku-choka	to be tired		
kwisha	to be finished	ku-lewa	to be intoxicated
ku-jaa	to be filled	ku-potea	to be lost
ku-kasirika	to be angry, vexed	ku-shiba	to be satisfied with food

A few verbs have exceptional stative forms with sometimes specialised meanings, for example

ku-nu*sa*   to smell, sniff   ku-nu*ka*   to smell bad

All the stative verbs in the above lists are used with the -ME- tense whenever the present tense is used in English. This gives the sense of 'has become'. (e.g. We are late = we have become late) The present -NA- tense is rarely used in this sense. (See next chapter.)

Statives with the 'possible' meaning.

Many of the above verbs can have alternative meanings such as the following:

ku-badilika	to be changeable
ku-chomeka	to be burnable, pierceable, etc.
ku-fungika	to be closeable
ku-funguka	to be openable
ku-kubalika	to be agreeable
ku-jibika	to be answerable, etc.

In fact any verb, provided its meaning allows it, can be made into a stative form, following the rules laid out above. The context will generally show whether the 'possible' meaning or the normal 'stative' meaning is implied.

The following verbs are also very common 'possible' types of statives, and they take an additional '-na' as a suffix:

ku-julikana	to be known,	(from ku-jua — to know).
ku-onekana	to be visible,	(from ku-ona — to see).
ku-patikana	to be obtainable,	(from ku-pata — to get).
ku-wezekana	to be possible,	(from ku-weza — to be able).

N.B. All 'possible' stative verbs can be, and generally are, used in the present tense, affirmative or negative. (Compare their other meanings which take the -ME- tense instead of the -NA- tense.)

26   Past Perfect Tense

The sign for this tense is -ME-. It is again used in the same way as the previous tense signs and as a basic guide as to when to use it in Swahili, it will always be used when the words 'has' or 'have' occur in the English. It is also used widely with the Stative verbs instead of the present tense used in English. See previous chapter.

The verb Ku-anza—to start, begin; would conjugate thus:

ni-me-anza	nimeanza	I have started
u-me-anza	umeanza	you have started
a-me-anza	ameanza	he/she has started
tu-me-anza	tumeanza	we have started
m-me-anza	mmeanza	you have started
wa-me-anza	wameanza	they have started

M- MI- class

u-me-anza	umeanza	it has started
i-me-anza	imeanza	they have started

KI- VI- class

ki-me-anza	kimeanza	it has started
vi-me-anza	vimeanza	they have started

Arabic verbs again create no exceptions:

ni-me-jibu	nimejibu	I have answered
ni-me-fikiri	nimefikiri	I have considered

Monosyllabic verbs again retain their 'infinitive'—'ku-':

ni-me-kula	nimekula	I have eaten
a-me-kuja	amekuja	He/she has come
wa-me-kwenda	wamekwenda	They have gone
ni-me-kuwa	nimekuwa	I have been (not the past of 'to go')/I have become

Use with stative verbs

As previously mentioned, stative verbs (apart from the 'possible' type) are rarely used with the present tense, either affirmative or negative. A little explanation as to why may make this clear.

If you have, say, a china cup, it will either be whole or broken. Even if it has a crack, it is no longer whole. It is not possible for a cup to be 'being' broken, because the moment the first crack appears in it, it will no longer be in a state of being whole. Thus by using this tense, the meaning is implied 'The cup has become split' or 'The cup has become broken'. (Kikombe ki*me*pasuka; kikombe ki*me*vunjika).

It is, of course, possible to be breaking a cup, but then you would not use the stative form of the verb for that statement. (Ninavunja kikombe.)

Similarly with the verb 'ku-lewa — to be intoxicated' you can either be sober or have become intoxicated. You can of course, consume liquor in the present tense, but the moment you do, you 'have become intoxicated' (umelewa), even though not necessarily be 'drunk'.

Hence you would translate the following thus:

Umechelewa.	You are late (you have become late).
Chakula kimekwisha.	The food is finished (has become finished).
Mlango umefunguka.	The door is open (has been opened).
Mtoto amepotea.	The child is lost (has become lost).
Nimechoka.	I am tired (I have become tired).
Chakula kimechomeka.	The food is burnt (has become burnt).

BUT you could also say —

Chakula ki*na*chomeka.	The food is roastable, burnable.
Mlango u*na*funguka.	The door is openable.

N.B. It is of course also possible to use any of these verbs with all other tenses, i.e. -LI- and -TA- and others yet to be learnt.

The verbs whose meanings are stative without having to be put into stative form, however, may NEVER be used with the present tense, (i.e. ku-chelewa, ku-choka, ku-potea, etc.), except in very rare cases which are best ignored at present.

Examples:
Kikombe kimoja kimepotea, lakini vingine vinaonekana.
   One cup is lost, but the others are in sight (visible).
Mkate ule umeharibika kabisa.
   That loaf is completely spoilt.
Mzee yule amekasirika sana kwa sababu nimechelewa.
   That old man is very angry because I am late.
Viazi vizuri sana vinapatikana mjini mwezi huu.
   Very good potatoes are obtainable in town this month.

Idiom
The verb 'kwisha' is often used in an idiom giving the sense of 'already'. It is followed in these cases by the verb stem only, without any tense sign. Monosyllabics keep their 'ku-' however. (In the past, the second verb was always placed in the 'infinitive', but the modern tendency is to leave the 'infinitive' off, apart from the monosyllabics.)

Modern Swahili makes great use of a new 'tense' '-mesha-' It is a merging of the verb 'kwisha' and the -me- tense, giving the sense of *'having already done'*. Monosyllabic verbs keep their ku-prefix.

Examples:
Juma ameshafika. *Juma has already arrived.*
Ng' ombe ameshakufa. *The cow has already died.*
Nimeshashiba, asante. *I am already full of food, thanks.*
Maria ameshakwenda. *Maria has already gone.*
Nimeshasoma kitabu kile. *I have already read that book.*

N.B. When you want to say 'I have finished doing something', you have to use the verb 'ku-maliza'. In this case, the second verb will be placed in the 'infinitive' form in full.

e.g. Amemaliza kusoma kitabu kile.
He has finished reading that book.

Exercise 25

(a) *Translate:* To be late; to be broken; to be burnt; to change; to be mistaken; to be satisfied with food; to be angry; to break; to get tired; to be visible; to be openable; to be finished; to be possible; to be destroyed; to be filled; to be intoxicated; to be forgotten; to be poured out; to turn over; to be lost; to be obtainable; to come apart; to be known; to be altered; to turn over; to be agreeable; to pour out; to roast.

(b) *Translate:* I am late; the baskets have been filled; the cup is broken; the children are lost; they are tired; potatoes are obtainable; are you satisfied with food?; you (pl.) are intoxicated; he has already gone; the doctor is well known; this tree will be sawn; he was very angry; we are mistaken; don't be late; those things have been forgotten; they are already tired; they were satisfied with that examination; don't tear that cloth; the mountain is clearly (well) visible now; the guests have already arrived.

(c) *Translate:* Don't sit on that chair, it is broken; he has failed to shut the door because it closes badly; they have already seen that big river; the food has already been cooked by that cook; don't put out more food because they are satisfied; 'Where is the Bwana?' 'He has gone out'.; the children have gone to bed because they are tired. (Note: 'to go to bed' is translated into Swahili as 'to lie down' or 'to sleep'.); the arm is completely broken; yesterday, Juma got completely drunk; if you have been to Nairobi, you have seen a beautiful city.

(d) *Translate:* Mkate umechomeka; wameshiba; mlango umeharibika; amekwenda; wamelala; mfereji umejaa; tutachelewa; amekosa kuandika cheti; usivunje chombo kile; Bwana amekasirika sana; kisu kilipotea Jumatano; shibeni!; mkate unachomeka jikoni; tumekwisha anza; wamemaliza; mlango ule unafunguka; kitanda hiki kimenunuliwa kwa sababu mgeni atafika leo; kiko hiki kimekatika; nimekula vidonge viwili; mtihani huu umekwisha.

(e) *Translate:* Usikose kurudi hapa Jumanne; wamesahau kumaliza kuchoma viazi vile; mtumishi huyu amekwisha maliza kusafisha vyombo; usiongeze tena kwa sababu vyombo hivi vimejaa; wawindaji hawa wanajulikana sana; nunua viazi vingine kwa sababu vimekwisha; ametafuta kisu kizuri kile lakini kimepotea; milima ile itaonekana kesho; 'Mzee yule amekufa?' 'Ndiyo, Bwana, amekwisha kufa'.; kama umemaliza mtihani huu, pumzika kidogo!

More useful nouns

M- WA- class

mchungaji	wachungaji	herdsman, pastor, shepherd
mke	wake	a wife
mkristo	wakristo	a Christian
mkulima	wakulima	a farmer, cultivator
mnyapara	wanyapara	a foreman, overseer
mume	waume	a husband
mwanachama	wanachama	a member (of a society etc.)
mwananchi	wananchi	a countryman, native, citizen
mwashi	washi	a bricklayer, stonemason

M- MI- class

mfupa	mifupa	a bone
mkia	mikia	a tail
mkoa	mikoa	an administrative district, region
mkuki	mikuki	a spear
mkutano	mikutano	a meeting
mnazi	minazi	a coconut palm
mpaka	mipaka	a boundary, limit
mpini	mipini	a wooden handle, large handle
mpira	mipira	a rubber tree, also anything made of rubber, e.g. ball, football, hosepipe, etc.
mpango	mipango	an arrangement, plan, programme
msaada	misaada	aid, assistance, help
msikiti	misikiti	a mosque
msitu	misitu	a forest, wood
mstari	mistari	a line, queue
mtelemko	mitelemko	a slope
muda	(miuda)	a period of time
mwavuli	miavuli	an umbrella, sunshade
mzizi	mizizi	a root

KI- VI class

chama	vyama	club, society, association, co-operative, etc.
kiasi	(viasi)	quantity, amount
kibanda	vibanda	shed, hut (but *not* a permanent dwelling)
kipini	vipini	a small handle
kiraka	viraka	a patch, (in clothing, tyre, etc.)
kisiwa	visiwa	an island
kitunguu	vitunguu	an onion
kivuli	vivuli	a shade, shadow

69

kiwanda	viwanda	a workshop
kiwanja	viwanja	a plot of ground, pitch
kizibo	vizibo	a cork, stopper

Exercise 26

(a) *Translate:* A husband; aid; shade; a pastor; an onion; members; a bricklayer; roots; a forest; boundaries; a plot of ground; a period of time; wives; Christians; a mosque; societies; a cork; a handle; football; a slope; an arrangement; a farmer; a spear; a coconut palm; a shadow; a quantity; a patch; countrymen; a region; a shed.

(b) *Translate:* Those Christians have a good pastor; we shall give out assistance for those farmers; that man has three wives; that animal has a very long tail; these coconut palms give out much shade; there are some bones in the forest; many members have entered that society; the children will play football on Saturday; the Muslims have gone to the mosque; we need a few onions.

(c) *Translate and give plurals to:* Mnyapara; mzizi; chama; kizibo; mke; mwashi; mwanachama; kitunguu; mpaka; mkia; msikiti; mchungaji; mume; kisiwa; Mkristo; kiraka; msaada; mnazi; msitu; muda.

(d) *Translate:* Wanachama wamefanya mpango mpya; mpira umeanza kiwanjani; atapata kiasi kidogo; mkulima yule ana mimea mizuri kabisa; mfupa ule umevunjika kabisa; tutakaa kwa muda mrefu pale; wanachama wamekwenda mkutanoni; kaeni kivulini!; mpaka uko wapi? kule msituni; nitaweka kiraka katika kitambaa kile.

27 'To have'—2

As mentioned in chapter 20 the 'infinitive' of this verb is 'kuwa na' which means literally, 'To be with'. With the exception of the present tenses (affirmative and negative) these two words are *always* kept separate no matter what the tense or context may be. Thus in the tenses already introduced, remembering that 'kuwa' is itself a mono-syllabic verb, we get:

-LI-	Nilikuwa na	I had, I did have
	Ulikuwa na	You had, you did have
	Alikuwa na	He/she had, he/she did have
	Tulikuwa na	We had, we did have
	Mlikuwa na	You had, you did have
	Walikuwa na	They had, they did have
-TA-	Nitakuwa na	I shall have
	Utakuwa na	You will have
	Atakuwa na	He/she will have

Tutakuwa na	We shall have
Mtakuwa na	You will have
Watakuwa na	They will have

-ME-		
	Nimekuwa na	I have had
	Umekuwa na	You have had
	Amekuwa na	He/she has had
	Tumekuwa na	We have had
	Mmekuwa na	You have had
	Wamekuwa na	They have had

The other noun classes follow the same patterns:

M- MI-		
	Ulikuwa na	It had, it did have
	Ilikuwa na	They had, they did have
	Utakuwa na	It will have
	Itakuwa na	They will have
	Umekuwa na	It has had
	Imekuwa na	They have had

KI- VI-		
	Kilikuwa na	It had, it did have
	Vilikuwa na	They had, they did have
	Kitakuwa na	It will have
	Vitakuwa na	They will have
	Kimekuwa na	It has had
	Vimekuwa na	They have had

PA-		
(Etc.)	Palikuwa na	There was/were (lit. The place had)
	Kulikuwa na	There was/were
	Patakuwa na	There will be
	Kutakuwa na	There will be
	Pamekuwa na	There has/have been
	Kumekuwa na	There has/have been

N.B. (1) You cannot use the '-na-' present tense with this verb.

(2) You must not leave the 'na' on its own without another word following it. Even though in English one could say 'I have had', without going on, the Swahili must have either a noun, or other construction following the word 'na'.

(3) Palikuwa na; kulikuwa na——cf. pana; kuna (there is). (See ch. 20.)

Examples:

Alikuwa na mke mwema.	He had a good wife.
Kiti kile kitakuwa na miguu mitatu.	That stool will have three legs.

Exercise 27

(a) *Translate:* I had much food; we shall have an examination tomorrow; there was a meeting yesterday; we shall have visitors on Wednesday; this

room will have three beds; those trees had sharp thorns; that farmer has
had good crops; he had a bad sore on the leg; there will be a forest on that
mountain; there have been many meetings this year; we have had three
cooks this month; these plants have had plenty of shade; I have one child,
but I shall have two; did you have some books?; there was a big fire on the
mountain; those villages had many inhabitants; these trees will have deep
roots; those youths had sharp knives; they have much material; we have
had great help.

(b) *Translate:* Tulikuwa na wanachama wengi mwaka ule; vibarua wale
watakuwa na mnyapara mkali sana; kulikuwa na mtelemko kule;
patakuwa na msikiti hapa; chumba kile kilikuwa na kioo; kitanda kile
kilikuwa na mto, lakini sasa uko wapi?; mto ule umekuwa na viboko
wengi; watu wale walikuwa na mikuki jana; nitakuwa na mpango mpya
kesho; kulikuwa na Waislamu wengi huku zamani.

28 Adverbs — 2

Besides the adverbs which can be formed by giving certain adjectives
'Ki- Vi-' agreements (ch. 16), there are many more which only exist in
adverbial form. The following are in common use:

baadaye	afterwards, later, and then
bado	not yet, still
halafu	afterwards, later, and then
hasa	especially
hivi, hivyo	this way, thus
kumbe!	fancy that! (expression of astonishment)
labda	perhaps, possibly
mapema	early, soon
pia	as well, also, too
polepole (cf.	slowly, slow, carefully, gently
'Pole!' in ch. 2)	
sikuzote	always
tu	only, just (must *always* come at the end of its phrase)
upesi	quickly, hurriedly
vilevile	as well, just the same, too, also

Besides the above, many other adverbs can be made up by using a
noun, or certain other adjectives, and preceding them by the word
'kwa ....'. If a Bantu adjective is used, it is again given 'Ki- vi-'
agreements.

kwa bahati	luckily, fortunately
kwa ghafula	suddenly (sometimes used without the 'kwa')
kwa haraka	quickly, speedily
kwa kawaida	usually, generally, customarily
kwa kifupi	shortly, in brief, briefly
kwa kusudi	purposely, on purpose (sometimes used without the 'kwa')
kwa kutwa	daily
kwa kweli	truthfully, truly
kwa sauti	loudly
kwa hiyo	therefore
kwa sababu hii	therefore

There is nowadays a very common phrase in use "Bado kidogo" ('not quite yet') It is virtually used as the stock answer to the question 'How long?'relating to time. It is freely used irrespective of the length of the actual waiting period etc. expected, for example "Chakula tayari?"(is the food ready?)reply "Bodo kidogo!"("not quite yet"), even if the cooking has yet to be started!!

Examples:

Kwa bahati, niliona kifaru mmoja tu.
Fortunately I saw just one rhino.
Kwa kawaida, vibarua wale wanakuja kwa kutwa.
Usually, those labourers come daily.
Kumbe amesahau leo, labda atakumbuka kesho.
Fancy that! He has forgotten today, perhaps he will remember tomorrow.

Note that the positions of Swahili adverbs are as in the English equivalent, except for 'tu' which must always come at the end of its phrase. Others may follow the verb.

Exercise 28

(a) *Translate:* Afterwards; fancy that!; luckily; especially; slowly; loudly; usually; as well; only; quickly; early; perhaps; just the same; daily; therefore; shortly; suddenly; always; not yet; truly; purposely.

(b) *Translate:* Go carefully!; I have only one child; come quickly!; he went to Nairobi, and then returned here; he went also; he likes potatoes, especially sweet potatoes; he entered suddenly; I fell over on purpose; speak (pl.) loudly!; truly, he is a trustworthy servant; usually he wakes up early; I had that book, perhaps he had one too; fancy that!; He is still living here!; he always comes here; do thus!; he spoke briefly; the tree suddenly fell; he came here, and afterwards went to Nairobi; I want only one loaf; he is not about, perhaps he has gone to town; the bread is finished, therefore buy another loaf.

(c) *Translate:* Njoo mapema kesho; alikwenda kwa haraka; kwa bahati nilipata mkate mjini jana; safisha vyombo hivi, baadaye fagia chumba kile, na hiki vilevile; mlango ulifunguliwa ghafula; kwa kawaida pana mikutano mingi kila mwezi lakini hasa mwezi huu; tulikwenda jana kwa kusudi kufika mapema; yeye anakuja hapa kwa kutwa; inua mzigo huu polepole; kwa kweli chama kile kinafaa sana.

73

29 Possessives

The possessive 'of' is translated into Swahili by a word whose stem has only one letter, '-A'. (This is, in fact, an additional concord which ends in '-a' added as a separate word.) But this word must take agreements with the possessed, not the possessor. Yet you cannot say, for instance, 'The child's toys' as we would in English. Such a phrase has to be turned round the other way to say 'The toys of the child', and the possessive here would have to agree with 'toys', and not the 'child'.

The agreement given to the possessive (or possessive marker) is closely related to the subject prefix of the appropriate noun class. The only exception to this rule is the singular agreement for the M- Wa-class.

M- Wa- class	Sing.	A+a	=Wa	(you might have expected just 'a')
	Plur.	Wa+a	=Wa	(the two 'a's merge)
M–Mi– class	Sing.	U+a	=Wa	
	Plur.	I+a	=Ya	
Ki–Vi– class	Sing.	Ki+a	=Cha	(Ki– changes before this vowel)
	Plur.	Vi+a	=Vya	(Vi– changes before this vowel)

(The vowels changing to consonants, such as in the M- MI- class will be found to come naturally if spoken aloud.)

We can now translate the phrase 'The toys of the child'—'Michezo ya mtoto.'

Word order:
This possessive comes after adjectives and the demonstrative.

Examples:

Visahani vikubwa vya vikombe hivi.	These cups' large saucers.
Miti michache ya msitu.	A few trees of the forest.
Watu wa Tanzania.	The people of Tanzania.
Mtoto wa mpishi wa Mzungu yule.	The child of that European's cook.
Vibarua wa mkulima.	The farmer's labourers.

N.B. The 'wa' here agrees with 'vibarua' as they are living beings.

Vitu vya Bwana Smith.	Mr. Smith's things.

Exercise 29
(a) *Translate:* A bag of potatoes; the farmer's crops; the guests' luggage; the wells of that village; the child's food; the trees of the forest; the door of the room; the labourers' wages; the mountains of Tanzania; the thorns of the

tree; the pupils' books; toes (of the foot); a finger (of the hand); the patient's body; the farmer's animals; the old man's pipe; the servant's reference; the teacher's chair; the members of the society; the farmer's potatoes.

(b) *Translate:* Mind the thorns of that tree. They are very sharp; the farmers of this village had good food crops; Mount Kilimanjaro (the mountain of Kilimanjaro) is visible now; the five-year plan has started for this period; those visitors' loads were quite heavy; Kenya's agricultural programme is progressing well; cut five pieces of bread for the guests' meal; the meeting of the Agricultural Society will start tomorrow; put two pillows on the children's beds; perhaps I shall try a Swahili examination this year.

(c) *Translate:* Kilimo cha sasa; viboko wa mto ule; mfupa wa mkono; mwisho wa kitabu kile; watoto wa mwanamke yule; kitambaa cha vyombo; chombo cha vitabu; kisu cha mkate; mchezo wa mpira; msikiti wa Waislamu; muda wa miezi miwili; kivuli cha mti ule; kiwanja cha mpira; mipaka ya mkoa huu; kipini cha kikombe hiki; mkia wa mnyama yule; mizizi ya mti huu; wananchi wa Kenya; mifereji ya mtelemko ule; kiasi kikubwa cha vitunguu.

(d) *Translate:* Wakulima wengi wa kijiji kile ni wanachama; watakuwa na miezi miwili ya msaada nasi, halafu tutarudi Nairobi; mtelemko wa mlima huu ni mkali sana; Mchungaji mzee wa Wakristo wa mji wa Tanga amekwisha kufa; nimenunua mkuki wa Mmasai yule; tumekaa Tanzania kwa muda wa miaka minane sasa; wenyeji wengi wa mji ule wamekwenda mkutanoni; usinunue mkate ule, ni wa jana; wageni wa Mzungu yule wanafanya mwendo wa muda wa mwezi mmoja; vitu vya watu hawa viko wapi? Vipo katika chumba cha wageni.

Personal possessives

The personal possessives in Swahili all take agreements which must be with the possessed, not the possessor.

-angu	my, mine
-ako	your, yours.
-ake	his, hers, its

N.B. This is the only occasion in the entire grammar of Swahili where the same word can be used for persons and things (cf. Personal Pronouns, ch. 18).

-etu	our, ours
-enu	your, yours
-ao	their, theirs

The agreements are exactly similar to those of the possessives dealt with in the previous section.

M- Wa- class

Mtoto wangu	My child	Watoto wangu	My children
Mtoto wako	Your child	Watoto wako	Your children
Mtoto wake	His/her/its child	Watoto wake	His/her/its children
Mtoto wetu	Our child	Watoto wetu	Our children

75

Mtoto wenu	Your child (pl.)	Watoto wenu	Your (pl.) children
Mtoto wao	Their child	Watoto wao	Their children

M- Mi- class

Mpango wangu	My arrangement	Mipango yangu	My arrangements
Mpango wako	Your arrangement	Mipango yako	Your arrangements
Mpango wake	His/her/its arrangement	Mipango yake	His/her/its arrangements
Mpango wetu	Our arrangement	Mipango yetu	Our arrangements
Mpango wenu	Your arrangement	Mipango yenu	Your arrangements
Mpango wao	Their arrangement	Mipango yao	Their arrangements

Ki- Vi- class

Kisu changu	My knife	Visu vyangu	My knives
Kisu chako	Your knife	Visu vyako	Your knives
Kisu chake	His/her/its knife	Visu vyake	His/her/its knives
Kisu chetu	Our knife	Visu vyetu	Our knives
Kisu chenu	Your knife (pl.)	Visu vyenu	Your knives (pl.)
Kisu chao	Their knife	Visu vyao	Their knives

Word order
Personal possessives follow immediately after the noun they qualify, but *before* any adjectives. Thus, to summarise, the order used is: Noun, personal possessive, adjectives, quantity, demonstrative, possessive.

> e.g. Kitabu changu kikubwa chekundu hiki cha Kiswahili.
> This big red Swahili book of mine.

(Reminder: should you ever hear alternative word orders, they are changed merely on account of stress. It would usually be the demonstrative which would change place, when it might we placed either before the noun or after the personal possessive).

Examples:
Weka mizigo yangu katika chumba changu.
> Put my loads in my room.

Kiazi hiki ni kizuri kabisa. Angalia mizizi yake.
> This potato is excellent. Look at its roots.

Mtoto huyu ana michezo mingi, lakini mpira wake umepotea.
> This child has many toys, but his ball is lost.

Mkulima yule amekwenda kuuza wanyama wake mjini.
> That farmer has gone to sell his animals in town.

Mikono yangu michafu.
> My hands are dirty.

Exercise 30

(a) *Translate:* My hands; his books; your (pl.) children; its door (the room's); your heart; its roots (the tree's); your bodies; her bread; our crops; their luggage; its forest (the mountain's); our cook; my wife; her husband; their foreman (the labourers'); its tail (the animal's); my chair; its shadow (the tree's) their examination; his onions.

(b) *Translate:* This is not Hamisi's book. His is red; the children have brought their food; there is a meeting of our Society today; their labourers started early today; that animal is known because its tail has been cut; that European is looking for his wife; the animals have lain down in the shade of that tree; this cup is broken. Its handle is lost also; these people are waiting for their salaries; if you have finished your food, have a rest.

(c) *Translate:* Mshahara wangu; miji yenu; mkono wake; kisahani chake; wageni wao; viatu vyangu; kitabu chako; vyeti vyenu; wake wao; wagonjwa wake; chumba chako; visima vyao; kitanda chake; msaada wenu; wanachama wake; mpira wao.

(d) *Translate:* Leteni mizigo yao; mganga amekwenda kuangalia wagonjwa wake; kisu chake si kikali, lakini changu kikali kabisa; niliweza kuingia msikiti wao juzi; vijana wa kijiji kile wanasaidia sana wazee wao; wamepanda miti katika mipaka yao; mwavuli wake umepotea; lete mto wa kitanda chako, na chandalua chake pia; ninaomba kutumia kiberiti chako; cheti chako kiko wapi? Kimo katika mfuko wangu Bwana.

30 Questions

In English, word order is slightly reversed when changing a statement into a question.

> e.g. You are going to Nairobi today. (statement)
> Are you going to Nairobi today? (question)

But in Swahili, as will have been seen, there is no change whatsoever in the formation of a question from a statement.

> e.g. Utakwenda Nairobi leo. (statement)
> Utakwenda Nairobi leo? (question)

When writing a question such as this, the only clue that it is a question is the question mark. But in speech, the intonation is quite changed. In a statement, the voice is kept on a monotone until the last syllable or so, when it then lowers. But in a question, the voice is used at a slightly higher level than normal, and the last two or three syllables are spoken on an even higher pitch, with the slight drop for the final syllable. There are, however, a number of interrogatory words which are commonly used:

> Gani?   What sort? Which kind of? Which?

Kwa nini?	Why? (For what?)
Lini?	When?
Mbona?	Why? (Used only either when greatly astonished or with impatience.)
Nani?	Who? Whom?
-ngapi?	How many? (see Ch. 9)
Nini?	What? (Used only for object.)
Wapi?	Where? (see Ch. 11.)

Position

Each of the above are used in a certain position in the sentence.

Gani?   is used as an adjective, normally coming last of the adjectives,

e.g. Umenunua mkate gani?—What sort of bread have you bought?

Mti mrefu gani ulianguka?—Which tall tree fell?

Kwa nini?   will always precede the sentence,

e.g. Kwa nini umechelewa tena?—Why are you late again?

Lini?   This word may either be used at the beginning, or the end of the clause,

e.g. Lini watakwenda Mombasa?

or   Watakwenda lini, Mombasa?—When will they go to Mombasa?

Mbona?   is used as for 'Kwa nini?',

e.g. Mbona umechelewa tena?—Why, for goodness' sake, are you late again?

Nani?   can either be placed at the beginning or end of a sentence. But in order to place it at the end of a long sentence, it requires the combined use of a relative. Thus, for the present we can only place it at the beginning of a sentence, or end of a very short phrase.

e.g. Nani atakwenda leo?

or   Atakwenda nani, leo?—Who will go today?

Nani alileta vitabu hivi?—Who brought these books?

If, however, it is used as 'whom?' then it will follow the verb.

e.g. Uliona nani?—Whom did you see?

-ngapi?   takes agreements, and is used as an adjective, (see Ch. 9)

Nini?   being used only for the object, will only be used after the verb.

e.g. Unataka nini?—What do you want?
Ulikwenda kuleta nini?—What did you go to bring?

N.B. If, however, you need to say 'what?' for a subject, they generally say 'what sort of thing?'.

e.g. Kitu gani kilianguka?—What fell?

Wapi?   will invariably follow the verb. (Remember that with the present of the verb 'to be', there is a special form as described in Chapter 11.)
e.g. Wageni wamekwenda wapi?—Where have the guests gone?
Bwana yuko wapi?—Where is the Bwana?

N.B. One may hear a common expression of disbelief 'Wapi!' or even 'Ah Wapi!' often uttered with considerable vehemence. It is comparable to the English expression 'Oh, get away with you!' It requires no particular comment in reply, other than, possibly 'Kweli!' (true!)

Je?

There is a very versatile interrogatory word, 'Je?'. According to its position, it has a number of varied meanings—

1. If used before any question, whether or not it uses an interrogatory word, it has no literal translation but merely serves as a warning to the listener that a question is coming up. (It is used a lot in rhetorical questioning.) Its sense might be equivalent to 'I say .....'
e.g. Je, utakwenda Nairobi leo?
Will you go to Nairobi today?
or I say, will you go to Nairobi today?
In fact, certain special words are often used to attract attention, such as 'Aisei!' (from the English 'I say') to address an equal, or 'Ebu!' or 'Ati!'.
e.g. Aisei/Ebu/Ati unakwenda mjini?
I say, are you going to town?

2. If '–je?' is suffix to a verb, then it has the meaning of 'How?' But although this is its general English translation in fact it is used in Swahili where we might not necessarily say 'How?' in English.
e.g. Watoto walichezaje leo?
How did the children play today?
Unauzaje viazi hivi?
How are you selling these potatoes? (i.e. by volume, or weight, or for how much?)
Unaonaje?
How do you feel? (or also, What do you think?)
Unasemaje?
What do you say? (lit. How do you say?)

N.B. Remember that because you have added a syllable to the verb with this '-je', the stress will move up one syllable accordingly.

3. If 'je' is used as the last word of a short verbless question, it takes on the meaning of 'How about?'.

    e.g. Mtoto huyu ni mgonjwa sana. Yule, je?
        This child is very sick, How about that one?
        Mimi, ninakwenda Nairobi leo. Wewe, je?
        As for me, I am going to Nairobi today. How about you?

Examples:
    Ninyi, mlikwenda wapi jana? Na ninyi, je?
        You (pl.), where did you go yesterday? And how about you
        (pl.)?
    Waliona wanyama gani Serengeti?
        What sort of animals did they see in Serengeti?
    Tutapandaje mlima mkali ule?
        How shall we climb that steep mountain?
    Je, umefanya nini na vitu vile?
        What have you done with those things?

Exercise 31

(a) *Translate:* What kind of bread? Who came? Why did you go? What does he want? How many bags? Where have you been? Whom did you see? How about those things? How did you answer? When will they arrive? I say, have you read this book? Who are you? What will do? What shall I buy? Why did you(pl.)forget? How do you open this door? Have you finished? Why have you become a doctor? When will the meeting start? Where is the European—and his guest?

(b) *Translate:;* When will your (pl.) guests arrive? Why did you cook potatoes again? What sort of person is that? (Often asked when implying 'What tribe?'). Whom do you wish to see here? What is this thing? When will he start? Did they go to Dar es Salaam yesterday? Where is my new pipe? What are you doing? When did they arrive in Kenya?

(c) *Translate:* Mbona umerudi tena? Ati! Unafanya nini hapa? Watawezaje kuchukua mzigo ule? Kitabu gani kimepotea? Nani Bwana Ali? Kitu gani, hiki? Kwa nini chakula kimechelewa? Chakula kitakuwa tayari lini? Mmea gani ule? Watoto wangapi wamekosa kuja leo?

31   Verbs—5

The causative

The Causative form of the verb is another very useful derivative from other verbs, or indeed sometimes from certain nouns, adjectives, or even conjunctions.

    This derivative is basically the addition of -SHA onto the stem, but unfortunately, there are exceptions such as the alteration of the preceding vowel, or in some cases, the addition of -ZA instead of the usual -SHA. But it is possible to give certain basic rules which are as follows (for meanings of the verbs given as examples, see the list following the rules):

1. As in the previous derivations, verbs containing A, I or U as the last vowel in the stem take an extra I. Thus the final vowel goes to '-isha',

e.g.	A	ku-hama	ku-hamisha
	I	ku-fika	ku-fikisha
	U	ku-rudi	ku-rudisha

2. Verbs containing an 'E' or 'O' in the stem to go '-esha',

e.g.	E	ku-enda	ku-endesha
	O	ku-kopa	ku-kopesha

3. Unfortunately, not all verbs take -SHA, but some take -ZA instead, seemingly without following any particular rule. It will either be '-iza' or '-eza', following the same principles as the first two rules,

e.g. ku-penda   ku-pendeza

4. Verbs which end in double vowels will usually take the -Z- which will simply go in between the two vowels,

e.g.	ku-jaa	ku-jaza
	ku-legea	ku-legeza
	ku-kaa	ku-kaza (can also occur as ku-kalisha—to cause to stay)

5. Many verbs which end either in '-ka' or '-ta' change their stems and substitute '-sha' in their stead,

e.g.	ku-waka	ku-washa
	ku-pata	ku-pasha

6. Nouns, adjectives, etc., which can be made into causative verbs invariably end in '-isha', but sometimes have extra letters or syllables inserted in between the stem and the derivative ending,

e.g.	lazima	ku-lazimisha
	sawa	ku-sawazisha

BUT, there are many exceptions to the above 'rules', and so the more common forms of Causative verbs are listed below together with the form from which they are derived:

Causative		*From*	
ku-amsha	to awaken (cause to awake)	ku-amka	to be/become awake
ku-angusha	to fell, (cause to fall)	ku-anguka	to fall
ku-bahatisha	to guess, try luck	bahati	luck (N class)

ku-chemsha	to boil (cause to boil)	ku-chemka	to be boiling
ku-chokesha	to tire	ku-choka	to be/get tired
ku-eleza	to explain	ku-elea	to be clear
ku-endesha	to drive (cause to go)	ku-enda	to go
ku-fikisha	to cause to reach/ arrive	ku-fika	to arrive
ku-fundisha	to teach, instruct	(kufunda)	(uncommonly used)
ku-geuza	to turn around (cause to)	ku-geuka	to turn
ku-hakikisha	to make certain, ensure	hakika	certainty (N class)
ku-hamisha	to cause to move (house)	ku-hama	to move away
ku-kausha	to cause to dry	ku-kauka	to dry
ku-ingiza	to insert, put in	ku-ingia	to enter
ku-jaza	to fill	ku-jaa	to be filled
ku-kaza	to fix, tighten	ku-kaa	to stay
ku-kopesha	to lend (cause to borrow)	ku-kopa	to borrow
ku-lainisha	to soften, smoothen	laini	soft, smooth (adj.)
ku-laza	to cause to lie down	ku-lala	to lie down
ku-lazimisha	to compel	lazima	obligation (N class)
ku-legeza	to loosen	ku-legea	to be loose
ku-lisha	to feed	ku-la	to eat
ku-oza	to cause to marry	ku-oa	to marry (used of man only)
ku-ozesha	to cause to rot, ferment	ku-oza	to rot, go bad
ku-pasha	to cause to get	ku-pata	to get
ku-pendeza	to please (cause to like)	ku-penda	to like, love
ku-poteza	to lose	ku-potea	to be lost
ku-punguza	to reduce	ku-pungua	to be/grow less
ku-rudisha	to return, send back	ku-rudi	to return
ku-sawazisha	to put right, put in order	sawa	right, equal
ku-shusha	to drop, discharge, let go	ku-shuka	to go down
ku-sikiliza (ku-sikiza)	to listen (to cause to hear)	ku-sikia	to hear

ku-simamisha	to erect, cause to stand, stop	ku-simama	to stand, stop
ku-tayarisha	to prepare, make ready	tayari	ready (adj.)
ku-tembeza	to cause to walk	ku-tembea	to walk
ku-telemsha	to lower	ku-telemka	to go down, descend
ku-valisha	to dress, put clothes on	ku-vaa	to wear
ku-washa	to light, itch	ku-waka	to be burning

N.B. *It is furthermore possible to make a passive derivative of these causatives. In this case, the same rules apply for rendering the above into passives as for all other verbs.*

e.g.	ku-angushwa	to be felled
	ku-tembezwa	to be taken for a walk
	ku-tayarishwa	to be prepared

N.B. *The passive -W- follows the causative -SH- or -Z- in each case.*

Examples:
Pasha moto chakula hiki.
  Heat up this food.
Amejaza vikapu vitatu kwa viazi.
  He has filled three baskets with potatoes.
Tumelisha watoto mapema leo.
  We have fed the children early today.
Vibarua wale wameangusha miti mingi kule.
  Those labourers have felled many trees over there.
Miti mingi imeangushwa na vibarua wale.
  Many trees have been felled by those labourers.

Exercise 32

(a) *Translate:* To be reduced; to listen; to light; to ensure; to cause to dry; to make smooth; to put right; to dress; to cause to drop; to feed; to send back; to drive; to fell; to compel; to be pleased; to teach; to insert; to guess; to cause to lie down; to loosen; to be lowered; to cause to wake; to cause to turn around; to reduce; to prepare; to be taken for a walk; to explain; to cause to get; to lend; to fill,

(b) *Translate:* These people were compelled to go today; cause these potatoes to get heat (i.e. heat these potatoes up); don't drop that load; she is feeding her child; dry these cloths quickly; their salaries have been reduced; prepare this room for the guest; my arm is itching; he will get married on Saturday; listen (pl.) to your teacher.

(c) *Translate:* Boil the potatoes for only a small period of time; that teacher is teaching blind children to read with their fingers; your book was returned yesterday; visitors are very pleased by the mountains of Tanzania; when did you lose your pocket knife?; send this basket back to the farmer; my servant has forgotten to put the furniture straight; those loads were lowered slowly because they were very heavy; would you prepare that room for my visitor?; don't wake the children up early tomorrow.

(d) *Translate:* Ku-kaza; ku-legeza; ku-simamisha; ku-tayarishwa; ku-oza; ku-endeshwa; ku-hakikisha; ku-chokesha; ku-amsha; ku- chemshwa; ku-fundishwa; ku-valisha; ku-kopesha; ku-pungua; ku-telemka; ku-geuza; ku-chemka; ku-angushwa; ku-fikisha; ku-waka.

(e) *Translate:* Rudisha kisu chake; ninalegeza msumari huu; mchungaji ana-oza mwanamke leo; uvalishe mtoto, tafadhali; fikisha cheti hiki kwa Bwana Mohammedi; kitabu hiki kimeeleza vitu vingi; simamisha mti huu pale; nimepoteza mwavuli wangu; moto ule unawaka sana; nenda kulisha wanyama wale.

32 Negative tenses

Negative subject prefixes

The majority of the negative tenses are used in combination with a negative Subject Prefix. With most of these prefixes, it is merely a question of adding HA- to the Subject Prefix already learnt. But the first few in the M- Wa- class are slightly different, so they are all given here:

si-	I ..... not	hatu-	we ..... not
hu-	you ..... not	ham-	you ..... not
ha-	he/she ..... not	hawa-	they ..... not

M- MI- class

hau–	it ..... not	hai–	they ..... not

KI- VI- class

haki–	it ..... not	havi–	they ..... not

The above prefixes are used in exactly the same way as the affirmative prefixes, but they can *only* be used with *certain negative tenses*.

N.B. (1) Note the difference between 'hu-' and 'hau-',in spite of the fact that in the affirmative they are the same.

(2) Before a vowel, 'ham-' takes a W- 'hamw-'.

The negative present tense

This tense is unusual in that it has no tense sign such as has been encountered up till now. Instead, the negative prefixes just shown are used directly onto the verb stem. In addition to this, the final -A of Bantu verbs is changed to an -I. This does not, however, occur with Arabic verbs.

(A useful rule to remember which applies to Arabic verbs in all tenses, though not the derivatives, is—'Once a 'U' always a 'U', once an 'I' always an 'I', once an 'E' always an 'E'.)

Thus, if we use the verb 'ku-jua' (to know), we get:

si-ju(a)i	sijui	I do not know
hu-ju(a)i	hujui	you do not know
ha-ju(a)i	hajui	he/she does not know
hatu-ju(a)i	hatujui	we do not know
ham-ju(a)i	hamjui	you do not know
hawa-ju(a)i	hawajui	they do not know

M- MI- class (using ku-ingia—to enter)

hau-ingi(a)i	hauingii	it does not go in
hai-ingi(a)i	haiingii	they do not go in

KI- VI- class

haki-ingi(a)i	hakiingii	it does not go in
havi-ingi(a)i	haviingii	they do not go in

With Arabic verbs (e.g. ku-faulu—to succeed), there is no alteration of the final vowel:

si-faulu	sifaulu	I do not succeed
hu-faulu	hufaulu	you do not succeed
ha-faulu	hafaulu	he/she does not succeed
hatu-faulu	hatufaulu	we do not succeed
ham-faulu	hamfaulu	you do not succeed
hawa-faulu	hawafaulu	they do not succeed

M- MI- class

hau-faulu	haufaulu	it does not succeed
hai-faulu	haifaulu	they do not succeed

KI- VI- class

haki-faulu	hakifaulu	it does not succeed
havi-faulu	havifaulu	they do not succeed

Monosyllabic verbs (e.g. ku-ja—to come), this time drop their 'infinitive' 'ku-' and, of course their final -A changes to -I as usual—

si-j(a)i	siji	I do not come
hu-j(a)i	huji	you do not come
ha-j(a)i	haji	he/she does not come
hatu-j(a)i	hatuji	we do not come
ham-j(a)i	hamji	you do not come
hawa-j(a)i	hawaji	they do not come

M- MI- class

| hau-j(a)i | hauji | it does not come |
| hai-j(a)i | haiji | they do not come |

KI- VI- class

| haki-j(a)i | hakiji | it does not come |
| havi-j(a)i | haviji | they do not come |

N.B. *Remember the Present negative of 'kuwa' which is 'si' (see Ch. 19).*

Examples:

Mganga haji Jumanne.
The doctor does not come on Tuesdays.
Watoto hawali chakula chao.
The children are not eating their food.
Mlango huu haufungiki vizuri.
This door does not close properly.
Viazi vile havionekani.
Those potatoes are not in sight.

Exercise 33:

(a) *Translate:* I do not think; he does not go; the book is not read; the door does not close; the knife does not cut well; they do not drink; are you (pl.) not playing?; do you (pl.) not see?; salaries are not being increased; he is not sick; he is not following; they are not gazing; the nails are not suitable; this loaf is not sufficient; I am unable to come today; this material does not dry quickly; those labourers do not tire; you do not hear; she is not lying down; I do not eat potatoes.

(b) *Translate:* I do not buy bread in town because it is not suitable; those animals do not live here; our salaries are not being increased this month; I do not wish to buy your things today; why does he not say something? because he does not hear; this fire is not burning well. Try again; I have heard that you cannot come today; she is happy because her meetings are not continuing; cloth is not sold here because it is not bought by the local people; potatoes are not obtainable in town this month.

(c) *Translate:* Hakopeshi; hawasimami; sijui kuendesha; harudi; moto hauwaki; vitunguu hivi haviozi; haamki; silimi mwaka huu; hamwingii? mnyama hali leo; hatukai hapa; watoto hawasikilizi; chombo hiki hakisimamishwi; sioni kitu; sipendi mkate, asante; wanafunzi hawachezi leo; haendelei vizuri.

'To have' present negative tense

The present negative tense of this verb is similar to its affirmative equivalent, in that it breaks away from its normal 'infinitive' form of 'kuwa na', and instead, the negative prefixes are added directly onto the word 'na' (cf. ch. 20).

| sina | I have not |
| huna | you have not |

hana	he/she has not
hatuna	we have not
hamna	you have not
hawana	they have not

M- MI- class

hauna	it has not
haina	they have not

KI- VI- class

hakina	it has not
havina	they have not

Similarly the construction for 'there is not' and 'there are not' follows suit with the addition of the negative 'ha-':

hapana	there is/are not (definite place)

N.B. This is where the 'Hapana' meaning 'No' comes from.

hakuna	there is/are not about
hamna	there is/are not inside

Examples:

Mwanamke yule hana watoto.	That woman has no children.
Hakuna kiwanja cha mpira huku.	There is no football ground hereabouts.
Kikombe hiki hakina kipini.	This cup has no handle.
Tutakwenda mjini kula kwa sababu sina chakula nyumbani.	We shall go to town to eat because I have no food in the house (at home).

Exercise 34

(a) *Translate:* He has no bread; I have no children; we have no books; they have no food; he has no nails; the chair has no legs; the bed has no pillows; there are no trees hereabouts; there is no doctor here; there are no nails in the basket; you (pl.) have no help; have you no children?; I have not; we have no cook; there are no Europeans about; this club has no women; there is no meeting today; we have no well in this village; these plants have not long roots; he has no guests today.

(b) *Translate:* That European has no wife; there is no bread in the house; there are no hippos in that big river; why has that bed no pillow? these plants do not have very big roots; there are no insects here in Nairobi; those labourers over there have no overseer; have you a lighter, because I haven't?; those new arrivals have no luggage; I see that you have no chit. How about you?

(c) *Translate:* Hawana chakula; kikombe hiki hakina kisahani; milima ile haina misitu; hapana kiberiti hapa; hatuna vibarua wengi, wachache tu; vitanda vile havina vyandalua; hakuna mto kule; sina mkutano leo; yeye hana mkate mwingine. Wewe je?; huna kisu mfukoni? Sina.

Negative future tense

The future is the only tense which has the same tense sign in both the affirmative and the negative. This is, as we have already seen, -TA-. In this tense the negative is expressed by using the negative prefixes. Note, however, that the final vowel on the verb is NOT affected. It is only the present tense in which this is affected. The verb 'ku-weza' therefore conjugates:

si-ta-weza	sitaweza	I shall not be able
hu-ta-weza	hutaweza	you will not be able
ha-ta-weza	hataweza	he/she will not be able
hatu-ta-weza	hatutaweza	we shall not be able
ham-ta-weza	hamtaweza	you will not be able
hawa-ta-weza	hawataweza	they will not be able

M- MI- class

hau-ta-weza	hautaweza	it will not be able
hai-ta-weza	haitaweza	they will not be able

Ki- Vi- class

haki-ta-weza	hakitaweza	it will not be able
havi-ta-weza	havitaweza	they will not be able

Arabic verbs are treated similarly:

si-ta-jibu	sitajibu	I shall not answer
ha-ta-rudi	hatarudi	he/she will not return

Monosyllabics, as with the affirmative tense, retain their 'infinitive' Ku-:

hawa-ta-kuja	hawatakuja	they will not come.
hatu-ta-kwenda	hatutakwenda	we shall not go
si-ta-kuwa	sitakuwa	I shall not be . . . . .
ha-ta-kuwa na	hatakuwa na	he shall not have . . . . .

Examples:

Mti mrefu ule hautaanguka hapa.	That tall tree will not fall here.
Chumba hiki hakitakuwa na vitanda viwili.	This room will not have two beds.
Mimi sitakwenda Dar es Salaam kesho.	I myself am not going to Dar es Salaam tomorrow.

Exercise 35

(a) *Translate:* I shall not go tomorrow; he shall not buy; we shall not take; they won't be able; will you not try?; you (pl.) will not come back; that chair will not be suitable; those nails will not be sufficient; he will not arrive today; you will not come; the food will not be ready; she will not have children; you will not succeed; I shall not read; he will not think; they will not travel; you (pl.) will not forgive; the animals will not eat; the visitors will not have luggage; the river will not be large.

(b) *Translate:* I shall not want to return home this year; they will not be able to finish this thing today; these dirty cups will not be suitable (will not do); the children's game will not be played today; I know that our Bwana will not agree to increase our salaries; we shall not want to buy another knife like that (one); bring more cups because these will not be enough; this nice tree will not be felled, not the slightest; the farmers of this village will not follow our programme; these loads will not be carried today.

(c) *Translate:* Mkutano hautakuwa kesho; hapatakuwa na watu pale; wadudu hawataonekana kule; kitabu kile hakitasomwa; sitakaa sana pale; viazi havitapatikana kijijini; msaada hautakuwa mkubwa; mchezo hautachezwa Jumamosi; visu havitatosha; mipango haitafaa.

Negative past tense
Theoretically, there is only one past negative tense to replace the two affirmative past tenses (-LI- and -ME-) and that is the -KU- tense. But in practice in modern Swahili, this past negative tense is only really used as a negative to the -LI- tense. Another tense is now commonly used as the negative equivalent to the -ME- tense, and will be dealt with in chapter 37.

It will be seen that this tense sign is identical to the 'infinitive' sign. In use, however, it creates no problem, and it must be used with the negative prefixes:

si-ku-anguka	sikuanguka	I did not fall
hu-ku-anguka	hukuanguka	you did not fall
ha-ku-anguka	hakuanguka	he/she did not fall
hatu-ku-anguka	hatukuanguka	we did not fall
ham-ku-anguka	hamkuanguka	you did not fall
hawa-ku-anguka	hawakuanguka	they did not fall

M- MI- class

hau-ku-anguka	haukuanguka	it did not fall
hai-ku-anguka	haikuanguka	they did not fall

KI- VI- class

haki-ku-anguka	hakikuanguka	it did not fall
havi-ku-anguka	havikuanguka	they did not fall

Arabic verbs again do not create any exception:

si-ku-faulu	sikufaulu	I did not succeed
hawa-ku-safiri	hawakusafiri	they did not travel

Monosyllabic verbs in effect drop their 'infinitive' 'ku-' to have it replaced by the tense sign '-ku-'. You will see that there is a slight difference where the 'infinitive' took a 'kw-':

ha-ku-fa	hakufa	he/she did not die

si-ku-enda	sikuenda	I did not go
hawa-ku-wa	hawakuwa	they were not .....
ham-ku-wana	hamkuwa na	you (pl.) did not have

Examples:

Mpishi wako hakupata mshahara wake.
Your cook did not get his salary.
Mgeni wangu hakuweza kufika jana.
My guest was unable to arrive yesterday.
Mkate haukuliwa jana.
The bread was not eaten yesterday.

Exercise 36

(a) *Translate:* He did not try; they did not come; the chair was not suitable; you did not remember; we did not think; you (pl.) did not eat; they did not have shoes; he was not an able cook; the patient did not die; I did not see anything; those trees were not felled; the mountain was not visible; the visitors were not late; the leg was not broken; my pipe was not lost; he did not move away; we did not enter; you did not ensure; didn't you (pl.) hear?; we did not hear.

(b) *Translate:* They did not awake early, but they were not late; Many insects entered the room because he did not shut the door; These potatoes were not bought in town; The game of football was not played on Thursday; The food is spoilt because it was not covered with a cloth; I did not know that you have a wife; They did not go to Mombasa to bring their luggage; That sick person did not eat his food; Mount Kenya was not visible yesterday.

(c) *Translate:* Hatukufaulu; hakuenda; hapakuwa na mkutano jana; mkate haukuletwa; hatukujaza vikapu vile; hamkukaa kule?; hakukuwa na mto kule; sikurudisha kitabu chake; moto haukuwaka vizuri; mgonjwa hakulazwa; mshahara haukuwa mzuri; viazi havikuharibika; sikuweza kulala; chakula hakikuchemshwa; hatukuanza; hakukasirika; hawaku-kosa; mtoto hakufunga mlango; hukutaka kwenda?; hawakukubali.

Exercise 37—Revision

(a) *Translate:* What animals did you see in Ngorongoro?; We are going to have many guests on Saturday; How did you find Dodoma? (i.e. what did you think?); He will not take his luggage because it is heavy; Only eighteen farmers came to our meeting the day before yesterday; Go quickly to fetch help. There is a big fire over there; Where is my new lighter? I do not know, perhaps it is lost; I need two pieces of that white cloth; Whom have you been to see in that town?; Don't fell those tall trees, they are not suitable.

(b) *Translate:* Patakuwa na mkutano kwa kila mmoja kesho; Mbona hukuja jana? Sikukumbuka; Viazi hivi havifai sasa kwa sababu vimekauka; Hukuenda mjini kununua vitu vyangu? Ndiyo, Bwana; Watoto wangu wamekwisha kwenda kucheza mpira; Kiwanja cha mpira kile hakifai kwa sababu kina mtelemko; Hakukubali kuingia chama chetu; Ulifanya nini jana? Na yeye je?; Ufikishe cheti hiki kwa Bwana Mongi; Kibarua yule amefanya vizuri kurudi hapa.

33 Nouns—4

The 'N' noun class

This is the largest of all the noun classes in the language. This is mainly as a result of the fact that nearly all words which are taken from other languages, chiefly English and Arabic, are placed in this class. In fact, words of Bantu origin occurring in this class are in the great minority.

If, therefore, you are stuck for the Swahili for an English noun, you may, on a number of occasions, get away with using the English word pronounced with Swahili intonation with, if necessary, the addition of an appropriate final vowel (this is generally '-i').
e.g. 'Cheese' would be understandable as 'Chizi'.
'Shirt' would be understandable at 'Shati'.
'Typewriter' would be understandable as 'Tapuraita'. (Note that an '-er' ending in English goes to "-a" in Swahili.)
But do not resort to this habit at the cost of the correct vocabulary!

NOTE that in this class there is no change in the concord (which is in any case absent on 'foreign' words) for singular and plural. Thus 'nyumba' means either 'house' or 'houses'. The singular or plural can, however, be shown on the subject prefixes etc. Therefore, in the following list, the nouns mentioned could be either singular or plural.

asubuhi	morning
baba	father
bahati	luck, fortune
barabara	road, main road
baridi	cold, coolness
barafu	refrigerator, ice
barua	letter (mail)
bia	beer (bottled)
bei	price
bilauri	tumbler, glass
chai	tea
chumvi	salt
chupa	bottle
dakika	minute
dawa	medicine, polish, chemical
habari	news
hatari	danger
hema	tent
homa	fever
inzi	fly (any sort)
jioni	evening (before sunset)
kahawa	coffee
kalamu	pencil, pen

kaptula	shorts (used in singular)
karabai	pressure lamp
karatasi	paper (not newspaper)
kazi	work
mama	mother
mbegu	seeds, planting material
mboga	vegetables, relish
mbu	mosquito
mbwa	dog
meza	table
motokaa	car
mvua	rain
nafasi	opportunity, spare time, space
nguo	garment, clothes
nyama	meat
nyoka	snake
nyumba	house
paka	cat
panga	machete
pasi	flat-iron
pesa	money, coin (generally used in plural)
pilipili	pepper, chilli
pombe	local beer
rafiki	friend
ratili	pound (weight)
ruhusa	permission
ruksa	permission
saa	clock, watch, hour
sababu	reason, cause
sabuni	soap
safari	journey
sahani	plate, dish
samaki	fish
sehemu	part, portion, fraction
shida	difficulty, trouble
siagi	butter
sigara	cigarettes
siku	day
suruali	trousers (used in singular)
taa	lamp
takataka	rubbish
tarehe	date (of calendar)
wiki	week

N.B. *Remember that all days of the week, as well as days of reference (leo, jana, etc.,) are also N class (see Ch. 23).*

The majority of individual species of animals (domesticated and wild) as well as birds and insects are also in this class. But remember that even though the noun may not be in the M- WA- class, all agreements must be M- WA- if relating to the Animal Kingdom.

Adjectival agreements (concord agreements).

Although most of the nouns in this class have no concords, it is nevertheless necessary to give regular agreements to the dependent adjectives. But as with nouns, adjectives in this class have no means of showing whether they are singular or plural. The basic concord is N- for singular and plural, but this is often absent as summarised below:

1. Firstly, the N- on its own can only be placed before certain consonants, namely D, G, and Z:

e.g.	-dogo	small	nyumba ndogo	a small house
	-gumu	hard	siagi ngumu	hard butter
	-zuri	good	habari nzuri	good news

2. Before the consonants B, V (and P if a monosyllabic stem) the N- changes to M-:

e.g.	-baya	bad	bahati mbaya	bad luck
	-vivu	lazy	kazi mvivu	lazy work
	-pya	new	motokaa mpya	a new car

3. Before all other consonants, no concord whatsoever appears:

e.g.	-chache	few	barua chache	a few letters
	-fupi	short	safari fupi	a short journey
	-kali	sharp	panga kali	a sharp machete
	-ngapi?	how many?	dakika ngapi?	how many minutes?
	-tamu	sweet	chai tamu	sweet tea

4. Before vowel stem adjectives, the N- becomes NY-:

e.g.	-eusi	black	kahawa nyeusi	black coffee
	-ingine	another	sigara nyingine	another cigarette

Exceptions to above rules.
The following are common irregular adjectives:

-ema	good	goes to *njema*	habari njema	good news
-refu	long	goes to *ndefu*	barua ndefu	a long letter
-wili	two	goes to *mbili*	meza mbili	two tables

N.B. Remember that Arabic adjectives never take agreements. Numerals apart from '-wili' (two) take no concord in this class, since they fall under Rule 3,
    e.g. Sahani tatu   Three plates

Subject prefixes

The subject prefixes in this class do show a difference between the Singular and Plural. They are:

I- Singular, or negative   Hai—
Zi- Plural, or negative   Hazi—

e.g. Barua moja *i*mefika.   One letter has arrived.
     Barua nyingi *zi*mefika.   Many letters have arrived.

Demonstratives

From these subject prefixes, we can now form the demonstratives thus:

This   Begin with an H, end with I, double the vowel, I—Hii.
These   Begin with an H, end with ZI, repeat the vowel,
       I—HIZI.
That   Begin with I, end with LE—Ile.
Those   Begin with ZI, end with LE—Zile.

N.B. Demonstratives are used more frequently in this class than the others, since they denote the difference between Singular and Plural, which compensates for the absence of a singular or plural marker in the nouns.

e.g. Chupa hii   This bottle
     Mbegu hizi   These seeds
     Hatari ile   That danger
     Wiki zile   Those weeks

BUT note—Kaptula *hii*   These shorts (i.e. one garment)
          Suruali *ile*   Those trousers (i.e. one garment)

N.B. Whilst the English is always plural with these words, the Swahili will always be singular unless several garments are implied ('kaptula hizi' or 'suruali hizi' would denote several pairs).

Verb 'to be' with locative

These are:

ipo   iko   imo
zipo   ziko   zimo

e.g. Chai iko wapi? Ipo hapa mezani.
     Where is the tea? It is here on the table.
     Kalamu ziko wapi? Zimo kikapuni.
     Where are the pencils? They are in the basket.

Possessives

Using agreements similar to the subject prefix, these are as follows:

I- + -A=YA   ZI- + -A=ZA

e.g. Dawa ya viatu   Shoe polish
     Taa za safari   Safari lamps

Personal possessives

These will also have agreements similar to the subject prefix:

Singular	yangu	my, mine	yetu	our, ours
	yako	your, yours	yenu	your, yours
	yake	his/hers, her, its	yao	their, theirs
Plural	zangu	my, mine	zetu	our, ours
	zako	your, yours	zenu	your, yours
	zake	his/hers, her, its	zao	their, theirs

e.g. Dawa yangu   My medicine
     Barua yake   His/her letter
     Nyumba yetu   Our house
     Sababu zao   Their reasons
     Mbegu zake   Its seeds (his seeds or her seeds)

and also Suruali yangu   My trousers (one garment)
         Kaptula yake   His shorts (one garment)

Examples:

Chupa hizi zimejaa pombe nyingi. — These bottles are filled with much local beer.

Mtumishi alipiga dawa ya mbu katika nyumba nzima. — The servant sprayed mosquito spray in the whole house.

Wiki hii tutakwenda katika safari ndefu sana. — This week we shall go on a very long journey.

Lete sukari nyingine kwa sababu hii imekwisha. — Bring some more sugar because this is finished.

Je, una nafasi kwenda kununua ratili mbili za mboga? — Have you the time to go to buy two pounds of vegetables?

Exercise 38

(a) *Translate:* Opportunity; cold; danger; tent; pound (weight); cat; friend; flies; coffee; clock; reason; tumbler; morning; work; mother; dog; fish; date (of calendar); cheese; table; vegetables; lamp; trousers; snake; shirt; tea; permission; car; fever; pressure lamp; paper; butter; soap; rubbish; day; plate; seeds; letter; price; salt.

(b) *Translate:* Great fortune; a fierce dog; a small house; white paper; many mosquitoes; a few vegetables; five plates; a long road; two cigarettes; a sharp machete; clean clothes; soft butter; many days; red soap; an empty bottle; many friends; eight pounds (weight); two minutes; every morning; good medicine.

(c) *Translate:* This opportunity; those trousers; a safari tent; the morning hours; my new car; furniture polish; news of many days; his mail; days of work; these vegetable seeds; a cup of tea; five pounds of sugar; his many houses; my shorts; your (pl.) difficulties; our dirty clothes; two bottles of beer; a meat dish; those dirty flies; that long snake.

(d) *Translate:* Be careful of this chemical, it has great danger; My cook cannot come to work today because he has a fierce fever; Go to the town to buy two pounds of dog meat; Where are my new clothes? They are on the bed; Those two pressure lamps are burning very well; This work is not bad, but it is not good just the same; This person has been cut on the leg with this sharp machete; There are very fierce dogs in that large house; Two friends will come this evening to drink beer with me; I have a problem because I have no money this week.

(e) *Translate:* Siagi nyingine; kazi ile ina hatari; barabara kuu hii; bei gani?; dakika ngapi?; sina nafasi leo; pesa ziko wapi?; bahati njema; una ruhusa?; barua za Mzungu; tarehe gani?; shida za kazi hii; bei ya nyama; chai au kahawa?; angalia mbwa mkali; suruali yangu iko wapi?; muda wa saa moja kamili; hapana nafasi ya kazi hapa; bahati mbaya; nyumba ile ni ya Bwana Rashidi.

(f) *Translate:* Ratili mbili za nyama zitatosha? Hazitatosha, nunua ratili moja nyingine; Barafu yake imejaa (na) chupa za bia; Lete karatasi kuandika cheti cha ruhusa; Anavaa nguo zake za kazi; Sipendi kunywa chai tamu, ninapenda chai bila sukari tu; Kuna hatari kuendesha motokaa vibaya; Nenda kupata dawa nyekundu ya viatu; Tutakuwa na rafiki wengi jioni hii; Meza ndogo ile imevunjika; Mgonjwa huyu ana homa kali sana kwa sababu hakupata dawa.

34   Useful expressions

The following are common and useful expressions:

ku-cheza mpira	to play football
ku-fanya kazi	to work (to do work)
ku-fua nguo	to wash clothes
ku-nyesha mvua	to rain (lit, to rain rain)
ku-pakua chakula	to serve up the food
ku-panga meza	to lay the table
ku-safisha vyombo	to do the washing up
ku-sikia baridi	to feel cold
ku-tandika kitanda	to make a bed
ku-vaa nguo	to dress (wear clothes)
ku-vua nguo	to undress
ku-vua samaki	to fish (lit. to fish fish)
ku-vuta sigara	to smoke (cigarette)

and the verb 'ku-piga' has almost unlimited use:

ku-piga dawa	to apply insecticide, etc.
or	to polish

ku-piga deki	to scrub the floor (deck)
ku-piga hema	to pitch a tent
ku-piga hodi	to say 'hodi' (when, say, approaching a house)
ku-piga pasi	to iron
	etc.

The verb 'kwenda' used with personal possessives with a plural N class agreement is often used for 'going on one's way'. It is often used in the imperative, but may be used with other tenses:

Nenda zako.	Be on your way.
Tulikwenda zetu.	We went on our way.
Anakwenda zake.	He is on his way (going away).

And the verb 'ku-taka' is often used in the sense of 'something is going to do something',

| e.g. Nyumba hii inataka kuanguka. | This house is going to fall. |
| Inataka kunyesha mvua. | It is going to rain. |

N.B. Some of the verbs mentioned above, being newly introduced here, require special mention.

ku-fua	means	to wash clothes, but must always be accompanied by 'nguo' or other garment. (It also means to work metal, in which case it must be followed by 'chuma'.)
ku-nyesha	means	to rain, but must always be followed by, or preceded by 'mvua — rain'
ku-pakua	means	to unload
ku-sikia	means	to hear or obey, but is also used when 'feeling' cold, hunger, heat, thirst, etc.
ku-tandika	means	to spread out, spread over
ku-vua	means	to catch fish, basically, but from a different stem (ku-vaa), also means to undress
ku-vuta	means	to pull, drag, tow

Unspecific agreements

Where, in English, we have a sentence beginning with 'It' such as 'It is not possible to do something', the 'It' is unspecified. In Swahili, the agreement used for that 'It' is the N class singular.

| e.g. Haiwezekani kufanya kitu. | It is not possible to do something. |
| Inaonekana kwamba ..... | It is clear that ..... |

Similarly, where a collection of nouns contribute towards the subject of the verb, if they fall in different noun classes the agreement given to them will be N class plural, or sometimes KI- VI- class plural:

e.g. Mkate, viazi, samaki na   Bread, potatoes, fish and
     mboga *zi*lipikwa.   vegetables were cooked.
But, Milima, mito na miti   Mountains, rivers and many
     mingi *i*lionekana.   trees were visible.

(All nouns in the same class.)

If, however, the miscellaneous nouns all refer to persons or animals, then the usual M- WA- concord rules will apply:

Vijana, watoto, mbwa na   Youths, children, dogs and cats
     paka *wa*nakaa hapa.   live here.

(All nouns descriptive of man or animal).

Living beings in the N class

As previously mentioned (in chapter 13), all nouns denoting living beings regardless of the class they are in, should be given M- WA- agreements.

BUT, there is *one* exception to this 'rule' and that is with the Personal Possessives *only*. Within this exception, however, we have to differentiate between humans and animals, for each have their own exception. 'Humans' which occur in the N class take N class agreements both in the singular and the plural. (Included here is the exception 'wake zake' (his wives) which is used in preference to 'Wake wake' which could be confusing.)

e.g. Rafiki yangu *a*mefika.   My friend has arrived.
     Rafiki zangu *wa*mefika.   My friends have arrived.

(Other 'Humans' occurring in the N class are listed below.)

Animals in the N class

Animals which occur in the 'N' class (and most do), take M- WA- agreements in the singular, but N class in the plural, for personal possessives only (see Ch. 13).

e.g. Mbwa *w*angu *m*moja *a*mefika.   My one dog has arrived.
     Mbwa zangu *wa*wili *wa*mefika.   My two dogs have arrived.

(For detailed list of animal species see Appendix II).

If these examples in the last two sections are learnt thoroughly, they can be used as a 'template' for all other occasions when fitting a personal possessive to a human or animal.

Persons occurring in the N class

askari   a soldier/policeman
baba   father

babu	grandfather
binadamu	human being (son of Adam)
binamu	cousin
binti	daughter
dada	sister (older)
jamaa	family member
kaka	brother (older)
mama	mother
ndugu	younger brother/sister, 'relative', friend

N.B. *The word 'ndugu' has a very wide meaning. Its true meaning is that of a close relative or younger brother or sister, but it is used freely for people coming from the same tribe (if away from that area), or if used within their tribal area, would suggest someone from the same clan.*

nyanya	grandmother
rafiki	friend
shangazi	aunt (father's sister only)
shemeji	in-law
yaya	nurse, nanny

Examples:

Mama yangu amekwenda kuona ndugu zake.	My mother has gone to see her relatives.
Askari zetu wanatembea na mbwa zao kila siku.	Our police walk with their dogs every day.
Jamaa yule ana binti watatu.	That member of the family has three daughters.

Contractions
The words 'Baba' and 'Mama' are usually contracted with the personal possessives 1st, 2nd, and 3rd persons singular *only*, thus:

Mamangu	My mother	Babangu	My father
Mamako	Your mother	Babako	Your father
Mamake	His/her mother	Babake	His/her father

BUT

Mama yetu	Our mother	Baba yetu	Our father
Mama yenu	Your mother	Baba yenu	Your father
Mama yao	Their mother	Baba yao	Their father

Another contraction
There is another word, this time from the M- WA- class, which is very rarely met without a contracted personal possessive, and that is:

Mwenzi	Wenzi (pl.)	A companion

Its contractions are as follows:

Mwenzangu	My companion	Wenzangu	My companions
Mwenzako }	Your companion	Wenzako }	Your companions
Mwenzio		Wenzio	
Mwenzake		Wenzake	
Mwenzie }	His/her companion	Wenzie }	His/her companions
Mwenziwe		Wenziwe	
Mwenzetu	Our companion	Wenzetu	Our companions
Mwenzenu	Your companion	Wenzenu	Your companions
Mwenzao	Their companion	Wenzao	Their companions

All other agreements will be normal M- WA- class.

e.g. Babangu amerudi.   My father has returned.

Umeona mamako?   Have you seen your mother?

Wenzetu watafika leo.   Our companions will arrive today.

Exercise 39

(a) *Translate:* Lay the table; I don't smoke, thanks; spray the mosquito spray; would you undress?; the children are playing football; it will rain tomorrow; don't dish up, not yet; make the guest's bed; I don't feel cold; don't forget to say 'hodi' at the door; wash these clothes, then do the ironing; they went fishing; those labourers are not working; be on your (pl.) way!; he is going to come tomorrow; don't (pl.) smoke here; they went on their way; we shall pitch our tent over there somewhere; unload this luggage; this car will be towed.

(b) *Translate:* It is not known if his companion will come; it rained hard the day before yesterday; the potatoes and bread are finished; it is under consideration (it is being considered); my father has arrived; would you feed my cat; their mother has died; is he your friend?; it is known that Juma was a thief; my sister is already married.

(c) *Translate:* My brother has brought his dog here; I think it will rain tomorrow; Where is your father? He is in the house; Make another bed now, because my friend will stay until Wednesday; Dish up the food and then carry on ironing; Your dog has eaten my cat's food; Our nurse has forgotten to remove the children's clothes; My family are working over there; These cups, plates, and bottles have become very dirty; My young brother is fishing over there in the river.

(d) *Translate:* Sijui kama itawezekana; mtumishi huyu amepanga meza vizuri; maliza kufanya kazi yako, halafu nenda zako; hawezi kufua nguo kwa sababu hapana sabuni; kitanda hiki hakikutandikwa; utapiga dawa ya mbu katika kila chumba kila jioni; wengine wanavua samaki huku kila Jumapili; yeye anaweza kufua chuma; hawawezi kufanya kazi kwa sababu inanyesha mvua; hapana ruhusa kuvuta sigara hapa.

35   Numerals—2

More numerals

The tens ascend in this manner:

kumi	ten
ishirini	twenty
thelathini	thirty
arobaini	forty
hamsini	fifty
sitini	sixty
sabini	seventy
themanini	eighty
tisini	ninety

The units following all these tens are added as with the teens, i.e. by inserting the word 'na' followed by the appropriate unit, remembering that those which take agreements are given the appropriate concord.

e.g. thelathini na mbili	32.
watu hamsini na watatu	53 people.
viti sabini na kimoja	71 chairs.

Hundreds, thousands, etc.,

mia	hundred (100).
elfu	thousand (1,000).
laki	a hundred thousand (100,000).
milioni	a million (1,000,000)

All the above are, in effect, N class nouns, so when giving several hundreds, agreements of the unit numbers are as for N class.

e.g. mia tatu	three hundred
elfu mbili	two thousand

When giving a number consisting of hundreds, tens and units, the word 'na' is only used once, and will occur between the last two words.

e.g. mia tatu, arobaini na tano	345
mia tisa, themanini na saba	987
but mia sita na thelathini	630 (no units)
mia moja na tatu	103

When using a number containing thousands, the word *na* is *never* used between thousands and hundreds, even though no tens or units may follow, but it will precede tens or units:

elfu moja, mia tatu na ishirini	1,320

elfu mbili, mia nne, tisini na moja	2,491
elfu nne na hamsini	4,050
elfu sita, sitini na tano	6, 065
elfu tano, mia saba	5,700

N.B. The word 'moja' is generally used after 'mia' and 'elfu' when appropriate, though it may occasionally be omitted.

When going into tens of thousands, certain steps are taken to avoid confusion, which are slightly contrary to the normal rules. If hundreds, tens or units follow the tens of thousands, then the number of thousands will take its normal place after the word 'elfu'.

e.g. elfu kumi na nane, mia mbili na kumi   18,210

But if you say 'Elfu kumi na nane', it could be mistaken for 1,018, and not 18,000 which is considerably different! In order to avoid this possible confusion, the tendency nowadays is to put the number of thousands BEFORE the word 'elfu'.

e.g. kumi na nane elfu—18,000

N.B. This procedure is only followed when there are no hundreds, tens or units.

The number 1,018 would be translated as – Elfu moja, kumi na nane.

Remember that these numbers take their usual place, i.e. after the noun they qualify, and after any adjectives that may be present.

Viti vidogo mia moja, kumi na viwili.   112 small chairs.

Fractions
Only halves, thirds and quarters have their own words (all derived from Arabic):

nusu	half
theluthi	third
robo	quarter

These are N class nouns, so agreements would follow accordingly.

e.g. theluthi mbili	two thirds
robo tatu	three quarters

These are added to a whole number, being separated by the word 'na', and they do not affect the whole number in any way.

e.g. Elfu moja, mia mbili, thelathini na nne na nusu   1,234½

Other fractions are made up using the word 'sehemu' meaning a part or portion (N class). Thus they say so many parts of so many.

e.g. Sehemu moja *ya* nane	⅛th. (Note singular possessive)
Sehemu saba *za* nane	⅞ths. (Note plural possessive)

Decimals
Whilst there is a word for a point or dot 'nukta', it is rarely used now, and the English word is used 'pointi'. Numbers following it are read out singly, as in the English.

e.g. Kumi na tisa pointi tatu, nne, moja, saba—19·3417

Zero
The Swahili for 'zero' is 'sifuri' (N class).

Percentages
No special words are used, but one merely quotes the appropriate number and follows it with '..... kwa mia'. (lit. '..... for a hundred').

e.g. Hamsini kwa mia   Fifty per cent.
     Sabini na tano kwa mia   Seventy five per cent

N.B. (1) Very small fractions, or very large numbers (say over 100,000) are not commonly used in Swahili, since such smallness or largeness would generally be inconceivable to the less educated. To them it would just be a matter of being 'Kidogo sana' (very minute) or 'Nyingi sana' (very many). Only the more educated people would be able to appreciate such minuteness or large quantity, and they most probably would speak English in any case!
(2) The symbols for numerals (1, 2, 3, etc.) are generally known, and one would not normally write them out in words.

Examples:
Mji ule una wenyeji elfu kumi, mia tano.
   That town has ten thousand, five hundred inhabitants.
Mwizi yule amefungwa kwa siku mia mbili, arobaini na tatu.
   That thief has been imprisoned for 243 days.
Kuna wanyama kumi na mbili elfu katika sehemu ile.
   There are 12,000 animals in that part.

Exercise 40
(a) *Translate:* 25%; 321; 2,394; 4,576; 29,000; 129,746; 487,007; ⁹⁄₁₆ths; 5·7685; 0·025; ⅜ths; ¾; ⅞; 22½; 328 chairs; 25 cups; 300,000 people; 15,000 coconut palms; 108 bottles of beer; 101 pieces.

(b) *Translate:* There are 365 days in one year; This road carries about 575 cars every day; 1966 years; This building (house) has about 2,500 books; This club has 321 members; There are only 53 farmers in this village; Every teacher teaches 35 children; We have planted 85 trees; There were 11,588 visitors that year; There are 25¾ bottles of chemicals.

(c) *Translate:* Mia nane, thelathini na nne; Mia tisa na saba; Ishirini elfu; Elfu moja na moja; Sehemu moja ya elfu kumi; Sifuri pointi sifuri, sifuri, saba; Laki nne; Ishirini na sita na theluthi; Elfu moja na kumi; Ishirini na tatu kwa mia.

36 Time

Throughout East Africa, there is very little variation during the year in the time of sunrise and sunset. To all intents and purposes, there are twelve hours of daylight, and twelve of darkness. It is therefore logical that time, in Swahili, is measured from daybreak and sunset, as was the custom in Biblical days. Since the sun usually rises at about 6 a.m., 7 a.m. is the first hour of daylight. Similarly, the sun generally sets between 6 p.m. and 7 p.m., so that 7 p.m. is the first hour of darkness. This means that Swahili time and 'Western time' are just 6 hours different. Thus, to arrive at one, 6 hours are either added or subtracted from the other.

When giving the time, in Swahili, the word 'saa' always precedes the time.

saa moja	7 o'clock	saa saba	1 o'clock
saa mbili	8 o'clock	saa nane	2 o'clock
saa tatu	9 o'clock	saa tisa	3 o'clock
saa nne	10 o'clock	saa kumi	4 o'clock
saa tano	11 o'clock	saa kumi na moja	5 o'clock
saa sita	12 o'clock	saa kumi na mbili	6 o'clock

The quarters are as follows:

na robo	quarter past	(lit. and a quarter)
na nusu	half past	(lit. and a half)
kasa robo	quarter to	(lit. less a quarter)

Minutes past the hour (generally only counted up to thirty) are added using the word 'dakika' (a minute) with 'na'.

na dakika kumi	ten past (lit. and ten minutes)
na dakika ishirini na tano	twenty five past

(Both the quarters and minutes are always added to the appropriate hour. They are never, like in English, used on their own.)

Minutes to the hour are given using 'dakika' with the word 'kasoro' (less).

kasoro dakika tano	five to (less 5 minutes)
kasoro dakika kumi na saba	17 minutes to (less 17 minutes)

(It is rare that minutes are added beyond the half hour, but it is occasionally heard). It is essential that minutes to the hour be subtracted from the following hour and not, as in English again, used on their own.

e.g. saa tatu kasoro dakika ishirini   twenty minutes to nine.

saa kumi na moja na dakika saba	seven minutes past five.
saa tano na nusu	half past eleven

N.B. The twenty-four hour clock is neither used, nor understood in Swahili.

For an exact hour, the word 'kamili' is used.

e.g. saa tisa kamili   exactly 3 o' clock, *or* 3 o'clock on the dot.

There is still a need, however, to differentiate between hours of darkness and hours of light; p.m. and a.m. are not of course used in Swahili time. Basically, the word 'mchana' is used following a day-time hour, and 'usiku' following an hour of darkness. But more specifically the following vocabulary is used with time:

tangu	since, from	(Preposition used only with time)
mpaka	until	(M- MI- noun class)
usiku	night	(U noun class)
mchana	daytime	(M- MI- noun class)
alfajiri	dawn	(5.45 a.m.—6.30 a.m. approx.)
asubuhi	morning	(6.30 a.m.—noon approx.)
adhuhuri	noon	(used mainly on the coast)
alasiri	afternoon	(2.00 p.m.—5.00 p.m. approx.)
jioni	late afternoon	(5 p.m. to sunset)

(There is no word for 'evening' in the English sense). The periods of the day around lunchtime are generally referred to simply as 'mchana', especially inland, where even 'alasiri' may not be commonly used. With the exception of the first four of the above list, all are N class nouns.

When using the above nouns with time, they are all used with the possessive 'ya' preceding them. (Note that it is *not* 'za' since time is a single hour, not hours). There is a strong tendency nowadays, however to omit the possessive altogether.

e.g. Saa kumi na nusu ya mchana
  or Saa kumi na nusu mchana 4.30 p.m.
Saa kumi na nusu ya usiku
  or Saa kumi na nusu usiku 4.30 p.m.
Saa tano ya asubuhi
  or Saa tano asubuhi 11.00 a.m.
Saa tano ya usiku
  or Saa tano usiku 11.00 p.m.

Note that no preposition (at, etc.,) is translated when referring to time.

e.g. Alifika saa tatu,
    He arrived at 9 o'clock.

Seconds.
There is no word in Swahili for seconds, and so they use the English word 'sekunde', although occasionally the word 'nukta' (a point or dot) is used. But once again, it is only the educated who would need to know such small fractions of time, and such persons would normally understand English sufficiently to use the English terms.

Points of interest concerning time
Although Swahili time is always 6 hours different from 'Western' time, it is strange to note that almost invariably, Africans set their clocks and watches to 'Western' time, and read it off automatically in Swahili time.

Africans who live outside the larger towns, are extraordinarily good at telling the time even without a watch or clock. A glance at the sun, and their shadow, is sufficient for them to gauge the time to within an hour, and more frequently to within half, or even a quarter of an hour. If the day is overcast, then their accuracy diminishes.

More vocabulary

Saa ngapi?	What is the time?
Zamani	A long time ago, once upon a time
Sikuzote	Always
Daima	Everlastingly, continually
Milele	For ever and ever, for eternity

e.g. Saa ngapi sasa?   What time is it now?
Sasa ni saa tano kamili.   Now it is exactly 11 o'clock.
ni kama saa kumi.   It is about 4 o'clock.

Periods of time
When measuring time, as opposed to telling the time, much the same vocabulary is used, but to avoid confusion, the words 'muda wa' (a period of) are always used,

> e.g. Fanya kazi kwa muda wa saa tatu na nusu.
> Work for a period of 3½ hours.

BUT Fanya kazi saa tatu na nusu.
Work at half past nine.

The quarters have words changed about when signifying periods of time,

e.g. robo saa   a quarter of an hour
nusu saa   half an hour

BUT a period of ¾ hour is given as 45 minutes — 'muda wa dakika arobaini na tano'.

Similarly, periods of minutes are also always preceded by the words 'muda wa' (a period of),

e.g. Muda wa dakika arobaini na tano.
   A period of 45 minutes.
   Muda wa nusu saa.
   A period of ½ an hour.
   Muda wa saa mbili na dakika kumi.
   A period of 2 hours and ten minutes.

Exercise 41

(a) *Translate:* 7.15 a.m.; noon; dawn; 6.30 p.m.; midnight; 2.10 p.m.; a period of three and a half hours; a period of 24 hours; what time is it? Now it is 25 to four; 17.00 hours; five past one (p.m.); he stayed for a quarter of an hour; nine o'clock on the dot; from 8.15 until 8.45; 10.30 at night; 6 a.m.; 6.50 p.m.; 8 o'clock in the evening; he died at 3 o'clock in the morning; come at half past twelve today.

(b) *Translate:* Would you come here at 7.30 a.m. tomorrow; We shall start to eat at a quarter to nine to-day; I awoke at 4.45 a.m.; The meeting will start at 16.30 hours; The journey continued for 4¾ hours; The time is about 20 past 2 now; They arrived at twenty five to five this morning; My labourers work for 8 hours every day; Cook this meat for half an hour only; It rained for 7½ hours.

(c) *Translate:* Saa kumi alasiri; saa kumi na moja jioni; muda wa saa kumi; alifika saa ngapi? Alifika saa saba kamili; rudi saa tatu kesho; endelea mpaka saa tisa na dakika ishirini; atafika saa za alasiri; wataanza saa kumi na mbili na robo alfajiri; kuna muda wa saa saba na nusu za kazi kila siku; saa ni kama saa nane sasa.

37   The -JA- tense

This is a negative tense which requires the use of the negative subject prefixes. It is most frequently used as the negative equivalent to the past perfect tense (-ME-), but it also has the sense of 'not yet'.

It conjugates regularly:

Si-ja-anza.	Sijaanza.	I have not (yet) started.
Hu-ja-anza.	Hujaanza.	You have not (yet) started.
Ha-ja-anza.	Hajaanza.	He/she has not (yet) started.
Hatu-ja-anza.	Hatujaanza.	We have not (yet) started.
Ham-ja-anza.	Hamjaanza.	You have not (yet) started.
Hawa-ja-anza.	Hawajaanza.	They have not (yet) started.

M- MI- class
Hau-ja-anza.	Haujaanza.	It has not (yet) started.
Hai-ja-anza.	Haijaanza.	They have not (yet) started.

KI- VI- class

Haki-ja-anza.	Hakijaanza.	It has not (yet) started.
Havi-ja-anza.	Havijaanza.	They have not (yet) started.

N class

Hai-ja-anza.	Haijaanza.	It has not (yet) started.
Hazi-ja-anza.	Hazijaanza.	They have not (yet) started.

Arabic verbs create no exception:

Si-ja-jibu	Sijajibu.	I have not (yet) replied.
Ha-ja-fikiri.	Hajafikiri.	He/she has not (yet) thought.

Monosyllabics, however, *drop* their 'infinitive' 'ku-':

Ha-ja-ja	Hajaja.	He/she has not (yet) come.
Hawa-ja-la.	Hawajala.	They have not (yet) eaten.
Si-ja-enda.	Sijaenda.	I have not (yet) gone.

Since this tense is now so commonly used as a straight negative to the -ME- tense, the word 'Bado' (not yet) is used either before or after the verb to give stress to the 'not yet' sense. But in spite of this, there is always the sense of 'yet' about this negative.

e.g. Hatujapanda mlima wa Kilimanjaro.
We have not (yet) climbed Mount Kilimanjaro.
Umekwisha kula? Sijala.
Have you already eaten? I haven't (yet).

More verbs

ku-acha	to leave off, abandon
ku-achisha	to dismiss, 'sack' (causative)
ku-ambia	to tell, inform
ku-fuga	to keep livestock

N.B. This verb must be followed by some appropriate type of livestock.

ku-fukuza	to drive off (chase)
ku-gusa	to touch
ku-iba	to steal
ku-imba	to sing
ku-ita	to call, summon
ku-kaza	to tighten
ku-kunja	to fold, wrinkle
ku-lia	to cry out, cry, bark (or make an animal sound)
ku-oga	to have a bath, shower
ku-okota	to find, come across
ku-ondoa	to remove, take away
ku-ondoka	to leave, go away, depart

ku-pa	to give to
ku-pangusa	to wipe lightly, dust
ku-peleka	to send, deliver
ku-pima	to measure, test
ku-pita	to pass (active)
ku-pokea	to receive
ku-zaa	to bear, give birth, yield
ku-zaliwa	to be born

N.B. *(1) The verbs 'ku-ambia', 'ku-ita' and 'ku-pa' can be used only together with an object infix. (See Ch. 38.)*
(2) 'Ku-pa' is basically a monosyllabic verb whose passive form is 'ku-pewa'.

Exercise 42

(a) *Translate:* To send; to measure; to leave off; to give; to bear; to cry out; to steal; to call; to touch; to tell; to leave; to remove; to find; to bathe; to dust; to receive; to sing; to keep livestock; to come across; to drive off.

(b) *Translate:* I have not stolen; they have not sung; do not fold yet; we have not passed; she has not yet given birth; he has not yet dusted the furniture; you have not yet received the mail; the cloth has not yet been folded; the vessels have not yet been removed; that mountain has not yet been climbed; the children have not yet taken a bath; this dog has not barked; those farmers have not yet kept livestock (animals); these things have not been abandoned; that lazy person has not yet been dismissed; that quantity has not yet been measured; he has driven off those insects; take these dirty plates away; take this letter to Mr. Smith; we have already passed his house.

(c) *Translate:* I have tried to do this work, but I have not succeeded; His car has not yet arrived; It has not yet rained this month; The food is not yet ready; The mail (the letters have) has not yet arrived. It (they) will come at 2 p.m.; We have not yet become used to using Swahili; That thief has not been caught; Those children have played since 8 o'clock this morning, but they are not yet tired; That student has not yet returned my book; Those farmers have not yet planted their vegetable seeds.

(d) *Translate:* Usiguse hii; mtoto alizaliwa saa tisa jana; msiondoke mpaka saa kumi; sijaokota kiko changu; hawajapokea ruhusa kuingia pale; wageni hawajaondoka; hajapeleka barua; wanyama wale hawajafukuzwa; nimepeleka barua lakini hajajibu; kibarua mvivu yule hana kazi kwa sababu ameachishwa.

38   Object infixes

As has already been mentioned (in chapter 18), there is no word in Swahili for 'It' as such. So far we have had to use it only in the form of a subject prefix. But where we have 'It' or 'Him' as an object (or any other pronoun), it must be inserted into the verb as an infix. The infixes used are these:

M- WA- class

-ni-	me	-tu-	us
-ku-	you	-wa-	you (pl.)
-m- (-mw- in front of a vowel)	him, her (it, if an animal)	-wa-	them

It will be noted that only the 1st person singular and plural present no problem. There is likely at first to be confusion brought about by the 2nd person singular being similar to the 'infinitive' and past negative signs; the 3rd person singular being similar to the 2nd person plural Subject prefix; and the 2nd and 3rd persons plural being identical.

It is essential, therefore, that at this stage, these infixes be thoroughly learnt before proceeding. The object infixes in all other noun classes, are identical to their Subject prefixes, namely:

M- MI- class	-u-	it	-i-	them
KI- VI- class	-ki-	it	-vi-	them
N class	-i-	it	-zi-	them

N.B. *(1) It is important to remember that '-ki-' and '-vi-' NEVER change to '-ch-' and '-vy-' in front of a vowel when used as an object infix,*

e.g. Ume*ki*ona kisu?	Have you seen the knife?
Ame*vi*ondoa vikombe.	He has removed the cups.

N.B. *(2) All transitive verbs may take an object infix, but the following three verbs MUST ONLY be used WITH one, and it MUST be from the M- WA- class:*

ku-ambia	to tell, inform
ku-ita	to call, summon
ku-pa	to give to

Position:
The object infix is placed between the tense sign and the verb stem. It never merges with other vowels,

e.g. A-li-*ni*-ona.	Ali*ni*ona.	He saw me.

Ni-me-*wa*-ambia.   Nime*wa*ambia.   I have told them.
Tu-ta-*u*-funga.   Tuta*u*funga.   We shall shut it (door).

These object infixes may be used with any transitive verb in any tense including the 'infinitive'. Thus if we use the N class singular object infix to represent 'it', we can get:

ku-i-leta	kuileta	to bring it
usi-i-lete	usiilete	don't bring it
u-i-lete	uilete	would you bring it
a-na-i-leta	anaileta	he is bringing it
a-li-i-leta	aliileta	he brought it
a-ta-i-leta	ataileta	he will bring it
a-me-i-leta	ameileta	he has brought it
ha-i-leti	haileti	he is not bringing it
ha-ku-i-leta	hakuileta	he did not bring it
ha-ta-i-leta	hataileta	he will not bring it
ha-ja-i-leta	hajaileta	he has not (yet) brought it.

(It may also be used with a direct imperative, but see the last section in this chapter.)

When using an object infix with a monosyllabic verb, its use forces out the 'infinitive' 'ku-',

e.g. ku-pa   to give   ni-li-m-pa   nilimpa   I gave (to) him
(NOT Nilimkupa)
ku-la   to eat   a-li-m-la   alimla   he ate him
(NOT Alimkula)

But where a monosyllabic verb is used in the 'infinitive', then of course the 'infinitive' sign must be used. In this case, the object infix's position will be normal. i.e. between the tense sign and verb stem:

Nenda ku-m-pa.   Nenda kumpa.   Go to give him.
Siwezi ku-ku-pa.   Siwezi kukupa.   I cannot give you.

Limitation of infixes.
In Swahili one may insert only *one* object infix into a verb. Where English may use two object pronouns (direct and indirect) such as 'He gave it me' or 'I gave it him', the corresponding Swahili will not translate the 'it'. Thus we get simply 'Alinipa'—he gave me, and 'Ni-limpa'—I gave him. The 'it' in both cases is left understood. In cases such as the ones shown here where two objects are found in English, Swahili will always use only the personal object, which takes precedence over the other (i.e. an object infix from the M-Wa-class will take precedence over object infixes from all other classes.) Where it is essential to lay particular emphasis on the non-personal object, this can be done by the use of either a demonstrative or a noun:

Nilimpa kitabu.   I gave him a/the book.
Alinipa hii.   He gave me this (N class).

This rule applies even in cases where the object personal noun is mentioned in combination with an 'it' as in 'I gave it to the child' 'Nilimpa mtoto'. (The 'it' is still left out as understood.)

Ambiguity of -WA-

As will have been noted, there is likely to be a confusion between the 2nd and 3rd person plural object infixes which are both '-wa-', i.e. the sentence 'Niliwaona jana' could mean either 'I saw you (pl.) yesterday' or 'I saw them yesterday'. In order to clarify which is intended, there are three alternative ways in which this can be expressed, two of which are strictly ungrammatical, but are now accepted as normal Swahili. Thus 'I saw you (pl.)' could be:

	Niliwaona ninyi	(using personal pronoun)
or	Niliwaoneni	(using same construction as with plural imperatives)
or	Nilikuoneni	(using 2nd person singular object, with plural imperative construction)

Of the three possibilities, the second one is the most common, and when learning, it is as well to stick to only one of these, preferably therefore, the second one. Where neither of these three constructions are used, then the 3rd person plural is implied, 'Niliwaona'—'I saw them'.

When to use object infixes

As has already been pointed out, there are no definite or indefinite articles to nouns in Swahili. By using an object infix, we can, to a certain extent, give an object noun a definite or specific sense. Since a noun accompanied by a demonstrative or personal possessive is automatically specific, there is a tendency to give such a noun an object infix within the verb as well,

e.g.	Nilinunua kitabu.	I bought a book.
	Nili*ki*nunua kitabu.	I bought *the* book.
	Nili*ki*nunua kitabu hiki.	I bought *this* book.
	Nili*ki*nunua kitabu chake.	I bought *his* book.

There is a greater tendency always to use an object infix when it agrees with a person or animal, but if one wishes to stress an indefinite person, it can be omitted,

e.g.	Niliona mganga jana.	I saw *a* doctor yesterday.
	Nili*mw*ona mganga jana.	I saw *the* doctor yesterday.

You will find that with things there is no ruling with regard to object infixes supporting nouns even with demonstratives accompanying them, and only experience in the language will clarify fully when to use it. It should, however, invariably be used for persons, but for things it should only be used where special emphasis is required on the object,

e.g. Alifungua mlango.   He opened the door.
     Ali*u*fungua mlango.   He opened *THE* door.

N.B. Do not forget the three verbs which MUST take the object infix.

Reflexive infix

In addition to the object infix specific to each noun class, there is a reflexive infix used when the object of a transitive verb is the same as the subject. It is -JI-, meaning 'oneself', 'itself', etc. It does not vary, being the same for all noun classes. Its position is the same as for other object infixes and no other object infix can be used in a verb containing it.

e.g. Alijiona kiooni   He/She saw him/herself in the mirror.
     Mlango umejifunga.   The door has shut itself.

Notice the English translation of the following verbs which incorporate this reflexive infix:

ku-jifunza   to learn (to educate oneself)
ku-jitolea   to volunteer (to put oneself out)
ku-jiua   to commit suicide (to kill oneself)

N.B. (1) The verb 'Ku-funza'—to educate, is now rarely encountered on its own.
(2) Ku-jitolea comes from the verb 'Ku-toa'—to put out, in its prepositional form (see ch. 43).

Infix order

A useful memoriser for the order of the infixes so far introduced is the word STOVE, whose letters stand for:

S Subject prefix
T Tense sign or marker
O Object infix
V Verb stem
E End of verb for derivatives etc.

e.g. Ni-me-ki-let-a   I have brought it.
     S T O V E

Examples using object infixes:

Ninataka kukupa nafasi kwenda mjini.
   I want to give you time to go to town.
Amemwambia kuinunua motokaa nzuri ile.
   He has told him to buy that good car.

Umeleta kisu changu? Nimekileta.
Have you brought my knife? I have brought it.
Alijikata kwa kisu.
He cut himself with a knife.

Exercise 43

(a) *Translate:* He called me; I saw him; he saw me; they told us; I gave you; you (pl.) folded it (the cloth); I sent you (pl.); he called us; have you seen it (the book); he has not yet received them (the letters); I told you (pl.); he has not yet hit it (the nail); we have not climbed them (the mountains); have you found it (the book)?; they gave you (pl.); we gave it (the book) to you; he measured himself; I have hit myself; I summoned you (pl.).

(b) *Translate:* We have given our cook new clothes; have you seen Hamisi? Yes, I saw him in town; they have told you (pl.) not to stay here. (Negative imperative); those labourers have not yet finished that work; he told me that he did not see you yesterday; can you see those animals there? I do not see them; I have read a very good book. Have you read it?; When did you plant these crops? I planted them a long time ago; Have you cleaned my shoes? I haven't cleaned them; My servant has ironed these new clothes of mine very well.

(c) *Translate*: Alinipa; nitawapimeni; tuliwaambia; nitawaita kesho; mgonjwa amejiua; watu wale wamejitolea kutoa msaada; siwezi kukupa kazi; sisi tunajifunza Kiswahili; vyombo viko wapi? Ameviondoa; umekunja nguo? Ndiyo, nimezikunja; aliniita saa tatu; nimejikata kwa kisu; utainunua motokaa ile? Nitainunua; mmepata ruhusa? Tumeipata; watawalipeni mishahara saa nane; hawezi kukuona leo, labda kesho; umemwona mbwa wangu? Sijamwona; mwalimu amejibuje? Sijamwuliza; walisemaje? Hatujawaambia; ulimwona saa ngapi? Nilimwona zamani kidogo.

The imperatives with an object

As was stated in the first section, object infixes may be used with a verb in any tense. This includes the imperatives, but a slight change occurs in the verb when the direct imperative is used with an object infix. In this case, the infix becomes in fact a prefix onto the imperative, and the final -A of Bantu verbs changes to an -E,

e.g. Piga!   Hit!   Mpige!   Hit him!

(Note that some of these imperatives are identical to the polite imperative; i.e. Mpige! could also mean 'Would you (pl.) hit!' Context, however, generally cancels out any possible confusion).

Arabic verbs are unaffected, since their terminal vowel never changes.

e.g. Mjibu!   Answer him!

Monosyllabic verbs, as previously, drop their 'infinitive' KU- and also change their final -A to -E.

e.g. Mpe!   Give him!
Nipe!   Give me!

N.B. Although this form is similar to the Subjunctive, in that the terminal A changes to E, it is still abrupt, and is not, in fact, the subjunctive. The polite imperative with an object creates no problem, since it is merely a matter of inserting the object infix between subject prefix and verb stem, in the normal way.

e.g.	Umpe!	Would you give him!
	Unipe!	Would you give me!
	Mmjibu!	Would you (pl.) answer him!

The negative imperative
This is in reality the negative subjunctive, and as such takes an object infix in the normal manner (i.e. between tense sign and verb stem).

e.g.	Usimjibu!	Don't answer him!
	Usimpige!	Don't hit him!
	Usimpe!	Don't give him!
	Msinipe!	Don't (pl.) give me!

(Remember that the final A changes to E, even without the Object infix).

Examples:

Chakula tayari? Ndiyo Bwana! Kilete basi!
Is the food ready? Yes, Bwana! Bring it then!
Usiwaambie kwamba nimefika.
Don't tell them that I have arrived.
Wape vitu vyao. Nimekwisha wapa.
Give them their things. I have already given them to them.

N.B. The final 'a' of 'wapa' is not changed to 'e' because this verb should strictly be in the infinitive (Kuwapa) see page 67.

Exercise 44
(a) *Translate:* Don't touch them (these things)!; give me that chit! would you bring it (the bread)!; don't anwer him!; seize him!; call them!; give them their money!; summon Mr. Rajabu!; don't fell them (those trees)!; tell him!; call me at 6 a.m.!; send them (the letters)!; bring them (the cups)!; would you look for them (the children)!; read it (the chit)!; don't forget them (the papers)!; give it to him (the letter)!; don't beat that child!; don't tear it (the book)!; finish it (the work)!;
(b) *Translate:* Msimpe kitu!; kisome (kitabu)!; uangushe (mti)!; tupe pesa!; waambie!; tuite!; mwangalie!; umwone kesho!; ijaribu! (mitihani); ziondoe (sahani)!; kitandike (kitanda)!; usiufunge (mlango)!; umwambie kwamba wamekwisha kwenda!; walipe sasa!; ilete (mizigo)!; mpe ruhusa!; mwogeshe!; vipanguse (vyombo)!; kikunje (kitambaa)!; mwache pale!

39   Weights and measures

There are virtually no Swahili words for weights and measures, and therefore most of these have to be borrowed from other languages. (All nouns are N class, unless otherwise stated).

Weights

aunsi (also rarely—wakia)	ounce
ratili (ratli)	pound
tan(i)	ton
kilo	kilo
frasila (frasla)	a unit of about 35 lb. used with certain agricultural commodities, especially onions, copra and jaggery (raw sugar).

Measures (volume)

debe	a 4-gallon tin (MA- class)
galoni	gallon (can also mean a gallon tin)
kibaba	½ litre (used mainly with flour and grain, KI- VI- class)
painti	pint
pishi	2 litres (used mainly with flour and grain)
lita	litre

Length and area

inchi	inch
futi	foot
yadi	yard
hatua	a pace (generally regarded as a yard)
maili	mile
kilometa	kilometre
meta	metre
sentimeta	centimetre
milimeta	millimetre
hekta(ri)	hectare
eka ⎫ ekari ⎭	acre
eneo	an area (geometric, MA- class)

Money

pesa	money
fedha	money, (really means silver)
senti	cent
shilingi	a shilling
paundi	a pound, £1 (not strictly used in East Africa.)

116

hela	money (used in certain districts), also used occasionally as a variable unit of approximately 2 cents in a few areas. (Comes from old German unit, 'Heller'.)
sumni ⎫	50 cents (used only in certain areas). (It is
thumni ⎬	strange that the root of this word comes
thumuni ⎭	from an arabic word, meaning an eighth).

N.B. The currency in each of the East African countries is 100 cents to 1 shilling, though each country has its own notes and coins. Slang words are often used for notes and coins, where the picture depicted on the back of the coin or note is quoted; e.g. 'Sungura' (a rabbit) means a Tanzania 50c. coin which depicts a rabbit on its reverse side.)

General Note. The metric system, though used, was by no means dominant in East Africa. Most market produce was traded in Kilos, but certain crops were still traded in pounds. Retail was generally carried out in ounces and pounds. All distances were measured in feet, inches, and miles. On the railways however, originally built by the Germans in Tanzania, distances have always been measured in kilometres, and the track is one-metre gauge. The metric system was adopted, however, in 1969.

Exercise 45

(a) *Translate:* Three pounds (weight); two kilos; five kilometres; one litre; ten hectares; how many shillings?; fifteen paces; three tons; two half-litre measures; five shillings and twenty cents; a few grams; 35 lbs. of onions; what (sort of) area?; a thousand pounds (£1,000); one hectare is 100 paces by 100 paces; give me 50 cents; a journey of 352 kilometres; I have bought five metres of cloth.

(b) *Translate:* Give us five kilos of potatoes. Would you put them here please; Tell your wife that garment needs 75 centimetres of cloth; That old man wants some money. Have you fifty cents? Give it to him, then; My brother has planted 15 hectares of food crops; Would you put 25 litres of petrol (petroli) in my car; How much are those vegetables? They are five shillings and seventy-five cents a kilo; Your price is not cheap. Reduce it a little; There are about 2¼ pounds in one kilo; He bought that house for shs. 8,000.00 only; Arusha is 296 kilometres from Nairobi; Give him shs. 1.80 to buy one kilo of bread.

40   The Subjunctive

The affirmative subjunctive

The subjunctive form of the verb is very commonly used in good Swahili, far more than it is in English. There are about seven instances in which the subjunctive should be used, but first let us see how it is made up.

We are not unfamiliar with the Subjunctive, since it is used in order to make up the Polite Imperative (see ch. 4). It has no tense sign, and so the Subject prefix is placed directly onto the verb stem. Then, with Bantu verbs, the final -A is changed to -E.

N.B. Remember that M- in front of a vowel takes -W- (see Ch. 4).

Thus the verb 'ku-ngoja' (to wait) would conjugate:

ni-ngoj(a)e	ningoje
u-ngoj(a)e	ungoje
a-ngoj(a)e	angoje
tu-ngoj(a)e	tungoje
m-ngoj(a)e	mngoje
wa-ngoj(a)e	wangoje

Arabic verbs are not affected in the final vowel (see rule on Arabic verbs in chapter 32.)

ni-jaribu	nijaribu
tu-fikiri	tufikiri

Monosyllabic verbs drop their 'infinitive' 'ku'.

ni-end(a)e	niende	(kwenda)
a-j(a)e	aje	(kuja)
tu-w(a)e	tuwe	(kuwa)

N.B. The Subjunctive can, of course, take the Object Infix where desired.

The same procedure is followed if using the Subjunctive with a prefix from another noun class:

i-futw(a)e	ifutwe	(plural M- MI- class)
ki-futw(a)e	kifutwe	(singular KI- VI- class)
zi-futw(a)e	zifutwe	(plural N class)
	etc.	

Uses and meanings

1. Polite imperative (used only in the 2nd person).
Ungoje.   Would you wait.   Mngoje.   Would you (pl.) wait.

2. The suggestion 'let me .....' etc.

Ningoje.   Let me wait.   Tungoje.   Let us wait.
Angoje.   Let him/her wait.   Wangoje.   Let them wait.
Twende.   Let us go (the U has changed to W for ease of speech).

N.B. This sense is rarely used in the 2nd person.

3. To translate the second of two commands, and indirect commands

Njoo uone.   Come and see.
Mwambie apike chakula.   Tell him to cook the food.

('Tell him' is the first command, and 'to cook' or 'that he must cook' is the indirect one.) Note that the subjects of the two verbs are invariably different in such cases.

Aliwaambia waje.   He told them to come.

4. Purpose or intention

('in order to' or 'in order that').

Mwite niseme naye.   Call him that I may speak with him.
Ninasoma kitabu hiki   I am reading this book in order
  nijifunze Kiswahili.   to learn Swahili.

There is a word 'ili' which also means 'in order to/that' (a direct equivalent to 'ut' in Latin), which can be inserted immediately before the Subjunctive verb (occasionally, nowadays, used even before an 'infinitive'). It is used merely to strengthen the sense of definite purpose or intention.

Tulikuja Tanzania kuona   We came to Tanzania to see animals.
  wanyama.
Tulikuja Tanzania tuone   We came to Tanzania so as to see
  wanyama.   animals.
Tulikuja Tanzania ili   We came to Tanzania specifically to
  tuone wanyama.   see animals.

or even nowadays—

Tulikuja Tanzania ili   We came to Tanzania in order to
  kuona wanyama.   see animals.

5. Questioned suggestion ('Am I to .....? etc.)

Ningoje?   Am I to wait?
Aingie?   Is he/she to enter?
Vitu hivi visafishwe?   Are these things to be cleaned?
Twende lini?   When are we to go?

6. Obligation

There are a few words in Swahili which express certain degrees of obligation.

lazima	necessity, must, to be bound, to be sure to
sharti	obligation
afadhali	better, preferable
bora	best
heri	advantage, blessing, fortune
yafaa	Lit. 'It is suitable' (from ku-faa). (This is a present tense not yet dealt with. See ch. 54.)

With the exception of the last word in the above list, the word 'Ni' (it is) can precede any of these words. It is, however, usually omitted as being understood.

(Ni) Lazima uende sasa.	You must go now.
	It is necessary that you go now.
(Ni) Sharti uende sasa.	You are obliged to go now.
(Ni) Afadhali uende sasa.	You had better go now.
(Ni) Bora uende sasa.	You had best go now.
(Ni) Heri uende sasa.	It would be an advantage to go now.
Yafaa uende sasa.	It is as well to go now.

It will be seen that only the first two examples are forceful, the other four have very little difference in implication, and are therefore more or less interchangeable.

7. Dependent clause after 'to want'.

Where a second verb follows the verb 'to want' and their subjects are different, it is often necessary to use the Subjunctive in order to show the subject of the second verb. If, on the other hand, the subject is the same for both verbs, the second is kept in the 'infinitive',

e.g. Ninataka kwenda sasa. I want to go now (same subject).
Ninataka uende sasa. I want *you* to go now (different subjects).

N.B. *It would be quite incorrect to say in the second case, 'Ninakutaka' (i.e. inserting the object infix for 2nd person singular), since the sense is not 'I want you', but 'I want that you go'. Hence the use of the Subjunctive for the second verb.*

Examples:

Amekwenda mjini *anunue* mboga. (Use No.4)
He has gone to the town so as to buy vegetables.
Twende Mombasa sasa ili *tupumzike*. (Use No. 4)
Let's go to Mombasa now in order to rest.

120

Anataka *nikuambie* kwamba (ni) lazima *uondoke* sasa. (Uses Nos. 7 and 6)
He wants me to tell you that you must leave now.
Watoto hawa *wacheze* mpira leo? Ndiyo, *wacheze*. (Use Nos. 5 and 2)
May these children play football today? Yes, let them play.
Usichukue viazi vingine *vibaki* kwa kesho. (Use No. 4)
Don't take more potatoes so that some may be left over for tomorrow.
Wageni wale wamefika Moshi *wapande* mlima wa Kilimanjaro. (Use No. 4)
Those visitors have reached Moshi so as to climb Mount Kilimanjaro.
Mwambie Hamisi *anipe* cheti chake. (Use No. 3)
Tell Hamisi to give me his chit/reference.

Exercise 46

(a) *Translate:* Let him go; are we to stay?; let the door be closed; would you bring; tell him to come; they must come; he wants me to buy bread; they came in order to see us; they had better come in; these letters must be returned; let those trees be felled; what am I to say?; would you help me; he wants to try; let us try; they came to Moshi to climb Mount Kilimanjaro; it would be an advantage for us to take this luggage now; is the food to be prepared?; should we write?; let us eat now.

(b) *Translate:* The farmer has planted good crops to get a large quantity; He wants us to stay here until tomorrow morning; What should we give that blind man?; Are the labourers to wait, or should they leave?; The cook has lit a fire in order to cook the food; You must remember to bring tea at 6.30 a.m.; Those chairs had better be put out for the ladies; Tell them to tell me so that I may know everything; Let the children return home at a quarter past five; I have bought a new car in order to learn to drive.

(c) *Translate:* Mishahara iongezwe?; bora arudi nyumbani; vitu hivi lazima viondolewe; yafaa sana tuoge kila siku; aipeleke mizigo wapi?; mwambie mpishi apange meza sasa; tujaze vyombo vile; kitu kile bora kisahaulike; lazima wawe tayari saa moja asubuhi; mkae; lazima inyeshe mvua leo; nitandike kitanda cha mgeni?; ununue ratili kumi za viazi; wanataka tuende kule ili wapate msaada; vyombo lazima vipanguswe kila siku; waende mjini sasa; tulishe wanyama sehemu gani leo?; ninataka watoto wawe na vitabu vyao kesho; afadhali tuanze sasa; waambie wakupe cheti.

The negative subjunctive.

This tense, like the affirmative subjunctive, is not new to us. We have seen that it is used in order to express the negative imperative (see Ch. 4).

It is made up in the same manner as the affirmative subjunctive, except that a negative subjunctive sign is inserted which is -SI-. The final -A of Bantu verbs again changes to -E. It is important to

121

remember, however, that although it is a negative tense, it does *not* take negative prefixes.

ni-si-ngoje	nisingoje
u-si-ngoje	usingoje
a-si-ngoje	asingoje
tu-si-ngoje	tusingoje
m-si-ngoje	msingoje
wa-si-ngoje	wasingoje

Arabic verbs are treated similarly:— (See Rule on page 85).

ni-si-fikiri	nisifikiri, (from Ku-fikiri)
wa-si-jibu	wasijibu, (from Ku-jibu)

Monosyllabic verbs again drop their 'infinitive' Ku-

a-si-je	asije, (from Ku-ja)
wa-si-ende	wasiende, (from Kwenda)
tu-si-we	Tusiwe, (from Ku-wa)

Uses and meanings
Its uses correspond in the main with those of the affirmative subjunctive. There are also two other special uses of this verb form.

1. Negative Imperative
(Which is automatically polite).

Usingoje. Don't wait.   Msingoje. Don't wait (pl.)

N.B. This will only be used in the 2nd person.

2. The suggestion 'Let me not . . . . .' etc.

Nisingoje.	Let me not wait.	Tusingoje.	Let's not wait.
Asingoje	Let him not wait.	Wasingoje.	Let them not wait.
Tusiende.	Let's not go.		

N.B. This sense is rarely used in the 2nd person.

3. To translate the second of two commands, and indirect commands when negative.

Mwambie asipike chakula.	Tell him not to cook the food.
Aliwaambia wasije	He told them not to come.
Jaribu usichelewe.	Try and not be late.

4. Purpose or intention

Ninaondoka nisiseme naye.	I am leaving so as not to talk to him.
Nimevaa nguo nyingi nisisikie baridi.	I have put on many clothes so as not to feel cold.

This negative can also take the word 'ili' to give weight to the purpose or intention.

| Nimevaa nguo nyingi ili nisisikie baridi. | I have put on many clothes in order not to feel cold. |

5. *Questioned suggestion ('Am I not to .....?').*

Nisingoje?	Am I not to wait?
Asiingie?	Is he/she not to enter?
Vitu hivi visisafishwe?	Are these things not to be cleaned?

6. *Negative obligation.*
Following the same words of obligation as mentioned in the affirmative subjunctive, the negative subjunctive should follow where appropriate:

Lazima usiende sasa.	You must not go now.
Sharti usiende sasa.	You are obliged not to go now.
Afadhali usiende sasa.	You had better not go now.
Bora usiende sasa.	You had best not go now.
Heri usiende sasa.	It would be advantageous not to go now.
Yafaa usiende sasa.	It is as well not to go now.

7. *Dependent clause after 'to want'*
Where a verb follows the verb 'to want' and a negative is required, it is customary to place only one of the verbs in the negative, otherwise a 'double negative' may result.

Where the same subject is assumed for both verbs, it is therefore usual to place the first in the negative tense, and the second in the 'infinitive' (cf. affirmative subjunctive).

| Sitaki kwenda. | I don't want to go. |

But where the subject is different for the second verb, it is usual to place the first verb in the affirmative tense, and the second in the negative subjunctive.

| Ninataka usiende. | I want you not to go. |

(which is the same sense as 'I don't want you to go')

8. *Verbs of restriction or prevention.*
This extra use of the negative subjunctive is one which, upon literal translation, appears to create a 'double negative'. There are two verbs in common use which are nearly always followed by the negative subjunctive:

| ku-kataza | to refuse, forbid |
| ku-zuia | to prevent |

e.g. Alinizuia nisitoke.
    He prevented me from coming out.

123

Tuliwakataza wasiingie.
We refused them entry.
We forbade them to come in.

(To translate these literally would make nonsense.)

9. Unsuccessful effort.
Another specialised use of this subjunctive is when recounting an incident which ended unsuccessfully.

Tulikwenda mjini kununua viazi tusipate.
We went to town to buy potatoes and did not get (any).
Mtoto alipanda mti asiweze kutelemka.
The child climbed the tree and was unable to come down.

N.B. The 'and' in these cases is not translated in Swahili.

Examples:

Yafaa upumzike sasa ili usichoke.	It is as well that you get some rest now so as not to get tired.
Askari polisi walizuia watu wasiingie nyumba ile.	The police prevented the people from entering that house.
Lazima watoto wasiguse vitu hivi.	The children must not touch these things.
Mpishi asinunue mkate leo?	Is the cook not to buy bread today?

Exercise 47

(a) *Translate:* Don't return; don't let them try again; tell them not to damage that car; I have written a chit so as not to forget; are they not to come?; you (pl.) must not touch; they did not want us to go today; we did not want to try again; prevent them from entering; he has forbidden me to go; I went to look for the children and was unable to see them; is he not to have assistance?; you must not fish about here; don't let them read this book; we must not forget the meeting tomorrow; they should not consider that that house is theirs; this stopper will prevent the seeds from coming out; you had better not tell them; are the servants not to unload that luggage?; don't let them go without seeing me.

(b) *Translate:* Tell your father not to give my children food; We tried to climb the mountain and were unable; Clean these plates well lest they be dirty; Wash your hands lest we eat dirty food; I have forbidden those people from returning here again; I want you not to use this tool again: This heavy door prevented the thieves from entering; You had better not plant those trees today because there is no rain about; Tell the labourers not to fell those tall trees; Let's not wait here. Let's return home.

(c) *Translate:* Msisahau; funga mlango wadudu wasiingie; waambie watoto wasicheze hapa; tufanyeje kuzuia nyumba isianguke; imekataliwa watu wasilime msituni; vibarua wasifanye kazi Jumapili; afadhali wakulima wasipande mbegu zao mwezi huu; alianguka mtoni asiweze kujiondoa; Memsabu anataka nisifue nguo leo; tuwakumbushe rafiki zetu kuja kesho wasisahau.

(d) *Translate:* Nimewaambieni msije hapa kuniona tena; Mganga hajaja leo.

Amechelewa sana; Watoto wamesoma kwa muda wa saa tano na nusu kamili; Mamangu na babake wamekuja hapa kuniona; Tumetafuta vitunguu sokoni tusipate kwa sababu havipatikani siku hizi; Wageni wako watafika hapa saa tisa na robo kesho; Mlango huu ni bure kwa sababu haufungiki; Mtumishi wako apige dawa katika kila chumba kuzuia wadudu wasiwe hapa; Utawapa chakula gani, wageni hawa?; Nilikuwa na bahati kubwa sana jana kwa sababu nilipewa pesa nyingi.

More Nouns

N class. (Some may occasionally be placed in the MA- class.)

afisi	office
akiba	reserve, store
akili	common sense, intelligence
alama	mark, stain, sign
bahari	sea
bahasha	envelope, bundle
bendera	flag
bidii	effort, energy
bunduki	rifle, gun
chapa	brand, trade-mark
damu	blood
faida	profit
fedha	silver, money
fulani	someone or other, something or other
furaha	joy, happiness
ghafula	suddenness
haraka	haste
hasara	loss
heri	fortune, luck, blessing
jasho	sweat
kamba	string, rope, cord
kawaida	normal, custom
kodi	tax, rent
kofia	hat, cap, headwear
koti	coat
kuku	hen, chicken
kusudi	purpose, intention
kutwa	daytime
kweli	truth
lugha	language
mali	possession, property, wealth
mara	times (multiplication)
mbuzi	goat
mchwa	termite (white ant)
namna	like, sort, kind
nchi	a country

ndege	bird, aeroplane
ndizi	banana
ndoo	bucket
ng'ombe	cow, ox, cattle
nguvu	strength, power
njia	way, path, road
nyanya	tomato, grandmother
orodha	list
rangi	colour, paint
salamu	greetings
sauti	voice, sound
serikali	government
simu	telephone, telegram
suti	suit
zawadi	present, gift

41   Position

Prepositions of Position

The following nouns and adverbs, when followed by the possessive 'ya' become prepositions, and are descriptive of position.

juu ya	on top of, above, over, on, upon
chini ya	underneath, below, beneath, under
ndani ya	inside, within, in
nje ya	outside, without (the sense of outside), on the surface of
mbele ya	in front of, before (of place), forward of, beyond
nyuma ya	behind, at the back of, in the rear of
kando ya	by the side of, beside, alongside, at the edge of, on one side of
kati ya	between, in the centre/middle of
katikati ya	among, amongst
ng'ambo ya	on the other side of, beyond, the far side of

N.B. (1) The possessive agreement will always be 'ya' and will never vary regardless of context.

(2) The words 'kati' and 'katikati' are more or less interchangeable since their meanings are practically the same.

Examples:

Weka kikapu juu ya meza.
Put the basket on top of the table.
Mbwa analala chini ya kitanda.
The dog is sleeping under the bed.
Nimeweka mizigo yangu ndani ya motokaa.
I have put my luggage inside the car.
Kuna mbwa mkali nje ya nyumba.
There is a fierce dog outside the house.
Panda mti huu mbele ya nyumba.
Plant this tree in front of the house.
Mtoto amejificha nyuma ya mti ule.
The child has hidden himself behind that tree.
Walifuata mfereji kando ya barabara.
They followed the ditch at the side of the road.
Wameangusha mti kati ya nyumba mbili hizi.
They have felled the tree between these two houses.
Kuna wanyama katikati ya miti ile.
There are animals amongst those trees.
Siwezi kufika ng'ambo ya mto ule.
I cannot reach the far side of that river.

Use of personal possessives.

Besides the possessive 'ya', it is also possible to use any of the personal possessives where appropriate. The agreement, once again, will always be 'y-' regardless of context.

e.g. juu yangu	above me (and also a specialized meaning of 'It is up to me' i.e. my responsibility)
juu yake, etc.	above him/her/it (his responsibility)
chini yangu	beneath/below me (also a special meaning of relation to status, e.g. Yeye ni chini yangu. —He is my subordinate.)
chini yake, etc.	below him/her/it
ndani yake	inside him/her/it
nje yake	outside him/her/it
mbele yao	in front of them
nyuma yako	behind you
kando yake	beside him/her/it
kati yao	between them
ng'ambo yake	on the other side of him/her/it

Adverbs

Besides the use with some sort of possessive, these words may be used without any possessive, in which case they are adverbs, thus having slightly different meanings:

chini	down	mbele	ahead
juu	up, on	ndani	in, inside
kando	at the side	ng'ambo	the other side
kati	between	nje	out, outside
katikati	in the midst	nyuma	behind

Examples:

Ndege alikwenda juu sana.	The bird went very high (up).
Weka mizigo hii chini.	Put these loads down.
Tafuta ndani.	Look inside.
Toa hii nje.	Put this outside.
Endelea mbele.	Proceed ahead.
Tazama nyuma.	Look behind.
Barabara ni mbaya kando.	The road is bad at the side.
Amesimama kati/katikati.	He/she has stood in the middle.
Hamisi anakaa ng'ambo.	Hamisi lives on the far side.

Exercise 48

(a) *Translate:* Profit; envelope; gift; a country; string; fortune; hat; voice; rain; brand; loss; reserve; coat; hen; bucket; colour; cow; truth; sea; someone or other; suddenness; list; mark; part; tomato; suit; haste; bananas; language; trade-mark.

(b) *Translate:* Behind; by the side of; on top of; the other side of; in front of; beneath; within; amongst; in between; outside of.

(c) *Translate:* In front of me; inside it; try the other side; stand behind him; on top of the house; inside the basket; wait outside; go in front; put it inside; it is his responsibility; these labourers are my subordinates; at the side of the river; he is inside; main road ahead; don't look behind you; he has climbed up; the teacher stood in front of his children; there are animals amongst the trees; on top of the hill; I have searched inside, and outside it too.

(d) *Translate:* That big house has been damaged because a tree fell on it; There are no cattle on the other side of that village; That old man stood at the side of the road; It is our responsibility to help them; I have put those labourers under that foreman; Halt! There is danger ahead!; Look for the children inside the house and outside also; I am standing in front of you (pl.) to tell you that there is a thief amongst you; There is a very beautiful bird at the top of that tree; It is up to everybody to try very hard.

(e) *Translate:* Haraka; kawaida; kodi; bendera; akili; namna; simu; afisi; kamba; ghafula; mali; kweli; mara; bahari; hasara; njia; nguvu; mchwa; furaha; chapa.

(f) *Translate:* Vaa kofia yako juu ya kichwa; acha koti lile nje; ameweka fedha juu ya meza; kama hujui, mwulize fulani; kuna ng'ombe ng'ambo ya kilima kile; twende mbele; lete ndoo kubwa ndani; tutatumia rangi hii nje ya nyumba, na ile ndani; usifanye kazi namna hii; ni juu yako kuondoa alama hizi; wanawake wale wanachukua ndizi juu ya vichwa vyao; tufuate njia hii kando ya mto; funga kamba hii nje; ni bendera gani juu ya nyumba ile?; ameweka kitu fulani ndani; mchwa wale wameharibu sehemu za chini ya mlango; amenipa zawadi nzuri sana; imenyesha mvua ng'ambo ya milima ile; ficha bunduki yake chini ya koti; nitafunga kuku wale ndani ya kibanda changu.

42 Adjectives—4

-OTE, -ENYE, -ENYEWE, -O -OTE

There are four adjectives in common use in Swahili which break away from the usual form of agreement. They are:

-ote	all, the whole
-enye	having, possessing, with
-enyewe	-self (i.e. myself, himself, itself, themselves etc.)
-o -ote	whatsoever, any . . . . . at all

Instead of these adjectives taking normal concord agreements with the noun they qualify, they take an agreement which closely resembles the object infix for that class.

-OTE

M- WA- class	no singular	
(plural)	wa-ote	wote

N.B. This adjective has a further unusual feature in that it can exist with 1st and 2nd person plural agreements:

sisi sote	all of us (or just 'sote')
ninyi nyote	all of you (or just 'nyote')

N.B. Since '-ote' and '-o -ote', deal with quantity, they will come last in the line of adjectives.

In some areas, 'sisi wote' is understood to mean 'both of us'.

M- MI- class	u-ote	wote
	i-ote	yote
KI- VI- class	ki-ote	chote
	vi-ote	vyote
N class	i-ote	yote
	zi-ote	zote

e.g. Sisi sote tumekwenda kule.   We have all gone there.

Kitambaa chote ni kichafu. { All the cloth is dirty.
                                  { The whole cloth is dirty.

Nyumba zote ni zangu   All the houses are mine.

-ENYE

M- WA- class	m(w)-enye	mwenye
	wa-enye	wenye

M- MI- class	u-enye	wenye
	i-enye	yenye
KI- VI- class	ki-enye	chenye
	vi-enye	vyenye
N class	i-enye	yenye
	zi-enye	zenye

e.g. Mwite yule mwenye kofia.   Call that person with the hat.
Kiti chenye miguu mitatu.   A chair with three legs. (A 3-legged chair)
Chai yenye sukari.   Tea with sugar.

-ENYEWE

M- WA- class	mw-enyewe	mwenyewe
	wa-enyewe	wenyewe
M- MI- class	u-enyewe	wenyewe
	i-enyewe	yenyewe
Ki- Vi- class	ki-enyewe	chenyewe
	vi-enyewe	vyenyewe
N class	i-enyewe	yenyewe
	zi-enyewe	zenyewe

e.g. Mimi mwenyewe nimemwona.   I myself have seen him.
Chumba chenyewe ni kidogo sana.   The room itself is very small.
Barua zenyewe zimepotea.   The letters themselves are lost.

N.B. The word 'mwenyewe' is also a noun meaning 'an owner'. (Plural 'wenyewe')

Thus 'mwenyewe mwenyewe' means 'the owner himself'.
There are two ways of saying 'an owner', however—

mwenye ng'ombe   the one having cattle
mwenyewe wa ng'ombe   the owner of cattle

Generally speaking, the first alternative is preferred as being shorter and easier to say.

-O -OTE

This adjective slightly breaks away from the rule as applied to the previous three:

M- WA- class	ye yote (may be written as one word 'yeyote')
	wo wote
M- MI- class	wo wote
	yo yote
KI- VI- class	cho chote
	vyo vyote

N.B. Where 'cho chote' is met without any qualifying noun, it is generally understood to agree with 'kitu' and thus means 'anything at all'. If there is food, then it could be assumed to agree with 'chakula' in which case it would mean 'a little taste of food' (i.e. a tit-bit) (lit. any food at all).

N class	yo yote
	zo zote

e.g. Uliza mtu ye yote mwenye saa.   Ask anyone with a watch.

Mpe mzee yule kitu cho chote.   Give that old man anything at all.

Ninahitaji msaada wo wote.   I need any help at all.

Exercise 49

(a) *Translate:* All the youths; all the books; any work at all; the house itself; a two-roomed house; all the bread; I went myself; all of you; remove all these things; all the cloth; it requires all your strength; any room will do; people with children; the owner of this house; look at all those parts; the present itself was money; you can follow any path; bring the chair with the cushion; would all those having their salaries wait outside; ask anyone with a watch.

(b) *Translate:* Would all those with children come with me; I myself went to Mombasa in order to fish, but did not get a fish at all; he wants you all to go there at 10.45 a.m. tomorrow; they passed the village but did not have a chance to see anyone at all; 'What should I give you?' 'Anything will do'; the owner of this house has prevented all from entering these doors; tell the owner of this car to remove it; we must all ask the farmer himself for permission; it has not rained any rain at all since Wednesday; bring all those things here without leaving anything behind.

(c) *Translate:* Uje saa yo yote; umesoma barua zote?; nipe barua ile yenye bahasha wazi; mimi mwenyewe sina motokaa lakini rafiki yangu ni mwenyewe wa motokaa hii; sisi sote tumeanza; sijui kama yeye ana mkate wo wote, mwulize mwenyewe; yule mwenye kofia nyeusi ni rafiki yangu; siwezi kukupa cho chote; yeye mwenyewe anapenda mkate wenye chumvi; waambie watoto wote wasicheze mpira katika kiwanja kile.

43   Verbs—6

The prepositional forms

There is a special form of verb in Swahili corresponding to verb and preposition sequences in English. No preposition is used with this form of verb in Swahili, and this verb generally takes an object infix.

If we take the phrase, 'Buy me some bread', we really mean 'Buy bread for me'. We cannot translate this as 'Ninunue mkate' as the verb then means literally 'buy me' i.e. 'I am up for sale'. The verb in these cases must therefore go into the prepositional form. We could say 'Nunua mkate kwa mimi' and although it would be understood, it is in fact unconventional.

The way in which a verb is made into the prepositional form is by the insertion of an I or E before the final vowel. Similar rules are followed by those given earlier for other derivations to determine whether to use an 'i' or 'e' (see Ch. 17). As will be seen in section 7 of this chapter, a combination of this derivation with others is possible.

1. E is inserted when the previous vowel is O or E and I is inserted when the previous vowel is A, I or U.

a	ku-kata	to cut	ku-kat*i*a	to cut for/for cutting
e	ku-leta	to bring	ku-let*e*a	to bring to/for
i	ku-pita	to pass	ku-pit*i*a	to pass for/over etc.
o	ku-soma	to read	ku-som*e*a	to read for/to
u	ku-anguka	to fall	ku-anguk*i*a	to fall in/on/upon etc.

2. Verbs ending in a double vowel have '-li-' or '-le-' inserted between the vowels, depending, once again, on the previous vowel:

a	ku-zaa	to bear	ku-zal*i*a	to bear for, etc.
e	ku-pokea	to receive	ku-pokel*e*a	to receive for
i	ku-fagia	to sweep	ku-fagil*i*a	to sweep for
o	ku-ondoa	to remove	ku-ondol*e*a	to remove for/to
u	ku-chukua	to carry	ku-chukul*i*a	to carry for/to

3. Arabic verbs change their final vowel to '-ia':

ku-rudi	to return	ku-rudia	to return to/for
ku-jibu	to reply	ku-jibia	to reply to/for

4. Monosyllabic verbs follow rule 1, and are then no longer treated as monosyllabics, since they now contain two syllables:

ku-la	to eat	ku-lia	to eat for/for eating

5. Some verbs are permanently prepositional and thus do not always need adjusting:

ku-ambia	to tell, tell to	ku-tafuta	to search for

| ku-ingia | to enter (into) | ku-tazama | to look at |
| ku-pa | to give to | ku-uliza | to ask (for/ about) |

e.g.

Mwambie Juma	Tell (to) Juma
Aliingia mfereji.	He entered (into) the ditch.
Alinipa mkate.	He gave (to) me bread.
Alitafuta watoto.	He looked for the children.
Alitazama milima.	He looked at the mountains.
Aliuliza habari	He asked for the news.

If action is done on behalf of somebody, then they can still be changed as with rule 1,

e.g.

| Alinitafutia watoto. | He looked for the children for me. |
| Aliniulizia habari. | He asked for the news for me. |

6. Some verbs have specialized meanings in their prepositional forms:

ku-amka	to wake	ku-amkia	to greet
ku-hama	to move away (emigrate)	ku-hamia	to move in (immigrate)
ku-nuka	to stink	ku-nukia	to smell sweet

7. Combination of the prepositional form and other verb derivatives, such as passives, causatives, and statives is possible:

ku-safisha	to clean	ku-safishwa	to be cleaned
		ku-safishiwa	to be cleaned for
ku-pata	to get	ku-pasha	to cause to get
		ku-pashia	to cause to get for
ku-choma	to roast	ku-chomeka	to be roasted
		ku-chomekea	to be roasted for

8. By virtue of its meaning, the prepositional verb almost invariably takes an object infix, but remember that a verb may only take *one* object infix.

Examples:

Ninunulie mkate.	Buy me some bread.
Niletee kisu changu.	Bring me my knife.
Rafiki yangu amenisafishia motokaa.	My friend has cleaned the car for me.
Amekwenda mjini kunipatia barua zangu.	He/she has gone to town to bring me my mail.
Amepata mpishi ampikie chakula kizuri.	He has got a cook to cook him good food.

133

Exercise 50

(a) *Translate:* Cut me some bread; would you carry this luggage for her; read me this letter, would you; pass me the salt!; he went to receive my gift for me; unload that car for me; she greets me every morning; the servant is sweeping the kitchen for the cook; we moved into this house a long time ago; that tree smells very sweet; that blind man wants me to read that letter to him; let me carry that load for you; you must wipe this table for me every day; we went into the ditch; bring them chairs; would you get me eight pounds of potatoes in town; my relative has asked me to sell this car for him; open the door for me; feed the children for me at 6 o'clock; the room has been cleaned for the guest.

(b) *Translate:* Let's go back to the town; wait for me until 4 o'clock; that car has brought me my luggage; I have no strength, please carry this load for me; put these plates on the table for me, would you?; this food smells very nice; would you open this door for us; he has made sure for us the time the aircraft will leave; they have gone to the doctor; take this letter to Mr. Jones.

(c) *Translate:* Nirudishie kitabu hiki; mfungie mlango; mimi ninampigia pasi Memsabu; yaya anatutembezea watoto wetu; nikatie kamba hii; tuwekee sukari katika chai yetu; alinikunjia kitambaa hiki vibaya; tuchemshie chakula; nipelekee cheti hiki afisini; nitafutie kisu; wamerudia mji; ananifanyia kazi; waombe vijana wale wanipigie hema; mzee aliangukia mto; niinulie mguu wako; msafishie vyombo vyote vile; tutawasaidia; nitamwendeshea motokaa yake; tutawafanyia mpango mpya; ninamwandikia barua kwa sababu hajui kuandika.

44 Adjectives — 5

Compound adjectives

Simple adjectives are not very numerous in Swahili, but there is a way in which nouns, verbs or other words can be made into compound adjectives. This is done by the addition of the possessive in front of the noun or other word chosen. The possessive must as usual agree with the noun being described.

1. Typical compound adjectives are:

-a	baridi	cold (sometimes now used without the possessive)
-a	bure	free (without possessive means 'useless')
-a	hatari	dangerous
-a	kawaida	normal, usual, regular
-a	kweli	true
-a	lazima	necessary, compulsory

-a	moto	hot (sometimes now used without the possessive)
-a	mwisho	last
-a	mwitu	wild (of the forest) (sometimes without possessive)
-a	pori	wild (of the bush) sometimes '-a porini'
-a	siri	secret
-a	zamani	old

In fact, you may take almost any noun and use it in this manner to form an adjective.

2. Verbs are also often used, in the 'infinitive':

-a	kutosha	sufficient, enough
-a	kupendeza	pleasing, pleasant
-a	kufaa	suitable

3. It is also used in this way for expressing the purpose of something, and these verbs are invariably placed in prepositional form:

-a	kukatia	for cutting
-a	kulimia	for tilling, cultivating
-a	kupimia	for measuring
-a	kusafishia	for cleaning

4. We also get left and right:

-a	kulia	right (lit. for eating)
-a	kushoto	left

(These may occasionally be used without the possessive if giving a direct direction, e.g. Pita kushoto—keep left.)

5. Also the sexes:

-a	kike	female
-a	kiume	male

6. Where a 'type' of thing is to be described, this construction is used after placing the noun in the singular KI- VI- class.

-a	Kihindi	Indian type
-a	Kizungu	European type
-a	kienyeji	native type
-a	kitoto	child type, childish
-a	kisasa	modern, modern type (sometimes '-a sasa')
-a	Kimasai	Masai type

135

7. The ordinal numbers also use this construction:

-a	kwanza	the first (lit. of starting)
-a	pili	second (note slight change in spelling from '-wili')
-a	tatu	third
-a	nne	fourth
-a	tano	fifth
-a	sita	sixth
-a	saba	seventh
-a	nane	eighth
-a	tisa	ninth
-a	kumi	tenth
-a	kumi na moja	eleventh (N.B. *not* kumi na kwanza)
-a	kumi na mbili	twelfth (N.B. *not* kumi na pili)
-a	mia	hundredth
-a	mia, ishirini na moja	hundred and twenty first
-a	mwisho	last

N.B. The numbers themselves never *take agreements in this form, and the possessive must always be given* singular *agreements only, except for the first and last, which can be used in the plural.*

Examples:
Wape watoto wale chakula cha kutosha.
   Give those children enough food.
Mtoto wa kwanza atapata kitabu, wa pili atapata pesa.
   The first child will get a book, the second will get money.
Watu wengine hawawezi kula chakula cha Kizungu.
   Some people are unable to eat European type food.
Ni kitu cha lazima wakulima wote wafuate kilimo cha kisasa.
   It is a necessary thing that all farmers follow modern agriculture.
Mkono wake wa kulia umevunjika kwa mara ya pili.
   His right arm is broken for the second time.

Exercise 51
(a) *Translate:* Hot potatoes; cold meat; free books; a secret meeting; a wild dog; an old house; the last day; a female cat; native type clothing; normal work; a measuring vessel; the left arm; a male child; true news (pl.); a cleaning cloth; the first thing; suitable plates; the second tree; a childish game; European food.
(b) *Translate:* Give me a carving knife (a knife for cutting meat); they have gone to look at the rain gauge (vessel for measuring rain); we do not want native type hens, we need European type; children's clothes are not obtainable in town; he told us the first thing; it is a very pleasant thing to go on safari to see wild animals; I have bought an old Masai spear; that cow has borne her second female offspring (child); people must not have secret meetings; there is a free book for showing all these things.

(c) *Translate:* Mguu wake wa kulia umevunjika; una karatasi za kutosha?; safari ya lazima; anakaa katika nyumba ya tano toka hapa; hiki ni chombo cha kulimia; amefanya kazi bure; amenunua motokaa ya kisasa kabisa; wageni wamefika Tanzania kuona wanyama wa porini; alirudi siku ya pili; pita barabara ya kushoto; yu mwanachama wa chama cha siri; wameanza mchezo wa nne sasa; ninahitaji kitu cha kufungulia mlango huu kwa sababu haufunguki; yule ana mke wa kupendeza; yeye ni mgeni wa pili kuja leo; mke wake amezaa mtoto wa kike juzi; leo ni siku ya mwisho ya mtihani; ninataka karatasi ya kuandikia barua; chakula cha Kihindi ni kikali kwa kawaida; mnalipwa mishahara ya kutosha.

45 Months and Dates

Months

The months, in Swahili, are taken directly from the English calendar. In each case 'Mwezi wa .....' precedes the name of the month.

Januari	January	Julai	July
Februari	February	Agosti	August
Machi	March	Septemba	September
Aprili	April	Oktoba	October
Mei	May	Novemba	November
Juni	June	Desemba	December

Note that the stress in Swahili follows the normal rule i.e. penultimate syllable.

Other vocabulary:

kalenda	calendar ('N' class)
tarehe	date ('N' class)

Although most Africans are quite familiar with these names of the month, most of them get a better picture of the time of year by referring to the months as the first, second, third, etc. up to the twelfth month. They thus prefer to use the ordinal numbers:

Mwezi wa kwanza	January (first month)
Mwezi wa pili	February (second month)
Mwezi wa tatu	March (third month)
	etc.
Mwezi wa kumi na mbili	December (twelfth month)

137

Dates

Dates are given in Swahili with the ordinal numbers, as in English, but they do not usually take the possessive, except the second. In each case, however, the word 'tarehe' precedes the number.

tarehe moja	the first (one will often hear 'Tarehe mosi' instead)
tarehe ya pili	the second (*may* be used without possessive 'tarehe pili' or even 'tarehe mbili')
tarehe tatu	the third
tarehe kumi na mbili	the twelfth
tarehe ishirini na moja	the twenty first
tarehe thelathini na moja	the thirty first

The year

Unlike the English when we recognise a year by the manner in which it is said (i.e. nineteen sixty six), the Swahili language uses the ordinal number in full, preceded by 'Mwaka wa . . . . .' (The year of . . . . .).

e.g. the year 1966
mwaka wa elfu moja, mia tisa, sitini na sita

The full date

Thus a full date would be given as follows:

Tarehe ishirini na saba, mwezi wa sita (or mwezi wa Juni) mwaka wa elfu moja, mia tisa, thelathini na moja
The 27th June 1931.

Exercise 52

(a) *Translate:* 22nd July 1933; 4th September 1954; 31st August 1958; 25th December 1901; 24th April this year; he goes to Nairobi every second of the month; to-day is the first; the exams will start on May 11th; there is a meeting on the 22nd of this month; I am going home on January 31st.

(b) *Translate:* Tarehe kumi na saba, mwezi wa saba, mwaka wa elfu moja mia tisa thelathini na nne; tarehe kumi na nne mwezi wa kumi na mbili mwaka wa elfu moja mia tisa thelathini na mbili; tarehe tisa, mwezi wa Desemba mwaka wa elfu moja mia tisa sitini na moja; tarehe mosi mwezi wa Julai mwaka wa elfu moja mia nane tisini na tisa; tarehe ishirini na tisa, mwezi wa pili, mwaka wa elfu moja mia tisa na sitini; mzee yule alikufa tarehe nne, mwezi wa kumi na moja, mwaka wa elfu moja mia tisa hamsini na tano; chama hiki kilianzishwa mwaka wa elfu moja mia tisa na arobaini; una kalenda ya mwaka huu?; Jumamosi itakuwa tarehe kumi na mbili; mchezo wa mpira utakuwa tarehe kumi na tatu.

46 Nouns — 5

MA–Noun class

This class is sometimes called the JI- MA- class, since a small minority of nouns in the class have the concord 'ji-' in the singular which may either be changed to 'ma-' in the plural, or have 'ma' added to it. The remaining nouns have no concord in the singular, and take 'ma-' in the plural.

The nouns in this class can be placed in different categories—

1. Those whose singular concord 'ji-' changes to 'ma-' in the plural:

   e.g. jicho   macho   an eye
         jiwe   mawe   a stone, a torch battery

2. The nouns whose singular concord is 'ji-' but have irregular plural concords:

   e.g. jiko   meko (or   a fireplace, kitchen, stove
                majiko)
         jino   meno   a tooth

3. One odd word with only a 'j-' concord in the singular:

   jambo   mambo   a matter

(This is the same word as is used in the common greeting.)

4. Nouns whose singular is 'ji-' but *add* 'ma-' to it for the plural:

   e.g. jibu   majibu   an answer
         jina   majina   a name
         jipu   majipu   a boil, abscess

5. The largest group, which has no concord in the singular, and which takes 'ma-' in the plural:

   e.g. baraza   mabaraza   a local court, verandah, meeting
         bati   mabati   corrugated iron, sheet iron
         blanketi   mablanketi   a blanket
         boma   maboma   fortification, government office block (outside capital city)
         bonde   mabonde   a valley
         bunge   mabunge   parliament
         daraja   madaraja   a bridge, staircase
         debe   madebe   a 4-gallon tin can
         dirisha   madirisha   a window (with or without glass)
         duka   maduka   a shop
         gari   magari   a vehicle

gazeti	magazeti	a newspaper, periodical
jani	majani	a leaf ('grass' when plural)
jembe	majembe	a hoe
jua		the sun
kanisa	makanisa	a church
pipa	mapipa	a barrel, oil drum
pori	mapori	the bush
sanduku	masanduku	a box, suitcase, boot of a car
shamba	mashamba	a farm, field, plantation
shauri	mashauri	a plan, advice, affair
shoka	mashoka	an axe
soko	masoko	a market
taifa	mataifa	a nation
tope	matope	mud (plural used for large quantities)
yai	mayai	an egg
zulia	mazulia	a carpet
(and many others!)		

6. Nearly all fruit, or produce of plants, is in this class, often using the same stem as the plant itself (the plant generally being in the M- MI-class. See appendix III),

e.g.	chungwa	machungwa	an orange
	hindi (rare)	mahindi	maize grain
	limau	malimau	a lemon
	nanasi	mananasi	pineapple
	papai	mapapai	pawpaw
	tunda	matunda	fruit
	ua	maua	a flower, blossom

7. Nouns indicating a person's occupation or status can be found in this class because of a skill or importance. Agreements will be M- WA- only,

e.g.	Bibi	Mabibi	Lady, grandmother
	Bwana	Mabwana	Mr., Sir, master, husband, gentleman.
	dereva	madereva	a driver
	fundi	mafundi	skilled worker, craftsman
	karani	makarani	a clerk, typist
	Memsabu	Mamemsabu	Madam, lady of the house
	Rais	Marais	a President
	seremala	maseremala	a carpenter, joiner
	tajiri	matajiri	an employer, merchant, businessman, rich person
	tarishi	matarishi	a messenger
	waziri	mawaziri	a government minister

8. Words denoting things which are uncountable, or only found in quantity, including liquids, which are only used in the plural and only take plural agreements:

e.g.	maarifa	knowledge, ingenuity
	mafuta	fat, oil (but not engine oil which is 'oili' in the 'N' class)
	maji	water
	majivu	ashes
	matata	trouble
	mavi	excrement, faeces
	maziwa	milk
	mazungumzo	conversation

9. Words indicating size or importance. This class is often the converse of the KI- VI- class, and is therefore also known as the augmentative class. Almost any noun can be changed into this class to stress size or importance. Occasionally, however, a noun in the N class will be put in this class simply to be able to signify a plural,

e.g.	dudu	madudu	a pest (i.e. even a hippo!)
	jitu	majitu	a giant (from 'mtu')
	jumba	majumba	a hall, mansion, palace etc. (from 'nyumba')
	or such words as		
		maelfu	thousands

Remember, too, that many nouns are not kept rigidly in either this or the N class, and may easily be placed in either class as considered appropriate (e.g. koti, hema, etc.).

Agreements — Adjectives

Consonant stem adjectives
In this class, consonant stem adjectives take *no* concord in the singular. Do not confuse this rule, however, with the N class rule. In the MA- class it makes no difference what the initial letter is.

Thus we get

duka kubwa	a big shop
dirisha chafu	a dirty window
daraja refu	a long bridge
jua kali	fierce sun (strong sunlight)
sanduku zuri	a good box

The only exception to a consonant stem adjective is the mono-syllabic stem. This takes the singular concord 'ji-':

| gari jipya | a new vehicle |

In the plural, all consonant stem adjectives take the concord 'ma-':

maduka makubwa	big shops
madirisha machafu	dirty windows
madaraja marefu	long bridges
masanduku mazuri	good boxes
magari mapya	new vehicles

and of course the liquids etc.:

maji machafu	dirty water
mazungumzo marefu	long conversation
majivu machache	a few ashes
maziwa mazuri	good milk

Vowel stem adjectives.
These go back to the 'ji-' singular concord, though in all cases, in fact, the 'i' is omitted, and so just the 'j' is added:

jiwe jeusi	a black stone
kanisa jeupe	a white church
jua jingi	much sun

but, we have one exception—'-ingine' becomes 'lingine' (which comes from the subject prefix):

shamba lingine	another field
jina lingine	another name

In the plural, the 'ma-' concord is modified:

ma+eusi =meusi	(a+e =e) cf. M- WA- class
ma+ingi =mengi	(a+i =e) cf. M- WA- class
mawe meusi	black stones
makanisa meupe	white churches
majani mengi	much grass/many leaves
majina mengine	other names
mambo mengine	other matters

The numbers are quite normal:

jambo moja	one matter
mambo mawili	two matters etc.

Subject Prefixes

These are

	affirmative		*negative*
	li-	singular	hali-
	ya-	plural	haya-

pipa moja limejaa	one barrel is full
mapipa mawili yamejaa	two barrels are full
maji yamechemka	the water has boiled

Demonstratives
From the subject prefixes, we get the following demonstratives:

Singular		Plural	
hili	this	haya	these
lile	that	yale	those

taifa hili	this nation
zulia lile	that carpet
meno haya	these teeth
machungwa yale	those oranges

and note:

maji haya	this water
maziwa yale	that milk

Verb 'to be' with locative

lipo	liko	limo
yapo	yako	yamo

Boma liko wapi?   Liko kule.
Where is the Government office block?   It is over there.

(in fact, 'boma' is often used in English with this meaning, throughout East Africa, e.g. 'Where is the boma?')

Maziwa yamo chomboni? Yamo.
Is the milk in the vessel? It is.
Shoka lipo hapa.
The axe is here.

Possessives
These are as follows:

li+a =la (singular)	ya+a =ya (plural)
bati la nyumba hii	this house's corrugated iron
mafuta ya taa	paraffin (lamp oil)

Personal possessives

Singular	langu	my, mine	letu	our, ours
	lako	your, yours	lenu	your, yours
	lake	his, hers, its	lao	their, theirs
Plural	yangu	my, mine	yetu	our, ours
	yako	your, yours	yenu	your, yours
	yake	his, hers, its	yao	their, theirs

gari langu	my vehicle	magari yangu	my vehicles
shamba lake	his/her farm	mashamba yake	his/her fields
taifa letu	our nation	majembe yetu	our hoes
shauri lao	their affair	mashauri yao	their affairs

Object infixes

These are the same as the subject prefixes — '-li-' (singular) and '-ya-' (plural).

>Umel*i*ona sanduku langu? Nimel*i*ona.
>>Have you seen my suitcase? I have seen it.
>Madirisha ni machafu. Huja*ya*safisha.
>>The windows are dirty. You have not yet cleaned them.

-OTE, -ENYE, etc.

The agreements for these are:

Singular		Plural	
	lote		yote
	lenye		yenye
	lenyewe		yenyewe
	lo lote		yo yote

>Pori lote limejaa na wanyama.
>>The whole bush (all the bush) is filled with game.
>Duka lenye vitu vingi.
>>A shop with many things.
>Boma lenyewe litafunga saa nane.
>>The boma itself will close at 2 o'clock.
>Nipe jina lo lote.
>>Give me any name at all.
>Mambo yote yamekwisha.
>>All the matters are finished.
>Sipendi machungwa yenye mbegu nyingi.
>>I don't like oranges with many seeds (pips).
>Mazulia yenyewe ni mazuri kabisa.
>>The carpets themselves are extremely good.
>Usilete matope yo yote nyumbani.
>>Don't bring any mud at all into the house.

Examples:

>Rais amesema kwamba atalisaidia taifa hili.
>>The President has said that he will help this nation.
>Ninahitaji gari la kuchukulia masanduku makubwa haya.
>>I need a vehicle for carrying these large boxes.
>Jina lako nani? Jina langu (ni) Smith.
>>What is your name? My name is Smith.
>(Note the way this question is asked; lit. 'Who is your name?')
>Jua kali lile limekausha majani haya katika shamba lao.
>>That strong sun has dried up this grass in their field.
>Mamangu amekwenda mtoni kuleta debe la maji ya kunywa.
>>My mother has gone to the river to bring a tin can of drinking water. ('Debe' is in fact used even in the English, throughout East Africa.)

144

Exercise 53

(a) *Translate:* Verandah; name; driver; parliament; shop; water; nation; carpet; bridge; stone; milk; window; boil; vehicle; affair; staircase; eggs; skilled person; a fruit; a hall; church; fort; eye; a matter; name; sun; President; fat; Government minister; an orange; a flower; newspaper; grass; barrel; suitcase; corrugated iron; hoe; axe; ashes; an answer.

(b) *Translate:* Much trouble; an empty 4-gallon tin; other fields; that large market; my name; another box; a new nation; a newspaper with much news; those dirty windows; that sharp axe; many difficult matters; two barrels of oil; his first name; those heavy vehicles; any reply; a butcher's shop; this big red carpet; that flower smells nice; those drivers; that carpenter is an able craftsman.

(c) *Translate:* The drivers of these vehicles have gone to the shops; these cattle do not give out much milk, but it is very good; the Minister of Housing (houses) will come tomorrow; the leaves of these flowers smell very nice; the messenger has not brought me any reply whatsoever; the rubbish bin has been knocked down by dogs; vehicles are unable to use this road because of this mud; these flowers must be put on our verandah; that clerk has a big abscess under his tooth; the eye itself of that sick person is very red.

(d) *Translate:* Madirisha: bunge; majani; tarishi; maarifa; dudu; matunda; mambo; mawe; kanisa; soko; meno; matope; nanasi; mazungumzo; jitu; papai; jipu; macho; karani.

(e) *Translate:* Gari lake jipya; duka la mkate; sanduku hili litafaa; kanisa la Wakristo; Bunge la Tanzania; bonde lenye mashamba mengi; jicho jekundu lile; jua kali hili; maji machafu haya; jambo gumu lenyewe; lete sanduku lo lote; shamba lako liko wapi? Ni lile pale; jina lake nani? Jina lake Hamisi; fundi wa chuma; malimau mabovu yale; maziwa machache; baraza la kijiji kile; ulilipata lini jibu lake? Nililipata jana; safisha jiko chafu lile.

(f) *Translate:* Majembe yanapatikana katika duka kubwa lile; mahindi mazuri haya yametoka shamba lile bondeni; meno yako si meupe kwa sababu maji haya si mazuri; nifungulie dirisha lile; toa zulia kubwa hili ili uweze kulisafisha vizuri; ng'ombe huyu ametoa madebe saba ya maziwa mazuri wiki hii; tulikuwa na mazungumzo mafupi barazani; ninahitaji tarishi kunipelekea jibu hili dukani; umeliona jina lako katika gazeti hili? La, sijaliona.

47   The -KI- Tense

Conditional and present participle tenses
The Conditional Tense
This tense sign is again used in the normal way, i.e. with the subject prefix preceding it, and the verb stem following it. Its sense is 'if'. It will invariably be followed by a future tense, or an imperative (which has future implication).

ni-ki-kaa	nikikaa	if I stay
u-ki-kaa	ukikaa	if you stay
a-ki-kaa	akikaa	if he/she stays
tu-ki-kaa	tukikaa	if we stay
m-ki-kaa	mkikaa	if you stay
wa-ki-kaa	wakikaa	if they stay

M- Mi- class

u-ki-kaa	ukikaa	if it stays
i-ki-kaa	ikikaa	if they stay

Ki- Vi- class

ki-ki-kaa	kikikaa	if it stays
vi-ki-kaa	vikikaa	if they stay

N class

i-ki-kaa	ikikaa	if it stays
zi-ki-kaa	zikikaa	if they stay

Ma- class

li-ki-kaa	likikaa	if it stays
ya-ki-kaa	yakikaa	if they stay

Arabic verbs create no exception:

ni-ki-jibu	nikijibu	if I reply
wa-ki-fikiri	wakifikiri	if they think/consider

Monosyllabic verbs, however, drop their 'infinitive' 'ku-':

a-ki-ja	akija	if he comes
tu-ki-enda	tukienda	if we go
u-ki-wa	ukiwa	if you are
u-ki-wa na	ukiwa na	if you have

Examples:
Ukienda Dar es Salaam utaona bahari.
    If you go to Dar es Salaam, you will see the sea.
Wakinywa pombe watalewa.
    If they drink local beer they will get drunk.
Ukifika mjini, nunua mkate.
    If you get to the town, buy some bread.
Mkimwona Hamisi, mwambieni aje hapa.
    If you (pl.) see Hamisi, tell (pl.) him to come here.

N.B. That the verb containing the condition is first in each case, (which is the order more commonly heard) though the sentence in each case could be reversed,

e.g. You will see the sea if you go to Dar es Salaam.
Utaona bahari ukienda Dar es Salaam.

There is a word which also means 'if' namely 'kama'. It may be used before the verb bearing the '-ki-' tense to strengthen the condition 'if'. It may also be used with other tenses 'kama ulikwenda'—'if you went'.

Kama ukienda Dar es Salaam, utaona bahari.
If (by any chance) you go to Dar es Salaam, you will see the sea.

The present participle tense

There is a second use of this same tense sign. It is made up in exactly the same way as the conditional tense, but instead of occurring within the first verb of a sentence, it is generally found in the second or subsequent verb.

In this second case it often corresponds to the Present Particle in English.

e.g. Tuliwaona wakicheza.	We saw them playing.
Walikuwa wakitembea.	They were walking.
Alikuja akiimba.	He came singing.

There is now a slight problem created, because in Swahili there are three ways in which, say, the word, 'playing' can be translated:

1. It can be a verbal noun, in which case in Swahili it would be translated as 'kucheza'.

    e.g. Playing football is easy.
    Kucheza mpira ni rahisi.

2. It can be a participle, in which case in Swahili one would use the -KI- tense:

    e.g. I saw him playing.
    Nilimwona akicheza.

(You could not say 'I saw him to play football'.)

3. It can be the present tense of the verb:

    e.g. He is playing.   Anacheza.

In order to ascertain which of the three is intended, perhaps the simplest way is by the process of elimination. The present tense is generally easy to see, and is always preceded by the present form of the verb 'to be'. The participle can easily be spotted because it can take the word 'while' or 'whilst' before it and not change the meaning in any way.

e.g. I saw him whilst playing.   Nilimwona akicheza.

But you could not say 'While playing football is easy'. Therefore if it is clear that neither of the other two senses are implied, one can safely assume that the word is a verbal noun and therefore takes the 'infinitive' in Swahili.

In a short time, however, these tenses will come automatically to your mind.

N.B. This participle can be used with any tense by using, as in English, the verb 'to be',

e.g. Alikuwa akicheza.	He was playing.
Atakuwa akicheza.	He will be playing.
Amekuwa akicheza	He has been playing.

Such tenses are known as compound tenses, and are frequently used in this language. For further compound tenses, see chapter 65.

N.B. You can still add 'while' or 'whilst' to these examples.

Examples:

Ukipanda mlima wa Kilimanjaro lazima uchukue nguo za kutosha.
   If you climb Mount Kilimanjaro you must take enough clothing.
Ukimwona Hamisi *akipumzika*, mwambie anione.
   If you see Hamisi resting, tell him to see me.
Amechoka kwa sababu amekuwa *akikimbia* sana.
   He is tired because he has been running a lot.
Mkienda Mombasa leo, mtawaona watoto wetu *wakicheza* mpira.
   If you (pl.) go to Mombasa to-day, you will see our children playing football.
Hatukuwa hapa jana kwa sababu tulikuwa porini *tukifanya* kazi.
   We were not here yesterday because we were in the bush working (doing some work).
Wamasai watakuwa *wakicheza* dansi kesho usiku.
   The Masai will be dancing to-morrow night.
Mwalimu alikuwa *akifundisha* kusoma na kuandika.
   The teacher was teaching reading and writing.

Exercise 54

(a) *Translate:* If you like; if they eat; if it is; if I drink; if the tree falls; if he replies; if you think; if you (pl.) arrive; if we give you; if he tells us; if you have permission; if the chairs are brought; if the flowers are cut; if eggs are obtainable; if he tells me his name; if a hoe is used; if the mail is brought; if you (pl.) touch; if his leg breaks; if he dies.

(b) *Translate:* He was reading; they like reading; we are reading; I saw him reading; I heard him singing; he likes singing; he will be singing on Saturday; they are playing to-morrow; they are tired because they have been playing; if they see the tree falling; they saw him coming; we were waiting for two hours; it was raining yesterday; the axe was being used; he was cooking in the kitchen; the food was being cooked in the kitchen; he will be waiting for me in town; we are learning Swahili; learning Swahili is easy in this country.

(c) *Translate:* If you come home now, I shall give you some tea; if you see animals on that road, you will be lucky (you will have luck); if you go tomorrow, the doctor will be examining (measuring) patients at that time; if that tree falls, it will damage your house; my servant was washing our clothes without hot water; if they try hard, they are bound to succeed; these flowers were growing badly, so I cut them; some people do not like learning languages; he broke the glass whilst cleaning the windows; we saw the animals lying in the shade under the trees.

(d) *Translate:* Ukienda Nairobi, ninunulie vitu vichache; alikuwa akiendesha gari lake vibaya; tuliwaona watoto wetu wakicheza; huwezi kuchukua jembe langu kwa sababu nitakuwa nikilitumia kesho; nilikasirika sana kwa sababu alikuwa akilala mkutanoni; mkikimbia kule mtamwona akifanya kazi shambani; ukiokota kiko changu, njoo hapa kuniambia; kama ukija saa nane, sitakwenda safarini; mzee alilala akiketi katika kiti chake; ukijaribu sana, utaweza kujifunza lugha hii bila kuona matata mengi.

Negative conditional tense ('if not'/'unless')

There are two ways in which it is possible to give a negative to the -KI-conditional tense, which in English is given as 'if not' or 'unless'.

1. The word 'kama' can be used together with a straightforward negative tense:

kama hutakwenda	if you do not go/unless you go
kama hawatakuja	if they do not come/unless they come
kama barua hazitafika	if the mail does not arrive/unless the mail arrives.

2. A tense exists which carries this meaning. It is -SIPO-.

It is in actual fact a negative relative tense of time (cf. Ch. 52) and as such, it takes *affirmative* subject prefixes, *not* negative.

ni-sipo-weza	nisipoweza	if I am not able/unless I can
u-sipo-weza	usipoweza	if you are not able/unless you can
a-sipo-weza	asipoweza	if he/she is not able/unless he/she can
tu-sipo-weza	tusipoweza	if we are not able/unless we can
m-sipo-weza	msipoweza	if you are not able/unless you can
wa-sipo-weza	wasipoweza	if they are not able/unless they can

M- Mi- class

u-sipo-weza	usipoweza	if it is not able/unless it can
i-sipo-weza	isipoweza	if they are not able/unless they can

Ki- Vi- class

ki-sipo-weza	kisipoweza	if it is not able/unless it can
vi-sipo-weza	visipoweza	if they are not able/unless they can

N class

i-sipo-weza	isipoweza	if it is not able/unless it can
zi-sipo-weza	zisipoweza	if they are not able/unless they can

Ma- class

li-sipo-weza	lisipoweza	if it is not able/unless it can
ya-sipo-weza	yasipoweza	if they are not able/unless they can

Arabic verbs are treated in the same way:

ni-sipo-jibu	nisipojibu	if I do not answer/unless I reply
a-sipo-fikiri	asipofikiri	if he does not think/unless he thinks

Monosyllabic verbs *retain* their 'infinitive' 'ku-'

ni-sipo-kuja	nisipokuja	if I do not come/unless I come
tu-sipo-kwenda	tusipokwenda	if we do not go/unless we go
a-sipo-kuwa	asipokuwa	if he is not/unless he is
wa-sipo-kuwa na	wasipokuwa na	if they do not have/unless they have
i-sipo-kuwa	isipokuwa	unless it be (i.e. except) (Frequently used as a conjunction as an alternative to 'ila'—except, unless)

N.B. Both constructions 1 and 2 are in common use.

It is important to note that these two constructions can only be used as a negative to the conditional tense use of -KI-. If a negative participle is required, two methods can be used:

1. The use of a normal present negative tense:

   Niliwaona hawafanyi kazi.   I saw them not working.

2. The use of a compound tense. In this case, either of the two verbs may be placed in the negative:

Walikuwa hawafanyi kazi.	They were not working.
Hawakuwa wakifanya kazi.	They were not working.
Watakuwa hawafanyi kazi.	They will not be working.
Hawatakuwa wakifanya kazi.	They will not be working.
Wamekuwa hawafanyi kazi.	They have not been working.

Hawajawa wakifanya kazi.   They have not yet been
working.
(The -SIPO- tense is never used in this context.)

Examples:
Hukuniona Jumapili kwa sababu sikuwa nikifanya kazi siku ile.
You did not see me on Sunday because I was not working that
day.
Watu hawa hawatakuwa wakicheza Jumanne.
These people will not be playing on Tuesday.
Hamkufaulu mtihani wenu kwa sababu mmekuwa hamjaribu
sana.
You (pl.) did not suceed your examination because you have
not been trying hard.
Mlango huu umekuwa haufungiki vizuri kwa muda mrefu.
This door has not been closing properly for a long time.

Useful idioms
There is a very useful idiom which employs the -KI- tense. It is the one
used for translating the expression 'Whether . . . or not'.

e.g. Whether you like it or not.

This is translated as 'Ukipenda, usipende'.

(Note that the word 'it' is omitted, though may be inserted by means
of an object infix if referring to a specific object 'Ukiipenda, usiipende'.)

Notice that the negative subjunctive is used to denote the negative part
of the expression.

Similarly, you can use this expression for any person:

akipenda, asipende   whether he/she likes it or not
tukipenda, tusipende   whether we like it or not
mkipenda, msipende   whether you (pl.) like it or not
wakipenda, wasipende   whether they like it or not

Or with other verbs:

ukienda, usiende   whether you go or not
ukijaribu, usijaribu etc.   whether you try or not

This idiom is often followed by a second idiom meaning

'It is all the same to me/to him/to us', etc.

This is turned into 'It is all one to . . .' in Swahili. For this the plural
concord 'ma-' is used with the stem '-moja' to give the suggestion of
'all one'. This is 'mamoja'. (This is the only occasion that a plural
agreement is given to '-moja'.)

For the second part, which may or may not be used, the personal possessives are used together with a 'kw-' agreement.

kwangu	to me	kwetu	to us
kwako	to you	kwenu	to you
kwake	to him/her	kwao	to them

Thus we get:

Ni mamoja kwangu.	It's all the same to me.
Ni mamoja kwake.	It's all the same to him/her.
Ni mamoja kwetu.	It's all the same to us.
	etc.

Examples:

Akija, asije, ni mamoja kwangu.
Whether he/she comes or not, it's all the same to me.
Tukifaulu tusifaulu, ni mamoja.
Whether we succeed or not, it's all the same.
Sijui nikienda, nisiende.
I don't know whether to go or not.
Mkijua, msijue jambo hili, ni juu yenu.
Whether you (pl.) know this matter or not, it is up to you.

Exercise 55

(a) *Translate:* Unless he comes; if it does not rain; whether or not you stay, it is all the same to us; he was not singing yesterday; whether you wear that hat or not; if you do not eat; unless we return now, we shall be late; if he does not bring the milk it is all the same to us; unless he tells me his name; if they are not given permission; unless you (pl.) are blind; whether that tree falls or not; if you do not read the newspapers; unless I have permission; whether it rains or not, it is all the same; if water is not brought; if the lamp is not lit, we shall not see; if that door is not closed I shall feel cold; we have not been buying bread in that shop; if we do not wake up early we shall not be able to go to church.

(b) *Translate:* Unless we try hard, we shall not succeed; I saw them on the road but they were not running; if at the beginning you do not succeed, try again; if you (pl.) do not read books, how will you know anything?; unless he arrives here early to-morrow we cannot start; my dog has not been eating anything since yesterday; unless he eats a little food he will die; my friend has been trying to give him food many times; the visitors will not be climbing Mount Kenya on Monday; if you do not work well, you will not be staying here long (much).

(c) *Translate:* Wasipopanda mbegu zao sasa hawatapata faida; wakiondoka wasiondoke ni mamoja kwao; usipofaulu mwanzoni, jaribu tena; usipojua saa, mwulize mwenye saa; siwezi kuwasaidieni msiponiambia kila kitu; asipomlisha mbwa wake chakula cha kutosha, atakufa tu; meno yasi-posafishwa vizuri yatakuwa meusi; barua isipopelekwa leo itachelewa; usipoweka sabuni katika maji haya, huwezi kufua nguo vizuri; akijitolea, asijitolee, ni juu yake, ni mamoja kwangu; nisipoacha kazi sasa, nitachoka sana.

48 Indeclinable Words—2

Prepositions, adverbs and conjunctions, 'alone' and 'because'

More prepositions, etc.
The following are more prepositions which are in common use:

baada ya	after (only of time)
badala ya	instead of
habari ya	concerning, about (lit. 'news of .....')

N.B. This can be 'habari za . . .' if much to tell, or to refer to.

kabla ya	before, prior to (only of time)
zaidi ya	more than

As with the previous prepositions given in chapter 41, these may be used with personal possessives instead of the possessive 'ya'. But these will still all begin with 'y-' (apart from 'habari' which could begin with 'z-' if there was much to tell).
The word which follows the above possessives will be either a noun, a verb in the 'infinitive' or a demonstrative.

> e.g. Alirudi nyumbani baada ya kumaliza.
> He returned home after finishing.
> Alirudi nyumbani baada yangu.
> He returned home after me.
> Alikwenda Nairobi badala ya kwenda Dar es Salaam.
> He went to Nairobi instead of going to Dar es Salaam.
> Alikwenda Nairobi badala yangu.
> He went to Nairobi in my stead (instead of me).
> Mwambie habari ya safari yako.
> Tell him about your safari.
> Mwambie habari za safari (if much to tell).
> Tell him all about your safari.
> Funga mlango kabla ya kuondoka.
> Close the door before leaving.
> Niliona zaidi ya watu kumi kule.
> I saw more than 10 people there.

Two of these prepositions may be used without the possessives, thus becoming conjunctions or adverbs etc.:

kabla	before
zaidi	more (or can be used to denote a comparative)

'Kabla' is often used with the -JA- tense:

> Kabla hujaondoka, funga mlango.
> Before you leave, shut the door.
> or c.f. Kabla ya kuondoka, funga mlango.
> Before leaving, shut the door.

'Zaidi'

Nipe sukari zaidi.	Give me more sugar.
Yeye ni mrefu zaidi.	He is taller.
Mzigo huu ni mzito zaidi.	This load is heavier.
Kitabu hiki ni bora zaidi.	This book is better still.

'badala' and 'habari' are strictly speaking N-class nouns.

There are four more common prepositions which instead of taking the possessive 'ya', take instead the word 'na':

karibu na	close to, near to, nearly, almost
mbali na	far from, different to (*may* be heard with 'ya')
pamoja na	together with (lit. 'in one place with')
sawa na	equal to, the same as

> e.g. Hamisi anakaa karibu na mji.
> Hamisi lives close to the town.
> Nairobi ni mbali na London.
> Nairobi is far from London.
> Rafiki yangu amekuja pamoja na watoto wake.
> My friend has come together with his children.
> Kitabu changu ni sawa na chako.
> My book is the same as yours.

These may all be used without the word 'na' in which case they become adverbs etc.:

karibu	close
mbali	far
pamoja	together
sawa	equal, the same, similar

Sisi sote tunakaa karibu.	We all live close.
Tulikwenda mbali sana.	We went very far.
Watakuja wote pamoja.	They will come all together.
Mizigo hii ni sawa.	These loads are equal/the same.

Adverbs
These adverbs may also be heard commonly:
        kisha   and then, afterwards (cf. halafu, baadaye)

mbalimbali	different (cf. mbali na)
sawasawa	equally, just the same, just so, just right

e.g. Nenda mjini, nunua mboga, kisha rudi hapa.
   Go to town, buy vegetables, then come back here.
   Walikwenda mbalimbali.
   They went separately.
   Kusoma na kuandika ni mambo mbalimbali.
   Reading and writing are different matters.

Alone
There is a word meaning 'alone' which is 'pekee':

e.g. Alikuja pekee.	He came alone.
Mti ulisimama pekee.	The tree stood alone.

This word, however, is dropping from common usage, and is more frequently used as 'peke' followed by the appropriate personal possessive. It has the meaning of 'by'...'self'.

Peke yangu	By myself	Peke yetu	By ourselves
Peke yako	By yourself	Peke yenu	By yourselves
Peke yake	By himself/ herself/itself	Peke yao	By themselves

Examples:
Nimekuja peke yangu.	I have come by myself.
Watoto walirudi peke yao.	The children returned by themselves.
Mti ulianguka peke yake.	The tree fell by itself.

Conjunctions
ama ..... ama	either ..... or (cf. au)
wala ..... wala	neither ..... nor

'Ama' can be used as an exact alternative to 'au', but is more frequently used when several alternatives are listed.

Example:
   Unaweza kuchagua ama kitabu hiki, ama hiki, ama kile.
   You can choose either this book, this one, or that one.

'Wala' can *only* be used with a negative tense, and *must* be introduced by one:

   Huwezi kwenda wala Nairobi, wala Dar es Salaam.
   You may go neither to Nairobi, nor to Dar es Salaam.

(Notice that in Swahili it gives the impression of being a double negative.)

155

Because

We have already introduced 'kwa sababu' for 'because', and the learner is advised to keep to it until more accustomed to the language, but there are three other ways of saying 'because' in Swahili—'kwa ajili ya', 'kwa kuwa' and 'kwa maana ya'. They are all more or less interchangeable, though not all can be used in any particular context.

Kwa ajili ya

This may be used in the context of 'on account of' as follows:

> Kwa ajili ya mvua hatukuja
>> We did not come on account of the rain, or We did not come because of the rain.
>
> (using 'ya' followed by a noun)

> Kwa ajili ilinyesha mvua hatukuja.
>> We did not come because it rained.
>
> (no 'ya' because a verb following)

> Kwa ajili ya kunyesha mvua hatukuja.
>> We did not come because of it raining.
>
> (using 'ya' followed by a verbal noun)

(Compare the word order above with the examples below.)

Kwa maana ya and Kwa sababu ya

These may be directly interchanged with 'kwa ajili ya' with or without the word 'ya' as above. In some cases the 'kwa' may be omitted as shown below:

> Hatukuja kwa maana ya mvua.
> Hatukuja (kwa) sababu ya mvua.
> Hatukuja (kwa) maana ilinyesha mvua.
> Hatukuja (kwa) sababu ilinyesha mvua.
> Hatukuja kwa maana ya kunyesha mvua.
> Hatukuja (kwa) sababu ya kunyesha mvua.

Kwa kuwa

This may only be used with a verb (not verbal noun.)

> Hatukuja kwa kuwa ilinyesha mvua.
>> We did not come because it rained.

More examples:

> Unaweza kurudi ama leo ama kesho kwa maana ni mamoja kwangu.
>> You can return either today or tomorrow because it is all the same to me.

Lete mizigo yangu yote, pamoja na yake pia.
Bring all my luggage, together with his too.
Safisha chumba chao kabla hawajafika, kisha pika chakula.
Clean their room before they arrive, then cook the food.
Tafuta kisu changu mbele zaidi ya hapa.
Look for my knife further ahead than here.
Sisi hatupendi kuja peke yetu kwa sababu ya wanyama wakali.
We do not like coming alone (by ourselves) because of danger-
ous animals
Sikuweza kula wala kunywa cho chote.
I was unable to eat or drink anything at all.

Exercise 56

(a) *Translate:* Instead of; close to; before (of time); equal to; by myself; far
from; more than; just right; together with; concerning; after; neither . . .
nor.

(b) *Translate:* He can neither read nor write; you have done (just) right; they
went by themselves; near the tree; after three o'clock; more than ten; tell
him about the meeting; we arrived together; this book is the same as that
one; buy bread then come home; this tree and that one are different; he lives
far from me; we saw almost 200 animals; don't start before 2 o'clock; take
this book instead of that one; he likes tea sweeter; we came with the
children; try by yourself without any help; he is unable to come either
today, or tomorrow; either he goes or I shall.

(c) *Translate:* My vehicle has broken down near the river; he does not know
either English or Swahili; whether we stay or not, it is all the same to him;
they have come far alone without any help at all; we have bought many
different things because we live far from the town; after leaving Nairobi, we
continued more than 50 miles; have you not yet heard about my examination?; why do you not sit in the shade instead of standing in the fierce sun?;
come and see me before you leave; let us go and have a chat (converse)
together.

(d) *Translate:* Mganga anakaa karibu na mji; alisahau kunieleza habari ya
chama kile; nenda mbele zaidi; unaweza kwenda ama peke yako ama
pamoja na mtumishi wako; sikujua kwa sababu/kwa maana/kwa kuwa
hakuniambia; nimekuja badala yake; njoo kuniona kabla hujaondoka;
usiende karibu zaidi; hana wala ndugu wala rafiki; watu wawili wale
wanakaa pamoja.

49 Relatives—1

'Amba-' and infixes

The relatives 'who', 'whom' and 'which' exist in Swahili in the form of either an infix, or a suffix. Whichever it is, its form is the same. But nevertheless, the relative must take agreements with the subject or object to which it refers. The agreements are as follows:

M- Wa- class	sing.	-ye-
	plur.	-o-
M- Mi- class	sing.	-o-
	plur.	-yo-
Ki- Vi- class	sing.	-cho-
	plur.	-vyo-
N class	sing.	-yo-
	plur.	-zo-
Ma-	sing.	-lo-
	plur.	-yo-

(It will be noticed that, with the exception of the singular 'M- Wa-' class, they all end in an 'o'. Furthermore, the consonant preceding the 'o' is closely correlated to the subject prefix, except that 'u' and 'w' disappear in the relative.)

Using the relative

The relative is used constantly in Swahili, even though it may not occur in the corresponding English. For example, we would say in English 'The man I saw yesterday.' This would have to be said as 'The man whom I saw yesterday' in Swahili.

The relative is also frequently used where English would use a present or past participle.

'A broken chair' would have to be translated as 'A chair which is broken' or 'which has been broken'. 'A falling tree' would have to be translated at 'A tree which is falling'.

It is of the utmost importance to be well acquainted with the relative and its usage. There are many different ways in which the above relative agreements can be used both as an infix to a verb or suffix. Only certain tenses, however, may contain this infix within the verb.

Amba-

There is a stem which can be used with any verb, with any tense, which takes the relative as a suffix. It is

amba-   which means 'who', 'whom', or 'which'.

It is not only very common, but very simple to use. Its position in a sentence is immediately before the verb which requires the relative.

N.B. The word 'amba-' must NEVER start a sentence. It must always be preceded by the subject or object it qualifies, either in the form of a noun, pronoun or demonstrative.

Examples:

huyu ambaye atasema	this person who will speak
mtu ambaye alikuja jana	the person who came yesterday
mti ambao ulianguka	the tree which fell

(Relatives agreeing with objects will be dealt with later.)

Thus this construction can be used in any tense or context:

mtu ambaye anakuja	the person who is coming
watu ambao wanakuja	the people who are coming
mtu ambaye atakuja	the person who will come
watu ambao watakuja	the people who will come
mtu ambaye amekuja	the person who has come
watu ambao wamekuja	the people who have come
mtu ambaye alikuja	the person who came
watu ambao walikuja	the people who came
mtu ambaye haji	the person who is not coming
watu ambao hawaji	the people who are not coming
mtu ambaye hatakuja	the person who will not come
watu ambao hawatakuja	the people who will not come
mtu ambaye hakuja	the person who did not come
watu ambao hawakuja	the people who did not come
mtu ambaye hajaja	the person who has not yet come
watu ambao hawajaja	the people who have not yet come
mtu ambaye akija	the person who, if he comes, . . .
	or if the person who comes
watu ambao wakija	the people who, if they come, . . .
	or if the people who come
mtu ambaye lazima aje	the person who must come
watu ambao lazima waje	the people who must come
mtu ambaye lazima asije	the person who must not come
watu ambao lazima wasije	the people who must not come

(Note that in the last four examples above, the relative qualifies the verb 'ni' which is in fact omitted.)

Similarly, the same relatives are used with 1st and 2nd person verb forms:

mimi ambaye nilikuja	I who came
wewe ambaye ulikuja	you who (sing.) came
sisi ambao tulikuja	we who came
ninyi ambao mlikuja	you (pl.) who came

Things in other noun classes follow the same pattern:

mti ambao unafaa	a tree which is suitable
miti ambayo inafaa	trees which are suitable
kiti ambacho kilifaa	a chair which was suitable
viti ambavyo vilifaa	chairs which were suitable
nyumba ambayo itafaa	a house which will be suitable
nyumba ambazo zitafaa	houses which will be suitable
duka ambalo halifai	a shop which is not suitable, *or* an unsuitable shop
maduka ambayo hayafai	shops which are unsuitable, *or* unsuitable shops
	etc.

The verb 'to be' and 'to have' can also be used thus:

mimi ambaye ni mwalimu	I who am a teacher
mzungu ambaye ana watoto	the European who has children
wao ambao walikuwa vibarua	they who were labourers
viti ambavyo vilikuwa na miguu mitatu	chairs which had three legs

The Relative with Object

Where the relative has to agree with the object of a verb, the word 'amba-' may still be used, but there is a reversal of word order. The object noun has to come first, as in English, followed by 'amba-' followed by the subject noun (if there is one) then the verb. Occasionally, one may even hear the subject noun following the verb. Finally, the object infix is almost invariably inserted into the verb, even with things.

e.g.	Nilinunua vitu.	I bought things.
	Mimi ambaye nilinunua vitu.	I who bought things.
but	Vitu ambavyo nilivinunua.	The things (which) I bought.
	Vitabu ambavyo alivinunua Hamisi.	} The books (which) Hamisi bought.
or	Vitabu ambavyo Hamisi alivinunua.	}
	Watu ambao niliwaona.	The people whom I saw.
	Mimi ambaye waliniona.	I whom they saw.

(In the last five examples above, the relative agrees with the object.)

N.B. The verb 'to be' cannot take a relative object, and the verb 'to have' creates a special case which will be dealt with in chapter 51.

Examples:

Wale ambao watakwenda Moshi, wataona mlima wa Kilimanjaro.
Those who will go to Moshi will see Mount Kilimanjaro.
Gari ambalo nimelinunua ni zuri sana.
The vehicle which I have bought is very good.
Mizigo ambayo ilifika jana ni yangu.
The loads which arrived yesterday are mine.
Viazi ambavyo ulivinunua jana ni vibovu.
The potatoes you bought yesterday are rotten.

Exercise 57

(a) *Translate:* They who came; the clothes which were washed; the river we saw; the man who is wearing a hat; those who were late; we who have been paid; the book I read; the door which was opened; the food which was eaten; the insects which ate the food; the water which was brought; those who do not know; the valley which is not visible; eggs which are obtainable; the spear I bought; the animals the farmer keeps; the milk the cows give (put out); the mountain I climbed; he who is my cook; the flowers which are growing.

(b) *Translate:* Would you look for the knife which I lost yesterday; dogs which eat much meat have much strength; is there anyone here who has a pencil?; your friend who came here the day before yesterday has returned again; the milk I got this morning has gone bad; the letter I wrote the other day has not yet arrived; would the people who know English not say anything; the road which goes to Tanga has been closed because of mud; the mountain we climbed is called Mount Meru; the child who broke the window which you saw lives over there.

(c) *Translate:* Motokaa ambayo niliinunua; watoto ambao wanafundishwa na mwalimu yule; mtihani ambao ulikuwa mgumu; chumba ambacho hujakisafisha; mgeni ambaye alifika jana; nguo ambazo unazivaa; mguu ambao umevunjika; milima ambayo inaonekana; kisu ambacho kimepotea; yule ambaye anaitwa Hamisi; simu ambayo niliipokea jana; mtihani ambao tutaujaribu; mzee ambaye alikufa; sisi ambao ni wageni; visu ambavyo ni vikali; mti ambao ulianguka; gazeti ambalo ulilisoma; mchezo ambao watoto wataucheza; kamba ambayo ilikatika; dawa ambayo uliila.

The relative used as an infix (-NA- and -LI- tenses)

To all intents and purposes, the 'amba-' relative is probably the easiest form to use. But for those who wish to develop and improve their Swahili, it is important to know that the relative does exist in other forms, being principally used as a verbal infix. The actual relative element is identical, but instead of being added to 'amba-' outside the verb, it is placed between the tense sign and the verb stem. It can *only* however, be used with certain tense signs, namely the present -NA-tense, and the past simple -LI- tense. (A special form exists for the future tense, and one negative tense, but these will be dealt with separately.)

Examples:

Nili*ye*fanya	I who did (cf. Mimi ambaye nilifanya)
Nina*ye*fanya	I who do (cf. Mimi ambaye ninafanya)
Tuli*o*fanya	We who did (cf. Sisi ambao tulifanya)
Tuna*o*fanya	· We who do (cf. Sisi ambao tunafanya)
Kitu kina*cho*faa	A suitable thing (Something which is suitable)
Kitu kili*cho*faa	Something which was suitable

This relative infix does *not*, like the object infix, affect the 'infinitive' 'ku-' of monosyllabic verbs:

Ninayekuja	I who am coming
Waliokuwa	They who were
Chakula walichokula	The food they ate

N.B. This construction cannot be used with the present tense of 'kuwa'.

-NA- tense relative infix
M-WA- class

ni-na-ye-cheza	ninayecheza	I who am playing
u-na-ye-cheza	unayecheza	you who are playing
a-na-ye-cheza	anayecheza	he/she who is playing
tu-na-o-cheza	tunaocheza	we who are playing
m-na-o-cheza	mnaocheza	you who are playing
wa-na-o-cheza	wanaocheza	they who are playing

M-MI- class

u-na-o-baki	unaobaki	it which remains
i-na-yo-baki	inayobaki	they which remain

KI- VI- class

ki-na-cho-baki	kinachobaki	it which remains
vi-na-vyo-baki	vinavyobaki	they which remain

N class

i-na-yo-baki	inayobaki	it which remains
zi-na-zo-baki	zinazobaki	they which remain

MA- class

li-na-lo-baki	linalobaki	it which remains
ya-na-yo-baki	yanayobaki	they which remain

Relative infix with the -LI- tense
M- WA- class

ni-li-ye-cheza	niliyecheza	I who played
u-li-ye-cheza	uliyecheza	you who played
a-li-ye-cheza	aliyecheza	he/she who played

tu-li-o-cheza	tuliocheza	we who played
m-li-o-cheza	mliocheza	you who played
wa-li-o-cheza	waliocheza	they who played

M- MI- class
| u-li-o-baki | uliobaki | it which remained |
| i-li-yo-baki | iliyobaki | they which remained |

Ki- Vi- class
| ki-li-cho-baki | kilichobaki | it which remained |
| vi-li-vyo-baki | vilivyobaki | they which remained |

N class
| i-li-yo-baki | iliyobaki | it which remained |
| zi-li-zo-baki | zilizobaki | they which remained |

Ma- class
| li-li-lo-baki | lililobaki | it which remained |
| ya-li-yo-baki | yaliyobaki | they which remained |

N.B. It is also possible to insert the relative of object in the same way. e.g. Kitu nilichoona—The thing which I saw.

The verb 'ku-pita' with -LI- tense and relative is often used to mean 'last. . . .'.

e.g. mwaka uliopita   last year
     wiki iliyopita   last week
     siku zilizopita   the past days, i.e. in the past.

Use with object infix

It is possible to use this relative infix with these two tenses, together with an object infix (which *will* cause monosyllabic verbs to drop their 'infinitive' 'ku-'). In this case, the relative infix will precede the object infix:

walionipa . . . .   they who gave me . . . .
kitu kinachonifaa   something which suits me
wanyama niliowaona   animals which I saw (them)

The memorizer introduced in chapter 38 for knowing the order of all infixes, etc. can now be modified to 'S T R O V E', whose letters stand for:

    S   for Subject prefix
    T   for Tense sign
    R   for Relative infix
    O   for Object infix
    V   for Verb stem
    E   for End of verb for derivatives etc.

e.g. Aliyenikatia mkate.
   A-li-ye-ni-kat-i-a mkate.   (He who cut the bread for me.)
   S T R O V E

Examples:
   Maua yanayoota katika shamba hili ni mazuri sana.
   The flowers which are growing in this field are very nice.
   Mzee aliyekuja jana anataka kazi.
   The old man who came yesterday wants work.
   Mtu yule aliyeniuzia kitu hiki ni mwizi.
   The person who sold this thing to me is a thief.
   Chakula unachokula kilipikwa na mpishi uliyemleta jana.
   The food which you are eating was cooked by the cook whom
      you brought yesterday.
   Hii ni barua niliyoiandika mwenyewe.
   This is the letter which I wrote myself.
   Yule anayekuja sasa ni mke wangu.
   That person coming now is my wife.
   (That person who is coming now . . . .)

Exercise 58
(a) *Translate by inserting the relative particle as an infix within the verb:* They
who came; the clothes which were washed; the river we saw; the man who
is wearing a hat; those who were late; we who are being paid; the book I
read; the door which was opened; the food which was eaten; the insects
which ate the food; the water which was brought; those who knew; the
valley which is visible; eggs which are obtainable; the spear I bought; the
animals which the farmer keeps; the milk the cows give (out); the mountain
I climbed; he who was my cook; the flowers which are growing.

(b) *Write these sentences in Swahili first without, then with the word 'amba-':*
The cows which were in that field have all died; the water which you put on
the stove has boiled; the pencil which you gave me is broken; the wages
which are being paid are this month's; the children whom you see (them)
live in that village; those who want to go to Nairobi are who?; the material
which I bought the other day was very cheap; the seeds which I am planting
were bought in the shop which opened in town; in the days which passed
(i.e. in the past) people lived in the houses which you see there; the car
which passed me knocked down that old man who is lying at the side of the
road.

(c) *Translate:* Gari nililolinunua; watoto waliofundishwa na mwalimu huyu;
mtihani uliokuwa mgumu; chumba unachokisafisha; mgeni anayefika leo;
nguo ulizozivaa; mguu uliovunjika; milima iliyoonekana; kisu kilicho-
potea; yule anayeitwa Hamisi; simu ninayoipeleka; mtihani walioujaribu;
mzee aliyekufa; sisi tuliokuwa wageni; visu vilivyokuwa vikali; mti ulio-
anguka; gazeti unalolisoma; mchezo watoto wanaoucheza; kamba iliyo-
katika; dawa unayoitumia sasa.

Relative infix with future tense
Beside the two tenses just dealt with, the relative infix may be used
within a verb containing the future tense -TA-. But this is only
permissible provided an extra syllable '-ka-' is also inserted:

| Ni-ta-*ka*-ye-fanya | Nitakayefanya | I who shall do |
| Mti u-ta-*ka*-o-anguka | Mti utakaoanguka | The tree which will fall |

It is most important to remember this extra syllable, since it would constitute a major 'howler' to omit it. Its origin is connected with the verb 'ku-taka'. It does not affect either the relative or object infixes in any way. If the relative is used on 'amba-' then there is no necessity to insert this extra syllable in the verb.

Conjugation of future tense with relative infix:

ni-taka-ye-fanya	nitakayefanya	I who shall do
u-taka-ye-fanya	utakayefanya	you who will do
a-taka-ye-fanya	atakayefanya	he/she who will do
tu-taka-o-fanya	tutakaofanya	we who shall do
m-taka-o-fanya	mtakaofanya	you who will do
wa-taka-o-fanya	watakaofanya	they who will do

M-Mi- class
| u-taka-o-faa | utakaofaa | it which will suffice |
| i-taka-yo-faa | itakayofaa | they which will suffice |

Ki- Vi- class
| ki-taka-cho-faa | kitakachofaa | it which will suffice |
| vi-taka-vyo-faa | vitakavyofaa | they which will suffice |

N class
| i-taka-yo-faa | itakayofaa | it which will suffice |
| zi-taka-zo-faa | zitakazofaa | they which will suffice |

Ma- class
| li-taka-lo-faa | litakalofaa | it which will suffice |
| ya-taka-yo-faa | yatakayofaa | they which will suffice |

And it is, of course, again possible to insert relatives of object in the same manner:

| | kitabu nitakachokinunua | the book which I shall buy |
| *or* | kitabu ambacho nitakinunua | the book which I shall buy |

Examples:
Wageni watakaofika kesho watakuja kuniona.
    The strangers who will arrive tomorrow will come to see me.
Miti itakayoangushwa itatumiwa hapa.
    The trees which will be felled will be used here.
Motokaa nitakayoinunua itakuwa ghali sana.
    The car which I shall buy will be very expensive.
Mwanamke nitakayemwoa lazima apendeze.
    The woman whom I will marry must be attractive (pleasing).

Exercise 59

(a) *Translate without the use of the word 'amba-':* The meeting which will start; the letter I shall write; the game which will be played; the guests who will arrive; the food which will be eaten; the presents I will give her; the salary you will be paid; the house I shall buy; the rent which will be paid; the water you will drink; the chit which you will be given; the journey we shall make; the pressure lamp which will be taken; the grass which will grow; the children who will play; things which will be suitable; the person who will be cook; the fire which will burn; the luggage they will take; the European who will come.

(b) *Translate the following first without, then with the word 'amba-':* The meeting which will start tomorrow will be short; the food which I shall bring will be ready soon; the journey we shall make will start on Thursday; the books the students will buy have not yet arrived; the name which I shall give him will be John; I shall come back for the box which the carpenter will finish tomorrow; the children who are going to Dar es Salaam tomorrow must come here first; the time which it will take will be only short; the doctor who will come today will arrive at 3 p.m.; the fruit which this tree will bear will be sold on the market.

(c) *Translate without using 'amba-' except where necessary:* The food he cooked; the book I am reading; the work he will do; the towns I have seen; the people who were forgotten; the nails which were not suitable; we who shall not be there; the examination I tried; the guests who are coming tomorrow; the flowers we planted; the milk which has gone bad; the door which will be open; the clothes he ironed; the child who was called Michael; the language we are learning.

(d) *Translate:* Maji yatakayotosha; maziwa utakayoleta; mlango utakaofunguliwa; barua nitakazoziandika; mizigo itakayokuwa mizito; sehemu utakazozisafisha leo; chama tutakachokiingia; faida watakayoipata; sisi tutakaokunywa kahawa; bonde litakaloonekana; nitapanda gari litakalofika saa sita; tutatumia miti yote itakayoangushwa; wote wenye majina yatakayoitwa waje hapa; mgeni atakayefika ni rafiki yangu; mshahara utakaopata utakuwa shilingi nne kwa kutwa; chakula nitakachokichukua lazima kitoshe kwa siku tatu; ninamngoja mgeni atakayefika saa yo yote; kisu nitakachokitumia ni chako; mbwa nitakayempata atakuwa mkali; kazi watakayoifanya itakuwa ngumu.

Relative in questions

As was mentioned in chapter 30 certain interrogatory words, in particular 'Nani?' are placed at the end of a question where possible. In a long sentence, it is possible to place 'Nani?' at the end of a question only by using the relative. We can do the same thing in English too:

> *Who* are the children who want to go to Nairobi?
> *or* The children who (relative) want to go to Nairobi are *who*?

These questions may be translated in exactly the same way in Swahili.

> Nani ni watoto wanaotaka kwenda Nairobi?
> Watoto wanaotaka kwenda Nairobi ni nani?

In Swahili, because it suits the interrogatory intonation better, the latter of the two is preferred so that more stress can be placed on the final word.

WHOSE? This word is used in English to express 'of who?' In Swahili it is expressed as '-a nani?',

e.g.	Kitabu cha nani?	Whose book?
	Watoto wa nani?	Whose children?

WHOSE as a relative statement in Swahili uses a relative plus a personal possessive. e.g.
The person whose children came yesterday.
Mtu ambaye watoto wake walikuja jana.

Examples:
Nani alikuja jana?
Who came yesterday?
Yule aliyekuja jana ni nani?
That person who came yesterday is who?
Unataka kumwona nani?
Whom do you want to see?
Unayetaka kumwona ni nani?
He whom you want to see is who?
Mizigo uliyoichukua ni ya nani?
Whose are the loads you took?

Exercise 60

(a) *Translate first without 'amba-' where possible, then with:* Who is coming with me? who are the people who arrived yesterday? who are the children you will see tomorrow? this dog that has not eaten is whose? who will speak at our meeting? who wants to buy a good vehicle? who has not yet heard the news? who are the pupils who failed to come on Saturday? whose is this book? who has broken this expensive cup?

(b) *Translate:* Yule atakayefanya kazi hii ni nani? mzee aliyekufa alikuwa nani? mtoto ambaye alilivunja dirisha hili ni nani? mgeni yule anayesimama mlangoni ni nani? vibarua ambao hawajalipwa ni nani? wanachama ambao hawakuenda mkutanoni ni nani? mwenye saa ni nani? yule aliyekupa zawadi hii ni nani? aliyechukua kalamu yangu ni nani? yule atakayeolewa ni nani?

The negative relative

The negative tense sign -SI- is used in verbs containing a relative infix. This -SI- has already been met in the negative subjunctive. It is preceded, as in the latter tense, by the *affirmative* subject prefix. The main disadvantage of this negative relative is that it is the only negative tense which can be used with a relative infix, and it can therefore stand for any of the tenses, past, present or future. Only context can give any suggestion as to which is meant. If there is still likely to be any confusion, or if it is necessary to stress a particular tense in the negative, then 'amba-' has to be used with the appropriate negative tense.

Thus 'wasiofanya' could mean either

> they who will not do
> or they who are not doing
> or they who did not do
> or they who have not done

The tense fully conjugates thus:

M- Wa- class

ni-si-ye-fanya	nisiyefanya	I who do not do, etc.
u-si-ye-fanya	usiyefanya	you who do not do, etc.
a-si-ye-fanya	asiyefanya	he/she who does not do etc.
tu-si-o-fanya	tusiofanya	we who do not do, etc.
m-si-o-fanya	msiofanya	you who do not do, etc.
wa-si-o-fanya	wasiofanya	they who do not do, etc.

M- Mi- class (Arabic verbs do not create any exception)

| u-si-o-baki | usiobaki | it which does not remain, etc. |
| i-si-yo-baki | isiyobaki | they which do not remain, etc. |

Ki- Vi- class

| ki-si-cho-baki | kisichobaki | it which does not remain, etc. |
| vi-si-vyo-baki | visivyobaki | they which do not remain, etc. |

N class

| i-si-yo-baki | isiyobaki | it which does not remain, etc. |
| zi-si-zo-baki | zisizobaki | they which do not remain, etc. |

Ma- class

| li-si-lo-baki | lisilobaki | it which does not remain, etc. |
| ya-si-yo-baki | yasiyobaki | they which do not remain, etc. |

Monosyllabic verbs *retain* their 'infinitive' 'ku-'

wasiokula   They who do not eat, etc.

N.B. The verb 'to be' has its own version for present tense (see page 175). Thus 'Nisiyekuwa' would only mean 'I who was not' or 'I who will not be'.

Once again, of course, the same pattern is followed when using an object relative within the verb:

Watoto usiowaona.   The children whom you did not see.

Examples:
Wale wasiojua Kiingereza wainue mkono.
Those who do not know English, raise (their) hand.
or Those who did not know English, . . .
or Those who will not know English, . . .
but
Wale ambao hawajui Kiingereza . . .
can now only mean 'Those who do not know English . . .'
Nenda kutafuta wale wasiofika.
Go to look for those who have not arrived.

(This is the most obvious sense, but it could also mean 'Go to look for those who will not arrive/who are not arriving/who did not arrive.)

Usiniletee kitu kisichofaa.
Don't bring me something which does not suit me. (Don't bring me something unsuitable.)

(This being the most obvious sense, but it could also mean 'Don't bring me something which will not suit me/has not suited me/did not suit me'.)

'Na' contractions with things
As mentioned in chapter 18 the word 'na' meaning 'with' or 'and' is generally contracted with the self-standing pronouns. (e.g. na mimi = nami).
As has been stated, there is no word in Swahili, for 'it'. Therefore in order to be able to say 'with it', an alternative construction has to be used. This construction consists of combining the word 'na' with the appropriate relative as a suffix:

	Singular		*Plural*	
M- Mi- class	nao	with it	nayo	with them
Ki- Vi- class	nacho	with it	navyo	with them
N class	nayo	with it	nazo	with them
Ma- class	nalo	with it	nayo	with them
	(or 'and it')		(or 'and them')	

It can now be seen that 'naye' (with him) and 'nao' (with them) are quite regularly formed by 'na' plus the relative.
This construction is used frequently with the verb 'to have' in relative form. This will be dealt with toward the end of Chapter 51.

Examples:
Kisu, umekuja nacho?
The knife, have you come with it?
Mizigo yote hii, umesafiri nayo yote?
All these loads, have you travelled with them all?

Nimeweza kuandika nayo, kalamu hii.
I have been able to write with it, this pencil.
Nimenunua gari jipya, nalo linanifaa sana.
I have bought a new car, and it does me very well.
Umevileta vikombe? Hamisi amekuja navyo.
Have you brought the cups? Hamisi has come with them.
Ninakihitaji kitabu hiki. Usiende nacho.
I need this book. Don't go with it.

Exercise 61

(a) *Translate the following using firstly the '-si-' tense, secondly 'amba-':* They who did not come; we who do not know; I who have not climbed; the clothes which were not washed; the food which was not cooked; the door which will not be closed; you who did not try; we who are not able; you (pl.) who are not working; the luggage which was not brought.

(b) *Translate the following to agree with the nouns in brackets:* With it (bread); with them (letters); with it (a flower); with it (milk); with them (things); with it (pencil); with them (loads); with it (a book); with them (children); with them (vehicles).

(c) *Write these sentences in Swahili first without, then with 'amba-':* People who don't smoke have much strength; the thief who was not caught is living in the bush now; the children who will not come are those who cannot read; this is a Muslim who does not eat beef; there is another vehicle which has not arrived; I shall destroy the trees which do not bear; there were a few women who did not go away; I do not like flowers which do not smell nice; call the labourers who have not given me their chits; I do not need a person who does not try hard.

(d) *Translate:* Tutatumia miti isiyoangushwa mwaka mwingine; tandika vitanda sasa usivyotandika asubuhi; nitajaribu tena mtihani nisiofaula mwezi wa Januari; wale wasiokwenda jana, waende leo; mizigo isiyofika jana italetwa baadaye; wale wasiokuwa hapa jana wasome karatasi hii; mguu mmoja ulivunjika, lakini ule usiovunjika una kidonda kibaya sana; pana mkutano leo kwa wale wasiojua kusoma na kuandika; mnyama yule asiyekula chakula chake ni mgonjwa; lazima tuseme Kiswahili kwa ajili ya hawa wasioweza kusema Kiingereza.

(e) *Translate:* Barua zilizoandikwa jana zimepotea; wanawake watakaofika kesho ni walimu; mimea ambayo mkulima yule aliipanda mwezi wa tatu haitafaa; mlima ambao hajaupanda ni Kilimanjaro; maji haya yaliyoletwa na Ali yamekuwa machafu; ua alilonileta linanukia sana; chama ambacho kilifunguliwa jana ni kwa wanaume tu; siwezi leo, kwa sababu chakula nilichokula jana kilikuwa kibaya; lugha tunayojifunza si ngumu kama Kiingereza; wote wasiokwenda Dodoma juzi wangoje nje.

50 Verbs—7

Additional verbs

The following verbs will be found useful, provided the ones previously given have been mastered:

ku-changanya	to mix
ku-cheka	to laugh
ku-chimba	to excavate, dig
ku-chinja	to slaughter
ku-fahamu	to know, understand
ku-gawa	to divide, share out
ku-jenga	to build
ku-kusanya	to collect, gather up
ku-kuta	to find, meet
ku-kwama	to get stuck (in mud etc.)
ku-linda	to guard, protect
ku-ng'oa	to uproot, pull out
ku-nyamaza	to keep quiet, silent
ku-nyoa	to shave hair
ku-ogopa	to fear, be afraid
ku-onyesha	to show, point out (causative of 'ku-ona')
ku-pona	to get better
ku-ruka	to jump, fly
ku-shika	to catch, hold (with less effort than 'kamata')
ku-shona	to sew
ku-sikitika	to be sorry, grieve
ku-sukuma	to push
ku-sumbua	to trouble, annoy
ku-tangulia	to precede, go in front/before
ku-tapika	to vomit
ku-tengeneza	to repair, put together
ku-tia	to put (same use as 'ku-weka')
ku-tuma	to send
ku-tumaini	to hope
ku-tupa	to throw, throw away
ku-ua	to kill (*not* 'slaughter', which see above)
ku-uma	to bite, to be in pain, sting, hurt
ku-vuja	to leak, run out (*not* run short of)
ku-vuka	to cross
ku-vuna	to harvest, gather a crop in, reap
ku-wahi	to be early
ku-ziba	to shut off, cork off, block off
ku-zima	to extinguish
ku-zunguka	to go round, encircle

Exercise 62

(a) *Translate:* To precede; to keep silent; to go round; to cross; to shave; to get stuck; to mix; to divide; to fear; to hope; to throw; to be early; to harvest; to build; to slaughter; to point out; to sew; to push; to vomit; to repair; to bite; to guard; to understand; to laugh; to extinguish; to leak; to uproot; to annoy; to fly; to sting.

(b) *Translate:* Slaughter that hen; don't annoy me!; if you cross that bridge; would you be early tomorrow; that dog bit him; don't extinguish that light; would you (pl.) precede; that patient has got better; keep quiet!; mix this medicine together with the food; we are very sorry; throw this outside!; this leg hurts; he wants to extract this tooth; don't forget to gather up those papers; the dog has vomited; my vehicle has got stuck in that mud; would you please push my car; my watch has been repaired; they are hoping that they will build their house here.

(c) *Translate:* Ku-tuma; ku-ua; ku-shika; ku-kusanya; ku-tia; ku-chimba; ku-fahamu; ku-ogopa; ku-vuna; ku-ziba; ku-pona; ku-kuta; ku-nyoa; ku-tupa; ku-vuja; ku-tangulia; ku-kwama; ku-gawa; ku-vuka; ku-tengeneza; ku-linda; ku-ruka; ku-tuma; ku-wahi; ku-zima; ku-ng'oa; ku-cheka; ku-shona; ku-uma; ku-sikitika.

(d) *Translate:* Tumechimba mfereji huu kwa sababu ya maji haya; yule aliyetupa takataka hii hapa ni nani?; wageni wale wamezunguka nchi hii yote; debe hili halivuji; msiogope kushika kitu hiki; ninasikitika, huwezi kuvuka mto huu; ukichoma majani haya yaliokusanywa, zima moto kabla hujaondoka; nikituma barua leo, ninatumaini kupata jibu kesho kutwa; ukimkuta njiani, mwambie akuonyeshe mti uliong'olewa; gari lililoharibika limekwisha tengenezwa sasa.

51 Relatives — 2

The general relative

A special form of the relative exists when a relative is required in an indefinite present tense. For example in a sentence such as — 'Cows which eat grass' or 'Farmers who grow crops'. This is a distinct tense as compared with the present definite whose tense sign is -NA-.

This specialised relative tense is called the General Relative. It has no tense sign as such, and instead, the relative is added on to the end of the verb stem as a suffix. The normal subject prefix is added directly on to the verb stem. Thus the verb 'ku-cheka' would conjugate:

ni-cheka-ye	nichekaye	I who laugh
u-cheka-ye	uchekaye	you who laugh
a-cheka-ye	achekaye	he/she who laughs
tu-cheka-o	tuchekao	we who laugh
m-cheka-o	mchekao	you who laugh
wa-cheka-o	wachekao	they who laugh

In other nouns classes this tense conjugates thus:

M- Mi- class

| u-faa-o | ufaao | it which suits |
| i-faa-yo | ifaayo | they which suit |

Ki- Vi- class

| ki-faa-cho | kifaacho | it which suits |
| vi-faa-vyo | vifaavyo | they which suit |

N class

| i-faa-yo | ifaayo | it which suits |
| zi-faa-zo | zifaazo | they which suit |

Ma- class

| li-faa-lo | lifaalo | it which suits |
| ya-faa-yo | yafaayo | they which suit |

N.B. Remember that by adding a syllable on to the end of a verb, the stress will also move up a syllable.

Arabic verbs are treated in a similar manner:

ni-fikiri-ye	nifikiriye	I who think
a-jibu-ye	ajibuye	he/she who answers
	etc.	

Monosyllabic verbs, however, drop their 'infinitive' 'ku-':

ni-ja-ye	nijaye	I who come
tu-la-o	tulao	we who eat
u-ja-o	ujao	it which comes (M- Mi- class)
zi-ja-zo	zijazo	they which come (N class)

N.B. (1) This construction is very commonly used to translate the word 'next' (i.e. the one which comes).

e.g. mwezi ujao	next month (the month which comes)
mwaka ujao	next year (the year which comes)
wiki ijayo	next week (the week which comes)
alhamisi ijayo	next Thursday (Thursday which comes)

N.B. (2) We cannot use the verbs 'to be' and 'to have' in this form, since a special construction is required.

Thus, to return to our original sentence, 'Cows which eat grass' this would be translated as 'Ng'ombe walao majani', and 'Farmers who grow crops' 'Wakulima waoteshao mimea'.

Examples:

Mwalimu afundishaye watoto wale . . .
The teacher who teaches those children . . .

Nyumba zijengwazo katika nchi hii . . .
Houses which are built in this country . . .
Mtu alindwaye ni Bwana Jones.
The person who is protected is Mr. Jones.
Mkutano utaanza Jumanne ijayo.
The meeting will start next Tuesday
Siku zijazo zitakuwa na mvua nyingi.
The following days will have much rain.
(The days which come will have much rain).
Nilifika mwaka uliopita, nitaondoka mwaka ujao.
I arrived last year, I shall leave next year.
(I arrived the year which passed.)

Exercise 63

(a) *Translate:* Those who fear; we who build; dogs who vomit; vehicles which
get stuck; a person who laughs; a debe-can which leaks; a leg which hurts;
food which is mixed; rubbish which is collected; letters which are sent;
people who annoy me; animals which are slaughtered; a door which is shut;
next year; next week; people who eat badly; next month; the doctor who
comes on Tuesdays; a book which is read; beds which are suitable.

(b) *Translate:* Bring me a suitable knife (a knife which is suitable); the things
which are sold in that shop are very cheap; bring your friend who is called
Hamisi; the people who live here are Americans; I shall marry the person
whom I love; he will help those who help themselves; the vehicles which
stop here all go to Nairobi; the road which goes round that mountain is not
good; we do not like people who are late; Europeans who come to
Tanzania help to build the nation.

(c) *Translate:* Wadudu waumao; siku zijazo; mimea ipandwayo hapa; nguo
zishonwazo vizuri; watoto wanyamazao; mtu ang'oaye meno; Jumapili
ijayo; maji yachemkayo; wagonjwa walalao; kijana aitwaye Juma; ua
linukialo; wanaume waoao; sisi tusomao sana; daraja livukalo mto; watu
wavutao sigara; wazee wawezao kusoma; maji yapatikanayo hapa; pombe
inywewayo sehemu hizi; kisu kikatacho vibaya; ndege warukao juu sana.

The relative with the verb 'to be'

Present tense

It will be remembered that the normal present tense of the verb 'to be'
is in general simply 'ni' (chapter 19).

When a relative is required, however, we have to use an entirely
different construction, using an old form of the verb which is never
now used except in this case. The stem is '-li', not to be confused with
the past simple tense sign. It is used in the form of the General
Relative. Thus the subject prefix is placed directly onto the verb stem
('-li-' in this case) and the appropriate relative added as a suffix. Thus:

ni-li-ye	niliye	I who am
u-li-ye	uliye	you who are
a-li-ye	aliye	he/she who is

tu-li-o	tulio	we who are
m-li-o	mlio	you who are
wa-li-o	walio	they who are

M- Mi- class

u-li-o	ulio	it which is
i-li-yo	iliyo	they which are

Ki- Vi- class

ki-li-cho	kilicho	it which is
vi-li-vyo	vilivyo	they which are

N class

i-li-yo	iliyo	it which is
zi-li-zo	zilizo	they which are

Ma- class

li-li-lo	lililo	it which is
ya-li-yo	yaliyo	they which are

Examples:

Mwite mtu aliye mganga.
  Call someone who is a Doctor.
Sisi tulio wageni hapa, hatujui njia.
  We who are strangers here, do not know the way.
Lete kiti kilicho pale.
  Bring the chair which is over there.
Angusha miti iliyo mirefu.
  Fell the trees which are tall.
Usilete mizigo iliyo mizito.
  Don't bring loads which are heavy.
Maduka yaliyo Nairobi ni mazuri kabisa.
  The shops which are in Nairobi are extremely good.

N.B. With all other tenses, the relative may be used as with the other monosyllabic verbs, apart from the present negative. Again, remember that 'Ninayekuwa' means 'I who am becoming' and due to its meaning, the relative is rarely used with the -NA- tense of this verb.

Present negative

Similarly, it will be recalled that the negative of this verb is simply SI in the present tense (see chapter 19). But where a relative is required with it, again the general relative is used, and -SI- becomes the 'stem' of the verb:

ni-si-ye	nisiye	I who am not
u-si-ye	usiye	you who are not
a-si-ye	asiye	he/she who is not

175

tu-si-o	tusio	we who are not
m-si-o	msio	you who are not
wa-si-o	wasio	they who are not

M- Mi- class
u-si-o	usio	it which is not
i-si-yo	isiyo	they which are not

Ki- Vi- class
ki-si-cho	kisicho	it which is not
vi-si-vyo	visivyo	they which are not

N class
i-si-yo	isiyo	it which is not
zi-si-zo	zisizo	they which are not

Ma- class
li-si-lo	lisilo	it which is not
ya-si-yo	yasiyo	they which are not

Examples:
  Sipendi mtu asiye mpishi.
    I do not want anybody who is not a cook.
  Watu wasio wanachama hawawezi kuingia.
    People who are not members cannot enter.
  Mpe mtoto kisu kisicho kikali.
    Give the child a knife which is not sharp.
  Tafuta vitu visivyo hapa.
    Look for the things which are not here.
  Ukisoma kwa taa zisizo kali, utaharibu macho.
    If you read with lamps which are not bright you will damage
    the eyes.

  Similarly, other negative tenses with a relative would use the
negative relative tense, whose sign is -SI-.

  Nisiyekuwa – I who was not/who will not be, etc.

It is, of course, possible in both the affirmative and negative tenses to
use 'amba-' and the verb 'to be' in the normal way:

e.g. Mwite mtu ambaye ni mganga = Mwite mtu aliye mganga.
  Lete kiti ambacho kipo pale = Lete kiti kilicho pale.
  Sipendi mtu ambaye si mpishi = Sipendi mtu asiye mpishi.
  Tafuta vitu ambavyo havipo hapa = Tafuta vitu visivyo hapa.

'Amba-' with these tenses, however, is not very often used in practice.

Exercise 64

(a) *Translate:* Children who are small; loads which are heavy; mountains which are high; things which are expensive; a door which is open; a basket which is empty; a stranger who is here; eggs which are cheap; water which is clean; shoes which are red; clothes which are dirty; news which is good; letters which are yours; a pencil which is mine; a book which is Hamisi's; smoke which is black; people who are late (careful!); a stranger who is German; the person who is last; the nation which is ours.

(b) *Translate:* An examination which is not difficult; work which is not good; a person who is not a European; books which are not mine; a vehicle which is not new; water which is not hot; a salary which is not large; people who are not sick; chairs which are not suitable (careful!); things which are not equal; a shop which is not near; fields which are not ours; a valley which is not wide; youths who are not Masai; sun which is not fierce; a well which is not deep; bread which is not white; servants who are not trustworthy; replies which are not ready; plates which are not clean.

(c) *Translate first with, then without, 'amba-':* The mountain which is over there is Kilimanjaro; bring the pillow which is on my bed; have you seen the fire which is on the mountain?; the man who is in that house is a stranger; I need only flowers which are red; would you give me the paper which is on the table; the houses which are the property of Hamisi have all burnt; the thorns which are on that tree have poison (sumu); you must drink only water which is clean; a well which is deep has cold water.

(d) *Translate first with, then without, 'amba-:* Everyone except those who are not drivers may leave; don't eat food which is not good; don't drink water which is not clean; write the names of the people who are not here today; give that child a load which is not heavy; don't use things which are not yours; you cannot use butter which is not soft; a knife which is not sharp does not cut well; don't bring me letters which are not mine; he cannot give out answers which are not easy.

(e) *Translate:* Kitambaa kisicho rahisi; mali zilizo zetu; miguu isiyo safi; vikombe visivyo vikavu; habari zilizo za kweli; chumba kilicho kidogo; mwalimu aliye mwema; duka lililo bora; kifaru aliye mkali; zulia lisilo safi; kisu kisicho changu; nyumba iliyo yao; kikapu kisicho kitupu; kazi iliyo bure; wote walio hapa; wengine walio mbali; lugha iliyo rahisi; jambo lililo la siri; samaki walio wa bahari; ng'ombe wasio zao.

(f) *Translate:* Sipendi chakula kisichopikwa vizuri; sitawaona watu watakaokuwa hapa kesho; hakuleta vitu visivyokuwa tayari; walitumia gari lililokuwa pale; alichukua kitabu kisichokuwa chake; tuliwauza ng'ombe wasiokuwa wa mkulima yule; mlango uliokuwa wazi jana umefungwa leo; kipande kilichotumiwa kilikuwa bure; alikuwa na motokaa isiyokuwa nzuri sana; mbwa mwenye miguu iliyokuwa michafu sana aliingia chumba.

The relative with 'to have'

Present tense

Up till now, no difference has been encountered between the relative when it agrees with the object, and the relative when it agrees with the subject.

With the verb 'to have', however, in all tenses a difference is made between the relative when agreeing with the subject, and the object.

Relative in agreement with the subject

When the relative agrees with the subject, no change is made from the normal construction used until now. Remember that the verb infinitive is 'kuwa na' and that it really means 'to be with'. When used with a relative, the word 'na' is *always* kept separate, even in the present tense (c.f. Ch. 20).

Present affirmative tense

The 'to be' portion of this verb is used as with the verb 'to be', and 'na' is added as a separate word:

niliye na	I who have (I who am with)
uliye na	you who have
aliye na	he/she who has
tulio na	we who have
mlio na	you who have
walio na	they who have

M- Mi- class

ulio na	it which has
iliyo na	they which have

Ki- Vi class

kilicho na	it which has
vilivyo na	they which have

N class

iliyo na	it which has
zilizo na	they which have

Ma- class

lililo na	it which has
yaliyo na	they which have

Present negative

M- Wa- class

nisiye na	I who have not
usiye na	you who have not
asiye na	he/she who has not
tusio na	we who have not
msio na	you who have not
wasio na	they who have not

M- Mi- class

usio na	it which has not
isiyo na	they which have not

Ki- Vi- class
kisicho na   it which has not
visivyo na   they which have not

N class
isiyo na   it which has not
zisizo na   they which have not

Ma- class
lisilo na   it which has not
yasiyo na   they which have not

Past simple tense
niliyekuwa na   I who had
waliokuwa na   they who had
iliyokuwa na   it which had ('N' class)
zilizokuwa na   they which had ('N' class)

Future tense
nitakayekuwa na   I who shall have
watakaokuwa na   they who will have
itakayokuwa na   it which will have ('N' class)
zitakazokuwa na   they which will have ('N' class)

Negative tense
nisiyekuwa na   I who did/shall not have
wasiokuwa na   they who did/will not have
isiyokuwa na   it which did/will not have ('N' class)
zisizokuwa na   they which did/will not have ('N' class)

N.B. The present tense '-na-' is never used with the relative of 'to have'. Thus 'Ninayekuwa na' does not exist. Instead they only use 'Niliye na' etc.

Once again, the relative can alternatively be used on 'amba-', in which case the verb 'kuwa na' would be treated normally being without a relative.

e.g. Mtu ambaye ana watoto = Mtu aliye na watoto . . .
A person who has children . . .
Mtu ambaye atakuwa na watoto = Mtu atakayekuwa na
watoto.
A person who will have children.

Examples:
Watu walio na ng'ombe wana mali.
People who have cattle, have wealth.
Mtu aliye na kofia ni mwalimu wangu.
The person who has the hat is my teacher.

Lete kiti kile kilicho na miguu mitatu.
Bring that chair which has three legs.
Usilete vikombe visivyo na visahani.
Don't bring cups which have no saucers.
Mti uliokuwa na miiba umeanguka.
The tree which had thorns has fallen.
Nyumba zitakazokuwa na vyumba vingi zitanifaa.
The houses which will have many rooms will suit me.

*N.B. It will be noted that in the present affirmative tense, the word
'-enye' could be substituted without changing the sense or meaning of
the sentence:*

Watu wenye ng'ombe = Watu walio na ng'ombe.
Mtu mwenye kofia = Mtu aliye na kofia.
Kiti chenye miguu mitatu = Kiti kilicho na miguu mitatu.

The present negative of this verb could similarly be substituted by the
word 'bila'.

Kikombe bila kisahani = Kikombe kisicho na kisahani.
A cup without a saucer = A cup which has no saucer.

In other tenses, the verb 'to have' has to be used, otherwise the tense
could not be shown.

Exercise 65

(a) *Translate:* They who have children; the leg which has a sore; the basket
which has potatoes; the fields which have crops; the beds which have
pillows; houses which have many rooms; a hoe which has a long handle; I
who had many difficulties; a society which will have many members; days
which had no rain.

(b) *Translate first with, then without 'amba-', then using '-enye' or 'bila' if
appropriate:* I who have a wife at home get good food!; those who had
letters yesterday, raise their hands; meat which has no salt is not good;
don't bring me food which has no heat; trees which will have many flowers,
will have much fruit; where is a shop which has bread?; work which has no
profit is useless; homeless people will be given help; would those who have
difficulties please wait outside; the roads which will have much mud are not
suitable.

(c) *Translate:* Kazi isiyokuwa na faida; chai iliyo na sukari; gari lililo na mzigo
mkubwa; mashamba yatakayokuwa na mimea mingi; mtu asiyekuwa na
kitu cho chote; barua iliyokuwa na habari nyingi; Mwislamu aliye na wake
wawili; mji ulio na wenyeji wachache; mzee asiye na nguvu; mito isiyo na
maji tele.

The relative in agreement with the object

When the relative within the verb 'to have' agrees with the object, not
only does the 'to be' part of the verb have to take the relative, but it is

also added on to the word 'na' as shown in the last section of chapter 49, in all tenses.

Remember that in these cases, the object noun precedes the verb, and the subject noun follows it.

This construction is best shown by examples:

Kitabu nilicho nacho.	The book which I have.
cf. Mimi niliye na kitabu.	I who have a book.
Watoto nilio nao.	The children whom I have.
cf. Mimi niliye na watoto.	I who have children.
Mke niliye naye.	The wife I have ('-ye' here agrees with 'mke' not 'ni-').
cf. Mimi niliye na mke.	I who have a wife (here, the '-ye' agrees with 'ni-')
Nyumba niliyokuwa nayo.	The house I had.
cf. Mimi niliyekuwa na nyumba.	I who had a house.
Shida nitakazokuwa nazo.	The difficulties I shall have.
cf. Mimi nitakayekuwa na shida.	I who shall have difficulties.
Kitu nisicho nacho	Something I don't have.
cf. Mimi nisiye na kitu.	I who have nothing.

Using 'Amba-'

Even if the word 'amba-' is being used, the relative particle must still be added to the word 'na', *except* when used in the present tense negative:

Kitu ambacho sikuwa nacho.	Something which I did not have.
Kitu ambacho sitakuwa nacho.	Something which I shall not have.
But Kitu ambacho sina.	Something which I do not have.
Kitu ambacho nilikuwa nacho.	Something which I had.
Kitu ambacho nitakuwa nacho.	Something which I shall have.
Kitu ambacho ninacho	Something which I have.

N.B. Amba is however rarely used in these cases, due to preference for:

Kitu nilicho nacho—Something which I have.

Use of the verb 'to have'

The present affirmative tense of the verb 'to have' has, in correct Swahili, a special form of use which is, strictly speaking, ungrammatical. The form consists of adding the relative particle on to the 'na' ending to agree with the object possessed, even though the phrase may not have any suggestion of a relative.

e.g.	Unacho kisu?	Have you a knife?
	Ninacho.	I have one.
	Wageni wale wanayo mizigo.	Those guests have luggage.
	Tunazo barua nyingi.	We have much mail.

In each of the above cases, except the second, it would not be considered a major error to omit the relative particle, and the question or statements would be perfectly understood. But in the reply 'I have one' we cannot say simply in Swahili 'Nina', because it really means 'I am with'. Even in English we would not say 'I am with'. We would go on to state who, or what we were with. Thus in Swahili where no object noun follows this verb, we *must* add an appropriate relative agreement, even though no relative as such is implied. In this type of context, such a particle would be added to the 'na' no matter what tense was being used, whereas in the other cases, where an object noun is given, it would not be necessary, nor indeed correct.

Ulikuwa na kisu?	Did you have a knife?
Nilikuwa nacho.	I had one.

But, where a *negative* reply is given, the relative particle is *not* added, even though logically it should be, in the present tense. In other tenses, however, it is added as normally.

e.g.	Unacho kisu?	Have you a knife?
	Sina	I have not.
	Ulikuwa na kisu?	Did you have a knife?
	Sikuwa nacho	I did not have one.
	Utakuwa na kisu?	Will you have a knife?
	Sitakuwa nacho.	I shall not have one.

Exercise 66

(a) *Translate:* The clothes he has; the roots the tree has; the salary I had; the help they will have; the answer I had; the cook we have; the profit we did not have; I have a guest; have you any matches? I have; have you (pl.) permission? We have not; the food we had; the letters we shall have; the patients the doctor has; I have a new vehicle; have you a vehicle? I have; have you the book which I have also? I did have, but now I have not; the jobs we have; the mountains which this country has; the first wife he had; the hoes they have are useless.

(b) *Translate:* The eggs I had were not good; this coat which I have was very expensive; the cook I shall have tomorrow will be a great help; the houses this town has are very clean; I sold the car I had last year; the roots this tree will have go very deep; the servants we have are very trustworthy; the dog Mr. Smith had was killed by a car; people who have dogs, are not robbed; the job he had did not suit him.

(c) *Translate:* Chai niliyo nayo ni baridi sasa; kiti alicho nacho si kizuri; mnao watoto? Tunao; shauri tulilokuwa nalo naye; pesa watakazokuwa nazo;

mazungumzo waliyokuwa nayo; mkate duka lile lilio nao; unaye mpishi? Ninaye; gazeti alilo nalo; nguvu waliyo nayo.

(d) *Translate:* The man who has a hat; the children we have; farmers who have good crops; the people who have tried; the shop which has good bread; bread which is sweet; the servants they have; Europeans who have servants; people who have no wealth; those who have not seen me; they who have luck; the luck which they have; he who has been a cook; the house I have; the doctor who has a big house.

52 Relatives—3

Relatives of manner and time

Relative of manner
We have seen several times up till now that any construction pertaining to 'manner' uses 'Ki- Vi-' agreements either singular or plural. (e.g. adverbs, and 'hivi'—'thus' etc.)

The same procedure is followed when a relative of manner is required, and the plural '-vyo-' is used. It is used exactly as other relatives, except that where possible it will be used as an infix or suffix on the verb, rather than as a suffix on 'amba-'. Its meaning is 'as', 'how', 'like', 'as far as', etc.

e.g. Nionavyo (general relative)   As I see it
Fanya ninavyofanya   Do as I am doing
Sijui alivyofika   I don't know how he arrived
Sikiliza atakavyosema   Listen how he will speak

There are certain words which can be used in conjunction with this relative to convey a special meaning:

jinsi   how, the manner in which
kadiri   as far as, to the limit of ability, etc.
kama   as, like

N.B. One will also frequently hear 'jinsi' used with the possessive 'ya' followed by the verb in the 'infinitive' giving the same meaning,

e.g. Hajui jinsi ya kufanya kazi hii.
He does not know how to do this work.

This form would be used whenever the infinitive is used in English, as in the example above.

These words are used to stress their particular meanings,

e.g. Sijui jinsi alivyoweza.
   I don't know how he was able.
Fanya jinsi atakavyofanya.
   Do how he will do.
Chukua mizigo hii mbali kadiri utakavyoweza.
   Carry these loads as far as you (can) will be able.
Jaribu kadiri unavyoweza
   Try as much as you can
Kama mnavyojua . . . .   As you (pl.) know . . .
Kama anavyoiona   As he sees it

Examples:
Hawezi kukimbia kama alivyoweza zamani.
   He can't run like he used to in the past.
Umeelewa nilivyosema?
   Have you understood what I said?
Lete ramani nione jinsi walivyojenga nyumba hii.
   Bring the plan so that I may see how they built this house.
Nitawasaidieni kadiri nitakavyoweza.
   I shall help you (pl.) as much as I can.
Umefanya hii jinsi nisivyotaka.
   You have done this how I did not want (it).

Relative of time
The relative of time also has frequent use in Swahili and is used to translate the word 'when' in the context of time as a statement, as opposed to 'when?'

For this relative, they use '-po-' which is taken from the locative class. It is also used exactly as other relatives, and again, where possible, is used on the verb rather than on 'amba-'.

In some tenses, when used with 'kila', 'po' takes the meaning of 'whenever'. In these cases, the subject would follow the verb, or precede 'kila'.

e.g. Nilipofika   When I arrived
   Kila nilipofika   Whenever I arrived
   Nitakapofika   When I shall arrive
   Ninapofika   When I am arriving
   Nifikapo   When I arrive
   Kila nifikapo   Whenever I arrive
   Nisipofika   When I don't arrive
                      Unless I arrive

(It is from here that the '-sipo-' tense comes (see Ch. 47).

Examples:
Kila alipofika mganga   Whenever the doctor arrived

Mgeni atakapofika, mpe chai	When the guest arrives, give him some tea.
Nitasafisha gari litakaporudi	I shall clean the vehicle when it returns
Kila nijapo ninakuona ukilala	Whenever I come, I find you lying down
Niletee barua zitakapokuwa tayari	Bring me the letters when they will be ready

N.B. Notice how the future tense is frequently used.

Exercise 67

(a) *Translate:* When the tree fell; the manner in which the tree fell; how to read; raise it as much as you can; as you know; whenever he comes; when the rain started; as you think; I don't know how he teaches; when the guest arrived; when the meeting will start; when will the meeting start?; the dog woke me up whenever the old man came; climb as high as you can; when you will reach the top; don't do it as he is doing (it); when they opened the door; when he eats; when the old man dies, come here as quickly as you can; when we received this letter.

(b) *Translate:* Call me when the labourers arrive; as you know, you must stand up when a guest enters the room; he does not remember when he arrived, or when he will leave; you must do this work how he will show you; that child will be very clever when he is big; I cannot remember what (how) he was called; whenever he comes he leaves the door open; try as much as is possible to come early every day; he will give me my money when he returns; as we told you (pl.) this road is closed when the rain starts.

(c) *Translate:* Watakapoondoka: walivyosema; kama watakavyofikiri; jinsi alivyofanya kazi; kila apitapo hapa; niliporudi nyumbani; wanyama watakapokula; wanavyolala sasa; nilipoingia, alikuwa akiketi anavyoketi sasa; gari lilipofika; kazi ilipokwisha; niambie utakapomaliza mpango huu; sijui atakavyonijibu; mzee yule hajui jinsi ya kuandika; hakufanya jinsi nilivyomwonyesha; utakapokwenda mjini, ninunulie gazeti; kama mjuavyo, chama hiki kilipoanzishwa . . .; sahani ilivunjika ilipoanguka; fanya nisemavyo sivyo kama ninavyofanya; chagua kama unavyopenda mwenyewe.

53   Nouns—6

U- noun class

All nouns in this class have the prefix U- in the singular. This U- may be changed to a W- when the stem begins with a vowel.

Not all nouns in this class have a plural, but if they do then the U- (or W-) is generally dropped and the noun becomes a plural N class

185

noun. Normal 'N' class rules are followed in that the N- concord will precede all nouns commencing with d, g, or z, M- before b, and v, and NY- before vowel stems.

The class may be divided into four groups of nouns.

1. Mainly abstract nouns made up of adjectival or noun stems from other classes, or even certain verb stems. These do not exist in plural form:

uaminifu	trustworthiness (from '-aminifu', trustworthy)
ubaya	badness, evil (from '-baya', bad)
ubovu	rottenness (from '-bovu', rotten)
uchache	scarcity (from '-chache', few)
uchafu	dirt (from '-chafu', dirty)
ufupi	shortness (from '-fupi', short)
ugeni	strangeness (from '-geni', strange)
ugumu	hardness (from '-gumu', hard)
uhodari	efficiency (from 'hodari', efficient)
uhuru	freedom (from 'huru', free)
wingi	plenty (from '-ingi', many)
Uislamu	Muslim religion (from 'Mwislamu', a Muslim),
ujamaa	relationship, brotherhood, socialism (from 'jamaa', family)
ujana	youth (from 'kijana', a youth)
ukali	ferocity, sharpness (from '-kali', fierce)
Ukristo	Christianity (from 'Mkristo', a Christian)
ukubwa	size (from '-kubwa', large)
umaskini	poverty (from 'maskini', poor)
umoja	unity (from '-moja', one)
unene	fatness, thickness (from '-nene', fat, thick)
upana	breadth, width (from '-pana', wide)
upendo	love (from 'ku-penda', to love)
urahisi	ease (from 'rahisi', easy)
urefu	length, height, depth (from '-refu', long etc.)

N.B. *Urefu is length, 'urefu wa kwenda juu' (or 'urefu juu') is height, and 'urefu wa kwenda chini' (or 'urefu wa chini') is depth.*

usafi	cleanliness (from 'safi', clean)
utajiri	wealth (from 'tajiri', a wealthy person)
utamu	sweetness (from '-tamu', sweet)
utoto	childhood (from 'mtoto', a child)
uvivu	laziness (from '-vivu', lazy)
uwezo	ability, power (from 'ku-weza', to be able)
uzee	old age (from 'mzee', an old person)
uzito	weight (from '-zito', heavy)
uzuri	goodness, beauty (from '-zuri', good)

(The same procedure can be followed for making up many other abstract nouns from other adjectives, nouns or verbs, not listed above.)

2. This is another group of nouns which have no plural, and are 'collective' nouns, descriptive of 'uncountable' matter,

e.g.

udongo	soil ('udongo ulaya' cement)
ugali	porridge
uji	gruel
umande	dew
umeme	lightning, electricity
usingizi	sleep
wali	cooked rice
wino	ink

3. This comprises nouns of many types, which have a plural,

e.g.

ua	nyua	courtyard, backyard
ubao	mbao	plank, board
udevu (rare)	ndevu	beard (used in plural for complete beard)
ufa	nyufa	crack
ufunguo	funguo	key
ukoo	koo	clan
ukuni (rare)	kuni	firewood (used mainly in plural)
ukurasa	kurasa	page (of a book, etc.)
ukuta	kuta	wall
ulimi	ndimi	tongue
uma	nyuma	fork (utensil)
unywele (rare)	nywele	hair (used mainly in plural)
upande	pande	side, part of the country
upepo	pepo	wind, compressed air ('evil spirits' in plural)
usiku	siku	night ('siku' in singular means 'a day')
uso	nyuso	face
uzi	nyuzi	string, thread
wakati	nyakati	period, time of year, etc., season
wembe	nyembe	razor, razor blade.

N.B. *The following, though having plurals, put their plurals into the MA- class (therefore taking MA- class agreements) since their presence in quantity creates a serious result. Hence the use of the amplicative class plural.*

ugomvi	magomvi	quarrel
ugonjwa	magonjwa	disease, sickness (could imply 'epidemic' in plural)

187

4. Names of countries. Many countries are given an U- prefix, but their agreements nevertheless are N class.

e.g.

Udachi	Germany
Ufaransa	France
Uganda	Uganda (ensure correct pronunciation 'ooganda', not the English 'Yewganda')
Uhindi	India
Uingereza	England (Britain)
Ulaya	Europe
Unguja	Zanzibar
Ureno	Portugal
Usukuma	Sukumaland (the homeland of the Wasukuma tribe) plus most other tribal areas.

Adjectival agreements

In the singular, the adjectival agreements are identical to those of the singular M- Mi- class. Therefore the concord M- (or MW- before a vowel) is used,

e.g.

ukuta mrefu	a long wall
ubao mzito	a heavy plank
upande mmoja	one side
wembe mkali	a sharp razor
uso mweusi	a black face
uzi mweupe	white string
ufunguo mwingine	another key

In the plural, the agreements, as with the nouns, are N class:

e.g.

kuta ndefu	long walls
mbao nzito	heavy planks
pande mbili	two sides
nyembe kali	sharp razors
nyuso nyeusi	black faces
nyuzi nyeupe	white strings
funguo nyingine	other keys

N.B. But remember the two nouns whose plural is MA- class:

magomvi makali	fierce quarrels
magonjwa makubwa	a large epidemic

Subject Prefixes

These are again, in the singular, like the M- MI- subject prefix, and like the N class plural in the plural, i.e.

	Affirmative	*Negative*
u-	(singular)	hau-
zi-	(plural)	hazi-

e.g. Ukurasa umepotea.   The page is lost.
Kurasa zimepotea.   The pages are lost.
Ufunguo uko wapi?   Where is the key?
Upo pale mezani.   It is there on the table.
Udongo haufai.   The soil is unsuitable.
Mbao hazitafaa.   The planks will not be suitable.

Demonstratives

From the subject prefixes, we can make up the demonstratives which are;

huu	this	ule	that
hizi	these	zile	those

e.g.	ukuta huu	this wall
	wakati ule	that period
	funguo hizi	these keys
	kuni zile	that firewood (lit. those firewoods)

Possessives

These are   wa   (singular)
            za   (plural)

e.g.	wakati wa mvua	the rain season
	ndevu za mzee	the old man's beard (remember 'beard' is plural)

Personal Possessives

These are

wangu	zangu	my, mine
wako	zako	your, yours
wake	zake	his/hers/her/its
wetu	zetu	our, ours
wenu	zenu	your, yours
wao	zao	their, theirs

e.g.	uhodari wake	his efficiency
	utoto wangu	my childhood
	uzito wako	your weight
	umoja wao	their unity
	funguo zetu	our keys
	pande zake	its sides
	nywele zake	his hair

Object infixes

Again, these are like the subject prefixes, i.e.

             -u-   and   -zi-

Ameuondoa uchafu ule.   He has removed that dirt.

Tumezipasua kuni hizi.   We have sawn this firewood.
Umeziona funguo zangu?   Have you seen my keys?

-Ote, -enye, etc.

These follow the object infix agreements;

wote	wenye	wenyewe	wo wote
zote	zenye	zenyewe	zo zote

e.g.

Utajiri wote	All wealth
Ugali wenye utamu	Porridge having sweetness
Uzito wenyewe ni kilo moja.	The weight itself is one kilo.
Nipe uma wo wote.	Give me any fork.
Tumetafuta pande zote.	We have searched all sides.
Watoto wanapenda kurasa zenye picha.	Children like pages with pictures.
Mbao zenyewe zilikuwa nzito.	The boards themselves were heavy.
Nyuzi zo zote zitafaa.	Any threads will do.

Relatives

Following the pattern of the subject prefix, they are

-o-   and   -zo-

Uhuru uliopatikana mwaka ule	The freedom which was obtained that year
Funguo tulizozipoteza	The keys which we lost
Usingizi tulio nao	The sleep we have
Udongo ulio hapa	The soil which is here

Examples:

Ukuta huu una urefu wa meta ishirini, urefu wa kwenda juu wa meta moja, na upana wa sentimeta ishirini.

This wall has a length of 20 meters, a height of 1 meter and a width of 20 cms.

Amezoea ugali tangu utoto mpaka uzee.

He has been accustomed to porridge from childhood to old age.

Mzee yule analala usingizi uani.

That old man is sleeping in the courtyard.

N.B. 'Ku-lala usingizi' is used for 'to sleep' as opposed to 'ku-lala' which could infer just 'lying down'.)

Wakati ule ulikuwa na upepo mkali kabisa.

That period (season) had an extremely strong (fierce) wind.

Nipe ufunguo wako wa mlango huu. Wangu umepotea.

Give me your key of this door. Mine is lost.

Kuni zote zilizoletwa juzijuzi zimekwisha sasa.

All the firewood which was brought the other day is finished now.

Ninahitaji kalamu ya wino.

I need a pen (as opposed to a pencil)

Exercise 68

(a) *Translate:* Poverty; old age; planks; fatness; Europe; tongue; dew; freedom; cleanliness; hair; a period of time; lightning; ink; quarrel; dirt; childhood; goodness; Zanzibar; soil; firewood.

(b) *Translate:* Another key; many pages; a strong (fierce) wind; its length; the efficiency of people; my beard; all sides; good soil; long threads; any time at all; the unity of this country; dry firewood; that face; a good sleep; those keys; this cooked rice; that dirt; those walls; that bad crack; that dark night.

(c) *Translate:* Where is the plank which was here?; the ink I had is lost; the ability he has is suitable; the planks which have been sawn; the soil which is about here is red; he has a disease of the tongue itself; the porridge is being cooked in the courtyard; the sweetness the food has; the eleventh page of this book; that red ink will be sufficient.

(d) *Translate:* There is much dirt on your face; bring a plank with a length of 15 feet and a width of 6 inches; her hair was black, but now it is white; I saw a lot of dew this morning; this wall has no strength because it has a large crack; that patient has a disease of the tongue which is very bad; I need a person with trustworthiness, not laziness; this box has not a big weight; the people of Sukumaland have good soil; we have travelled in all parts of this country.

(e) *Translate:* Uislamu; Udachi; uji; wembe; wali; wingi; uaminifu; ukoo; ugomvi; uzi; unene; utajiri; upendo; upande; ubovu; Ureno; uma; ufa; uso; uwezo; ujamaa.

(f) *Translate:* Ugumu wa kazi; watu wale wale wali wao; pasua kuni zote zile; funguo ziko wapi? Hamisi anazo; ubao wenye urefu wa futi saba; udongo mzito ulio hapa haufai; umesahau kuweka nyuma mezani; ngoja mpaka umande uondoke; kuna uchache wa nyembe huku; anatoka ukoo ulio na umoja wenye nguvu.

(g) *Translate:* Ninahitaji ufunguo wa mlango ulio uani; nimenunua kuni nyingine kwa sababu hizi haziwaki sawasawa; siwezi kuzinyoa ndevu zangu kwa sababu nyembe hazipatikani; mwalimu ataweza kuandika kwa urahisi katika ubao mweusi huu; Bwana analala usingizi sasa, basi rudi tena wakati wa jioni; Uingereza imetoa uhuru kwa nchi hii sasa; ni uchafu gani, ule ulio ukutani? ng'ombe wale wana ugonjwa ulioletwa na wadudu; ukitaka kuotesha maua mazuri lazima uwe na udongo wenye uzuri; ukuta ule una urefu wa futi ishirini na tano, urefu wa kwenda juu wa futi nne, na upana wa futi moja na nusu.

54 The Present Indefinite Tense

So far in this book, we have been only using one present tense, the '-na-' tense. There are, in fact three present tenses in the affirmative in Swahili. But for the beginner, only one is really essential, and that is the one we have been using. In fact, from a study of the Swahili press in Tanzania, the '-na-' tense is used three times out of four.

The other two tenses, therefore, are not essential for the beginner, but do nevertheless have a place in the language. There is, however, only one negative tense for all these affirmative tenses (see Ch. 32).

The present indefinite tense, whose sign is -A- is used to signify an action made periodically, without necessarily implying that it is going on at that moment. e.g. 'Cows eat grass' (as opposed to 'The cows are eating grass') means that they do often eat grass, but may not necessarily be eating it at this moment.

The conjugation of this tense is slightly complicated by the fact that its sign is a vowel.

ni-a-soma	nasoma	I read
u-a-soma	wasoma	you read
a-a-soma	asoma	he/she reads
tu-a-soma	twasoma	we read
m-a-soma	mwasoma	you read ('m-' before a vowel)
wa-a-soma	wasoma	they read

N.B. In speech, one will often hear 'Nasoma' where 'Ninasoma' is intended. This is because 'Ninasoma' has a habit of being shortened to 'Nasoma' in much the same way as in English when we say 'I'm reading' for 'I am reading'. This applies only to the 1st person singular and occurs with any verb.

It will be noted that 'u-' before this vowel changes to a 'w-'.

The other noun classes follow the same pattern:

M- MI- class	u-a-faa	wafaa	it is suitable
	i-a-faa	yafaa	they are suitable
KI- VI- class	ki-a-faa	chafaa	it is suitable
	vi-a-faa	vyafaa	they are suitable
N class	i-a-faa	yafaa	it is suitable
	zi-a-faa	zafaa	they are suitable
MA- class	li-a-faa	lafaa	it is suitable
	ya-a-faa	yafaa	they are suitable
U- class	u-a-faa	wafaa	it is suitable
	zi-a-faa	zafaa	they are suitable

Notice here, that the vowel '-i-', if the second letter of the subject prefix, is dropped in forming this tense. Object infixes may be added as usual.

Arabic verbs follow the same pattern and are not altered:

e.g. twahitaji   we need
     wajaribu   they try
     asamehe   he/she forgives
            etc.

Monosyllabic verbs

These present a slight variation from the normal tenses, in that they drop their 'infinitive' 'ku-' when used with this tense;

ni-a-ja	naja	I come
u-a-ja	waja	you come
a-a-ja	aja	he/she comes
tu-a-ja	twaja	we come
m-a-ja	mwaja	you come
wa-a-ja	waja	they come

N.B. (1) This tense is not used with 'kuwa' when meaning 'to be'. The only present tense which is used is the 'ni' form (see Ch. 19).
(2) The General Relative (Ch. 51) is the relative form of this tense.
(3) Note that with monosyllabic verbs, the 1st person singular form in this tense is distinct from the abbreviated present definite tense, i.e. 'Nakuja' would be the abbreviated form of 'Ninakuja' as opposed to 'Naja' of this tense.

Examples:

Ng'ombe wala majani.
   Cows eat grass.
Mganga aja hapa Jumanne.
   The doctor comes here on Tuesdays.
Vitu hivi vyatufaa sana.
   These things suit us a lot.
Nyumba ile yampendeza.
   That house pleases him.
Wenyeji wa hapa waotesha mimea mizuri.
   The local inhabitants grow good crops.
Sisi twasoma Kiswahili.
   We ourselves study Swahili.
Mvua yanyesha mwezi wa tatu.
   The rain rains the third month. (It rains in March)

Exercise 69

(a) *Translate:* He goes; they eat; we live (stay); I smoke cigarettes; it suits; the knife cuts badly; he drinks local beer; you (pl.) work well; cups break if you drop them; the mail arrives at 9 o'clock; dew descends at night-time; cattle are kept about here; bread is sold in that shop; you teach my children; those houses are suitable; salaries are paid on Saturdays; he eats any meat, but I do not eat chicken; permission is obtainable in that office; these trees give out plenty of shade; that shop is closed at 5 o'clock.

(b) *Translate:* He awakens at 6.30 every morning; that old man writes very well; the children play football on Saturdays; vehicles go every day to Dar es Salaam; this knife cuts badly; those flowers smell very nice; heavy vehicles get stuck in mud; I am very sorry to hear that you borrow money; this road goes round that mountain; he rejoices when he sees me.

(c) *Translate:* Mganga aja hapa kila Alhamisi; mikutano yaanza saa saba kamili; barabara hii yafika Dar es Salaam; udongo huu wafaa sana; milima ile yaonekana toka hapa; taa hii yazimika mlangoni; vibarua wale wasaidia sana; mimea hii yapandwa mwezi wa pili; kazi yaanza saa moja, yaisha saa tisa; aniita kila afikapo.

55 Verbs—8

Reciprocal verbs

A special derivative form of the verb occurs in Swahili to denote a reciprocated action, such as 'to hit one another' or 'to see one another'.

This derivative, with verbs of Bantu origin, is very simple to make up. The procedure is simply to add the suffix '-na' onto the verb.

> e.g. ku-piga to hit ku-pigana to hit one another
> (i.e. to fight)

The following are in fairly common use:

ku-ambia	ku-ambiana	to tell one another
ku-fuata	ku-fuatana	to follow one another
ku-fundisha	ku-fundishana	to teach one another
ku-kuta	ku-kutana	to meet one another (to hold a meeting)
ku-ngoja	ku-ngojana	to wait for one another
ku-ona	ku-onana	to see one another
ku-pata	ku-patana	to get together, to agree
ku-piga	ku-pigana	to hit one another, fight
ku-saidia	ku-saidiana	to help one another
ku-shinda	ku-shindana	to conquer one another, to compete
ku-ua	ku-uana	to kill one another
ku-vuta	ku-vutana	to pull one another

Arabic verbs follow the same procedure, but first they have to be put into their prepositional forms (see Ch. 43).

ku-jibu	ku-jibia	ku-jibiana	to answer one another
ku-rudi	ku-rudia	ku-rudiana	to return to one another

N.B. The 'possible' types of stative verbs (lu-onekana, etc.) are really reciprocal stative forms, hence their final '-na' (see end of chapter 25). This reciprocal form, in use, is often followed by the word 'na' repeated as a separate word, e.g.

Ninataka kuonana na Rashidi.
I want to meet (with) Rashidi.

cf. Ninataka kuona Rashidi (I want to see Rashidi)
(You could *not* say 'Ninataka kuonana Rashidi')

Exception
The verb 'ku-pa' goes to 'ku-peana' (not ku-pana)

Examples
Waliambiana habari zao.
They told each other their news.
Wanachama watakutana kesho.
The members will meet (one another) tomorrow.
Siwezi kuonana nawe leo.
I cannot meet you to-day.
Yafaa watu wote wasaidiane.
It is good that all people help one another.
Watu walipeana zawadi.
The people gave each other gifts.

Exercise 70
(a) *Translate:* To take leave of one another; to teach one another; to fight; to agree; to write to one another; to play *with* one another; to wait for one another; to follow one another; to understand one another; to seize one another; to compete; to remember one another; to love one another; to ask one another; to pull one another; to return to one another; to give one another; to see one another; to help one another; to call one another.
(b) *Translate:* Tell them to wait for one another when they climb the mountain; the children pulled one another up the hill; prevent those children from fighting; we shall meet again to-morrow; these animals follow one another in forests; we shall wait for one another at 5.15 p.m.; those people do not like each other; they taught each other their languages; we shall compete with you (pl.) in that game; they want to get together to prevent those people from killing one another.
(c) *Translate:* Nilionana naye jana; watoto wanapigana uani; tumeambiana habari zote; wamepatana nasi; wanyama walifuatana; tulionana mjini; wanachama wanakutana chamani; sisi na wenzetu tulisaidiana; tuliachana saa saba; hatukubaliani; lazima watu wote wapendane; watoto wanashindana kwa kikombe cha fedha; mwizi alipigana na mwenyewe wa duka; tutaonana tena kesho; watu wote waweza kufundishana; watoto

wanacheza pamoja; siku zafuatana; ni jambo baya kwa watu kuuana;
tutangojana chini ya daraja; vijana wale wanaangushana.

56 Nouns—7

The 'mahali' (locative) class

This noun class, though containing essentially one noun, is the most
complicated of all the noun classes as far as its agreements are
concerned.

We are already familiar, however, with the three agreements since
they were introduced in chapter 11 when dealing with the location of
things, etc.

To recapitulate the agreements contain either of three consonants,
namely

'P'   where definite location is implied
'K'   where indefinite location is implied
'M'   where inside location is implied

Note, however, that no differentiation can be made between the
singular and plural agreements. Context generally suggests singular or
plural, but if singular or plural stress is necessary, then appropriate
adjectives have to be used.

The word 'mahali' is a noun meaning 'place'. But although place
can be described with either of the three agreements mentioned above,
whenever the word 'mahali' itself is used in a sentence, only the P
agreements are used with it.

When the K or M agreements are used, the locative noun is left
understood. In fact, the word 'mahali' itself is often omitted as
understood, even with P agreements except in one or two cases where
it has to be used to avoid confusion.

We shall deal with each of the three agreements in turn.

'P' Agreements
Adjectival prefix. This is 'pa-' (note there is no 'concord' on the noun)

e.g. mahali pazuri	a good place (or simply 'pazuri')
mahali pabaya	a bad place (or simply 'pabaya')
mahali padogo	a small place (or simply 'padogo')
mahali pakubwa	a large place (or simply 'pakubwa')
mahali pachache	a few places (or simply 'pachache')
mahali patupu	an empty place (or simply 'patupu')

mahali pamoja	one place (or simply 'pamoja')
mahali pawili	two places (or simply 'pawili')

Vowel stem adjectives.

mahali pa+ingi=mahali pengi	many places (or 'pengi')
mahali pa+eupe=mahali peupe	a light place (or 'peupe')
mahali pa+eusi=mahali peusi	a dark place (or 'peusi')
mahali pa+ingine=mahali pengine	another place

The word 'pengine' has also a special meaning of 'sometimes' or 'maybe'. Therefore, if used on its own, it will be understood to mean 'sometimes'. So if to be used as 'another place,' it should be accompanied by the noun 'mahali'. In a sentence 'pengine' meaning 'sometimes' will generally come before the verb, whereas when meaning 'another place' it will generally follow it.

> e.g. Pengine alikwenda—Sometimes he went.
> Alikwenda mahali pengine—He went to another place.

N.B.   All the above examples could be in the plural (except 'pamoja').

Subject prefixes
These are pa- (affirmative) and hapa- (negative)

e.g. Mahali panafaa.	The place is suitable.
Mahali palikuwa padogo.	The place was small.
Mahali palikuwa na miti.	The place had trees.
(Mahali) pana miti hapa.	The place has trees here. (i.e. There are trees here)
Hapafai hapa.	It is unsuitable here.

Demonstratives
From the subject prefix we get

hapa	this place	i.e. here (definite)
pale	that place	i.e. there (definite)

Possessives
pa + a = pa (of)

e.g. Mahali pa hatari	a place of danger (a dangerous place)
Mahali pa kuwekea hema	a place of putting a tent, i.e. a camp site

Personal possessives

pangu	my place(s)
pako	your place(s)
pake	his/her place(s)
petu	our place(s)
penu	your place(s)
pao	their place(s)

N.B. These are often used in reference to one's home (house).

Object Infix.
Like the subject prefix, it is '-pa-',

e.g. Ninapapenda hapa.   I like the place here. (I like it here).
     Amepatafuta mahali.   He has looked for the place.

-Ote, -enye, etc.
pote   all places, i.e. everywhere
penye   the place having, i.e. by (near)
penyewe   the place itself
po pote   anywhere any place at all

e.g. Nimetafuta pote.   I have looked everywhere.
     Ningoje penye daraja.   Wait for me by the bridge.
     Mahali penyewe panafaa.   The place itself is suitable.
     Sijaona po pote penye maji. I have not yet seen any place
                               at all having water.

Relative
This is '-po-'. We have already met this in two constructions. In chapter 11 it is always used with the verb 'to be' when location is implied,

e.g. Mkate upo mezani.   The bread is on the table.

Secondly, we have met it being used as the relative of time (see Ch. 52),

Nilipofika   When I arrived.

This relative is used in the same manner as all other relatives, but has to be used with the word 'mahali' where it might be confused with the relative of time,

e.g. Mahali nilipofika   The place where I arrived
     cf. Nilipofika   When I arrived
     Mahali apendapo   The place he likes
     cf. Apendapo   When he likes
     Mahali tutakapokwenda   The place where we shall go
     cf. Tutakapokwenda   When we shall go
     Mahali tusipofika   The place(s) where we did not
                              reach

     cf. Tusipofika   Unless we arrive
                              If we do not arrive
                              When we do not arrive

Examples

Pote nilipokwenda, niliona wanyama.
Everywhere I went, I saw animals.
Hapa ni mahali alipoanguka.
Here is the place where he fell.
Hapa ni pazuri, sitaki kwenda pengine.
Here is a nice place, I don't want to go elsewhere.
Petu pana udongo safi.
Our place has good soil.
Hapana ruhusa kuvuta sigara hapa.
There is no permission to smoke here. (lit. The place has no permission to smoke here)
Pengine ataniletea maua atakapokuja hapa.
Maybe he will bring me flowers when he comes here.

Exercise 71

(a) *Translate:* A good place, another place, draw near (to) our place; I have looked in all places; by the tree; sometimes; there is a light patch over there; they were waiting for one another in two different places; many places have cattle; his place which I saw yesterday; put that load anywhere; a suitable place (a place which is suitable); a secret place; take this letter to your place; there are a few places with water; he looked for another place; the place itself was very small; the stranger is here; that place will not be suitable; the place where they stayed.

(b) *Translate:* When I go to Moshi, I sometimes go to his place; I like it a lot where I am staying; there are a lot of animals over there (in) the dark place; this place is unsuitable because it is small; they did not like it there, so they went to another place; he went to sit in his usual place; the place itself was small but it had no dirt; your keys are there on the table; there is no work here; all wait in one place, not in many places.

(c) *Translate:* Penye daraja; pale patakuwa na miti michache; hapana nafasi hapa; usisimame po pote hapa; nenda pale penye motokaa ile; mahali pake pana miti mingi; nilipoondoka; mahali tutakapokwenda; aliokota kisu changu mahali tusipotafuta; pana mahali pengi hapa penye Wazungu.

'K' Agreements

Remember, the word 'mahali' is not used here

Adjectival prefix.
This is 'ku-'

kuzuri	a nice area	kuchache	a few areas
kubaya	a bad area	kutupu	an empty area
kudogo	a small area	kumoja	one area
kukubwa	a large area	kuwili	two areas

N.B. The word 'area' is used here meaning 'an indefinite place'.

Vowel stem adjectives:
ku + ingi = kwingi   many areas

199

```
ku + eupe   = kweupe      a light area (a clearing)
ku + eusi   = kweusi      a dark area
ku + ingine = kwingine    another area
```

Subject prefixes.

These are 'ku-' (affirmative) and 'haku-' (negative),

e.g. Kunafaa.	The area is suitable.
Kulikuwa kudogo.	The area was small.
Kulikuwa na miti.	The area had trees.
Kuna miti huku.	The area has trees here. There are trees about here.
Hakufai.	The area is unsuitable.

Demonstratives

huku	this indefinite place (hereabouts)
kule	that indefinite place (thereabouts)

Possessives

ku + a = kwa	of
huku kwa hatari	this area of danger

N.B. This is the derivation of the preposition 'kwa' when it is used in the sense of 'towards', 'to' since its true meaning is 'the area of',

e.g. Nenda kwa Bwana Smith.
    lit. Go to the place (indefinite) of Mr. Smith
    (i.e. Go to Mr. Smith's).

Personal possessives

kwangu	my area
kwako	your area
kwake	his/her area
kwetu	our area
kwenu	your area
kwao	their area

The singular possessives here are frequently used with reference to one's 'homestead'.

The plural possessives are frequently used with reference to one's 'homeland'.

Thus anyone saying

'Amerudi kwake' 'means	'He has returned home' (his homestead).

but if a 'foreigner' in East Africa were to say 'Kwetu', he/she would be referring to his/her homeland, i.e. England, America, Germany, or wherever he/she comes from. If an African says 'Kwetu', however, he would be referring to his tribal area, such as Usukuma, Uchagga, Umasai, etc. Similarly, the 2nd and 3rd persons plural would refer to the same.

Object infix
This is again '-ku-'.

    Unakupenda huku?   Do you like it hereabouts?

N.B. *Note that it is the same object infix as the 2nd person singular. This could lead to confusion, and as a result, one does not come across it very often.*

-OTE, -ENYE, etc.

kote	all around
kwenye	in the area having, around, round about
kwenyewe	the area itself
ko kote	anywhere abouts

e.g. Nimetafuta kote.	I have looked all around.
Ningoje kwenye daraja.	Wait for me round about the bridge somewhere.
Kule kwenyewe kulifaa.	That area itself was suitable.
Unaweza kuwinda ko kote.	You can hunt anywhere about.

Relative
This is '-ko-'. This relative, unlike the '-po-' relative has no alternative use. Its use is therefore straightforward:

Kule nilikofika
    That area where I arrived
Kote nilikokwenda, niliona wanyama.
    All around where I went, I saw animals.

Examples
Alikoanguka kulikuwa huku.
    Where he fell was somewhere about here.
Huku ni kuzuri, sitaki kwenda kwingine.
    This is a nice area, I don't want to go to another area.
Kwetu hakuna nyoka.
    In our homeland, there are no snakes.
Hakuna ruhusa kuvuta sigara huku.
    There is no permission to smoke around here.

Exercise 72
(a) *Translate the following treating the word 'area' as indefinite location:* A good area; another area; draw near to our home; I have looked in all areas; round about that Baobab tree; there is a light (coloured) area somewhere over there; they were waiting for one another over there by those houses; many areas have cattle; his home-area which I saw yesterday; put that load

anywhere about here; a suitable area; this letter has come from our homeland; there are a few areas with water; he looked for another area; the area itself was very small; the stranger is somewhere about here; that area will not be suitable; the area where they stayed; I have been to all areas; I don't know where he went.

(b) *Translate:* Around there where we went hunting, there were many hills; take this luggage over there to my home; these animals do not like it about here, so we must look for another area for them; are there mountains about in your homeland?; a long time ago, there were many insects about there; there is no permission to fish about here; the news is good in our home area. How about yours?; where is our wealth? It is all around; there was a fire over there where it is dark; the Bwana is not about here. How about over there?

(c) *Translate:* Kwenye daraja; kule kutakuwa na miti michache; hakuna ruhusa kuvuta sigara huku; usiende kokote kule; nenda kule kwenye motokaa zile; kwao kulikuwa pori tupu; nilikokwenda; watakakokwenda; aliokota kiko changu nisikotafuta mwenyewe; tutakwenda kwenye wanyama kesho.

M Agreements
These are less frequently used.

Adjectival prefix.
This is 'm-' ('mw-' before a vowel)

mzuri	nice inside	mwingine	inside another place
mbaya	bad inside	mweupe	a light inside place
mdogo	small inside	mweusi	a dark inside place

(Adjectives are in fact rarely used with this agreement.)

Subject prefixes.
These are 'm-' (affirmative) and 'ham-' (negative)
('mw-' before a vowel)

Mnafaa mle.	It is suitable in there.
Mle mna nyoka.	In there there is a snake.
Hamna nyoka mle.	There is no snake in there.

Demonstratives

humu	in here
mle	in there

Aliingia humu.	He entered in here.
Iweke mle.	Put it in there.

(These *are* commonly used.)

Possessive
mu- + -a = mwa   of
(Uncommon)

202

Personal possessives

mwangu	in my
mwako	in your
mwake	in his, in her
mwetu	in our
mwenu	in your
mwao	in their

(These are very commonly used, but their use will be explained in the general notes in the next section.)

Object infix.
This is almost never used, but would be '-m-'

-OTE, -ENYE, etc.

mwote	all inside places (rare)
mwenye	inside place having
mwenyewe	the inside place itself (rare)
mo mote	any inside place (very rare)

e.g. Mle mwenye nyoka In there with the snake

Relative
This is '-mo-'

e.g. Mle alimoingia In there where he entered

N.B. It will be seen from the above, that the only constructions in common use are the subject prefixes, demonstratives, the personal possessives and the relative.

Examples
Tulimoingia mlikuwa humu.
   Where we entered was in here.
Humu ni mzuri, sitaki kuiweka mwingine.
   In here is good, I don't want to put it in anywhere else.
Hamna ruhusa kuvuta humu.
   There is no permission to smoke in here.

General notes
1. When using any of the agreements in this class, care should be taken never to mix the agreements within any phrase. If this were to be done, implications of location would be contradictory. e.g. One should never say:

   Hapana ruhusa kuvuta sigara *huku*
or *Hakuna* ruhusa kuvuta sigara *hapa* etc.

Thus it should be either
   Hapana . . . hapa/pale

or Hakuna . . . huku/kule
or Hamna . . . humu/mle

(N.B. You will, no doubt, see notices everywhere forbidding this and that, written wrongly with conflicting agreements!)

It is, however, possible to have 'hamna' with any of the three agreements, if it is used meaning 'you (pl.) have not'.

e.g. Hamna ruhusa kuingia hapa.
You (pl.) have no permission to enter here.

2. Whilst theoretically this noun class has only one noun in it (mahali), there is potentially a very large number of nouns which can be put into the class.

It will be recalled that up till now, whenever we have had a noun used with the prepositions 'in, on, to' etc., we have either been able to add the suffix '-ni', or use the preposition 'katika'. Furthermore, we had *had* to use 'katika' whenever there has been any other word used to qualify that noun, such as a demonstrative or adjective. But we have not been able to add these to a noun bearing the preposition suffix '-ni'. The reason for this is that by adding the suffix '-ni' we are, in effect, putting that noun into the locative class (the Mahali class). It therefore then qualifies for either of the three agreements, P, K, or M. This is, in fact, the greatest use of the M agreements, especially its personal possessives.

Thus we can now either say:

Katika chumba kile alichoingia
or Chumbani mle alimoingia   In that room where he entered
Katika mfuko mkubwa wangu
or Mfukoni mkubwa mwangu   In my big pocket/bag
Katika nyumba ndogo yangu
or Nyumbani pangu padogo   At/in my small house
or Nyumbani kwangu kudogo   At my small homestead
or Nyumbani mwangu mdogo   Inside my small house

Exercise 73

(a) *Translate using the prepositional suffix '-ni':* In his pocket; in that room; in that town; in those valleys; in their baskets; in my box; inside your house; the ditch in which he fell; on his table; the room in which he entered.

(b) *Translate using prepositional suffix '-ni':* There are many fish in that river; put those potatoes in that large basket; don't put those plates on that table; there are many inhabitants in those villages; don't put his money in your pocket; put this towel in the guest's room; don't fall in the ditch where the water went in; I have written my name in my book; Serengeti is a very nice area. There is very much game; you had better not put your hand in there where there are snakes.

(c) *Translate:* Ameongeza kuni motoni pale; acha barua ile mezani kwake; nilipofika alikuwa akifanya kazi nyumbani mwake; pengine ninakwenda kwake, pengine anakuja kwangu; niweke kisu hiki wapi? Sandukuni mtafaa; hamtakuwa na mtu ye yote nyumbani mle; anaogopa kuingia msituni wanyama wale walipoingia; umesoma habari gazetini humu?; umeona alipokwenda Mohamedi? La, sikuona; atakapofika, mwambie ninapokaa.

57 Comparison of Adjectives

In English, in order to make a comparison we generally alter the end of the adjective by the addition of a suffix, '-er' or '-est'.

e.g. big, bigger, biggest

In Swahili, we cannot change the adjective. Instead, we have to make an ordinary statement, followed by a word (which is often a verb) giving the suggestion of surpassing something else.

e.g. This tree is big, to surpass that one.
Mti huu ni mkubwa kupita ule.

It will be seen that the demonstratives, as well as the personal possessives are often used in making comparisons.

Comparatives
There are three words in common use for suggesting the comparison:

kupita	(to pass)
kuliko	(not a verb infinitive)
kushinda	(to conquer/excel)

Either of these three words can be used in a comparison, but it is recommended that the learner stick to only one of these. Possibly the most common of the three is 'kuliko'.

Thus we can show this in use in the following:

Mlima wa Kilimanjaro ni mrefu kuliko mlima wa Kenya.
Mount Kilimanjaro is higher than Mount Kenya.
Nyumba yangu ni kubwa kuliko yako.
My house is bigger than yours
Tuna watoto wengi kuliko nyinyi.
We have more children than you.

Mtihani ule ulikuwa mgumu kuliko huu.
That examination was harder than this one.

If, on the other hand, we want to say simply that something is bigger, or smaller, or heavier, etc. without necessarily comparing it with anything else, the word 'zaidi' is used:

Mlima wa Kilimanjaro ni mrefu zaidi.
Mount Kilimanjaro is higher.
Nyumba yangu ni kubwa zaidi.
My house is bigger.
Tuna watoto wengi zaidi.
We have more children.
Mtihani ule ulikuwa mgumu zaidi.
That examination was harder.

Superlatives

A similar procedure is followed for the superlatives. But this time, one has to follow the initial statement by the verb, followed by '-ote' (all) with the appropriate plural agreement.

e.g. Mlima wa Kilimanjaro ni mrefu kushinda yote.
Mount Kilimanjaro is the tallest. (Mount Kilimanjaro is tall to conquer all (mountains).)

N.B. *For superlatives, the verb 'kushinda' is probably the most appropriate, though again either of the three could be used.*

Nyumba yangu ni kubwa kushinda zote.
My house is the largest of all (houses).
Tuna watoto wengi kushinda wote.
We have the most children of all (people).
Mtihani huu ulikuwa mgumu kushinda yote.
This examination was the hardest of all (examinations).

N.B. *There must always be a plural agreement on the word '-ote', even though the initial subject may in the singular.*

Exercise 74

(a) *Translate:* I am taller than you; he is richer than we (he is a rich man to surpass us); this box is the smallest; this tea is sweeter; you are stronger than I; this house has the most rooms; that cloth is more expensive than this; their dog is fiercer than ours; our homeland is smaller than yours (pl.); your box is longer than his, but his is wider.

(b) *Translate:* They get higher salaries than we; Kenya is a bigger country than Uganda, but Tanzania is the biggest; Nairobi has more inhabitants than Mombasa; that road is shorter than this one; that plate is big, but this one is bigger; let the children carry the light loads. We shall carry those which are heavier; it is quicker to go by car than to walk; bring the largest vehicle which you can get; Swahili is an easier language to learn than English; it takes longer to go to New York than to go to London.

(c) *Translate:* Kitabu hiki ni kizuri kuliko kile; shamba hili lilitoa mimea mingi
kuliko lako; mbuyu huu ni mkubwa kushinda yote; dawa ile inafaa, lakini
hii ni nzuri zaidi; mimi ninakimbia upesi kuliko wewe; mpishi wake ana
uwezo mwingi kuliko wetu, lakini mpishi wa Bwana John anawashinda
wote; wamefanya kazi nyingi kuliko ninyi; nyumba ile itakuwa kubwa
kuliko hii; Hamisi anakaa mbali kuliko Juma, lakini Ali anakaa mbali
kushinda wote; amekuwa hodari kuliko wewe.

58 The -KA- Verb Tense

There are three quite separate uses of this tense sign:

The narrative past tense '
The expeditious tense (going to do something)
The 'headline' tense (used in newspapers etc).

The narrative tense
With this use, the sign is used in the normal manner, i.e. between the
subject prefix and the verb stem. It may take normal object infixes as
well, but *not* a relative infix.

e.g.	ni-ka-weka	nikaweka	(and) I put
	u-ka-weka	ukaweka	(and) you put
	a-ka-weka	akaweka	(and) he/she put
	tu-ka-weka	tukaweka	(and) we put
	m-ka-weka	mkaweka	(and) you put
	wa-ka-weka	wakaweka	(and) they put

similarly

M- Mi- class
	u-ka-anguka	ukaanguka	(and) it fell
	i-ka-anguka	ikaanguka	(and) they fell

Ki- Vi- class
	ki-ka-anguka	kikaanguka	(and) it fell
	vi-ka-anguka	vikaanguka	(and) they fell

N class
	i-ka-anguka	ikaanguka	(and) it fell
	zi-ka-anguka	zikaanguka	(and) they fell

Ma- class
	li-ka-anguka	likaanguka	(and) it fell
	ya-ka-anguka	yakaanguka	(and) they fell

etc.

Arabic verbs follow suit:

ni-ka-jaribu	nikajaribu	(and) I tried
wa-ka-fikiri	wakafikiri	(and) they thought
a-ka-samehe	akasamehe	(and) he forgave
	etc.	

Monosyllabic verbs, with this tense, drop their 'infinitive' 'ku-' sign:

ni-ka-la	nikala	(and) I ate
a-ka-ja	akaja	(and) he came
tu-ka-enda	tukaenda	(and) we went
wa-ka-wa	wakawa	(and) they were/became
ni-ka-wa na	nikawa na	(and) I had

Use

As the name of this tense suggests, it is used in re-counting narratives. It *must*, however, be introduced by an ordinary past tense, affirmative or negative. In practice, however, it is generally the -LI- tense which is used for this introduction:

> Tulikwenda mjini, tukamwona rafiki yetu, tukamwomba aje nasi, akaja.
>
> We went to town, we saw our friend, and we asked him to come with us, and he came.

It will be seen from the above example, that the word 'and' is not translated into Swahili. This is because there is a sort of 'built-in' 'and' within the tense sign.

It is not essential to use this tense when recounting a narrative, but it does improve the standard of Swahili, and is, in fact, used considerably particularly along the coast. It has a negative form, which is the negative subjunctive. This is the same use as 'unsuccessful effort' described in the 9th use of negative subjunctive in chapter 40.

> Tulikwenda mjini, tukaenda soko, tukatafuta viazi, tusipate.
>
> We went to town, we went to the market, and looked for potatoes, and didn't get (any).

Examples

> Zamani, Jack na Jill walipanda kilima, wakaleta ndoo ya maji, wakatelemka, Jack akaanguka, akapasua kichwa chake, Jill akamfuata.
>
> Once upon a time, Jack and Jill climbed the hill and fetched a pail of water, they came down, Jack fell and cracked his head, and Jill followed him.

Mdogo Bo Peep alipoteza kondoo zake akawatafuta asijue walipokwenda. Akawaacha, wakarudi wakiileta mikia yao nyuma yao.

Little Bo Peep lost her sheep and looked for them and did not know where they went. She left them and they returned bringing their tails behind them.

(N.B. These are free renderings of the English nursery rhymes for the purpose of illustrating this tense, and are not necessarily generally known amongst Africans).

Expeditious tense
The construction of this tense differs from the previous use. It is, in this case, incorporated within the normal affirmative subjunctive tense. Its sense is that of "going" to do a job, though nothing to do with the future tense, which can be suggested in English by the use of the words 'going to do something'.

ni-ka-lete	nikalete	let me go and bring
u-ka-lete	ukalete	would you go and bring
a-ka-lete	akalete	let him go and bring
tu-ka-lete	tukalete	let us go and bring
m-ka-lete	mkalete	would you go and bring
wa-ka-lete	wakalete	let them go and bring

(Its sense does not allow it to be used with other noun classes as subject.)

With Arabic verbs, the final vowel is not changed, as is also the case in the normal subjunctive.

u-ka-jaribu	ukajaribu	would you go and try
tu-ka-keti	tukaketi	let us go and sit down

(Although the above examples might be mistaken with the narrative tense, the fact that they are not introduced by a past tense is sufficient to suggest the expeditious tense.)

With monosyllabics, as with the normal subjunctive, the 'infinitive' 'ku-' sign is dropped:

ni-ka-le	nikale	let me go and eat
u-ka-nywe	ukanywe	would you go and drink

Note. This tense may often be used in conjunction with the verb 'kwenda'. If so, it merely stresses the action of going, without actually altering the sense of the '-ka-' within the verb subjunctive.

e.g. Twende tukale.   Let's go and eat (or just 'Tukale').
Aende akamwite.   Let him go and call him (or just 'Akamwite').

At the same time, one could use the verb 'kwenda' in such cases without following it with the -KA- subjunctive, and this would still be understandable, having the same meaning, but it is not strictly grammatically correct to omit it.

Variation

This -KA- tense can also be used with the same meaning when added to the abrupt imperative. This has the same effect on the imperative as using it with an object infix, i.e. it changes the final '-a' to '-e' on Bantu verbs. It also causes monosyllabic verbs to drop their 'infinitive' 'ku-'.

Kalete!	Go and bring!
Kamwambie!	Go and tell him!
Kampe!	Go and give it to him!
Kajaribu!	Go and try!

Once again, these could be preceded by 'nenda' merely to give accent to the 'going' part.

e.g. Nenda kalete!   *Go* and bring!

Examples:

Twende tukawalete watoto wetu hapa.
  Let's go and bring our children here.
Tulifika Mombasa, tukanunua nguo mpya halafu tukaenda kula.
  We went to Mombasa, we bought some new clothes and
    afterwards went to eat.
Nenda kamwambie alete chai.
  Go and tell him to bring the tea.
Ukanunue sigara dukani.
  Would you go and buy some cigarettes at the shop.
'Bwana yupo?' 'Ndiyo'. 'Kamwite, basi!'
  'Is the Bwana there?' 'Yes'. 'Go and call him then!'

'Headline' tense

This is not a tense you are personally likely to use, but since you are likely to come across it in the press, it is useful to know about it.

In the same way that the English press makes headline verbs as brief as possible, so does Swahili. To do this, they use the KA- tense without any subject prefix, and without altering the verb stem in any way.

e.g.	Mtu kauma mbwa	Person bites dog
	cf. Mtu aliuma mbwa	A person bit a dog
	Waziri kafa	Minister dies
	cf. Waziri alikufa	A minister died
	Mwizi kakamatwa	Thief seized
	cf. Mwizi alikamatwa	A thief was seized.

Exercise 75

(a) *Translate:* Go and call the teacher!; would you go and clean the vehicle; let us go and eat now!; let them go and look for the children; the guest arrived at 7 o'clock and ate at our home; AEROPLANE CRASHES (falls); would you (pl.) go and read this book; go and buy me some cigarettes at the shop; I saw him in town, told him the news, he went away and did not return; let's go and rest.

(b) *Translate:* Would you go and bring me some water, please; go and see if they will go to Nairobi tomorrow; he went fishing, fell into the river, and was unable to get himself out; they went hunting, killed an animal and ate it; go and give him a reply; we did not go to Nairobi, we stayed at home and read many books; let us go and drink some coffee now; let them go and bring us some more firewood; they went to buy a new vehicle, brought it home and showed it to everybody; if you don't know, go and ask.

(c) *Translate:* Tulifika katika nchi hii kwa ndege. Tulipofika Nairobi tukaona kwamba mji wenyewe ulikuwa mji mkubwa kabisa. Baada ya mizigo kuangaliwa, tukaingia mji, tukajaribu kupata chumba hotelini tusipate. Basi tukajaribu hoteli nyingine tukafaulu kupata chumba kidogo kimoja. Tukataka kukaa Nairobi kwa muda wa siku mbili, halafu kuendelea katika safari yetu. Baada ya kununua vitu vingi mjini, tukanunua motokaa mpya, tukaijaza petroli, tukaanza safari yetu ndefu kwenda Dar es Salaam. Njiani, tukaona mlima mrefu kabisa uliokuwa mweupe juu. Nikamwuliza mwenzangu 'Mlima gani ule?' Akajibu, 'Ninafikiri ni mlima wa Kilimanjaro, lakini tukamwulize mzee yule'. Tulipomwuliza akasema kwamba ulikuwa Kilimanjaro, tukaenda zetu.

59   More conditional tenses

We have, so far, learnt one conditional tense using 'if' followed by a future or imperative tense.

There are, however, other conditional tenses which put forward a hypothesis either present, or past. There are special tense signs in Swahili for these tenses.

Present
The tense sign for the present conditional is -NGE-. It is used as normal:

ni-nge-kaa	ningekaa	if I were to stay
u-nge-kaa	ungekaa	if you were to stay
a-nge-kaa	angekaa	if he/she were to stay
tu-nge-kaa	tungekaa	if we were to stay
m-nge-kaa	mngekaa	if you were to stay
wa-nge-kaa	wangekaa	if they were to stay

M- MI- class

u-nge-kaa	ungekaa	if it were to stay
i-nge-kaa	ingekaa	if they were to stay

Arabic verbs

ni-nge-jaribu	ningejaribu	if I were to try
wa-nge-fikiri	wangefikiri	if they were to think

Monosyllabic verbs retain their 'infinitive' 'ku-'

ni-nge-kula	ningekula	if I were to eat
a-nge-kwenda	angekwenda	if he/she were to go
tu-nge-kuwa	tungekuwa	if we were to be
wa-nge-kuwa	wangekuwa	if they were to have . . . .
na	na	

This condition is invariably followed by a second condition (this is really a hypothesis, but Swahili uses the same tense sign for it as for a condition).

> e.g. If I were to go now, I would see him.

In Swahili, the same construction is used for the second condition. In this case, the second one is also the present tense.

> Ningekwenda sasa ningemwona.

Examples

Ningejaribu sana, ningeweza kumaliza upesi.
If I were to try hard, I would be able to finish quickly.
Ungekuja leo, ningepika keki.
If you were to come to-day, I would cook a cake.
Mvua ingenyesha leo, ningepanda mbegu zangu.
If it were to rain to-day, I would sow my seeds.
Angeanguka mtini, angekufa.
If he were to fall from the tree, he would die.
Ungesoma gazeti hili, ungejua habari zote.
If you were to read this paper, you would know all the news.

Past conditional

The tense sign for the past tense incorporates the -LI- sign, and is -NGALI-.

ni-ngali-kaa	ningalikaa	if I had stayed
u-ngali-kaa	ungalikaa	if you had stayed
a-ngali-kaa	angalikaa	if she/he had stayed
tu-ngali-kaa	tungalikaa	if we had stayed
m-ngali-kaa	mngalikaa	if you had stayed
wa-ngali-kaa	wangalikaa	if they had stayed

M- MI- class

u-ngali-kaa	ungalikaa	if it had stayed
i-ngali-kaa	ingalikaa	if they had stayed

Arabic verbs

ni-ngali-jaribu	ningalijaribu	if I had tried
wa-ngali-fikiri	wangalifikiri	if they had thought

Monosyllabic verbs again retain their 'infinitive' 'ku-':

ni-ngali-kula	ningalikula	if I had eaten
a-ngali-kwenda	angalikwenda	if he had gone
tu-ngali-kuwa	tungalikuwa	if we had been
wa-ngali-kuwa	wangalikuwa na	if they had had

(Alternative translations could be 'If I were to have stayed', etc.)

As with the present conditional tense, this tense is invariably followed by another condition (hypothesis). This again uses the same construction:

> If I had known you, I would have asked you.
> Ningalikujua, ningalikuuliza.

Examples:

> Ningalijaribu sana, ningaliweza kumaliza upesi.
> If I had tried hard, I would have been able to finish quickly.
> Ungalikuja jana, ningalipika keki.
> If you had come yesterday, I would have cooked a cake.
> Mvua ingalinyesha jana, ningalipanda mbegu zangu.
> If it had rained yesterday, I would have sown my seeds.
> Angalianguka mtini, angalikufa.
> If he had fallen from the tree, he would have died.
> Ungalisoma gazeti hili, ungalijua habari zote.
> If you had read this paper, you would have known all the news.

Mixtures.
It is, of course, possible to mix up the two tenses, so that a condition in one tense is followed by a condition in another tense.

> e.g. Ungalisoma gazeti hili, ungejua habari zote sasa.
> If you had read this paper, you would know all the news now.
> Ningekuwa mzee sasa, ningalikuambia habari ya ile.
> If I were an old man now, I would have told you about that.

Present negative conditional
The equivalent negative tense to the -NGE- tense has the sign -SINGE-. This is the '-si-' negative tense added to '-nge-' hence its

213

normal rule of taking affirmative subject prefixes. This tense does not, similarly, take the negative subject prefixes, but the normal affirmative ones.

ni-singe-kaa	nisingekaa	if I were not to stay
u-singe-kaa	usingekaa	if you were not to stay
a-singe-kaa	asingekaa	if he/she were not to stay
tu-singe-kaa	tusingekaa	if we were not to stay
m-singe-kaa	msingekaa	if you were not to stay
wa-singe-kaa	wasingekaa	if they were not to stay

M-MI- class

| u-singe-kaa | usingekaa | if it were not to stay |
| i-singe-kaa | isingekaa | if they were not to stay. |

Arabic verbs

| ni-singe-jaribu | nisingejaribu | if I were not to try |
| wa-singe-fikiri | wasingefikiri | if they were not to think |

Monosyllabic verbs still retain their 'infinitive' 'ku-'

ni-singe-kula	nisingekula	if I were not to eat
a-singe-kwenda	asingekwenda	if he were not to go
tu-singe-kuwa	tusingekuwa	if we were not to be/become
wa-singe-kuwa na	wasingekuwa na	if they were not to have

(N.B. Sometimes, an alternative negative form is used which uses the normal affirmative tense sign, but the negative subject prefixes: Singe-kaa, Hungekaa, Hangekaa, Hatungekaa, etc. But it is less common, and the learner is recommended to learn and use the '-singe-' version.)

As with the previous examples, this condition may be followed by another, even though a different tense.

Examples;

Nisingejaribu sana, nisingeweza kumaliza upesi.
    If I were not to try hard, I would not be able to finish quickly.

Usingesoma gazeti hili, usingejua habari zote.
    If you were not to read this paper, you would not know all the news.

Mvua isingenyesha leo, nisingeweza kupanda mbegu zangu.
    If it were not to rain today, I would not be able to sow my seeds.

Nisingekuwa mzee sasa, ningeweza kupanda Kilimanjaro.
    If I were not an old man now, I would be able to climb Kilimanjaro.

Isingekuwa mwezi wa Desemba, ungaliweza kwenda Ulaya.
    If it were not the month of December, you would have been able to go to Europe.

Ungalimwambia habari, asingekuwa hapa sasa.
If you had told him the news, he would not be here now.
Wangepumzika, wasingechoka.
If they were to rest, they would not be tired.

Past negative conditional

The equivalent negative tense sign to the -NGALI- tense is -SINGALI-.
This is the '-si-' tense added to '-ngali-' hence its normal rule of taking
affirmative subject prefixes. Like the present negative tense, it does not
take negative subject prefixes, but affirmative:

ni-singali-kaa	nisingalikaa	if I had not stayed.
u-singali-kaa	usingalikaa	if you had not stayed.
a-singali-kaa	asingalikaa	if he/she had not stayed.
tu-singali-kaa	tusingalikaa	if we had not stayed.
m-singali-kaa	msingalikaa	if you had not stayed.
wa-singali-kaa	wasingalikaa	if they had not stayed.

M- Mi- class

u-singali-kaa	usingalikaa	if it had not stayed.
i-singali-kaa	isingalikaa	if they had not stayed.

Arabic verbs

ni-singali-jaribu	nisingalijaribu	if I had not tried.
wa-singali-fikiri	wasingalifikiri	if they had not thought.

Monosyllabic verbs, again, retain the 'infinitive' 'ku-'

ni-singali-kula	nisingalikula	if I had not eaten.
a-singali-kwenda	asingalikwenda	if he had not gone.
tu-singali-kuwa	tusingalikuwa	if we had not been/become
wa-singali-kuwa na	wasingalikuwa na	if they had not had.

(Alternative translations could be 'If I were not to have stayed', etc.)
As with the present negative tense, an alternative form does exist,
using negative subject prefixes with the affirmative tense sign: Singa-
likaa, Hungalikaa, Hangalikaa, Hatungalikaa, etc. But again being
less common, the learner is recommended to learn and use the
-SINGALI- form.
This condition may also be followed by another. Thus either of
these four tenses may be used in combinations with another.

Examples:

Nisingalijaribu sana, nisingaliweza kumaliza upesi.
If I had not tried hard, I would not have been able to finish
quickly.

215

Usingalisoma gazeti hili, usingalijua habari zote.
If you had not read this paper, you would not have known
all the news.
Mvua isingalinyesha jana, nisingaliweza kupanda mbegu
zangu.
If it had not rained yesterday, I would not have been able to
sow my seeds.
Nisingalikuwa mzee sasa, ningaliweza kupanda Kilimanjaro.
If I had not become an old man now, I would have been able
to climb Kilimanjaro.
Ungalimwambia habari zote, asingalikuwa hapa jana.
If you had told him all the news, he would not have been
here yesterday.
Wangalipumzika, wasingalichoka.
If they had rested, they could not have got tired.

*N.B. With all these tenses, the word 'kama' can be used to stress the
'if'.*

Exercise 76

(a) *Translate:* If you were to read; if you had climbed; if the tree had not
fallen; if the house was not here; if you were not a teacher; if we had eaten;
if the old man had not died; if they had tried; if you were to forgive him; if
he was not sick; if the arm had not broken; if this door had been closed; if
the mail were to be brought; if I had the key; if the bridge had not fallen; if
our journey had been shorter; if there had been a meeting to-day; if the
water was boiling; had the guest not arrived; if he had not lost his
opportunity.

(b) *Translate:* If you had come yesterday, you could have helped me; if they
were to go to Moshi now, they would see him; if he were a teacher, he
would have gone to the meeting; if he had been brought, we would be able
to ask him; if he had not fallen, he would not have died; if this house were
not large, we would not live here; if he were not a sick person, the doctor
would not have come; if the tree had not fallen, we would not have this
firewood; if they had not come here, we would have gone there; I would
catch that animal if it were not dangerous.

(c) *Translate:* Usingevuta sigara; ungeniuliza; angeweza kuja leo; ungalituma
barua; mlima usingeonekana; mizigo ingaliletwa hapa; gari lisingalipi-
nduka; nyumba ingalikuwa yangu; tungalilipwa mishahara; ungetandika
kitanda hiki; nisingaliambiwa; ungalikunywa pombe ile; asingaliingia
chumba kile; tusingalikuwa na msaada; saa isingaliharibika; kikombe
kisingekuwa kichafu; wenyeji wasingalipatana; tungejua Kiswahili; mbegu
zingepandwa; usingalikosa kufika.

(d) *Translate:* Ungevaa koti la mvua usingesikia baridi; angalipanda mimea ile
mapema zaidi, angalipata faida kubwa; wangefanya bidii leo, wangeweza
kupumzika kesho; ungalifika jana ungalimwona waziri wetu; ningalifika
jana, nisingalikosa kupata mshahara wangu; ungalimwambia shida zako,
angaliweza kukusaidia; ungaliniambia zamani, nisingalikwenda kumwuliza; isingalinyesha mvua leo, tungalikwenda kumwona; kisu kingekuwa
kikali, kingeweza kukata nyama hii; ningekuwa wewe, nisingevaa nguo ile.

216

60   Demonstratives of Reference

We have now been long familiar with the ordinary demonstrative ('huyu' this person; 'yule' that person, etc.). It will be remembered that they were made up by either beginning with an 'h', ending with the subject prefix (except the 'M- Wa-' class which is irregular) and repeating the vowel in between, or by starting with the subject prefix and adding '-le', depending on which demonstrative was required.

Demonstrative of proximity (This, these)

If, however, the demonstrative of proximity (this and these) is used in reference to someone or something which has already been mentioned or referred to, then a special form of the demonstrative exists. (It would not be considered a major error to omit this special demonstrative, but its use where appropriate greatly improves one's standard of the language).

e.g. There is a good shop in town. Now *this* (referred to) shop sells many things.

The construction of this special demonstrative is made up as follows:

The original first syllable of the ordinary demonstrative is taken, but instead of adding the subject prefix, the *relative* is added as appropriate. (The vowel used in the first syllable, however, remains as that which matched with the subject prefix). The M- WA- class singular, is again an exception:

	Ordinary	*Reference*	
M- Wa-	huyu	huyo	this person
	hawa	hao	these people
M- Mi-	huu	huo	this
	hii	hiyo	these
Ki- Vi-	hiki	hicho	this
	hivi	hivyo	these
N	hii	hiyo	this
	hizi	hizo	these
Ma-	hili	hilo	this
	haya	hayo	these
U-	huu	huo	this
	hizi	hizo	these
Mahali	hapa	hapo	this place
	huku	huko	this area
	humu	humo	this inside place

N.B. *The word 'huko' has a second specialised meaning used in the sense of 'down in' or 'over in' or 'up in' in the context of 'Down in Dar*

es Salaam' (Huko Dar es Salaam), 'Up in Nairobi' (Huko Nairobi),
'Over in the Serengeti' (Huko Serengeti), etc.

Word order
Whereas the demonstrative in normal use is generally placed at the
end of the line of adjectives, the demonstrative of reference normally
precedes the noun where there are no adjectives.

hilo duka	this (referred to) shop
hao watoto	these (referred to) children
hicho kiti	this (referred to) chair
etc.	

But one may often hear it placed after the noun but before any
adjectives:

duka hilo kubwa	this (referred to) large shop
watoto hao wadogo	these (referred to) small children
kiti hicho kilichovunjika	this (referred to) broken chair

Personal possessives, however, still follow immediately after the noun:

duka langu hilo	my (referred to) shop	*or* this (referred to) shop of mine
watoto wao hao	their (referred to) children	*or* these (referred to) children of theirs
kiti chake hicho	his (referred to) chair	*or* this (referred to) chair of his

Demonstrative of distance (that, those)
No special form of this demonstrative exists. Instead the normal
demonstrative is used, but in different word order. Like the demonstrative just mentioned, it can be used either before the noun, or just
after it, preceding any adjectives that might be present:

	lile duka	that (referred to) shop
	wale watoto	those (referred to) children
	kile kiti	that (referred to) chair
or	duka lile kubwa	that (referred to) big shop
	watoto wale wadogo	those (referred to) small children
but	kiti kile kilichovunjika	that broken chair

*N.B. There is nothing here to suggest reference, so that in this case,
since there are no adjectives, it would have to precede the noun, 'kile
kiti kilichovunjika'.*

Similarly, where only personal possessives are used without adjectives,
the demonstrative, if used in reference, would precede the noun:

lile duka langu	that (referred to) shop of mine

wale watoto wao	those (referred to) children of theirs
kile kiti chake	that (referred to) chair of his

In Swahili, one will often hear the normal demonstrative of proximity (this, these) used before the adjectives,

i.e. kiti hiki kikubwa   this large chair
watoto hawa wadogo these small children
etc.

This word order is used also in a sense of reference, but whereas the special demonstrative of reference (which uses the relative) tends to be used only with things referred to in the past, the normal demonstrative is used in this reversed word order when referring to something or someone being pointed to, or referred to by obvious direct connection,

e.g. Chukua kiti hiki kizuri.
Take this good chair (which is being offered).
Lete sanduku hili kubwa.
Bring this large box (at which I am pointing). etc.

Exercise 77

(a) *Give the demonstrative of reference agreeing with the following nouns:*
Shop; book; soap; water; sleep; keys; child; cook; women; bread; mountains; village; medicine; dew; knives; dates (calendar); planks; farmers; thorns; member.

(b) *Translate each sentence assuming the demonstrative is being used in reference:* I went to that shop and bought these things; if you see this man, tell me; have you read this good book?; these Europeans come from Germany; this bread is not sweet. I do not like it; these cattle are the property of that able farmer; spray the insecticide to drive off these flies; that letter took three months to arrive; these houses were bought by that African; the leaves of that tree are good to eat.

(c) *Translate:* Pana duka jipya mjini; hilo duka lauza mkate; huo mkate una utamu; huo utamu ni kwa sababu ya sukari iliyowekwa; hiyo sukari inapatikana katika mashamba ya nchi hii; hayo mashamba lazima yawe na maji ya kutosha; hayo maji lazima yasiwe na chumvi; hiyo chumvi inaweza kuharibu mimea; hiyo mimea ni mali ya wakulima; hao wakulima ni wenyeji wa Tanzania.

61   Emphatics

An emphatic is a word used to add stress to a person or thing, which in English is often a word such as 'indeed', or 'the very' or 'the self-same' etc.

> i.e.   Indeed the book I read
> The very man I saw
> The self-same medicine

The word used in Swahili takes agreements, and its stem is 'ndi-'.

The agreement it takes is the relative:

M- WA-	ndiye	the very person
	ndio	the very people

M- MI-	ndio	the very
	ndiyo	the very

KI- VI-	ndicho	the very
	ndivyo	the very (can also refer to manner)

N	ndiyo	the very
	ndizo	the very

N.B. 'Ndiyo' here is the very word used in the sense of 'yes' or 'no' as mentioned near the end of chapter 11.

MA-	ndilo	the very
	ndiyo	the very

U-	ndio	the very
	ndizo	the very

Mahali	ndipo	the very place (can also refer to time)
	ndiko	the very area
	ndimo	the very 'inside place'

The personal pronouns also have emphatic forms in the singular:

	ndimi	indeed I/me
	ndiwe	indeed you
	ndiye	indeed he/she, him/her
but	ndio sisi	indeed us/we
	ndio ninyi	indeed you
	ndio wao	indeed they/them

Word order
This may be used either before or after the noun (or after personal possessive if present). It is, however, frequently used in conjunction with demonstratives of reference, in which case it generally comes before the noun. But, whether before the noun or after it, it will always follow the demonstrative:

> Hicho ndicho kitu nilichokitafuta.
> This is indeed the thing I was looking for.
> Huyu ndiye mtu niliyemwona jana.
> This is the very person I saw yesterday.
> Kitabu hiki ndicho kizuri kabisa.
> This book is indeed excellent.
> Nani alileta barua? Ndimi, Bwana.
> Who brought the letters? It was indeed I, Bwana.
> Nani atakwenda Nairobi? Ndiwe utakayekwenda.
> Who will go to Nairobi? It is indeed you who will go.
> Dawa hii ndiyo nzuri sana.
> This medicine is indeed very good.
> Habari zile ndizo nilizozisikia jana.
> That news (pl.) is just what I heard yesterday.

Exercise 78

(a) *Give the emphatic agreeing with the following nouns:* Answer; pills; portion; game; animals; European; I; milk; well; chit; you; crop; they; dirt; firewood; cloth; driver; shade; flowers.

(b) *Translate:* That is indeed my luggage; those are the very children he teaches; that is the very place where I am going; this (place) is the very end; this is the very cash I was given; it was indeed she who told me; this is just as I thought; that is just the salary he is paid; those are the very keys I lost last week; this is just the food I like best.

(c) *Translate:* Hicho ndicho kisu nilichopewa; mgeni huyu ndiye mtu niliyemwona jana; dawa hii ndiyo nzuri sana; ndivyo nilivyosema; saa moja ndipo alipofika; kazi hii ndiyo ngumu sana; mpishi yule ndiye hodari; viazi hivi ndivyo vile nilivyopanda mwezi wa tatu; huo ndio mto tuliotafuta; hilo ndilo gari lililopinduka.

62 The HU- Verb Tense

The habitual tense

As mentioned in chapter 54, there are three present tenses in Swahili. We have now covered two of them, (the '-na-', and '-a-' tenses), and here we come to the third. Basically, it is the simplest of all tenses to use, since it never takes any agreement or subject prefix. Its sign is 'hu-' and this is added as a prefix onto any verb stem. It can, if required, take an object infix, between the tense sign and verb stem as is the normal practice, but, of course, may never take the relative. Thus, if we take the verb 'ku-penda' with this sign, we get:

hu-penda   hupenda   which could mean

I usually like	we usually like
you usually like	you usually like
he/she usually likes	they usually like
it usually likes	

Note that the sense of this tense is habitual or usual action. It can almost invariably be interchanged with the -A- tense. If we require to define the subject of the verb, this has either to be done by using the appropriate noun or a self-standing pronoun:

mimi hupenda	I usually like
wewe hupenda	you usually like
yeye hupenda	he/she usually likes
sisi hupenda	we usually like
ninyi hupenda	you usually like
wao hupenda	they usually like
watoto hupenda	children usually like
mwalimu hupenda	the teacher usually likes
mti hupenda	the tree usually likes
miti hupenda	trees usually like
etc.	

Arabic verbs are treated in the same manner:

Hufikiri	I usually think, you usually think, etc.
Hujibu	I usually reply, you usually reply, etc.

Monosyllabic verbs drop their 'infinitive' 'ku-':

Huja	I usually come, you usually come, etc.
Hula	I usually eat, you usually eat, etc.
Huenda	I usually go, you usually go, etc.

Examples:
Mganga huja hapa Jumanne.
    The doctor usually comes here on Tuesdays.
Ng'ombe hula majani.
    Cattle habitually eat grass.
Mkulima yule hufanya kazi hodari.
    That farmer usually works efficiently.
Duka lile huuza mkate.
    That shop usually sells bread.
Barua hufika hapa kila siku.
    Mail usually arrives here daily.

N.B. Do not confuse this tense with the second person singular negative subject prefix which is also 'hu-'. On Bantu verbs, the ending would be '-i' in the latter case, and '-a' in the former;

Wewe hufiki Jumanne.	You don't come on Tuesdays.
Wewe hufika Jumanne.	You usually come on Tuesdays.

With Arabic verbs, no difference is seen, but the context is generally sufficient to show which is implied:

Wewe hufikiri?	Don't you think?
Wewe hufikiri	You usually think

Negative.
The normal present negative tense is used for the negative of this tense.

Proverbs.
This tense is frequently used in proverbs and sayings in Swahili. To quote a few:

Mwizi hushikwa na mwizi mwenziwe.
    A thief is usually caught by his fellow thief.
    (cf. Set a thief to catch a thief)
Haba na haba hujaza kibaba.
    A little and a little fills the kibaba measure.
    (cf. Every little counts; take care of the pence, and the pounds
        will look after themselves)

Paka akiondoka, panya hutawala.
    If the cat goes away, the rats rule.
    (cf. While the cat's away, the mice are at play)

Mpanda ovyo, hula ovyo.
    He who plants any old how, eats any old how.
    (cf. You reap what you sow)

Exercise 79
(a) *Translate:* I usually go; mail usually arrives every day; we generally rest on Sundays; meetings usually start at 7 o'clock; dew generally comes at night-time; he usually thinks; they generally come; do you usually eat at this time?; I usually read a lot; she is generally late.
(b) *Translate:* Farmers usually plant their seeds this month; salaries are generally paid every end of the month; I usually go to Nairobi twice monthly; this chemical usually kills these insects; two gallons of paraffin usually is enough for two weeks; eggs are usually obtainable on the market; mosquitoes usually bring disease; Kilimanjaro is generally visible from here; it generally rains in March; they usually come on Sundays.
(c) *Translate:* Milima ile huonekana; mayai hupatikana siku hizi; kazi hii hupendwa sana; maji huingia mfereji; milango hufunguliwa saa mbili; mtu apandaye hutelemka; wadudu hufa kwa dawa hii; kiti hiki huwekwa hapa; nguo hufuliwa Jumatatu; motokaa huhitaji petroli.

63 Which?

There is a word in Swahili for 'which?' (the interrogative, not to be confused with the relative 'which') which has been omitted until now, since it seems to be fast becoming obsolete. It is -pi?

The agreements it takes are unusual in that they are subject prefixes, *not* concords as might be expected.

The 'M- Wa-' class, however, follows the normal exception:

M- WA-	yupi?	which person?
	wepi?	which people?

N.B. Note that it is 'wepi?' and not 'wapi?' which might otherwise be confused with 'where?'

M- MI-	upi?	which?
	ipi?	which?
KI- VI-	kipi?	which?
	vipi?	which?
N-	ipi?	which?
	zipi?	which?
MA-	lipi?	which?
	yapi?	which?
U-	upi?	which?
	zipi?	which?
Mahali	kupi?	which area? (only usually used with 'ku-' agreement)

See also page 4 for a new form of popular Tanzanian greeting that uses this word in its Vipi? form.

Examples

Mkate upi?	Which bread?
Nyumba ipi?	Which house?
Nilete chakula kipi?	Which food am I to bring?
Kisu kiko wapi?	Where is the knife?
Kipi?	Which one?
Kile nilicholeta jana.	That one which I brought yesterday
Kipo pale	It is there

N.B. As stated above, this word is falling into disuse in preference for 'gani?' which really means 'what sort?' but is used very commonly now with the meaning of 'which?' (see Ch. 30.)

i.e. Mkate gani?   Which loaf?
      Nyumba gani?   Which house?
      Nilete chakula gani?   What food am I to bring?
      Kisu kiko wapi?   Where is the knife?
      Kisu gani?   Which knife?

The learner is therefore advised to use 'gani?' in preference to '-pi?'

Exercise 80
(a) *Translate using -pi?:* Which meeting? which rivers? which servant? which
animals? which bed? which keys? which dirt? which nails? which shop?
which grass? which area? which knives? which lamp? which marks? which
water? which seeds? which field? which cup? which garment do you want?
which letters did you bring?
(b) *Translate:* Baraza lipi? mbwa yupi? kiti kipi? viazi vipi? nyumba ipi? moto
upi? miiba ipi? Wazungu wepi? chombo kipi? mfupa upi? siku zipi?
bendera ipi? mlango upi? sanduku lipi? maziwa yapi? mafundi wepi? kijana
yupi? mto upi? ndizi zipi? mwaka upi?

64 Nouns—8

KU- noun class (gerunds)

As mentioned in chapter 3 the verb 'infinitive' in Swahili is not strictly
speaking an infinitive, hence the use of the inverted commas throughout this book. A verb, when prefixed by 'ku-' is really a verb-noun, or
'gerund', which in English is generally identical to the present participle, e.g. reading, working, thinking, playing, etc.
  But to the learner of Swahili, since the use of this verb-noun in
Swahili is so often used in much the same context as the verb infinitive
in English, it is more convenient to treat it as an 'infinitive'.
  Once you have become reasonably fluent in this language, there are
occasions when you may want to use these verb 'infinitives' as nouns
within their own rights. If this is the case, then they will almost
certainly want to be given agreements.
  The agreements given to all these verb-nouns are identical to the
'ku-' agreements met in the 'mahali' class, i.e. adjectival concords are
'ku-',

        e.g. kusoma kuzuri   good reading
             kufikiri kubaya   bad thinking

  Subject prefix is also 'ku-',

e.g. Kusoma kunafaa kwa watoto.   Reading is suitable for
children.

Demonstratives are 'huku' and 'kule',

    e.g. kusoma huku   this reading
         kusoma kule   that reading

Possessives are 'kwa'

    e.g. kusoma kwa Kiswahili   reading of Swahili (Swahili
reading).

Personal possessives are: kwangu, kwako, kwake, kwetu, kwenu, kwao,

    e.g. kusoma kwangu   my reading
         kucheza kwake   his playing
         kufikiri kwao   their thinking, and so on.

The Swahili student is, however, advised not to use this noun class until quite certain of its use and context. This cannot properly be appreciated until one has a reasonable comprehension of the language. In everyday simple Swahili, this noun class is rarely, if ever, used.

Negative 'Infinitive'

When this noun class is used as an 'infinitive', there are occasions when its negative equivalent is also required. The construction of this negative 'infinitive' is formed by inserting the element '-to-' as an infix between the 'infinitive' 'ku-' and the verb stem.

Thus we get:

Affirmative		*Negative*	
ku-soma	to read	ku-tosoma	not to read
ku-fika	to arrive	ku-tofika	not to arrive
ku-weka	to put	ku-toweka	not to put
ku-gusa	to touch	ku-togusa	not to touch

Arabic verbs follow suit:

ku-jaribu	to try	ku-tojaribu	not to try
ku-fikiri	to consider	ku-tofikiri	not to consider
ku-samehe	to forgive	ku-tosamehe	not to forgive

Monosyllabic verbs retain their 'infinitive' 'ku-', thus having, in fact, two 'infinitive' tense signs:

ku-la	to eat	ku-tokula	not to eat
ku-wa	to be/become	ku-tokuwa	not to be/ become

ku-fa	to die	ku-tokufa	not to die

Deviation

One may occasionally meet any verb, not only monosyllabics with the 'ku-' sign repeated thus:

kutokusoma	not to read	kutokufika	not to arrive

No definite ruling exists regarding either of these two forms, but it is more common to omit the repetition of the 'ku-' except with the monosyllabic verbs.

Examples:

Kuwa au kutokuwa, hilo ndilo swali.
   To be, or not to be, that is (indeed) the question.
Lazima kutogusa kitu hiki.
   It is necessary not to touch this thing.
Ni bora kutokwenda leo.
   It is better not to go today.
Tunataka kutoangusha mti huu.
   We want to not fell this tree.

65   Compound Tenses

We have already seen in chapter 47 that there are some compound tenses in use in combination with the -KI- tense. There are other compound tenses also found in fairly common use, also using the verb 'to be' to take the first of the tenses.

Pluperfect tense (had)

nilikuwa nimefanya	I had done
ulikuwa umefanya	you had done
alikuwa amefanya	he/she had done
tulikuwa tumefanya	we had done
mlikuwa mmefanya	you had done
walikuwa wamefanya	they had done

Negative pluperfect

sikuwa nimefanya	I had not done
hukuwa umefanya	you had not done
hakuwa amefanya	he/she had not done
hatukuwa tumefanya	we had not done

hamkuwa mmefanya	you had not done
hawakuwa wamefanya	they had not done

Conditional participle

ningekuwa nikifanya	I would be doing
ungekuwa ukifanya	you would be doing
angekuwa akifanya	he/she would be doing
tungekuwa tukifanya	we would be doing
mngekuwa mkifanya	you would be doing
wangekuwa wakifanya	they would be doing

Past conditional participle

ningalikuwa nikifanya	I would have been doing
ungalikuwa ukifanya	you would have been doing
angalikuwa akifanya	he/she would have been doing
tungalikuwa tukifanya	we would have been doing
mngalikuwa mkifanya	you would have been doing
wangalikuwa wakifanya	they would have been doing

Negative conditional participle

nisingekuwa nikifanya	I would not be doing
usingekuwa ukifanya	you would not be doing
asingekuwa akifanya	he/she would not be doing
tusingekuwa tukifanya	we would not be doing
misingekuwa mkifanya	you would not be doing
wasingekuwa wakifanya	they would not be doing

Past negative conditional participle

nisingalikuwa nikifanya	I would not have been doing
usingalikuwa ukifanya	you would not have been doing
asingalikuwa akifanya	he/she would not have been doing
tusingalikuwa tukifanya	we would not have been doing
msingalikuwa mkifanya	you would not have been doing
wasingalikuwa wakifanya	they would not have been doing

Exercise 81

(a) *Translate:* They had tried; we had not written; the water would be entering the ditch; the letters would not have been coming; he would have been sleeping; they had not finished their work; when I got there, they had gone; the children would not have been playing if they had been told; the water would not have been boiling if you had not lit the fire; it would not be raining in the valley now.

(b) *Translate:* Walikuwa wamejaribu mara nyingi; mngalikuwa mkilala sasa tusingalifika; moto ungekuwa ukiwaka vizuri kuni zingalikuwa kavu; ungaliwauliza wasingalikuwa wakiondoka sasa; tusingekuwa tukienda sasa tungaliambiwa jana; ningalikuwa nikipanda mlima sasa ningalipewa ruhusa; wangekuwa wakija sasa wangalipata nafasi; watu wale walikuwa wamekuja mwaka uliopita; usingalikuwa ukikaa hapa, nyumba nyingine ingalipatikana; ningekuwa nikifanya kazi nyumbani nisingetakiwa hapa.

66 Summary of Verb Derivatives

We have covered at different stages throughout this book all the various verb derivatives which exist, namely,

Active verbs, chapters 3 and 4
Passive verbs, chapter 17
Stative verbs, chapter 25
Causative verbs, chapter 31
Prepositional verbs, chapter 43
Reciprocal verbs, chapter 55

It is, as may have been gathered by now, possible to combine one or more of these derivatives together.

A full summary of the various derivatives is given hereunder:

ku-piga	to beat (active)
ku-pigwa	to be beaten (passive)
ku-pigia	to beat for (prepositional)
ku-pigiwa	to be beaten for (passive prepositional)
ku-pigana	to beat one another (reciprocal)
ku-piganiwa	to be fought for/over (reciprocal-passive-prepositional)
ku-pigika	to be in a beatable state (stative)
ku-pigisha	to cause to beat (causative)
ku-piganisha	to cause to beat one another (reciprocal causative)
ku-piganika	to be in a fightable state (reciprocal stative)

Remember that Arabic verbs may also be treated in a similar way, and that, by being modified with Bantu derivations, which subsequently have an '-a' ending, therefore change to '-i' with the present negative, or '-e' with subjunctives.

e.g. ku-jibu	to answer (active)
ku-jibiwa	to be answered (passive)
ku-jibia	to answer to/for (prepositional)
ku-jibiliwa	to be answered for (passive prepositional)
ku-jibiana	to answer one another (reciprocal)
ku-jibika	to be answerable (stative)
ku-jibiza	to cause to answer (causative)
ku-jibizana	to cause to answer one another (reciprocal causative)
ku-jibikana	to be answerable to one another (reciprocal stative)

Monosyllabics are also used with these derivatives and since a derivative has one or more syllables, the verb is therefore no longer monosyllabic when in derivative form:

e.g.
ku-la	to eat (active)
ku-liwa	to be eaten (passive)
ku-lia	to eat for (prepositional)
ku-liwia	to be eaten for (passive prepositional)
ku-lana	to eat one another (reciprocal)
ku-lika	to be edible (stative)
ku-lisha	to cause to eat (causative)
ku-lishana	to feed one another (reciprocal causative)
ku-likana	to be edible to one another (reciprocal stative)

Owing to their meanings, not all verbs may necessarily be able to be put into all of the above derivative forms, but the above is a guiding form which many verbs can follow and which, with the development of the use of this language, you will gradually be able to include in your Swahili.

English verbs

There is a fast growing tendency, especially up-country, to hear English verbs used in Swahili, with proper Bantu prefixes, and on occasions, derivative suffixes. This is especially the case with Africans having a knowledge of both English and Swahili. It is purely colloquial, and generally frowned upon by pure Swahili speakers. For example, one will often hear such verbs as:

ku-pasi (mtihani)	to pass an examination
ku-feli (mtihani)	to fail an examination
ku-admiti (hospitali)	to admit to hospital
ku-admitiwa (hospitali)	to be admitted to hospital
ku-cheki	to check
ku-miksi	to mix

This tendency is also moving to nouns, especially technical words, for which there would be no actual Swahili word. But do not let this become an excuse for not learning the language properly!

Additional Exercises

Exercise 82

Vocabulary:

maji maji	watery stuff
Morani (wa-)	a Moran (Masai warrior)
mshale (mi-)	arrow
simba	lion

Morani na simba

Mwaka mmoja ambapo mvua haikunyesha kabisa na ng'ombe wa Wamasai walikuwa katika shida kubwa, ng'ombe wengi walikufa na waliobaki hawakuwa na nguvu yo yote, hata walipochomwa mshale hawakutoa damu ila maji maji tu. Hali ya watu na wanyama ilikuwa mbaya sana, na shida hii iliendelea kwa muda wa miaka miwili na zaidi.

Lakini palikuwa na msitu mkubwa uliokuwa karibu na mlima ambao ulikuwa na majani tele na mito midogo michache, na ulikuwa mwendo wa siku tatu au zaidi kutoka nyumba za Wamasai. Watu wote waliogopa kupeleka ng'ombe zao huko, maana kulikuwa na simba mkali sana ambaye alikuwa na watoto wawili wakubwa kidogo. Simba huyo alikuwa mkali kabisa hata wanyama wengine waliogopa kuingia msitu ule.

Siku moja, wazee wa Kimasai na Wamorani walikuwa wakizungumza nje ya boma wakifanya mashauri juu ya shida yao. Mwishoni Morani mmoja, jina lake Ol Kidongoi, akakubali kwenda kujaribu kumwua yule simba. Siku ya pili, yule Morani alifanya safari yake akaenda mpaka msituni. Mle akakutana na yule simba na baada ya kupigana naye kwa muda mrefu akafaulu kumwua.

Exercise 83

Vocabulary:

jeraha (ma-)	wound
ku-enea	to spread
mshipa (mi-)	blood vessel/muscular tissue
sumu	poison

Kuumwa na nyoka

Nyoka akimwuma mtu, huingiza sumu kwa meno yake mpaka iingie ndani ya mishipa midogo ya damu. Humo yapita upesi mpaka ndani ya mishipa mikubwa zaidi na kuenea katika mwili mzima. Kwa hiyo, msaada wa kwanza lazima ufanyike upesi kabisa pale pale mtu alipoumwa kuzuia sumu ili isiingie zaidi mwilini.

Basi kama kwa bahati upo pale ambapo mtu ameumwa fanya hivi:– Hatua ya kwanza: Mfunge kamba, uzi au kitambaa upesi sana, au cho chote ulicho nacho. Ifunge katika mguu au mkono ulioumwa karibu na jeraha, lakini upande wa moyo. Hivyo utazuia sumu isipite zaidi ndani ya mishipa ya damu. Hatua ya pili: Mlaze mtu chini, asisimame. Hatua ya tatu: Chukua kisu, mkate pale penye jeraha mpaka itoke damu. Ni lazima ukate kwa nguvu kidogo ili damu itoke kwa wingi. Hatua ya nne: Tumia maarifa kuzuia mtu asiogope. Mpe moyo, pia mwambie kwamba atasaidiwa kupona. Hatua ya tano: Funga jeraha kwa kitambaa chenye maji ya chumvi. Hatua ya sita: Mpeleke mgonjwa hospitali kwa haraka iwezekanavyo.

Kama mtu akipata sumu jichoni na nyoka, msafishie jicho lake ama kwa maji mengi, ama kwa maziwa. Halafu mfungie jicho kwa kitambaa kilichowekwa maji baridi, baadaye mpeleke hospitali vilevile.

Ingawa nyoka wenye sumu ni wachache katika nchi hii, ni bora kufuata hatua hizo za msaada wa kwanza kuliko kumwacha aliyeumwa afe.

Exercise 84

Vocabulary:

ajabu	wonder/marvel
asali	honey
bawa (ma-)	wing
kifua (vi-)	chest
kipepeo (vi-)	butterfly/moth
tumbo	stomach
ulimwengu	world

Vipepeo

Kipepeo ndiye mdudu aliye mzuri kupita wote katika ulimwengu. Ziko namna nyingi za vipepeo katika nchi hii, wengine wakubwa na wengine wadogo, lakini wote wenye rangi nzuri. Siku yo yote, hasa baada ya mvua, utawaona wakiruka huko na huko penye maua.

Kama ukimtazama kipepeo, utaona kwamba mwili wake ni katika sehemu tatu; kichwa, kifua na tumbo. Kichwa chake kina macho mawili, moja kila upande. Macho hayo ni ya ajabu sana. Kama ungeweza kuyatazama kwa karibu sana, ungeweza kuona kwamba kila jicho si jicho moja hasa, kama lile la mtu, lakini ni kwa kweli macho madogo mengi kama elfu moja, mia saba yaliyo pamoja. Kwa hiyo mdudu huyu anaweza kutazama mbele na nyuma kwa mara moja. Mtu lazima ageuze kichwa chake kama akitaka kuona nyuma yake, lakini kipepeo aweza kuona pande zote bila kugeuza kichwa.

Mara nyingi huonekana akisimama juu ya ua, na kama ukiweza kusimama na kunyamaza kabisa asikusikie, utaona ulimi wake mrefu ukiingizwa ndani ya lile ua, kipepeo akitafuta asali. Wakati wa kusimama uani, utaona mabawa yake wazi, yenye rangi nyingi. Rangi hizo husaidia kumficha kipepeo asionekane na wadudu wengine au ndege ambao wangependa kumla.

Exercise 85

Vocabulary:

ku-shukuru	to thank, be grateful
pango (ma-)	cave

Pango

Tulipofika nyumbani kwa yule mwenye shamba lililo na pango tulimkuta mke wake tu, Bwana mwenyewe alikuwa hayuko. Tukamwomba mke wake atupe

ruhusa tuingie pangoni akakataa, akisema, 'Bwana wangu hataki mtu yeyote aingie pango hili.' Tukaendelea kumwomba mpaka akakubali akisema, 'Kama mjuavyo, Bwana ni mkali kabisa na sitaki kupigwa kwa ajili yenu. Mkitaka kuingia, ingieni tu. Lakini kama Bwana wangu akirudi kabla hamjatoka nitamwambia kwamba mliingia kwa nguvu bila ruhusa yangu. Mkikubali hivyo, ingieni. Msipokubali nendeni zenu, msiendelee kunisumbua.'
Tukamshukuru tukaenda kwenye pango. Tulipofika pangoni, tukaokota jiwe kubwa sana lililoanguka mlangoni lililotuzuia tusiweze kuingia. Nikamwambia mwenzangu, 'Ebu, nisaidie kuondoa jiwe hili tuweze kuingia.' Basi tukajaribu pamoja kuliondoa jiwe lile tukafaulu kwa shida. Tulipoingia, mwenzangu akawasha karabai yake tukaingia ndani kabisa.

Exercise 86

Vocabulary:

thirst	kiu
use	matumizi

Water

In some countries there is always plenty of water so that men and animals have no danger of dying from thirst. In some countries it rains often, there is plenty of grass, the wells and rivers are full, and the people do not go far from their houses in order to get water for drinking and cooking. But in other countries, water is not plentiful like this. In those places, there is very little rain for a period of several months in the year, the grass dries up and dies, the wells dry up, the quantity of water in the rivers diminishes, the people have to carry their water vessels far in order to get water to drink and to cook with. In countries with plenty of water, people do not look after their water, but in dry countries, they do not use it without thinking, because they know that if they use it too quickly, there will be none left for their use nor their cattle and perhaps either they or their cattle will die.

Exercise 87

Our journey

The other day we went to see my friend called Hamisi, who lives near the Ruvu river. When we got there, we saw that he had gone away to Mombasa. So we came back home again. On the way, we passed two men who were planting maize seeds. 'Why are you planting now?' we asked, and they replied 'We always plant our seeds this month on account of the rain which comes early this side of the valley.' We continued on our way. After walking for about four hours, we got very tired and sat under a tree in the pleasant shade. My companion said to me 'I need some food. Do you think any food at all is obtainable about here?' 'I don't know.' I replied. 'Go and ask that farmer over there if he can tell us where we shall be able to get some.' So he went to ask that farmer who told him that there was a shop in the village which was very suitable for a meal. So we continued to walk to the village where we saw the shop, had a hearty meal (satisfied ourselves with food) and went on our way.

Exercise 88

How I came to Kenya

After hearing that I had been given this job, I went to pack my luggage so as to be ready to leave at any time. When I heard the date of my journey, which was the 31st August, I told all my friends that I was going to a country called Kenya. When that day arrived, I took all my things and went to the airport (aeroplane ground) and waited to board the aircraft. Unfortunately, the aircraft was a little late, but it eventually departed at 6.30 p.m. It was a very strong aircraft which went with fierce speed and very high too. But because it was night-time, I was unable to see anything at all until dawn the next day. When I saw Nairobi below us, I was very happy, and after a few minutes the aircraft descended to arrive in Nairobi, which is called 'The City in the Sun'. After my luggage was looked at, I was given permission to leave, I boarded a vehicle which took me into the town, and there I walked about a little then went to have a rest.

Exercise 89

Vocabulary:

crown	taji
guide	mwongozi (wa-)
hire, to	ku-ajiri
porter	mpagazi (wa-)
summit, peak	kilele (vi-)
that is to say	yaani

Climbing Kilimanjaro

Every visitor to Tanzania wants to climb this huge and beautiful mountain which is called Kilimanjaro. Its height is nineteen thousand, three hundred and forty-one feet above the sea, and is the highest mountain in Africa. You need about five days to climb this mountain that is to say three days to climb up, and two days to come down. If you carry some of your loads, the journey will not be very expensive, perhaps one hundred shillings or more. But if you get hired porters to carry all your luggage, the journey will be more expensive. Also, you must hire a guide (who also needs a porter), because you would easily lose your way without a person to show you the path itself. Again, on the last day of climbing, people set off at about midnight, or 1 a.m., so as to reach the summit at dawn. There is a lot of cold there at the top, so it is necessary to wear suitable clothes to prevent the cold from entering your body. If you reach the summit, you will find a book for putting your name to show everybody that you have succeeded in climbing this great mountain. When you reach the bottom part again, the porters give you a crown of flowers which grow on the slopes of the mountain. This crown shows that you have indeed conquered the highest mountain in Africa.

Appendix 1

Summary of verb tenses

Kupiga—to beat

Tenses marked   * retain 'ku-' in the monosyllabic verbs
              † take a relative infix
              ‡ take a relative infix with '-taka-'.

Present indefinite
Affirmative*‡†
Napiga   I beat
Wapiga   They beat
Yapiga   It beats

Negative
Sipigi   I do not beat
Hawapigi   They do not beat
Haipigi   It doesn't beat

Present continuous
Affirmative†*
Ninapiga   I am beating
Wanapiga   They are beating
Inapiga   It is beating

Negative
Sipigi   I am not beating
Hawapigi   They are not beating
Haipigi   It is not beating

Future
Affirmative*‡†
Nitapiga   I shall beat
Watapiga   They shall beat
Itapiga   It shall beat

Negative*‡
Sitapiga   I shall not beat
Hawatapiga   They shall not beat
Haitapiga   It shall not beat

Past simple
Affirmative†*
Nilipiga   I did beat
Walipiga   They did beat
Ilipiga   It did beat

Negative
Sikupiga   I did not beat
Hawakupiga   They did not beat
Haikupiga   It did not beat

Past perfect
Affirmative*
Nimepiga   I have beaten
Wamepiga   They have beaten
Imepiga   It has beaten

Negative
Sijapiga   I have not beaten (yet)
Hawajapiga   They have not beaten (yet)
Haijapiga   It has not beaten (yet)

Subjunctive
Affirmative
Nipige   That I may beat
Wapige   That they may beat
Ipige   That it may beat

Negative
Nisipige   That I may not beat
Wasipige   That they may not beat
Isipige   That it may not beat

Conditional ('IF')
Affirmative
Nikipiga   If I beat
Wakipiga   If they beat
Ikipiga   If it beats

Negative
Nisipopiga   If I do not beat
Wasipopiga   If they do not beat
Isipopiga   If it does not beat

Narrative
Affirmative
Nikapiga   And I beat
Wakapiga   And they beat
Ikapiga   And it beats

Negative

(Use other past tenses.)

Expeditious
Affirmative
Nikapige   That I go and beat

Negative
Nisiende kupiga   That I don't go and beat

Wakapige   That they go and beat

Ikapige   That it goes and beats

Wasiende kupiga   That they don't go to beat

Isiende kupiga   That it does not go to beat

Habitual
Affirmative
Hupiga   I habitually beat
Hupiga   They habitually beat
Hupiga It habitually beats

Negative
(Use present negative tense.)

Conditional future
Affirmative*
Ningepiga   If I were to beat
Wangepiga   If they were to beat
Ingepiga   If it were to beat

Negative*
Nisingepiga   If I were not to beat
Wasingepiga   If they were not to beat
Isingepiga   If it were not to beat

Conditional past
Affirmative*
Ningalipiga   If I had beaten
Wangalipiga   If they had beaten
Ingalipiga   If it had beaten

Negative*
Nisingalipiga   If I had not beaten
Wasingalipiga   If they had not beaten
Isingalipiga   If it had not beaten

Past continuous
Affirmative
†Nilikuwa nikipiga   I was beating
  Walikuwa wakipiga   They were beating

  Ilikuwa ikipiga   It was beating

Negative
Sikuwa nikipiga   I was not beating
Hawakuwa wakipiga   They were not beating
Haikuwa ikipiga   It was not beating

Pluperfect
Affirmative
†Nilikuwa nimepiga   I had beaten
  Walikuwa wamepiga   They had beaten

  Ilikuwa imepiga   It had beaten

Negative
Sikuwa nimepiga   I had not beaten
Hawakuwa wamepiga   They had not beaten
Haikuwa imepiga   It had not beaten

Incomplete past
Affirmative

Use appropriate affirmative tense (-ME-)

Negative
Sijapiga   I have not yet beaten
Hawajapiga   They have not yet beaten
Haijapiga   It has not yet beaten

General Relative

Nipigaye   I who beat
Wapigao   They who beat
Ipigayo   It which beats

Negative relative
(all tenses)
Nisiyepiga   I who don't beat
Wasiopiga   They who don't beat
Isiyopiga   It which doesn't beat

Order of infixes etc.
Subject prefix
Tense sign
Relative
Object infix
Verb stem
End of verb for derivatives etc. (These spell STROVE.)

   e.g. Niliyempiga—I who beat him.

Appendix 2

Use of kupiga

Without a doubt the most common verb found in the Swahili language is ku-piga. Although of course, its true meaning is to hit or to strike, its greatest use in the language is, in fact, rarely used for that translation.

By far its most common usage is to make up for the shortage of proper verbs, in which case it is generally combined with an appropriate noun to convey the sense of a special action which does not necessarily imply anything to do with hitting or striking.

The best way to describe its use is by examples, and the following list gives numerous such examples including some of the most common.

kupiga bandi   to stitch a hem
kupiga chapa   to print, type
kupiga chiafya*   to sneeze
kupiga dawa ya mbu   to spray
  mosquito insecticide
kupiga filimbi   to play/blow a whistle
  (or similar musical instrument)
kupiga fundo   to tie a knot
kupiga hema   to pitch a tent
kupiga hodi   to call out 'hodi' to
  attract attention
kupiga kofi   to box round the ears
kupiga kelele   to make a racket/noise,
  to shout
kupiga kengele   to ring a bell
kupiga kura   to vote, cast lots
kupiga kinanda   to play the piano
kupiga mabawa   to flap wings
kupiga magoti   to kneel down
kupiga makofi   to clap the hands
kupiga mikono   to wave hands about,
  gesticulate
kupiga mluzi   to whistle

kupiga moyo   to take courage
kupiga mstari   to draw a line
kupiga pasi   to iron clothes
kupiga picha   to take a photograph
kupiga ponta   to stitch
kupiga pua   to turn up one's nose
  (in contempt)
kupiga randa   to plane wood
  (carpentry)
kupiga shauri   to take counsel/advice
kupiga shabaha   to take aim
kupiga simu   to telephone
kupiga teke   to kick
kupiga miayo*   to yawn
kupiga umeme   to flash lightening
kupiga wendo   to beat time to music

and many more!
Of course kupiga can be used for such
  phrases as:
  kupiga msumari
  to hit a nail
etc.
*onomatopoeic word

Appendix 3

Agricultural crops and produce

N.B. Grasses have been omitted from this list since they generally only have local names which therefore vary over the country.

	Plant	Produce
apple	mtofaa, mi-	tofaa, ma-
aubergine	mbiringani, mi-	biringani, ma-
avocado pear	mparachichi, mi-	parachichi, ma-
bambarra nut	njugu mawe	njugu mawe
bamboo	mwanzi, mi-	mwanzi, mi-
banana	mgomba, mi-	ndizi
barley	shayiri	shayiri
beans, Bonavist	mfiwi, mi-	fiwi
kidney (French)	maharagwe	maharagwe
soya	njegere	njegere
sword (Jack)	magobi	magobi
velvet	upupu	upupu
cabbage	kebichi; kobishi	kebichi; kobishi
carrot	karoti	karoti
cashew	mkorosho, mi-	korosho
cassava, manioc	muhogo, mi-	muhogo, mi-
castor	mbarika, mi-; nyonyo	nyonyo
cauliflower	koliflari	koliflari
chick peas	dengu	dengu
citrus, grapefruit	mbalungi, mi-	balungi, ma-; danzi, ma-
lemon	mlimau, mi-	limau, ma-
lime	mlimu, mi-	ulimu; ndimu (Pl.)
orange	mchungwa, mi-	chungwa, ma-
orange, bitter	mdanzi, mi; mdaranzi, mi-	danzi, ma-; daranzi, ma-
tangerine	mchenza, mi-	chenza, ma-
clove	mkarafuu, mi-	karafuu
clover	klova	klova
cocoa	mkakao, mi-	kakao
coconut (see also 'palm')	mnazi mi-	nazi
cocoyam	maole	maole
coffee	mbuni, mi-	kahawa
cotton	pamba	pamba
cowpea	mkunde, mi-	kunde
egg plant (aubergine)	mbiringani, mi-	biringani, ma-
elephant grass	mabingobingo	mabingobingo
flax	kitani	kitani
ginger	mtangawizi, mi-	tangawizi
grams	choroko; pojo	choroko; pojo
grape	mzabibu, mi-	zabibu
groundnuts	karanga, njugu	karanga; njugu
guava	mpera, mi-	pera, ma-
hemp, bowstring	mkonge wa pori	katani ya pori
Indian	bangi	bangi
Jack fruit	mfenesi, mi-	fenesi
Java plum	mzambarao, mi-	zambarao
kapok	msufi, mi-	sufi
kudzu,	kuzu	kuzu
ladies' fingers	mbamia, mi-	bamia
linseed	kitani	kitani
lucerne	luseni	luseni
maize	mhindi, mi-	hindi, ma-; gunzi; bunzi (cob)
mango	mwembe, mi-	embe, ma-

manioc	muhogo, mi-	muhogo, mi-
millet, bulrush	uwele	mawele
finger	ulezi; mbege, mi-	ulezi; mbege
okra	mbamia, mi-	bamia
onion	kitunguu, vi-	kitunguu, vi-
paddy	mpunga, mi-	mpunga, mi- (unshelled)
		mchele, mi- (shelled)
palm, coconut	mnazi, mi-	{ nazi (mature)
		dafu, ma- (immature)
		mbata (copra)
date	mtende, mi-	tende
oil	mchikichi, mi-	chikichi
pawpaw	mpapai, mi-	{ papai, ma-
		utomvu wa papai
		(papain)
pea, chick	dengu	dengu
cow	mkunde, mi-	kunde
garden	njegere	njegere
pigeon	mbaazi, mi-	mbaazi
peanuts (groundnuts)	karanga; njugu	karanga; njugu
pepper, black	pilipili manga	pilipili manga
red	pilipili hoho	pilipili hoho
sweet	pilipili tamu	pilipili tamu
pineapple	mnanasi, mi-	nanasi, ma-
potato	kiazi, vi-	kiazi, vi-
European	kiazi Ulaya, vi-	kiazi Ulaya, vi-
sweet	kiazi kitamu, vi-	kiazi kitamu, vi-
pumpkin	boga	boga, ma-
pyrethrum	pareto	pareto
rice (paddy)	mpunga, mi-	{ mpunga, mi- (unshelled)
		mchele, mi- (shelled)
sann hemp	marejea	marejea
sesame (simsim)	ufuta	ufuta
sisal	mkonge, mi-	katani
simsim (sesame)	ufuta	ufuta
sorghum	mtama, mi-	mtama, mi-
soursop	mtopetope, mi-	topetope, ma-
	mstafeli, mi-	stafeli, ma-
sugar cane	muwa, miwa	{ muwa, miwa (cane)
		sukari (sugar)
		sukari guru (jaggery)
sunflower	alizeti	alizeti
tea	mchai, mi-	chai
tobacco	tumbako	tumbako
tomato	nyanya	nyanya
turmeric	manjano	manjano
vegetables (general)	mboga	mboga
water melon	tango	tango, ma-
wheat	ngano	ngano
yams	viazi vikuu	viazi vikuu

Appendix 4

Summary of grammar for noun classes

	Class	Typical word	Affirmative Subject Prefix	Negative Subject Prefix	He/it is here etc. definite	He/it is thereabouts etc. indefinite	He/it is within etc. inside	this, these	that, those
Singular	—	—	ni-	si-	nipo	niko	nimo	—	—
	(M(W)-)	—	u-	hu-	upo	uko	umo	—	—
	M(W)-	mtu	a-	ha-	yupo	yuko	yumo	huyu	yule
Plural	—	—	tu-	hatu-	tupo	tuko	tumo	—	—
	(WA-)	—	m(w)-	ham(w)-	mpo	mko	mmo	—	—
	WA-	watu	wa-	hawa-	wapo	wako	wamo	hawa	wale
Singular	M(W)-	mti	u-	hau-	upo	uko	umo	huu	ule
Plural	MI-	miti	i-	hai-	ipo	iko	imo	hii	ile
Singular	KI-(CH-)	kitu	ki-	haki-	kipo	kiko	kimo	hiki	kile
Plural	VI-(VY-)	vitu	vi-	havi-	vipo	viko	vimo	hivi	vile
Singular	N-	nyumba	i-	hai-	ipo	iko	imo	hii	ile
Plural	N-	nyumba	zi-	hazi-	zipo	ziko	zimo	hizi	zile
Singular	(JI-)	duka	li-	hali-	lipo	liko	limo	hili	lile
Plural	MA-	maduka	ya-	haya-	yapo	yako	yamo	haya	yale
Singular	U-	uma	u-	hau-	upo	uko	umo	huu	ule
Plural	N-	nyuma	zi-	hazi-	zipo	ziko	zimo	hizi	zile
Singular and Plural	PA-	mahali	pa-	hapa-	papo	—	—	hapa	pale
	(locative)	—	ku-	haku-	—	kuko	—	huku	kule
		—	m(w)-	ham-	—	—	mumo	humu	mle
	KU-	kusoma	ku-	haku- (kuto-)	kupo	kuko	kumo	huku	kule

240

Class	-zuri	-baya	-eupe	-ingine	of	-angu	object infixes
Singular							
—	mzuri	mbaya	mweupe	mwingine	wa	wangu	-ni-
M(W)-	mzuri	mbaya	mweupe	mwingine	wa	wangu	-ku-
	mzuri	mbaya	mweupe	mwingine	wa	wangu	-m(w)-
Plural							
—	wazuri	wabaya	weupe	wengine	wa	wangu	-tu-
WA-	wazuri	wabaya	weupe	wengine	wa	wangu	-wa-
	wazuri	wabaya	weupe	wengine	wa	wangu	-wa-
Singular M(W)-	mzuri	mbaya	mweupe	mwingine	wa	wangu	-u-
Plural MI-	mizuri	mibaya	myeupe	mingine	ya	yangu	-i-
Singular KI-(CH-)	kizuri	kibaya	cheupe	kingine	cha	changu	-ki-
Plural VI-(VY-)	vizuri	vibaya	vyeupe	vingine	vya	vyangu	-vi-
Singular N-	nzuri	mbaya	nyeupe	nyingine	ya	yangu	-i-
Plural N-	nzuri	mbaya	nyeupe	nyingine	za	zangu	-zi-
Singular (JI-)	zuri	baya	jeupe	lingine	la	langu	-li-
Plural MA-	mazuri	mabaya	meupe	mengine	ya	yangu	-ya-
Singular U-	mzuri	mbaya	mweupe	mwingine	wa	wangu	-u-
Plural N-	nuzuri	mbaya	nyeupe	nyingine	za	zangu	-zi-
Singular and plural PA-	pazuri	pabaya	peupe	pengine	pa	pangu	-pa-
—	kuzuri	kubaya	kweupe	kwingine	kwa	kwangu	-ku-
locative	mzuri	mbaya	mweupe	mwingine	mwa	mwangu	-m(w)-
KU-	kuzuri	kubaya	kweupe	kwingine	kwa	kwangu	-ku-

Class	-ote	-enye	relative	I who am etc.	this, these ref.	this is indeed he etc.	Which?
Singular { —	—	mwenye	-ye-	niliye	—	ndimi	—
{ —	—	mwenye	-ye-	uliye	—	ndiwe	—
{ M(W)-	—	mwenye	-ye-	aliye	huyo	ndiye	yupi?
Plural { —	sote	wenye	-o-	tulio	—	ndio	—
{ —	nyote	wenye	-o-	mlio	—	ndio	—
{ WA-	wote	wenye	-o-	walio	hao	ndio	wepi?
Singular M(W)-	wote	wenye	-o-	ulio	huo	ndio	upi?
Plural MI-	yote	yenye	-yo-	iliyo	hiyo	ndiyo	ipi?
Singular KI(CH-)	chote	chenye	-cho-	kilicho	hicho	ndicho	kipi?
Plural VI(VY-)	vyote	vyenye	-vyo-	vilivyo	hivyo	ndivyo	vipi?
Singular N-	yote	yenye	-yo-	iliyo	hiyo	ndiyo	ipi?
Plural N-	zote	zenye	-zo-	zilizo	hizo	ndizo	zipi?
Singular (JI-)	lote	lenye	-lo-	lililo	hilo	ndilo	lipi?
Plural MA-	yote	yenye	-yo-	yaliyo	hayo	ndiyo	yapi?
Singular U-	wote	wenye	-o-	ulio	huo	ndio	upi?
Plural N-	zote	zenye	-zo-	zilizo	hizo	ndizo	zipi?
Singular PA-	pote	penye	-po-	palipo	hapo	ndipo	—
and plural —	kote	kwenye	-ko-	kuliko	huko	ndiko	kupi?
(locative)	mwote	mwenye	-mo-	mlimo	humo	ndimo	—
KU-	kote	kwenye	-ko-	kuliko	huko	ndiko	kupi?

Appendix 5

Simplified glossary of grammatical terms

Adjective   A word which describes a noun or a pronoun, e.g. a *good* book.
Adverb   A word which qualifies a verb, adjective, or another adverb, e.g. he read *badly*.
Cardinal number   Number signifying quantity, e.g. one, three.
Causative   The form of verb which suggests the action was caused to be done, e.g. 'he woke me up', i.e. 'he caused me to wake up'.
Clause   A sub-section of a sentence, e.g. the book, *which I bought*, was expensive.
Concord   A prefix used on most Bantu nouns and adjectives which denotes singular or plural, e.g. *M*tu *m*kubwa, *wa*tu *wa*kubwa.
Conjunction   A word which joins up two words or sentences, e.g. We came to Tanzania *and* saw much game.
Contraction   The merging together of two words, e.g. 'it is' to 'it's'.
Demonstrative   A word serving to point out a noun, etc., e.g. *this* book, *that* hill.
Derivative   The changed form of a word with a common root, e.g. 'an onlooker', from 'to look'.
Emphatic   A word adding stress onto another, e.g. the *very* book.
Gerund   A verb-noun, e.g. *Reading* and *Writing*.
Imperative   An order, e.g. *Go!*
Infinitive   A form of verb showing no subject, e.g. *to read*.
Infix   An element inserted into the middle of a word, e.g. ku*mw*ona ('-mw-' added into 'kuona').
Intransitive   A verb which takes no object, e.g. 'to walk'.
Noun   Word descriptive of a thing or person, e.g. a *book*.
Object   The word usually to which the action of a verb usually points, e.g. I saw a *book*.
Ordinal number   Number signifying position, e.g. *first, third*.
Participle   Verbal adjective e.g. a broken lamp, I saw him *coming*.
Passive   Form of verb suggesting an action suffered, e.g. *to be cut, to be told*, etc.
Phrase   A sub-section of a sentence commencing with a preposition, e.g. he ran *across the road*.
Possessive   Word pointing to ownership, e.g. *of, my, your*.
Prefix   An element added onto the front of a word, e.g. *Ku*fanya (Ku- added onto '-fanya').
Preposition   Word serving to mark relationship between a noun and another word, e.g. the book is *on* the table.
Pronoun   Word used in place of a noun, e.g. '*It* is good' in place of 'The book is good'.
Reciprocal   A type of verb suggesting a reciprocating action, e.g. *to hit one another*.
Relative   Word referring a word or phrase to another, e.g. the book *which* I bought.
Sentence   Set of words complete in themselves, containing a verb and subject, though not necessarily an object.
Stative   A type of verb descriptive of resultant state of a subject, e.g. a *broken* chair.
Subject   The noun or word with which the verb of a sentence has to agree, e.g. the *guest* is coming.
Subjunctive   A verb tense, or mood, usually suggesting '*in order to*', '*so that*, or '*let . . .*'.
Suffix   An element added onto the end of a word e.g. 'mji*ni*' ('ni' added onto 'mji')
Transitive   A verb which takes an object, e.g. I *read* the book.

Appendix 6

Writing letters in Swahili

It is becoming the practice nowadays to follow the pattern of English letter format, when writing letters in Swahili. Below is a table summarizing three different types of letter formation, and it will be noticed that a literal translation of the opening 'Dear . . .' can be used other than in letters of endearment.

	Normal letters	Formal letters	Endearing letters
Openings	'Salaam', It is possible to start a normal letter with Mpendwa Juma meaning Dear Juma	'Bwana', or 'Bwana Mohamedi', (if to a male) 'Bibi', or 'Bibi Mariam', (if to a woman) 'Dada', (if to a female of approx. equal age and status)	'Mpenzi wangu', (to a beloved one) 'Mpenzi Baba/Mama', (to a parent) 'Mpenzi ndugu/Daudi', (to a relative or close friend)
Body of Letter	First paragraph to consist of greetings etc. e.g. 'Je, habari ya siku nyingi? U mzima? Mke na watoto wako hawajambo? Mimi sijambo sana, hata mke na watoto hawa- jambo. Hofu yangu (my worry) ni kujua hali yako tu'. Final para. would also convey greetings to all.	First para. straight to the point. e.g. 'Kwa mintaarafu ya barua yako ya tarehe 15 Juni 1980, ninakujibu kwamba . . .' (Con- cerning your letter of 15th June 1980, I reply (to you) that . . .) or 'Asante kwa barua yako niliyoipokea jana kuhusu ombi lako'. (Thank you for your letter which I received yesterday concern- ing your request.) etc.	First paragraph in form of greetings as with normal letters. Similarly, last para. also to convey good wishes to all.
Closures	'Wasalaam', (signature)	'Wako mtiifu', (Yours obediently/faith- fully) 'Mtumishi wako' (your servant) (Signature)	'Wako akupendaye' (Yours who loves you) 'Mimi rafiki yako' (Me your friend) (Sig- nature)

Vocabulary used in connection with letters

Kupokea barua—to receive a letter
Kuandika barua—to write a letter
Kupeleka barua—to send a letter
Kutumbukiza barua—to post a letter

Kubandika stempu—to stick on a stamp
Anwani—address
Ada nauli/gharama ya posta—postage
Bahasha—envelope

Kwa ndege—by air
Kwa meli—by sea (ship)
Sanduku la posta (S.L.P.)—P.O. Box
Hundi ya posta—Postal Order

Answers to Exercises

Exercise 1

(a) Furahini!; Lete!; Kaa or Keti!; Simameni!; Nenda!; Njooni!; Baki!; Kula!; Jibu!; Fanya!; Fungua!; Uzeni!; Tafuteni!; Jibuni!; Jaribu!; Kunywa!; Njoo!; Kuleni!; Pigeni!; Nunua!; Fikeni!; Semeni!; Fuateni!; Simameni!; Weka!; Kaeni!; Pika!; Ngoja!; Safisha!; Sameheni!; Kata!; Leteni!; Rudini!; Jibu!; Jaribu kujibu!; Nenda kununua!; Keti, Bwana Juma!; Njoo kuleta!; Ngoja kujaribu!; Ketini!; Jaribuni kufikiri!; Kunyweni!; Fungueni!; Ngoja kwenda!; Fika!; Kaa!; Jaribu kusamehe!

(b) Follow!; (pl.); Open!; Beat (pl.); Come!; Drink! (pl.); Stay!; Go! (pl.); Speak! (pl.); Wait! (pl.); Come back! (pl.); Seize! (pl.); Eat!; Search (pl.); Put! (pl.); Remain!; Buy!; Try! (pl.); Answer!; Think! (pl.); Open! (pl.); Wait!; Shut!; Try to sell!; Sit to wait!; Come! (pl.); Cook!; Bring!; Go to buy!; Follow!

Exercise 2

(a) Usikae!; Msiweke!; Msife!; Msiuze!; Usiharibu!; Simameni!; Usikate!; Msilete!; Ngoja!; Msingoje!; Usifanye!; Usijaribu!; Usifungue!; Msikae!; Usiuze!; Usifike!; Usitafute!; Usingoje kwenda!; Usijibu!; Msifungue!; Msijaribu!; Msinywe!; Msiseme!; Msibaki!; Usije!; Msiketi!; Msile!; Usingoje kujaribu!; Msipige!; Usije kuleta!; Usinunue!; Usiwe!; Msifike!; Usiende kununua!; Msifuate!; Usijaribu kujibu!; Usianguke! Msijibu!; Usisimame!; Msirudi!; Usiweke!; Usilete!; Msikae!; Usikate!; Usipike!; Usisafishe!; Msiwe!; Usisafiri!; Usifungue!; Msije!

(b) Don't follow!; Don't go to buy!; Don't open!; Don't bring!; Don't beat! (pl.); Don't cook!; Don't come!; Don't follow! (pl.); Don't come! (pl.); Don't drink! (pl.); Don't sit!; Don't stay!; Don't try to sell!; Don't go! (pl.); Don't shut!; Don't speak! (pl.); Don't become! (be); Don't wait!; Don't love!; Don't open! (pl.); Don't wait! (pl.); Don't think! (pl.); Don't come back! (pl.); Don't answer!; Don't seize! (pl.); Don't buy!; Don't eat!; Don't remain!; Don't search! (pl.); Don't put! (pl.)

Exercise 3

(a) Mwe!; Uketi!; Mwende!; Ule!; Tafadhali ulete!; Msimame!; Tafadhali mje!; Ubaki!; Mjibu!; Mfanye!; Tafadhali ufungue!; Mwuze!; Tafadhali mtafute!; Ujibu!; Tafadhali mjaribu!; Unywe!; Uje!; Mle!; Mpige!; Tafadhali ununue!; Mfike!; Tafadhali mseme!; Tafadhali mfuate!; Uanguke!; Usimame!; Uweke!; Mkae!; Upike!; Tafadhali ungoje!; Usafishe!; Msamehe!; Ukate!; Ulete!; Mrudi!; Ujibu!; Ujaribu kujibu!; Uende kununua!; Ukae, Bwana Juma!; Tafadhali uje kuleta!; Ungoje kujaribu!; Mketi!; Tafadhali ujaribu kufikiri!; Mnywe!; Mfungue!; Tafadhali ungoje kwenda!; Ufike!; Tafadhali ukae!; Ujaribu kusamehe!

(b) Would you follow! (pl.); Would you open; Would you beat! (pl.); Would you come!; Would you drink! (pl.); Would you stay!; Would you go! (pl.); Would you speak! (pl.); Would you wait! (pl.); Would you return! (pl.); Would you seize! (pl.); Would you eat!; Would you please search! (pl.); Would you put! (pl.); Would you remain!; Would you please buy!; Would you try! (pl.); Would you reply!; Would you think! (pl.); Would you please open! (pl.); Would you wait!; Would you shut!; Would you try to sell!; Would you sit to wait!; Would you come! (pl.); Would you cook!; Would you please bring!; Would you go to buy!; Would you follow!

Exercise 4
(a) Wazungu; wanafunzi; mdudu; wageni; wanawake; mgonjwa; watoto; mwanamume; walimu; wezi; wanaume; Waafrika; mtu; watumishi; mnyama; mwenyeji; Mwingereza; wawindaji; mwana; watoto Waamerika.

(b) Kamata mwizi!; Lete watoto!; Usipige mwalimu!; Msiharibu!; Fuateni mnyama!; Tafuta mganga!; Uwe mpishi!; Piga mtoto!; Ungoje mgeni!; Usile wadudu!; Uza wanyama!; Usilete wageni!; Usifuate mzee!; Jaribu kutafuta watoto!; Leteni wagonjwa!

(c) Insects; an inhabitant; thieves; a cook; a German; European children; an old cook; teachers; a woman; a sick person; African inhabitants; a teacher; a hunter; animals; Muslims; a Greek; a stranger/visitor/new-comer; a man; a servant; pupils/students.

Exercise 5
(a) Anza!; Fagia!; Usifute!; Ingieni!; Lipeni!; Msisahau!; Someni!; Panda!; Usianze!; Usichukue!; Msitumie!; Usilale!; Usifagie sasa!; Usilipe leo!; Soma tena!; Pata kabisa!; Amka na anza!; Futa sana!; Msianze kusoma sasa!; Tunza watoto.

(b) Anafanya; tunajaribu; wananunua; unatafuta; anafikiri; ninahitaji; mnachukua; tunasoma; anawinda; analipa; wanatumia; analala; tunaanza; ninakaa; unaleta; anakula; wanakuja; anakwenda; anakuwa; mnabaki.

(c) Mzungu anawinda; ninapenda sana kusoma; wanafurahi kabisa; mpishi anapika leo; usingoje sasa; sasa ninahitaji mtumishi; lipa sasa!; mgeni anakaa leo; jaribu sana kujifunza; mnaweza kwenda sasa; wanawake na watoto wanalala; mganga anakuja leo; tunafunga kabisa; wawindaji wanafuata wanyama; Mwamerika analeta walimu; tunajifunza sana leo; mgonjwa anasema tena; mnauza mnyama; mtoto anakuwa mwizi; wageni wanajaribu kuja leo.

(d) Wake up!; Take! (pl.); Would you get!; Would you (pl.) begin!; Climb! (pl.); Would you tend!; Sweep!; Would you (pl.) enter!; Don't beat! (pl.); Don't get!; Would you read!; Don't enter!; Don't start now!; Lie down! (pl.); Don't use! (pl.); Wipe!; Would you learn!; Would you (pl.) take!; Read (pl.); Go back now! (pl.)

(e) He/she is coming; we are starting; you are reading; they are hunting; I am cultivating; you (pl.) are taking; he/she is getting; they are sweeping; we are entering; he/she is sleeping/lying down; you are climbing/sowing; I am taking/carrying; we are needing; I am thinking/considering; he/she is waiting; you are trying; you (pl.) are eating; I am becoming; they are cooking; I am buying.

(f) The European is coming now; the woman is looking after the children; the men are cultivating today; the servants are sweeping and cleaning; the students/pupils are reading/studying a lot; the visitors are returning to Nairobi today; the animals are eating a lot now; the women are carrying the children; the patient is waking up now; they are staying in Dar es Salaam.

Exercise 6
(a) Mfereji; misumari; mto; mzigo; milima; miguu; moshi; mwaka; moto; mito; miti; mlango; mimea; mshahara; mikono; mbuyu; mwiba; michezo; mkate; mwisho.

247

(b) Mbuyu unasitawi; mkate unatosha; moto unapoa; mti unanukia; mimea inaiva; mfereji unafaa; mshahara unatosha; milima inaficha; mto unanuka; mwaka unaanza.

(c) Mtoto anafunga mlango; mfereji unafaa; mimea inaota; mlima unaficha mji; miembe inasitawi; fungua mlango sasa!; lete mkate leo!; msifunge mlango!; misumari inatosha; mtoto anapanda mti sasa; mtoto ananusa mmea.

(d) Miti, tree(s); watu, person, people; mito, river(s)/pillow(s); misumari, nail(s); watoto, child(ren); milima, mountain(s); miezi, months(s)/moon(s); miili, body(ies); wezi, thief(ves); waganga, doctor(s); mifereji, ditch(es); mimea, crop(s), plant(s); miguu, leg(s)/foot, feet; wanawake, woman, women; mishahara, salary(ies); miaka, year(s); walimu, teacher(s); wanaume, man, men; mioshi, smoke(s); wadudu, insect(s).

(e) I am buying bread; the child is hiding hands; we are bringing the bags; we are able to see the moon; he is helping the children to climb the mountain; shut the door; the European is paying salaries today; the tree is falling now; put the hands out; the examination is starting today; the servants are carrying the luggage (loads); the Baobab tree is flourishing well; the people are sufficient; you (pl.) need bread; the crops are drying up; the end is coming; the fire is bringing smoke; we are planting crops now; don't use the foot to shut the door; the child is buying bread; the animal is smelling (sniffing at) the visitor.

Exercise 7

(a) -tupu; -nene; -chache; -chafu; -kubwa; -gumu; -baya; -tamu; -zuri; -vivu; -kali; -dogo; -bovu; -kali; -refu; -kuu; -pana; -ngapi?; -refu; -fupi.

(b) Mlango mbaya; mikate michache; mtu mrefu; mpishi mvivu; mkate mzima; mfuko mtupu; milima mirefu; mwalimu mgeni; mwanamke mnene; mchezo mpya; mji mkubwa; miguu mirefu; mshahara mdogo; mizigo mizito; mkate mtamu; mlima mkali; mikono michafu; miiba mikali; mioto mikali; wenyeji wangapi?

(c) Mkate mdogo mbaya; mshahara mzuri sana; misumari mirefu michache; moto mkubwa mkali; mikono mirefu na miguu mifupi; wadudu wadogo wakali wachache; wazee wavivu; mkate mkubwa mzima; wanawake wanene wangapi?; wawindaji Wazungu wageni; ninapanda mimea mizuri mipya; anajaribu mtihani mgumu; funga milango mikubwa!; watoto wadogo wananunua mchezo mzuri; watu wangapi wanakuja leo?; misumari mirefu inalegea; tunatafuta mto mkavu; milango midogo mizito inafaa; ulete mizigo michache sasa!; usipike na mikono michafu.

(d) Dry; dirty; whole; how many?; new; bad; few; rotten; sweet; heavy; small; strange; large; fat; hard; short; great; empty; lazy; long/deep.

(e) A short man; wide rivers; dry bread; a good game; how many children?; a large baobab tree; a great doctor; a few nails; tall crops/plants; a whole month.

(f) We are entering a large town; bring an empty bag; the new crops/plants are flourishing; the fat child is carrying a small load; a few loaves are sufficient; how many guests are coming today?; the servant is cleaning the dirty door; the rotten bread is stinking; I need a small pillow; you are trying a fierce speed.

Exercise 8

(a) Watu hawa; mtoto yule; mkate huu; miti ile; mwezi huu; mguu ule; misumari ile; mwaka huu; mganga yule; wanawake wale; moyo huu; miiba hii; moto ule; mizigo hii; mlango ule; mshahara ule; Wazungu wale; mwalimu yule; wezi wale; milima ile.

(b) Mlima mrefu ule; mikate michache hii; mikono michafu ile; mimea mizuri hii; mwaka mpya huu; mwendo mkali ule; mwili mnene ule; mji mkubwa ule; wadudu wadogo wale; mfereji mkavu ule; mfuko mtupu ule; miguu mirefu ile; mbuyu mkubwa ule; Mwingereza mdogo huyu; moto mkali ule; mtihani mgumu huu; misumari mikali ile; watoto wadogo hawa; wanafunzi wageni hawa; mnyama mkubwa yule.

(c) Leteni mzigo mzito ule!; mwalimu yule anangoja watoto hawa; kamata mwizi yule!; mkate mbaya ule unanuka sana; miti mirefu hii inanukia sana; mikate midogo ile inatosha; mtihani mdogo huu unafaa sana!; mtoto yule anajaribu sana mwaka huu; usifiche mikono ile!; ufunge mlango ule!

(d) That old man; this cook; those Greeks; this mountain; that person; this plant/crop; those years; that bread; those games; this bag; those inhabitants; this patient/sick person; this tree; these visitors; that smoke; these men; those insects; those salaries; this animal; this hand/arm.

(e) That small door; this long loaf; that small mountain; that new cook; this new year; those few inhabitants; that good game; that wide river; this tall tree; that strict teacher; this German doctor; this big salary; that good heart; this lazy servant; this small mango tree; those dirty feet/legs; these European new-comers; these sharp thorns; this fat body; that heavy load.

(f) They are seizing that bad thief; these good people are very suitable; those few children are going to Nairobi; don't come with empty hands; those small trees are flourishing a lot; I like this sweet bread; those visitors are climbing that big mountain; these few nails are enough; this servant is helping a lot; these 'fierce' insects are looking for those animals.

Exercise 9

(a) Mkate upo; misumari ipo; watoto wapo; mfuko upo; Mzungu yupo; mto upo; miti ipo; mwisho upo; wageni wapo; mizigo ipo.

(b) Mgonjwa yuko wapi?; Misumari iko wapi?; Mto uko wapi?; Mwalimu yuko wapi?; Watoto wako wapi?; Mishahara iko wapi?; Mpishi yuko wapi?; Mwezi uko wapi?; Mdachi yuko wapi?; Wanawake wako wapi?; mchezo upo hapa; milango ipo pale; wanyama wako kule; mgeni yuko huku; wanaume wapo hapa; mtumishi yuko kule; mizigo ipo pale; mimea iko kule; mlima upo pale; mzee yupo hapa; mwisho upo hapa.

(c) Mlangoni; mikononi; mwakani; mtini; mchezoni; mguuni; mbuyuni; mferejini; mlimani; mjini; mezani; mwishoni; mifukoni; kikapuni; jikoni; nyumbani; mtoni; motoni; moshini; mguuni; sokoni.

(d) Michezo haipo hapa; watoto hawako; mwisho haupo hapa; mganga hayuko huku; wadudu hawapo hapa; mwembe hauko kule; mikate haipo hapa; wanafunzi hawako huku; mwanamke yule hayupo hapa; mizigo ile haipo pale.

(e) Mto uko wapi? Upo pale (or uko kule); Michezo mipya iko wapi? Ipo mezani; Wanyama wako wapi? Hawapo hapa wako mibuyuni; Mtumishi yuko wapi? Anafagia nyumbani; Wadudu wabaya wale wako wapi? Hawako huku, wako mtoni; Mzee yuko wapi? Ananunua mkate mjini; watumishi wale wako wapi? Wanasaidia kuleta mizigo hapa; Mzungu yupo? Hayupo hapa, yupo/yuko mlimani; Wanyama hawako? Hawako huku; Mizigo haipo hapa? Haipo hapa, ipo/imo nyumbani; Wanawake wako sokoni.

(f) The mango tree is over there; the thorns are thereabouts; the game is on the table; a stranger is at the door; the children are thereabouts; a thief is about; the door is there; the bread is in the kitchen; the salary is in the bag/pocket; the river is not here.

(g) Where is the bread? There on the table; Where are those large animals? They are about among/in the trees; Where are those long nails? They are in the bag; Are those few students here? They are not (here). They are studying/reading in town; Where is that bad thorn? It is here on the arm; Where is the sick child? He is in the house; Where is that heavy load? It is there; Is the servant here? He is not here; Is the guest about? He/she is lying down/sleeping; Where is the town? It is there.

Exercise 10

(a) Niliandika; alikumbuka; tuliongeza; ulifunika; waliinua; mlizoea; niliuliza; alipata; tulijaza; mlikohoa; alikimbia; tulikula; walikwenda; alicheza; nilifyeka; ulileta; walitoka; tulizungumza; alikubali; waliangalia; nilichagua; tuliendelea; tulifikiri; ulimaliza; alinawa; waliomba; alijibu; ulipanga; mlipumzika; alitazama; walitembea; tulijaribu; niliuliza; alisahau; alilala; niliota; walianza; ulisoma; aliona; walilipa.

(b) Uandike; anaangalia; toka!; usikohoe; mwinue!; msijaze; ananawa; ulizeni; wanacheza.

(c) Mnyama alikula wadudu; nilinunua mikate midogo michache; mtoto mdogo alianguka mferejini; mshahara ule ulitosha; alipenda mwanamke yule; wawindaji wale waliwinda wanyama wakali; tulipanda mlima mrefu ule; mliona miti mirefu ile?; miti ile ilinukia sana; aliweza kuuza mzigo ule mjini?; nililipa watu wale; watoto wale waliendelea kucheza; mpishi alitoa mkate ule mezani; wanafunzi wale walikwenda mjini; watoto hawa walitaka kujaribu kucheza mchezo mpya ule; tulikubali kujaribu tena leo; mzee alikaa hapa mwaka mzima; ulikumbuka kufunika mkate ule?; tunazoea kukaa hapa; mwanafunzi yule alimaliza mtihani ule leo.

(d) We slept; they used; he hunted; he is asking; they conversed; he wrote; he is walking; would you run; don't (pl.) play!; they got; I liked; we were; remember! (pl.); we are begging; he arrived; continue!; rest! (pl.); I needed; they entered; we agree.

(e) Don't play (pl.) in the house; that child is finishing to write the examination now; this animal climbed that Baobab tree; that old man was a good cook; that dry ditch stank a lot; those people were sufficient to help; a few crops flourished this year; we like a lot to play that game; he put the bread there on the table; he swept in the house and now he is resting.

Exercise 11

(a) Vidole; kiberiti; kilimo; Kilatini; kioo; visahani; vidonge; kijiko; viatu; viazi; kisu; vikapu; kibarua; kichwa; vijana; Kiswahili; kisima; kijiji; Kiingereza; kifaru; kiko; choo; kioo; chumba; chakula; kiboko; kipimo; cheti; kisima; kilima.

(b) Kijiji hiki; vyumba vile; kitanda hiki; vibarua hawa; kikombe hiki; kikapu kile; viboko wale; cheti hiki; kilimo hiki; Kiswahili hiki; kiko kile; vipande vile; vilima hivi; kitu hiki; kiti kile; chakula hiki; kisu hiki; kiberiti kile; kitambaa hiki; viazi hivi.

(c) Kijiko kidogo kile; kidonda kibaya hiki; kilugha kigumu kile; vikapu vitupu hivi; kiti kidogo hiki; viatu vichafu vile; chumba kikubwa kitupu kile; kiko kirefu kipya hiki; vitabu vizuri vingapi?; chuma kizito kile.

(d) Chumba kile kilikuwa kidogo sana; safisha vyombo; angalia kisu kikali hiki; mzee yule anasema kilugha; upange chumba hiki; usisahau kwenda

250

kijijini kununua viazi; wanawake walinunua viatu vipya Arusha; jaza kikapu hiki (na) viazi sokoni; kidonda kile kidoleni kilikuwa kibaya sana; toa vikombe na visahani vipya vile; kidonda kiko wapi? Kipo pale mguuni; viazi vikubwa hivi vinafaa sana; vibarua wale walikuja kusafisha chumba kile; mganga alileta vidonge hivi; tuliona kifaru mkali sana Manyara; kitanda kile kinahitaji mto mpya; weka vitu hivi kikapuni; choo kiko wapi? Kipo pale; unahitaji vipande vingapi? Vichache; vijana warefu wale walikwenda kuleta viti vichache.

(e) Finger, vidole; a thing, vitu; a vessel, vyombo; a mirror/sheet of glass, vioo; a sore/ulcer, vidonda; a basket, vikapu; a saucer, visahani; a W.C., vyoo; a rhinoceros, vifaru; a village, vijiji; a mosquito net/tarpaulin, vyandalua; a labourer, vibarua; a shoe, viatu; a potato, viazi; a hill, vilima; a pipe (tobacco), viko; a note, vyeti; a match-box/lighter, viberiti; a room, vyumba; a head, vichwa; a hippopotamus/whip, viboko; a pill, vidonge; a youth, vijana; a teaspoon, vijiko; a cup, vikombe; a blind person, vipofu; a piece, vipande; a deaf person, viziwi; a piece of iron, vyuma; a measuring device, vipimo; a book, vitabu; a knife, visu; a lame person, viwete; a cloth/material, vitambaa; a well, visima; a chair, viti; a bed, vitanda; food, vyakula; a local language/dialect, vilugha.

(f) An extremely good reference/chit; that large book; this sweet food; how many good chairs?; those small rooms; that blind old man; that deep well; these dirty spoons; a few empty baskets; that big vessel/container.

(g) I got some new material in town today; those good labourers succeeded to raise this heavy iron; that large tarpaulin is suitable to cover these things; that child likes to gaze in the mirror; don't forget to take (eat) those tablets/pills; this labourer is asking for a reference; those inhabitants are becoming used to this agriculture; this good food is quite enough; this sharp knife is very suitable to cut bread (for cutting bread); where is the pipe? It is there on the chair.

Exercise 12

(a) -ingi; -erevu; -eusi; -ingine; -aminifu; -eupe; -embamba; -ema; -epesi; -ingi; -ekundu.

(b) Watumishi waminifu; mkate mweupe; mwanamke mwema; viatu vyekundu; mwezi mwingine; (watu) wengi; mti mwembamba; mzigo mwepesi; kitabu cheusi; Mwafrika mwaminifu; kitambaa kingi; vitu vingi; kitabu chembamba; mwizi mwerevu; miili myembamba; vitambaa vyeusi; vyumba vingi; Kiswahili chepesi; kifaru mwingine; vibarua werevu.

(c) Mto mrefu mwembamba huu; Mzee yule anajua kilimo kizuri kingi; Lete kikombe chekundu kikubwa kingine; Vyandalua vidogo vyeupe vingapi?; Moto mkubwa ule unatoa moshi mweusi mwingi; Mtihani ule ulikuwa mwepesi sana; Mnyama mwerevu yule anakula mimea myekundu ile; Ninahitaji vibarua waminifu wengine; Tuliona kifaru mweusi mkali Serengeti; Ninajaribu kujifunza Kiswahili hiki; Watoto wengine wanacheza mchezo; Alikwenda mjini kununua viazi; Wageni wengi wanakuja kula hapa leo; Tunahitaji vijana wengine kusaidia kukamata mnyama mwerevu yule; Alipata msumari mwembamba sana mguuni; Mzee yule alikuwa mwema sana; Tuliweka kitambaa chekundu chumbani; Anahitaji mnyama mwamanifu kukaa nyumbani; Ninahitaji mikate myeusi michache; Wenyeji wengine walikaa pale miaka mingi.

(d) A red sore; narrow beds; another door; black smoke; white hands; a cunning youth; many crops/plants; another thing (something else); dark people; dark/black mountains.

251

(e) I bought that other book; Some things were red, others were black; Many women were in the town, others stayed at home; You can (are able to) take this light luggage (these light loads), those can remain here; An honest/trustworthy servant is able to get a big wage; Those white insects are eating rotten trees; Many visitors arrived in Tanzania that year; The tall slender tree fell over there; Bring some more food here!; Would you clean those other black shoes.

Exercise 13

(a) Laini; sawa; wazi; bora; ghali; maridadi; kila; maskini; bure; hodari; kamili; tele; safi; laini; rahisi; tayari; hodari; bora; kamili; maskini.

(b) Kitambaa safi; kila mwezi; chakula maridadi; mpishi hodari; kitabu rahisi; chombo bure; mito laini; watu bora; vibarua tele; mlango wazi; wanafunzi sawa; kiwete maskini; kila mtu; mchezo bure; viti bora; vikombe safi; viatu laini; viazi tele; watoto hodari; kilimo bora.

(c) Kila mtoto hodari; Mikate mitamu maridadi ile; Chakula kamili kilikuwa tayari; Watoto wadogo maskini wale; Milango wazi hii; Mizigo midogo sawa hii; Vibarua hodari wengi; Msumari bure huu; Kila mti ulikuwa mrefu; Kila chombo kitupu.

(d) A very clean saucer; those cheap things were best; every pupil was ready; mind that open door!; some books were expensive, others were cheap; I got another mosquito net, this (one) was useless; where are the clean shoes?; he wants something fancy; that year he was very poor; don't bring those useless things here.

Exercise 14

Mwezi ulianza vibaya sana; Mzungu anaongeza mishahara kidogo; Mnatumia vibaya sana visu vile; Mtihani ule ulikuwa mgumu kidogo; Mimea hii inakauka vizuri sana; Uliweka vibaya kioo kile; Mtumishi alisafisha vizuri chumba hiki; Mtoto yule alikata kidogo kidole; Mwendo ule ulikuwa mgumu kidogo; Ulete mkate. Vizuri!

Exercise 15

(a) Kukatwa; kulipwa; kuolewa; kujibiwa; kuliwa; kuandikwa; kupigwa; kutumiwa; kukamatwa; kupendwa; kuwindwa; kusahauliwa; kufikiriwa; kufunguliwa; kufungwa; kusamehewa; kununuliwa; kuanzwa; kuletwa; kwisha (kumalizwa).

(b) Kukatwa kwa kisu; kukatwa na mwingine; kujuliwa na walimu; alijibiwa na mtoto; walizaliwa mwaka ule; mlima ulipandwa kwa miguu; chakula kilifunikwa kwa kitambaa; chakula kilipikwa na mpishi hodari yule; kusemwa kwa Kiswahili; wanyama waliwindwa.

(c) Viazi vipya vile vililetwa na kijana yule; Mnyama mkali huyu alikamatwa kwa miguu; Mchezo ule unachezwa na watoto; Cheti hiki kiliandikwa na mganga mzungu; Kitabu kizuri kile kinasomwa sana; Walimu hodari wanatakiwa Tanzania; Vyumba vikubwa hivi vinasafishwa kila mwezi; Mti ule ulianguka na mtoto huyu alipigwa kwa kipande kile; Vikombe hivi vilitolewa na mtumishi; Niliombwa kwenda Dar es Salaam.

(d) To be refused (kukataa); to be arranged (kupanga); to be obtained/got (kupata); to be cleaned (kusafisha); to be started (kuanza); to be followed (kufuata); to be drunk (not intoxicated) (kunywa); to be needed (kuhitaji); to be wiped (kufuta); to be bought (kununua); to bear (—); to be cultivated (kulima); to be asked (kuomba); to be read (kusoma); to be eaten (kula); to marry (of man) (—): to be remembered (kukumbuka); to be put out (kutoa); to be forgotten (kusahau).

(e) Those small children are being searched for; Salaries were increased by the Greeks; Those labourers were hired by that European; These games were started this month; These cups were cleaned with this dirty cloth; That cunning thief was caught by those people; That good woman is very much liked by children; This food is eaten a lot by Africans; That door was badly opened; Those heavy loads are being carried by those labourers.

Exercise 16

(a) Mimi nilikwenda; yeye alikuja; yeye anasoma; wewe uingie; ninyi msirudi; wao wanajaribu; sisi tulifuata; wewe usingoje; mimi ninakunywa; yeye alikufa; ninyi mlisema; sisi tunafanya; wewe ulitumia; yeye alipanda nami; sisi tuliingia naye; mimi ninawinda nanyi; wao wanakaa nasi; yeye alisema naye; mimi nilisoma nao; sisi tunakaa/tunabaki nawe.

(b) Ninyi, mnapata mishahara mizuri; Yeye nami, tulikwenda Serengeti; (Wao) walikuja nami; Wao, wanasoma sana; watoto wale walikuja nasi; Yeye, alisoma Makerere; Ulikuja naye? Ndiyo, nilikuja naye; Yeye ali-kwenda Nairobi, mimi nilikaa hapa; Uje nami.

Exercise 17

(a) Hamisi ni mpishi; sisi ni wanafunzi; wao ni vibarua; yeye si mbaya; mti ule ni mbuyu; sisi si Waamerika; u mwalimu (wewe ni mwalimu); kile ni kiti; kikapu hiki ni kitupu; u David? (wewe ni David?); yu mwindaji (yeye ni mwindaji); kitabu hiki si rahisi; mimi ni mgeni; wewe si hodari; mimi si Mwingereza mtihani huu si mgumu; chakula hiki ni kitamu kile si kitamu; mpishi yupo/yumo nyumbani; watoto hawapo hapa; tunakuja.

(b) Wanyama wale (ni) wakali; Kisu hiki si kikali; Mkate huu (ni) mgumu; Kikapu kile (ni) kitupu; Kiswahili (ni) rahisi sana; Yule (ni) Hamisi; Hivi si viazi vizuri; Kidonda kile kilikuwa kibaya sana; Mshahara ulikuwa mzuri; Mizigo hii si mizito.

Exercise 18

(a) Una; ana; wana; tuna; nina; mna; ana.

(b) Ana mpishi mwema/mzuri; chumba hiki kina vitanda vingi; una kitabu?; mguu ule una kidonda kibaya; milima ile ina miti mingi; nina vipande vichache; kikombe kile kina kisahani bure; mganga ana vidonge vingi; kitanda kile kina chandalua; kijana yule ana kisu; ana kitabu, ni kizuri; hiki ni kiti, kina miguu mifupi; mtoto yule ana kichwa kikubwa; mzee ana moyo mwema/mzuri; chumba hiki kina kioo; tuna wanyama wengi; wanawake wana watoto wengi; watoto wale wana mwalimu mwema/ mzuri; mna viazi?; Juma ana viatu vichafu; nina kikombe hapa; kijiji kile kina wenyeji wengi; mnyama huyu ana wadudu wengi; mna mikono michafu; vitanda hivi vina mito; moto huu una moshi mwingi; mti ule una miiba mikali; vibarua wana vyeti; tuna mtihani leo; una kiberiti?

(c) I have a good pipe; he/she has luggage there; the room has small doors; the children have a new game; the doctor has many patients; you (pl.) have many books; that hill has very sharp thorns; that youth has a thin body; I have an examination today; have you a bag?

Exercise 19

Pana mbuyu mkubwa pale; kuna milima mirefu Tanzania; mna viazi kika-puni; pana kisu mezani; pana mgeni mlangoni; kuna mibuyu mikubwa

Kenya; kuna mkate jikoni?; pana mganga hapa? (or) kuna mganga huku?; hapa, pana wanafunzi hodari wengi; kuna Wazungu wachache Tanzania.

Exercise 20

(a) Usije leo; lete chakula; nenda mjini; fikiri sana; njoo tena!; uwe tayari!; safisha chumba hiki vizuri!; tafuteni watoto; njooni!; kula!; ninasoma; wanawake wanalima; wanaume wanawinda; msumari huu unalegea; mikate ile inatosha; (watu) wengi walikuja; tulikwenda Nairobi; mti mrefu ulianguka mtoni.

(b) Vijiko hivi; mito ile; chumba hiki; mlango ule; mizigo hii; vitanda vizuri hivi; Wazungu wangapi?; wenyeji wale; moshi mweusi ule; mchezo mpya huu; mwaka ule; mwezi huu; mzee maskini yule; milima hii, vyombo vile; vibarua hodari wale; kifaru mkali huyu; mtihani rahisi ule; vitabu vizuri na kiko kizuri; viatu vyekundu.

(c) Mimi ni mwalimu; sisi ni Waingereza; wanakuwa hodari; Hamisi ni mpishi mzuri/nwema; kuna mto kule; ana watoto wengi; yumo chumbani (yeye yumo chumbani); tunaendelea; u mgonjwa (wewe ni mgonjwa); mti huu (ni) Mbuyu; moshi ule (ni) mweusi; msumari ule si mkali; yeye si mganga; alikuwa mtoto mkubwa; wanyama wale si viboko; angalia, pana msumari hapa!; mguu ulikatwa hapa; kidonda kilikuwa kibaya kidogo; kile ni kiti kizuri; kuna wadudu wengi huku.

(d) Shut the door!; bring (pl.) the luggage (the loads)!; don't return here again!; take (carry) this book!; would you stand there!; don't (pl.) destroy those crops!; come here!; drink again!; would you (pl.) wait a little!; would you (pl.) enter!; don't (pl.) fall!; write a chit!; don't (pl.) fill other baskets!; would you increase the salary!; don't be (become) a thief!; get out (pl.) of here!; sit/stay! (pl.); he is cooking; we wanted; some died.

(e) How many children have you?; where are the loads?; that door is not open; this bread is new; that European has a long pipe; that hill has many animals; that room has a bed; those youths have long bodies; the hippo is in the river; that old man has empty pockets (bags).

Exercise 21

(a) (mtu) mmoja; miti miwili; vyumba vitatu; watoto wanne; misumari sita; vitabu vinane; miezi kumi; wanafunzi kumi na wawili; mizigo kumi na mmoja; miaka ishirini; vijiko kumi na vinane; vidole kumi; mikono miwili; milima mitano; vipande saba; vikapu kumi na vitatu; vikombe kumi na vitano; visu kumi na viwili; Wazungu kumi na mmoja; mkate mmoja; vijana kumi na wawili; vitanda kumi na tisa; kioo kimoja; viboko kumi na watano; mikate myeupe miwili na myeusi mitatu; mizigo mizito mitano na myepesi mitatu; vitanda vinne ne vyandalua vinane; watoto kumi na mmoja na mwalimu mmoja; wanaume saba na mwanamke mmoja; kiwete mmoja.

(b) Vikombe vyeupe sita na visahani viwili; viatu vyekundu viwili vile si safi; kila mkono una vidole vitano; walikaa hapa miezi kumi na miwili; chumba hiki kina mlango mdogo mmoja; alisoma vitabu tisa mwezi huu; Mwafrika mmoja ana vibarua kumi na mmoja; lete mikate mingine miwili; ninahitaji vijiko vidogo kumi na viwili; uliona vijana kumi wale?

(c) Two doctors and twenty patients; ten children; three loaves; five years; one river; eleven guests; one cook and four servants; eight lazy labourers; six rooms; nine books; thirteen Europeans and eighteen Africans; twelve animals; bring the two other loaves; he forgot three things; these inhabitants have three wells; he closed five doors; eight tall trees fell; how many rivers are there over there? Four; that labourer has seven chits/references; there is one stranger/guest at the door.

Exercise 22

(a) Nitaamka; tutahitaji; atapanda; nitapiga; utauza; utangoja?; tutakaa; mti utaanguka; visu hivi vitafaa; mikate ile itatosha; tutakufa; atakuwa mpishi; utasahau; mtasema; atarudi?; tutakuja leo; watakwenda; chakula kitaletwa; mchezo utachezwa; mishahara itaongezwa.

(b) Mti ule utaanguka pale; nitahitaji mpishi na watumishi wengine wawili; vikombe vile vitafaa; mizigo ile itakuwa mizito sana, usipike chakula, nitakula mjini; watakwenda Nairobi tena mwezi huu; wageni wangapi watakuja hapa?; kijana mmoja atajaribu kupanda mlima ule; kisima hiki kitakuwa kirefu kidogo; viazi vile vitatosha.

(c) Will you remember?; we shall write a chit; a chit will be written; I shall buy bread; bread will be bought; the food will be brought by Ali; the room will be swept; we shall be able to go to-day; he will drink; they will finish today; the door will be closed; they will want to travel today; these chairs will be needed; we shall get food in town; the shoes will dry well here; the examination will be started today; they will climb that mountain; you (pl.) will be happy; this youth will become a doctor; will you (pl.) try to return again?

Exercise 23

(a) Jumatatu; Alhamisi; jana; Jumatano; kesho kutwa; Ijumaa; juzi; Jumamosi; kesho; Jumanne; zamani; Jumapili; juzijuzi.

(b) Alikuja jana; tutakwenda Jumanne; mganga atakuja Jumapili nitakwenda kesho kutwa, watajaribu tena Alhamisi; nilikuja jana, ninakaa leo, nitarudi kesho; utarudi Jumatano; mchezo utachezwa kesho; nilizungumza naye juzi juzi; mkate huu ulipikwa Jumatatu.

(c) Walipanda mlima mrefu ule Alhamisi; tulifika Tanzania juzi; mwizi alikamatwa jana; kuna moshi mwingi mlimani leo; mtihani utaanza kesho; viatu vile vilinunuliwa Jumatano; mchezo utachezwa kesho kutwa; mishahara inalipwa kila Jumamosi; mzee alikufa zamani; mtoto yule aliletwa jana.

(d) The cook brought the food quite some time ago; they will be paid on Saturday; don't forget to come on Tuesday; this chit was written the other day; they will travel the day after to-morrow; the guest will arrive on Friday; we go to town every Monday; in the past, I lived in Nairobi; come back tomorrow!; these rooms are cleaned every Wednesday.

Exercise 24

(a) Kama; (kwa) sababu; toka/kutoka; bila; au; mpaka; katika; hata; ingawa; lakini; ila; kwa; basi!; au; basi!; kama.

(b) Alisema kwamba . . . ; mkate au viazi; kama miaka miwili; toka hapa mpaka Dar es Salaam; katika kitabu kile; hata wewe; mpaka mwaka ule; vikombe hivi, ila hiki, ni vichafu; ninajua kwa sababu nilikwenda; wageni (ni) tayari, basi lete chakula; lete kama mikate mitatu; kitabu hiki au kile; yeye si mwema/mzuri, hata kidogo; toka sasa mpaka/hata Jumanne; mgeni atakaa mpaka/hata kesho kutwa; kama utakwenda Jumatano, chukua vitu hivi; walikwenda lakini walisahau; mfuko ni mzito kwa sababu una viazi vingi; mtihani ni rahisi ingawa ni mrefu.

255

(c) Alikuja bila watoto kwa sababu walikuwa wagonjwa; tulisafiri toka London mpaka Nairobi; mnaweza kuona kwamba (yeye) hayuko, basi nendeni!; wanafunzi wale watasoma kwa kama mwaka mmoja; wanataka kuona (au) Mombasa, au Dar es Salaam; mganga aliweka kama vidonge kumi katika chombo kidogo kile; anapenda kula viazi vingi, hata viazi vitamu; mti mrefu ule ulianguka katika mto mpana ule; walifaulu mtihani bila kujaribu sana; Kiswahili si kigumu, hata kidogo!

(d) He came on foot (lit. he came by means of feet/legs); don't come without a chit; even I went; put this pillow on that bed; the animals from that village are extremely good; I shall eat about two potatoes. Is that all? Yes; I see that those mountains are very high; he is going today, but we shall go on Thursday (we are going on Thursday); if he will come tomorrow, don't forget to speak with him; the tree fell because it was rotten.

Exercise 25

(a) Kuchelewa; kuvunjika; kuchomeka; kubadili; kukosa; kushiba; kuka-sirika; kuvunja; kuchoka; kuonekana; kufunguka; kwisha; kuwezekana; kuharibika; kujaa; kulewa; kusahaulika; kumwagika; kupindua; kupotea; kupatikana; kukatika; kujulikana; kubadilika; kukubalika; kumwaga; kuchoma.

(b) Nimechelewa; vikapu vimejaa; kikombe kimevunjika; watoto wamepotea; wamechoka; viazi vinapatikana; umeshiba?; mmelewa; amekwisha kwenda; mganga anajulikana sana; mti huu utapasuliwa; alikasirika sana; tumekosa; usichelewe; vitu vile vimesahauliwa; wamekwisha choka; walitosheka na mtihani ule; usipasue kitambaa kile; mlima unaonekana vizuri sasa, wageni wamekwisha fika.

(c) Usikae katika kiti kile, kimevunjika; amekosa kufunga mlango kwa sababu unafungika vibaya; wamekwisha ona mto mkubwa ule; chakula kimekwisha pikwa na mpishi yule; usitoe chakula kingine kwa sababu wameshiba; 'Bwana yuko wapi?' 'Ametoka'; watoto wamelala kwa sababu wamechoka; mkono umevunjika kabisa; jana, Juma alilewa kabisa; kama umekwenda Nairobi, umeona mji mzuri (sana).

(d) The bread is toasted; they are satisfied with food; the door is damaged; he has gone; they have gone to bed/they have laid down; the ditch is full; we shall be late; he has failed to write a chit; don't break that vessel; the Bwana is very angry; the knife was lost on Wednesday; satisfy yourselves with food!; the bread is toasted in the kitchen; we have already started; they have finished; that door is openable; this bed has been bought because the guest will arrive today; this pipe has come apart; I have taken (eaten) two pills; this examination is finished.

(e) Do not fail to return here on Tuesday; they have forgotten to finish roasting those potatoes; this servant has already finished washing up (washing the vessels); don't increase any more because these containers are full; these hunters are well known; buy more potatoes, because they are finished; he has looked for that good knife but it is lost; those mountains will be visible to-morrow; 'Has that old man died?' 'Yes, Bwana (Sir,) he has already died'; if you have finished this examination, rest a little!

Exercise 26

(a) Mume; msaada; kivuli; mchungaji; kitunguu; wanachama; mwashi; mi-zizi; msitu; mipaka, kiwanja; muda; wake; Wakristo; msikiti; vyama; kizibo; mpini; mpira; mtelemko; mpango; mkulima; mkuki; mnazi; kivuli; kiasi; kiraka; wananchi; mkoa; kibanda.

(b) Wakristo wale wana mchungaji mwema; tutatoa msaada kwa wakulima wale; mwanamume yule ana wake watatu; mnyama yule ana mkia mrefu sana; minazi hii inatoa kivuli kingi; kuna mifupa msituni; wanachama wengi wameingia chama kile; watoto watacheza mpira Jumamosi; Waislamu wamekwenda msikitini; tunahitaji vitunguu vichache.

(c) A foreman (wanyapara); a root (mizizi); a club/society (vyama); a cork/ stopper (vizibo); a wife (wake); a mason (washi); a member (wanachama); an onion (vitunguu); a boundary (mipaka); a tail (mikia); a mosque (misikiti); a herdsman/pastor (wachungaji); a husband (waume); an island (visiwa); a Christian (Wakristo); a patch (viraka); help, aid (misaada); a coconut palm (minazi); a forest (misitu); a period of time (miuda).

(d) The members have made a new arrangement; football has started on the pitch; he will get a small amount; that farmer has extremely good crops; that bone is completely broken; we shall stay a long time there; the members have gone to the meeting; stay/sit (pl.) in the shade!; where is the boundary? There in the forest; I shall put a patch on that material.

Exercise 27
(a) Nilikuwa na chakula kingi; tutakuwa na mtihani kesho; palikuwa na mkutano jana; tutakuwa na wageni Jumatano; chumba hiki kitakuwa na vitanda vitatu; miti ile ilikuwa na miiba mikali; mkulima yule amekuwa na mimea mizuri; alikuwa na kidonda kibaya mguuni; kutakuwa na msitu katika mlima ule (patakuwa na msitu . . . .); pamekuwa na mikutano mingi mwaka huu; tumekuwa na wapishi watatu mwezi huu; mimea hii imekuwa na kivuli kingi; nina mtoto mmoja, lakini nitakuwa na wawili; ulikuwa na vitabu?; palikuwa na (kulikuwa na) moto mkubwa mlimani; vijiji vile vilikuwa na wenyeji wengi; miti hii itakuwa na mizizi mirefu; vijana wale walikuwa na visu vikali; wana kitambaa kingi; tumekuwa na msaada mkubwa.

(b) We had many members that year; those labourers will have a very strict foreman; there was a slope somewhere over there; there will be a mosque here; that room had a mirror; that bed had a pillow, but where is it now?; that river has many hippopotami; those people had spears yesterday; I shall have a new programme to-morrow; there were many Muslims hereabouts some time ago.

Exercise 28
(a) Baadaye/halafu; kumbe!; kwa bahati; hasa; polepole; kwa sauti; kwa kawaida; pia/vilevile; tu; kwa haraka/upesi; mapema; labda; vilevile/pia; kwa kutwa; kwa hiyo/kwa sababu hii; kwa kifupi; kwa ghafula; sikuzote; bado; kwa kweli; kwa kusudi.

(b) Nenda polepole; nina mtoto mmoja tu; njoo upesi/kwa haraka; alikwenda Nairobi, halafu/baadaye alirudi hapa; (yeye) alikwenda pia/vilevile; anapenda viazi, hasa viazi vitamu; aliingia kwa ghafula; nilianguka kwa kusudi; semeni kwa sauti; kwa kweli, yu mtumishi mwaminifu (yeye ni mtumishi mwaminifu); kwa kawaida anaamka mapema; nilikuwa na kitabu kile, labda yeye alikuwa na kimoja pia/vilevile; kumbe, bado anakaa hapa!; anakuja hapa sikuzote; fanya hivi/hivyo; alisema kwa kifupi; mti ulianguka kwa ghafula; alikuja hapa, halafu/baadaye alikwenda Nairobi; ninataka mkate mmoja tu; hayuko, labda amekwenda mjini; mkate umekwisha kwa hiyo nunua (mkate) mwingine.

(c) Come early tomorrow; he went quickly/hurriedly; fortunately I got some bread in town yesterday; clean these vessels (do the washing up) and then

257

sweep that room, and this one too; the door was opened suddenly; usually there are many meetings every month, but especially this month; we went yesterday on purpose to arrive early; he comes here daily; lift this load carefully; truly that club is very suitable.

Exercise 29

(a) Mfuko wa viazi; mimea ya mkulima; mizigo ya wageni; visima vya kijiji kile; chakula cha mtoto; miti ya msitu; mlango wa chumba; mishahara ya vibarua; milima ya Tanzania; miiba ya mti; vitabu vya wanafunzi; vidole vya mguu; kidole cha mkono; mwili wa mgonjwa; wanyama wa mkulima; kiko cha mzee; cheti cha mtumishi; kiti cha mwalimu; wanachama (wa chama); viazi vya mkulima.

(b) Angalia miiba ya mti ule. Ni mikali sana; wakulima wa kijiji hiki walikuwa na mimea mizuri ya chakula; mlima wa Kilimanjaro unaonekana sasa; mpango wa miaka mitano umeanza kwa muda huu; mizigo ya wageni wale ilikuwa mizito kidogo; mpango wa kilimo wa Kenya unaendelea vizuri (N.B. It is Kenya's plan, hence . . . wa Kenya . . .); kata vipande vitano vya mkate kwa chakula cha wageni; mkutano wa chama cha kilimo utaanza kesho; weka mito miwili katika vitanda vya watoto; labda nita-jaribu mtihani wa Kiswahili mwaka huu.

(c) Agriculture of now (i.e. modern agriculture); the hippopotami of that river; the bone of the arm; the end of that book; that woman's children; a dish-cloth (for example); a book-case; a bread-knife; a football-game; the Muslim's mosque; a period of two months; the shade of that tree; a football ground; the boundaries of this region; the handle of this cup; the tail of that animal; the roots of this tree; the citizens of Kenya; the ditches of that slope; a big quantity of onions.

(d) Many farmers of that village are members; they will have two months of aid with us, and then we shall return to Nairobi; the slope of this mountain is very steep; the old pastor of the Christians of Tanga town has already died; I have bought the spear of that Masai; we have stayed in Tanzania for a period of eight years now; many inhabitants of that town have gone to the meeting; don't buy that bread, it is yesterday's; that European's guests are making a one month's journey; where are these people's things? They are in the guests' room.

Exercise 30

(a) Mikono yangu; vitabu vyake; watoto wenu; mlango wake; moyo wako; mizizi yake; miili yenu; mkate wake; mimea yetu; mizigo yao; msitu wake; mpishi wetu; mke wangu; mume wake; mnyapara wao; mkia wake; kiti changu; kivuli chake; mtihani wao; vitunguu vyake.

(b) Hiki si kitabu cha Hamisi. Chake ni chekundu; watoto wameleta chakula chao; kuna (or pana) mkutano wa chama chetu leo; vibarua wao walianza mapema leo; mnyama yule anajulikana kwa sababu mkia wake umekatwa; Mzungu yule anatafuta mke wake; wanyama wamelala katika kivuli cha mti ule; kikombe hiki kimevunjika. Kipini chake kimepotea pia; watu hawa wanangoja mishahara yao; kama umemaliza chakula chako, pumzika.

(c) My salary; your (pl.) towns; his/her hand; his/her/its saucer; their guests; my shoes; your book; your (pl.) chits; their wives; his/her patients; your room; their wells; his/her bed; your (pl.) help; his/her/its members; their ball.

(d) Bring (pl.) their luggage; the doctor has gone to see his patients; his knife is not sharp, but mine is extremely sharp; I was able to enter their mosque the day before yesterday; the youths of that village are helping their elders a lot; they have planted trees on their boundaries; his/her umbrella is lost; bring the pillow of your bed, and its mosquito net too; I am asking to use your lighter/matches; where is your reference? It is in my pocket, Bwana.

Exercise 31

(a) Mkate gani?; Nani alikuja?; Kwa nini ulikwenda?; Anataka nini?; Mifuko mingapi?; Umekwenda wapi?; Uliona nani?; Vitu vile, je?; Ulijibuje?; Watafika lini?; Je!/Ebu!/Ati!/Aisei! Umesoma kitabu hiki?; U nani? (Wewe ni nani?); Kitu gani kitafaa?; Nitanunua nini?; Kwa nini mlisahau?; Unafunguaje mlango huu?; Umemaliza?; Kwa nini umekuwa mganga?; Mkutano utaanza lini?; Mzungu yuko wapi? Na mgeni wake, je?

(b) Lini wageni wenu watafika? (or) Wageni wenu watafika lini?; Kwa nini ulipika viazi tena?; Mtu gani yule?; Unapenda (unataka) kuona nani hapa?; Kitu gani hiki?; Ataanza lini?; (Je?) Walikwenda Dar es Salaam jana?; Kiko changu kipya kiko wapi?; Unafanya nini?; Walifika lini, Kenya? (or) Lini walifika Kenya? (N.B. Any, or all, of above could have been preceded by 'Je?')

(c) Why (surprised) have you returned again?; I say, what are you doing here?; How will they be able to carry that load?; What book is lost?; Who is Mr. Ali?; What is this (thing)?; Why is the food late?; When will the food be ready?; What sort of plant is that?; How many children have failed to come to-day?

Exercise 32

(a) Ku-punguzwa; ku-sikiliza; ku-washa; ku-hakikisha; ku-kausha; ku-lainisha; ku-sawazisha; ku-valisha; ku-shusha; ku-lisha; ku-rudisha; ku-endesha; ku-angusha; ku-lazimisha; ku-pendezwa; ku-fundisha; ku-ingiza; ku-bahatisha; ku-laza; ku-legeza; ku-telemshwa; ku-amsha; ku-geuza; ku-punguza; ku-tayarisha; ku-tembezwa; ku-eleza; ku-pasha; ku-kopesha; ku-jaza.

(b) Watu hawa walilazimishwa kwenda leo; pasha moto viazi hivi; usishushe mzigo ule; analisha mtoto wake; kausha vitambaa hivi upesi/kwa haraka; mishahara yao imepunguzwa; tayarisha chumba hiki kwa mgeni; mkono wangu unawasha; ataoa Jumamosi; sikilizeni mwalimu wenu.

(c) Chemsha viazi kwa muda mdogo tu; mwalimu yule anafundisha watoto vipofu kusoma kwa vidole vyao; kitabu chako kilirudishwa jana; wageni wanapendezwa sana kwa milima ya Tanzania; lini ulipoteza kisu chako cha mfukoni?; rudisha kikapu hiki kwa mkulima; mtumishi wangu amesahau kusawazisha vyombo; mizigo ile ilitelemshwa polepole kwa sababu ilikuwa mizito sana; utayarishe chumba kile kwa mgeni wangu; usiamshe watoto mapema kesho.

(d) To tighten; to loosen; erect; to be prepared; to rot/cause to marry; to be driven; to ensure; to tire; to cause to awake; to be boiled; to be taught; to dress; to lend; to grow less; to go down; to cause to turn; to be boiling; to be felled; to cause to arrive; to burn.

(e) Return his knife; I am loosening this nail; the pastor is marrying a woman today; would you dress the child please; get this chit to Mr. Mohammed; this book has explained many things; erect this pole over there; I have lost my umbrella; that fire is burning well/a lot; go to feed those animals.

Exercise 33

(a) Sifikiri; haendi; kitabu hakisomwi; mlango haufungi; kisu hakikati vizuri; hawanywi; hamchezi?; hamwoni?; mishahara haiongezwi; yeye si mgonjwa; hafuati; hawatazami; misumari haifai; mkate huu hautoshi; siwezi kuja leo; kitambaa hiki hakikauki upesi; vibarua wale hawachoki; husikii; halali; sili viazi.

(b) Sinunui mkate mjini kwa sababu haufai; wanyama wale hawakai hapa; mishahara yetu haiongezwi mwezi huu; sipendi kununua vitu vyako leo; kwa nini hasemi kitu? Kwa sababu hasikii; moto huu hauwaki vizuri. Jaribu tena; nimesikia kwamba huwezi kuja leo; anafurahi kwa sababu mikutano yake haiendelei; kitambaa hakiuzwi hapa kwa sababu hakinunuliwi na wenyeji; viazi havipatikani mjini mwezi huu.

(c) He does not lend; they are not standing; I do not know to drive; he is not returning; the fire is not burning; these onions do not rot; he/she is not waking up; I am not cultivating this year; are you (pl.) not entering?; the animal is not eating today; we do not live/stay here; the children are not listening; this vessel will not be made to stand; I see nothing (I do not see a thing); I do not like bread, thanks (I do not desire any bread, thanks); the pupils are not playing to-day; he/she is not progressing well.

Exercise 34

(a) Hana mkate; sina watoto; hatuna vitabu; hawana chakula; hana misumari; kiti hakina miguu; kitanda hakina mito; hakuna miti huku; hapana mganga hapa; hamna misumari kikapuni; hamna msaada; huna watoto? Sina; hatuna mpishi; hakuna. Wazungu; chama hiki hakina wanawake; hapana mkutano leo; hatuna kisima katika kijiji hiki; mimea hii haina mizizi mirefu; hana wageni leo.

(b) Mzungu yule hana mke; hakuna mkate nyumbani; hamna viboko katika mto mkubwa ule; kwa nini kitanda kile hakina mto? mimea hii haina mizizi mikubwa sana; hakuna wadudu huku Nairobi (or) hapana wadudu hapa Nairobi; vibarua wale kule (or pale) hawana mnyapara; (Je?) una kiberiti kwa sababu (mimi) sina; wageni wale hawana mizigo; ninaona kwamba huna cheti. Wewe, je?

(c) They have no food; this cup has no saucer; those mountains have no forests; there are no matches here (there is no lighter here); we have not many labourers, just a few; those beds have no mosquito nets; there is no river thereabouts; I have no meeting today; he has no more bread (other bread). How about you?; have you no knife in the pocket? I haven't.

Exercise 35

(a) Sitakwenda kesho; hatanunua; hatutachukua; hawataweza; hutajaribu?; hamtarudi; kiti kile hakitafaa; misumari ile haitatosha; hatafika leo; hutakuja; chakula hakitakuwa tayari; hatakuwa na watoto; hutafaulu; sitasoma; hatafikiri; hawatasafiri; hamtasamehe; wanyama hawatakula; wageni hawatakuwa na mizigo; mto hautakuwa mkubwa.

(b) Sitataka kurudi nyumbani mwaka huu; hawataweza kumaliza kitu hiki leo; vikombe vichafu hivi havitafaa; mchezo wa watoto hautachezwa leo; ninajua kwamba Bwana wetu hatakubali kuongeza mishahara yetu; hatutataka kununua kisu kingine kama kile; lete vikombe vingine kwa sababu hivi havitatosha; mti mzuri huu hautaangushwa, hata kidogo; wakulima wa kijiji hiki hawatafuata mpango wetu; mizigo hii haitachukuliwa leo.

(c) The meeting will not be tomorrow; there will be no people there; insects will not be seen thereabouts; that book will not be read; I shall not stay there much; potatoes will not be obtainable in the village; the help will not be great; the game will not be played on Saturday; the knives will not be sufficient; the arrangements will not be suitable.

Exercise 36

(a) Hakujaribu; hawakuja; kiti hakikufaa; hukukumbuka; hatukufikiri; hamkula; hawakuwa na viatu; hakuwa mpishi hodari; mgonjwa hakufa; sikuona kitu; miti ile haikuangushwa; mlima haukuonekana; wageni hawakuchelewa; mguu haukuvunjika; kiko changu hakikupotea; hakuhama; hatukuingia; hukuhakikisha; hamkusikia? Hatukusikia.

(b) Hawakuamka mapema, lakini hawakuchelewa; wadudu wengi waliingia chumba kwa sababu hakufunga mlango; viazi hivi havikununuliwa mjini; mchezo wa mpira haukuchezwa Alhamisi; chakula kimeharibika kwa sababu hakikufunikwa kwa kitambaa; sikujua kwamba una mke; hawakuenda Mombasa kuleta mizigo yao; mgonjwa yule hakula chakula chake; mlima wa Kenya haukuonekana jana.

(c) We did not succeed; he did not go; there was no meeting yesterday; the bread was not brought; we did not fill those baskets; didn't you (pl.) stay there?; there was no river thereabouts; I did not return this book; the fire did not burn well; the sick person (patient) was not made to lie down (put to bed); the salary was not good; the potatoes were not spoilt; I was unable to sleep; the food was not boiled; we did not start; he was not angry; they were not wrong (they did not fail); the child did not shut the door; didn't you want to go?; they did not agree.

Exercise 37

(a) Uliona wanyama gani Ngorongoro?; tutakuwa na wageni wengi Jumamosi; ulionaje Dodoma?; hatachukua mizigo yake kwa sababu ni mizito; wakulima kumi na wanane tu walikuja katika mkutano wetu juzi; nenda kwa haraka kuleta msaada. Kuna moto mkubwa kule (or) pana moto mkubwa pale; kiberiti changu kipya kiko wapi? Sijui, labda kimepotea; ninahitaji vipande viwili vya kitambaa cheupe kile; umekwenda kuona nani katika mji ule?; usiangushe miti mirefu ile, haifai.

(b) There will be a meeting for everyone tomorrow; why (surprised) did you not come yesterday? I did not remember; these potatoes are not suitable now because they have dried up; didn't you go to town to buy my things? No (indeed not), Bwana (sir); my children have already gone to play football; that football ground is unsuitable because it has a slope; he did not agree to enter our club/society; what did you do yesterday? And what about him?; would you send (cause it to arrive) this note to Mr. Mongi; that labourer has done well to return here.

Exercise 38

(a) Nafasi; baridi; hatari; hema; ratili; paka; rafiki; inzi; kahawa; saa; sababu; bilauri; asubuhi; kazi; mama; mbwa; samaki; tarehe; chizi; meza; mboga; taa; suruali; nyoka; shati; chai; ruhusa (ruksa); motokaa; homa; karabai; karatasi; siagi; sabuni; takataka; siku; sahani; mbegu; barua; bei; chumvi.

(b) Bahati kubwa (kuu); mbwa mkali; nyumba ndogo; karatasi nyeupe; mbu wengi; mboga chache; sahani tano; barabara ndefu; sigara mbili; panga kali; nguo safi; siagi laini; siku nyingi; sabuni nyekundu; chupa tupu; rafiki wengi; ratili nane; dakika mbili; kila asubuhi; dawa nzuri.

(c) Nafasi hii; surali ile; hema ya safari; saa za asubuhi; motokaa yangu mpya; dawa ya vyombo; habari ya/za siku nyingi; barua zake; siku za kazi; mbegu hizi za mboga; kikombe cha chai; ratili tano za sukari; nyumba zake nyingi; kaptula yangu; shida zenu; nguo zetu chafu; chupa mbili za bia; sahani ya nyama; inzi wachafu wale; nyoka mrefu yule.

(d) Angalia dawa hii, ina hatari kubwa; mpishi wangu hawezi kuja kazini leo kwa sababu ana homa kali; nenda mjini kununua ratili mbili za nyama ya mbwa; nguo zangu mpya ziko wapi? Zipo kitandani; karabai mbili zile zinawaka vizuri sana; kazi hii si mbaya, lakini si nzuri vilevile; (mtu) huyu amekatwa mguuni kwa panga kali hii; pana mbwa wakali sana katika nyumba kubwa ile; rafiki wawili watakuja jioni hii kunywa bia nami; nina shida kwa sababu sina pesa wiki hii.

(e) Other (more) butter; that work has danger; this main (great) road; how much? (what [sort of] price?); how many minutes; I have no opportunity/ time today; where is the money?; good fortune/luck; have you permission?; the European's mail; what date?; the difficulties of this work; the price of meat; tea or coffee?; mind the fierce dog; where are my trousers?; a period of exactly one hour; there is no vacancy of work here; bad luck; that house is Mr. Rashidi's.

(f) Will two pounds of meat be sufficient? They will not be enough, buy another pound; his refrigerator is filled with bottles of beer; bring paper to write a permit (chit of permission); he is wearing his work clothes; I don't like to drink sweet tea, I like tea only without sugar; there is danger in driving (to drive) a car badly; go to get red shoe polish; we shall have many friends this evening; that small table is broken; this patient has a very fierce fever because he did not get any medicine.

Exercise 39

(a) Panga meza; sivuti (sigara), asante; piga dawa ya mbu; uvue nguo; watoto wanacheza mpira; itanyesha mvua kesho; usipakue chakula, bado; tandika kitanda cha mgeni; sisikii baridi; usisahau kupiga hodi mlangoni; fua nguo hizi, halafu piga pasi; walikwenda kuvua samaki; vibarua wale hawafanyi kazi; nendeni zenu; anataka kuja kesho (atakuja kesho); msivute sigara hapa; walikwenda zao; tutapiga hema yetu kule; pakua mizigo hii; motokaa hii itavutwa.

(b) Haijulikani kama mwenzake atakuja; ilinyesha mvua nyingi juzi; viazi na mkate zimekwisha; inafikiriwa; babangu amefika; ulishe paka wangu; mama yao amekufa; yu rafiki yako?; inajulikana kwamba Juma alikuwa mwizi; dada yangu amekwisha olewa.

(c) Kaka yangu ameleta mbwa wake hapa; ninafikiri kwamba itanyesha mvua kesho; babako yuko wapi? Yumo nyumbani; tandika kitanda kingine sasa kwa sababu rafiki yangu atakaa mpaka Jumatano; pakua chakula, halafu (or baadaye) endelea kupiga pasi; mbwa wako amekula chakula cha paka wangu; yaya yetu amesahau kuvua nguo za watoto; jamaa zangu wana-fanya kazi kule/pale; vikombe, sahani, na chupa hizi zimekuwa chafu sana; ndugu yangu anavua samaki kule/pale mtoni.

(d) I don't know if it will be possible; this servant has laid the table well; finish doing your work, then be on your way; he cannot wash the clothes because there is no soap; this bed was not made; you will spray mosquito repellant in every room every evening; some people fish about here every Sunday; he knows (how) to work iron (metal); they are unable to work because it is raining; there is no permission to smoke here.

Exercise 40

(a) Ishirini na tano kwa mia; mia tatu, ishirini na moja; elfu mbili, mia tatu tisini na nne; elfu nne, mia tano, sabini na sita; ishirini na tisa elfu; laki moja, elfu ishirini na tisa, mia saba, arobaini na sita (or elfu mia ishirini na tisa, mia saba, arobaini na sita); laki nne, elfu themanini na saba, na saba (or elfu mia nne, themanini na saba, na saba); sehemu tatu za kumi na sita; tano, pointi saba, sita, nane, tano; sifuri pointi sifuri, mbili, tano; sehemu tatu za nane; robo tatu; sehemu saba za nane; ishirini na mbili na nusu; viti mia tatu, ishirini na vinane; vikombe ishirini na vitano; watu laki tatu; minazi kumi na tano elfu; chupa za bia mia na nane; vipande mia na kimoja

(b) Pana siku mia tatu, sitini na tano katika mwaka mmoja; barabara hii inachukua kama motokaa mia tano, sabini na tano kila siku; miaka elfu moja, mia tisa, sitini na sita; nyumba hii ina kama vitabu elfu mbili, mia tano; chama hiki kina wanachama mia tatu, ishirini na mmoja; kuna/pana wakulima hamsini na watatu tu, katika kijiji hiki; kila mwalimu anafundisha watoto thelathini na watano; tumepanda miti themanini na mitano; palikuwa na/kulikuwa na wageni elfu kumi na moja, mia tano themanini na wanane mwaka ule; pana/kuna chupa ishirini na tano na robo tatu za dawa.

(c) 834; 907; 20,000; 1,001; one ten thousandths; 0.007; 400,000, 26⅓; 1,010; 23%.

Exercise 41

(a) Saa moja na robo asubuhi; adhuhuri; alfajiri; saa kumi na mbili na nusu jioni; saa sita usiku; saa nane na dakika kumi (ya) mchana/alasiri; muda wa saa tatu na nusu; muda wa saa ishirini na nne; saa ngapi? Sasa ni saa kumi kasoro dakika ishirini na tano; saa kumi na moja alasiri/jioni: saa saba na dakika tano mchana; alikaa kwa muda wa robo saa; saa tatu kamili; tangu/toka saa mbili na robo mpaka saa tatu kasa robo; saa nne na nusu usiku; saa kumi na mbili alfajiri; saa moja kasoro dakika kumi jioni; saa mbili usiku; alikufa saa tisa usiku; njoo saa sita na nusu leo.

(b) Uje hapa saa moja na nusu (ya) asubuhi kesho (or kesho asubuhi); tutaanza kula saa tatu kasa robo leo; niliamka saa kumi na moja kasa robo (ya) usiku; mkutano utaanza saa kumi na nusu (ya) mchana/alasiri; safari iliendelea kwa muda wa saa nne na dakika arobaini na tano (or mwendo uliendelea . . . etc.); sasa ni kama saa nane na dakika ishirini (or 'sasa' at the end); walifika saa kumi na moja kasoro dakika ishirini na tano usiku; vibarua wangu wanafanya kazi kwa muda wa saa nane kila siku; pika nyama hii kwa muda wa nusu saa tu; ilinyesha mvua kwa muda wa saa saba na nusu.

(c) 4 p.m.; 5 p.m.; (a period of) 10 hours; what time did he arrive? He arrived at one o'clock exactly; come back at nine o'clock tomorrow; continue until twenty past three; he will arrive in the afternoon hours; they will start at 6.15 in the morning; there is a period of 7½ hours of work every day; the time is about two o'clock now.

Exercise 42

(a) Ku-peleka; ku-pima; ku-acha; ku-pa; ku-zaa; ku-lia; ku-iba; ku-ita; ku-gusa; ku-ambia; ku-ondoka; ku-ondoa; ku-okota; ku-oga; ku-pangusa; ku-pokea; ku-imba; ku-fuga; ku-okota; ku-fukuza.

(b) Sijaiba; hawajaimba; usikunje bado; hatujapita; hajazaa; hajapangusa vyombo; hujapokea barua; kitambaa hakijakunjwa; vyombo havijaondolewa; mlima ule haujapandwa; watoto hawajaoga; mbwa huyu hajalia; wakulima wale hawajafuga wanyama; vitu hivi havijaachwa; (mtu) mvivu yule hajaachishwa; kiasi hakijapimwa; amefukuza wadudu wale; ondoa sahani chafu hizi; peleka barua hii kwa Bwana Smith; tumekwisha pita nyumba yake.

(c) Nimejaribu kufanya kazi hii, lakini sijafaulu; motokaa yake haijafika; haijanyesha mvua mwezi huu; chakula hakijawa tayari; barua hazijafika. Zitafika saa nane (ya) mchana; hatujazoea kutumia Kiswahili, mwizi yule hajakamatwa; watoto wale wamecheza toka saa mbili asubuhi (hii) lakini hawajachoka; mwanafunzi yule hajarudisha kitabu changu; wakulima wale hawajapanda mbegu zao za mboga.

(d) Don't touch this; the child was born at three o'clock yesterday; don't go away (pl.) until four o'clock; I have not yet come across my pipe; they have not yet received permission to enter there; the visitors have not yet gone away; he has not yet sent the letter(s); those animals have not yet been driven off; I have sent a letter but he has not yet replied; that lazy labourer has no work because he has been dismissed.

Exercise 43

(a) Aliniita; nilimwona; aliniona; walituambia; nilikupa; mlikikunja (kitambaa); niliwapelekeni; alituita; umekiona (kitabu); hajazipokea (barua); niliwaambieni; hajaupiga (msumari); hatujaipanda (milima); umekiokota? (kitabu); waliwapeni; tulikupa (kitabu) (N.B. the '-ku-' here is 2nd person singular infix, *not* the 'infinitive' 'ku-'); alijipima; nimejipiga; niliwaiteni.

(b) Tumempa mpishi wetu nguo mpya; umemwona Hamisi? Ndiyo, nilimwona mjini; wamewaambieni msikae hapa; vibarua wale hawajaimaliza kazi ile; aliniambia kwamba hakukuona jana; unaweza kuwaona wanyama wale pale/kule? Siwaoni; nimesoma kitabu kizuri sana. Umekisoma?; lini ulipanda mimea hii? Niliipanda zamani; umevisafisha viatu vyangu? Sijavisafisha; mtumishi wangu amezipiga pasi nguo zangu mpya hizi vizuri sana.

(c) He gave (it) to me; I shall measure (weigh) you (pl.); we told them; I shall summon them tomorrow; the patient has committed suicide; those people have volunteered to give aid/assistance; I cannot give you work (I am unable to give you work); we are learning Swahili; where are the vessels? He has removed them; have you folded the clothes? Yes, I have folded them; he called me at nine o'clock; I have cut myself with a knife; will you buy that car? I shall buy it; have you (pl.) obtained permission? We have obtained it; they will pay you (pl.) salaries at two o'clock; he is unable to see you today, perhaps tomorrow; have you seen my dog? I have not seen him; how has the teacher replied? I have not yet asked him; how (what) did they say? We have not yet told them; what time did you see him? I saw him quite a while ago.

Exercise 44

(a) Usiviguse! (vitu hivi); nipe cheti kile!; uulete (mkate)!; usimjibu!; mkamate!; waite!; wape pesa zao!; mwite Bwana Rajabu!; usiiangushe (miti ile)!; mwambie!; niite saa kumi na mbili alfajiri/asubuhi!; zipeleke (barua)!; vilete (vikombe);! uwatafute (watoto);! kisome (cheti)!; usizisahau (karatasi)!; mpe (barua)!; usimpige mtoto yule; usikipasue (kitabu)!; imalize (kazi)!

(b) Don't (pl.) give him a thing (anything); read it (the book)!; fell it (the tree)!; give us (the) money!; tell them!; call us!; look after him!; would you see him tomorrow!; try them (the examinations)!; remove them (the plates)!; make it (the bed)!; don't shut it (the door)!; would you tell him that they have already gone!; pay them now!; bring them (the loads)!; give him permission!; bathe him!; dust it (the furniture)! or dust them (the vessels)!; fold it (the cloth)!; leave him there!

Exercise 45

(a) Ratili tatu; kilo mbili; kilometa tano; lita moja; hekta(ri) kumi; shilingi ngapi?; hatua kumi na tano; tani tatu; vibaba viwili; shilingi tano na senti ishirini; gramu chache; frasila moja ya vitunguu (ratili thelathini na tano za vitunguu); eneo gani?; paundi elfu moja; hekta(ri) moja ni hatua mia kwa hatua mia; nipe sumni/thumni (senti hamsini); mwendo wa kilometa mia tatu, hamsini na mbili (safari ya kilometa mia tatu, hamsini na mbili); nimenunua meta tano za kitambaa.

(b) Tupe kilo tano za viazi. Uviweke hapa tafadhali; Mwambie mke wako kwamba nguo ile inahitaji sentimeta sabini na tano za kitambaa; Mzee yule anataka fedha/pesa. Una senti hamsini/sumni/thumuni? Mpe, basi. Kaka yangu amepanda hekta(ri) kumi na tano za mimea ya chakula; Uweke lita ishirini na tano za petroli katika motokaa yangu; Mboga hizi (ni) bei gani? (or Bei gani, mboga hizi?) (Ni) shilingi tano na senti sabini na tano (kwa) kilo moja; Bei yako si rahisi. Ipunguze kidogo; Kuna kama ratili mbili na robo katika kilo moja; Alinunua nyumba ile kwa shilingi nane elfu (elfu nane) tu; Arusha ni kilometa mia mbili tisini na sita (ku)toka Nairobi; Mpe shilingi moja na senti themanini kununua kilo moja ya mkate.

Exercise 46

(a) Aende; tukae?; mlango ufungwe; ulete; mwambie aje; lazima waje; anataka ninunue mkate; walikuja ili watuone; afadhali waingie; barua hizi lazima zirudishwe; miti ile iangushwe; niseme nini?; unisaidie; anataka kujaribu (same subject); tujaribu; walikuja Moshi ili wapande mlima wa Kilimanjaro; heri tuchukue mizigo hii sasa; chakula kitayarishwe?; tuandike?; tule sasa.

(b) Mkulima amepanda mimea mizuri (ili) apate kiasi kikubwa; anataka tukae hapa mpaka kesho asubuhi; tumpe nini kipofu yule?; vibarua wangoje au waondoke?; mpishi amewasha moto (ili) apike chakula; lazima ukumbuke kuleta chai saa kumi na mbili na nusu asubuhi; afadhali viti vile vitolewe kwa wanawake; waambie waniambie nijue kila kitu; watoto warudi nyumbani saa kumi na moja na robo; nimenunua motokaa mpya ili nijifunze kuendesha.

(c) Are the salaries to be increased?; he had best return home; these things must be removed; it is as well for us to bathe every day; where is he to send the luggage/loads?; tell the cook to lay the table now; let us fill those vessels/containers; that thing is best forgotten; they must be ready at seven o'clock in the morning; would you (pl.) sit; it must rain today (i.e. it is bound to rain today); am I to make the guest's bed?; would you buy ten pounds of potatoes; they want us to go there in order that they get help; the furniture/vessels must be dusted every day; let them go to town now; in what/which part are we to feed/pasture the animals today?; I want the children to have their books tomorrow; we had better start now; tell them to give you a chit.

265

Exercise 47

(a) Usirudi; wasijaribu tena; waambie wasiharibu motokaa ile; nimeandika cheti nisisahau; wasije?; lazima msiguse; walitaka tusiende leo; hatukutaka kujaribu tena; wazuie wasiingie; amenikataza nisiende; nilikwenda kuwatafuta watoto nisiweze kuwaona; asiwe na msaada? (asipate msaada?); lazima usivue samaki huku; wasisome kitabu hiki; lazima tusisahau mkutano kesho; wasifikiri kwamba nyumba ile ni yao; kizibo hiki kitazuia mbegu zisitoke; afadhali usiwaambie; watumishi wasipakue mizigo ile?; wasiende bila kuniona.

(b) Mwambie babako asiwape watoto wangu chakula; tulijaribu kupanda mlima tusiweze; safisha (zisafishe) sahani hizi vizuri zisiwe chafu; nawa mikono yako tusile chakula kichafu; nimewakataza watu wale wasirudi hapa tena; ninataka usitumie (usikitumie) chombo hiki tena; mlango mzito huu uliwazuia wezi wasiingie; afadhali usipande miti ile leo kwa sababu hakuna mvua; waambie vibarua wasiangushe miti mirefu ile; tusingoje hapa, turudi nyumbani.

(c) Don't (pl.) forget; shut the door so that the insects do not come in; tell the children not to play here; what/how are we to do to prevent the house from falling?; it has been refused that people cultivate in the forest; don't let the labourers work on Sunday(s)/the labourers are not to work on Sunday(s); the farmers had better not plant their seeds this month; he fell into the river and was unable to get himself out; the Mistress does not want me to wash the clothes today; let us remind our friends to come tomorrow lest they forget.

(d) I have told you (pl.) not to come here to see me again; the Doctor has not (yet) come today. He is very late; the children have read (studied) for (a period of) exactly five and a half hours; my mother and her father have come here to see me; we have looked for onions on the market and not found any because they are not obtainable these days; your guests will arrive here at a quarter past three tomorrow; this door is useless because it does not close; let your servant apply insecticide in every room to prevent insects from being here; what sort of food will you give these guests?; I had great luck yesterday because I was given a lot of money.

Exercise 48

(a) Faida; bahasha; zawadi; nchi; kamba; heri; kofia; sauti; mvua; chapa; hasara; akiba; koti; kuku; ndoo; rangi; ng'ombe; kweli; bahari; fulani; ghafula; orodha; alama; sehemu; nyanya; suti; haraka; ndizi; lugha; chapa.

(b) Nyuma; kando ya; juu ya; ng'ambo ya; mbele ya chini (ya); ndani (ya); katikati ya; kati ya; nje ya.

(c) Mbele yangu; ndani yake; jaribu ng'ambo; simama nyuma yake; juu ya nyumba; ndani ya kikapu; ngoja nje; nenda mbele; iweke ndani; ni juu yake; vibarua hawa ni chini yangu; kando ya mto; yumo ndani; barabara kuu mbele; usitazame nyuma yako; amepanda juu; mwalimu alisimama mbele ya watoto wake; kuna wanyama katikati ya miti; juu ya kilima; nimetafuta ndani na nje yake pia.

(d) Nyumba kubwa ile imeharibika kwa sababu mti ulianguka juu yake; hakuna ng'ombe ng'ambo ya kijiji kile; mzee yule alisimama kando ya barabara; ni juu yetu kuwasaidia; nimeweka vibarua wale chini ya mnyapara yule; simama! Pana/Kuna hatari mbele!; watafute watoto ndani ya nyumba na nje pia/vilevile; ninasimama mbele yenu kuwaambia/kuwaambieni (or niwaambie/niwaambieni) kwamba kuna mwizi katikati yenu;

pana/kuna ndege mzuri kabisa juu ya mti ule; ni juu ya kila mtu kujaribu/ ajaribu sana.

(e) Haste; normal/custom; tax/rent; flag/banner; common sense; like/sort; telephone; office; rope/cord; suddenness; possession/property; truth; times; sea; loss; path/way; strength; white ants; joy; mark/brand.

(f) Wear your hat on top of (your) head; leave that coat outside; he has put the money on top of the table; if you don't know, ask someone or other; there are cattle the other side of that hill; let us go ahead; bring the big bucket inside; we shall use this colour outside the house, and that inside; don't work like this; it is up to you to remove these stains; those women are carrying bananas on top of their heads; let us follow this path at the side of the river; tie this rope outside; what is the flag on top of that house?; he has put something or other inside; those termites have damaged the bottom parts of the door; he has given me a very good present; it has rained the other side of those mountains; hide his gun under the coat; I shall close up those chickens inside my hut.

Exercise 49

(a) Vijana wote; vitabu vyote; kazi yo yote; nyumba yenyewe; nyumba yenye vyumba viwili; mkate wote; nilikwenda mwenyewe (or mimi mwenyewe nilikwenda); ninyi nyote; ondoa vitu vyote hivi; kitambaa chote; inahitaji nguvu yako yote; chumba cho chote kitafaa; (watu) wenye watoto; mwenyewe wa nyumba hii/mwenye nyumba hii; tazama vipande vyote vile/tazama sehemu zote zile; zawadi yenyewe ilikuwa pesa/fedha; unaweza kufuata njia yo yote; lete kiti chenye mto; wale wote wenye mishahara yao wangoje nje; uliza (mtu) yeyote mwenye saa.

(b) Wote wenye watoto waje nami; mimi mwenywe nilikwenda Mombasa ili nivue samaki lakini sikupata samaki ye yote; anataka ninyi nyote mwende pale/kule saa tano kasa robo kesho asubuhi; walikipita kijiji lakini hawakupata nafasi kuona ye yote; 'Nikupe kitu gani?' 'Cho chote kitafaa'; mwenyewe wa nyumba hii (mwenye nyumba hii) amezuia wote wasiingie milango hii; mwambie mwenyewe wa motokaa hii (mwenye motokaa hii) aiondoe; lazima (sisi) sote tumwombe mkulima nwenyewe kwa ruhusa/ ruksa; haijanyesha mvua yo yote tangu/toka (siku ya) Jumatano; vilete vitu vyote vile hapa bila kuacha cho chote nyuma.

(c) You may come at any time; have you read all the mail/letters?; give me that letter with the open envelope; I myself have no car but my friend is the owner of this car; we have all started; I don't know if he has any bread at all, ask him yourself; that person with the black hat is my friend; I am unable to give you anything at all; he himself likes bread with salt (salted bread); tell all the children not to play football on that ground.

Exercise 50

(a) Nikatie mkate; umchukulie mizigo hii; unisomee barua hii; nipitishie chumvi; alikwenda kunipokelea zawadi yangu; nipakulie motokaa ile; ananiamkia kila asubuhi; mtumishi amanfagilia mpishi jiko; tulihamia nyumba hii zamani; mti ule unanukia sana; kipofu yule anataka nimsomee barua ile; nikuchukulie mzigo ule; lazima unifutie meza hii kila siku; tuliingia mfereji; waletee viti; unipatie ratili nane za viazi mjini; ndugu yangu ameniomba nimwuzie motokaa hii; nifungulie mlango; nilishie watoto saa kumi na mbili; chumba kimemsafishiwa mgeni.

(b) Turudie mji (or turudi mjini); ningojee mpaka saa kumi; motokaa ile imeniletea mizigo yangu; sina nguvu, unichukulie mzigo huu (tafadhali);

uniwekee sahani hizi mezani; chakula hiki kinanukia sana; utufungulie mlango huu; ametuhakikishia saa ndege itaondoka; wamentwendea mganga (or wamekwenda kwa mganga); mchukulie barua hii Bwana Jones (cf. chukua barua hii kwa Bwana Jones).

(c) Return this book for me; shut the door for him; I am ironing for the Mistress; the nanny is taking our children for a walk for us; cut this rope for me; put sugar in our tea for us; he folded this cloth badly for me; boil us the food; take this chit to the office for me; look for the knife for me; they have returned to the town; he is working for me; ask those youths to pitch the tent for me; the old man fell into the river; lift your foot for me; clean all those vessels for him; we shall help them; I shall drive his car for him; we shall make them a new programme/arrangement; I am writing a letter for him because he does not know (how) to write.

Exercise 51

(a) Viazi (vya) moto; nyama ya baridi; vitabu vya bure; mkutano wa siri; mbwa wa mwitu/porini; nyumba ya zamani; siku ya mwisho; paka wa kike; nguo za kienyeji; kazi ya kawaida; chombo cha kupimia; mkono wa kushoto; mtoto wa kiume; habari za kweli; kitambaa cha kusafishia; kitu cha kwanza; sahani za kufaa; mti wa pili; mchezo wa kitoto; chakula cha Kizungu.

(b) Nipe kisu cha kukatia nyama; wamekwenda kutazama (kuangalia) chombo cha kupimia mvua (or kipimo cha mvua); hatutaki (hatupendi) kuku wa kienyeji, tunahitaji (kuku) wa Kizungu; nguo za kitoto hazi-patikani mjini; alituambia kitu cha kwanza; ni kitu cha kupendeza sana kwenda safarini kuona wanyama wa porini/mwitu; nimenunua mkuki wa zamani wa Kimasai; ng'ombe yule amezaa mtoto wa kike wa pili; lazima watu wasiwe na mikutano ya siri; kuna/pana kitabu cha bure kuonyesha vitu vyote hivi.

(c) His right leg is broken; have you enough paper?; a necessary journey; he lives in the fifth house from here; this is a cultivating tool/vessel; he has done useless work; he has bought an extremely modern car; visitors have come to Tanzania to see wild animals (game); he returned on the second day; take the left hand road (pass by the left hand road); he is a member of a secret society; they have started the fourth game now; I need something to open this door as it does not open; that person has a pleasant wife; he is the second visitor to come today; his wife has given birth to a female child the day before yesterday; today is the last day of the examination; I want some writing paper (letter writing paper); Indian food is generally hot (fierce); you (pl.) are paid sufficient wages.

Exercise 52

Tarehe ishirini na mbili, mwezi wa saba (Julai) mwaka wa elfu moja mia tisa thelathini na tatu; tarehe nne mwezi wa tisa (Septemba) mwaka wa elfu moja mia tisa hamsini na nne; tarehe thelathini na moja, mwezi wa nane (Agosti) mwaka wa elfu moja, mia tisa hamsini na nane; tarehe ishirini na tano, mwezi wa kumi na mbili (Desemba) mwaka wa elfu moja mia tisa na moja; tarehe ishirini na nne, mwezi wa nne (Aprili) mwaka huu; ana-kwenda Nairobi kila tarehe pili (ya mwezi); leo ni tarehe mosi; mitihani itaanza tarehe kumi na moja, mwezi wa tano (Mei); pana mkutano tarehe ishirini na mbili (ya) mwezi huu; nitakwenda nyumbani tarehe thelathini na moja, mwezi wa kwanza (Januari).

(b) 17th July, 1934; 14th December, 1932; 9th December, 1961; 1st July, 1899; 29th February, 1960; that old man died on 4th November, 1955; this club was started in 1940; have you this year's calendar?; Saturday will be the 12th; the football game (match) will be on the 13th.

Exercise 53

(a) Baraza; jina; dereva; bunge; duka; maji; taifa; zulia; daraja; jiwe; maziwa; dirisha; jipu; gari; shauri; daraja; mayai; fundi; tunda; jumba; kanisa; boma; jicho; jambo; jina; jua; Rais; mafuta; Waziri; chungwa; ua; gazeti; majani; pipa; sanduku; bati; jembe; shoka; majivu; jibu.

(b) Matata mengi; debe tupu; mashamba mengine; soko kubwa lile; jina langu; sanduku lingine; taifa jipya; gazeti lenye habari nyingi; madirisha machafu yale; shoka kali lile; mambo magumu mengi; mapipa mawili ya mafuta/oili; jina lake la kwanza; magari mazito yale; jibu lo lote; duka la nyama; zulia jekundu kubwa hili; ua lile linanukia; madereva wale; seremala yule ni fundi hodari.

(c) Madereva wa magari haya wamekwenda madukani; ng'ombe hawa hawatoi maziwa mengi, lakini ni mazuri sana; waziri wa nyumba atakuja kesho; majani ya maua haya yananukia sana; tarishi hajaniletea jibu lo lote; pipa la takataka limeangushwa na mbwa; magari hayawezi kutumia barabara/njia hii kwa sababu ya matope haya; lazima maua haya yawekwe katika baraza letu; karani yule ana jipu kubwa chini ya jino lake; jicho lenyewe la mgonjwa yule ni jekundu sana.

(d) Windows; parliament; grass/leaves; a messenger; knowledge/ingenuity; a pest; fruit (pl.); matters; stones; a church; a market; teeth; mud (much of it); a pineapple; conversation; a giant; a pawpaw; a boil; eyes; a clerk/typist.

(e) His/her new vehicle; a bread shop; this box will do; a Christian church/a Christian's church; the Tanzanian parliament; a valley having many fields/farms/plantations; that red eye; this fierce sun (strong sun); this dirty water; the difficult matter itself; bring any box at all; where is your field/farm? It is that one over there; what is his name? His name is Hamisi; a metal-worker/craftsman; those rotten lemons; a little milk; that village's local court; when did you get his reply? I got it yesterday; clean that dirty cooker/stove.

(f) Hoes are obtainable in that large shop; this good maize has come from that field in the valley; your teeth are not white because this water is not good; open that window for me; take this big carpet out in order that you can clean it well; this cow has given out seven debes (4-gallon tins) of good milk this week; we had a short conversation on the verandah; I need a messenger to send this reply for me to the shop; have you seen your name in this newspaper? No, I haven't seen it yet.

Exercise 54

(a) Ukipenda; wakila; ikiwa; nikinywa; mti ukianguka; akijibu; ukifikiri; mkifika; tukikupa; akituambia; ukiwa na ruhusa; viti vikiletwa; maua yakikatwa; mayai yakipatikana; akiniambia jina lake; jembe likitumiwa; barua zikiletwa; mkigusa; mguu wake ukivunjika; akifa.

(b) Alikuwa akisoma; wanapenda kusoma; tunasoma; nilimwona akisoma; nilimsikia akiimba; anapenda kuimba; atakuwa akiimba Jumamosi; watacheza kesho; wamechoka kwa sababu wamekuwa wakicheza; wakiona mti ukianguka; walimwona akija; tulikuwa tukingoja kwa muda wa saa mbili; ilikuwa ikinyesha mvua jana; shoka lilikuwa likitumiwa; alikuwa akipika jikoni; chakula kilikuwa kikipikwa jikoni; atakuwa akiningoja mjini; tunajifunza Kiswahili; kujifunza Kiswahili ni rahisi katika nchi hii.

(c) Ukija nyumbani sasa, nitakupa chai; ukiona wanyama katika barabara/ njia ile, utakuwa na bahati; ukienda kesho, mganga atakuwa akiwapima wagonjwa saa ile; mti ule ukianguka, utaharibu nyumba yako; mtumishi wangu alikuwa akifua nguo zetu bila maji (ya) moto; wakijaribu sana, lazima wafaulu; maua haya yalikuwa yakiota vibaya, basi niliyakata; (watu) wengine hawapendi kujifunza lugha; alivunja (alikivunja) kioo akisafisha (akiyasafisha) madirisha; tuliwaona wanyama wakilala kivulini chini ya miti.

(d) If you go to Nairobi, buy me a few things; he was driving his vehicle badly; we saw our children playing; you cannot take my hoe because I shall be using it tomorrow; I was very angry because he was sleeping at the meeting; if you (pl.) run over there, you will see him working in the field; if you come across my pipe, come here to tell me; if you come at 2 o'clock, I shall not go on safari; the old man fell asleep (slept) sitting in his chair; if you try hard, you will be able to learn this language without seeing/feeling much trouble/difficulty.

Exercise 55

(a) Asipokuja; isiponyesha mvua; ukikaa usikae ni mamoja kwetu; hakuwa akiimba jana/alikuwa haimbi jana; ukivaa usivae kofia ile; usipokula; tusiporudi sasa, tutachelewa; asipoleta maziwa, ni mamoja kwetu; asiponiambia jina lake; wasipopewa ruhusa; msipokuwa vipofu; mti ule ukianguka usianguke; usiposoma magazeti; nisipokuwa na ruhusa; ikinyesha isinyeshe (mvua) ni mamoja; maji yasipoletwa; taa isipowashwa, hatutaona; mlango ule usipofungwa nitasikia baridi; tumekuwa hatununui mkate katika duka lile/hatujawa (hatukuwa) tukinunua mkate katika duka lile; tusipoamka mapema hatutaweza kwenda kanisani.

(b) Tusipojaribu sana, hatutafaulu (or) kama hatujaribu sana, hatutafaula; niliwaona barabarani/njiani, lakini walikuwa hawakimbii (or) lakini hawakuwa wakikimbia; kama mwanzoni hufaulu, jaribu tena (or) usipofaulu mwanzoni, jaribu tena; kama hamsomi vitabu, mtajuaje cho chote! (or) msiposoma vitabu, mtajuaje cho chote?; kama hatafika hapa mapema kesho, hatutaweza kuanza (or) asipofika hapa mapema kesho . . .; mbwa wangu amekuwa hali cho chote tangu/toka jana; kama hali chakula kidogo atakufa (or) asipokula chakula kidogo, atakufa; rafiki yangu amekuwa akijaribu kumpa chakula mara nyingi; wageni hawatakuwa wakiupanda mlima wa Kenya Jumatatu (or) wageni watakuwa hawaupandi mlima wa Kenya Jumatatu; kama hufanyi kazi vizuri, utakuwa hukai sana hapa (or) usipofanya kazi vizuri, hutakuwa ukikaa sana hapa. (The second halves of these sentences are interchangeable).

(c) Unless they plant/sow their seeds now, they will not get a profit; whether they leave or not it is all the same to them; if you do not succeed in the beginning, try again; if you do not know the time, ask someone with a watch; I cannot help you (pl.) unless you tell me everything; unless he feeds his dog enough food, it will just die; if teeth are not cleaned well they will become black; unless the letter is sent today, it will be late; unless you put soap in this water, you cannot wash clothes properly; whether he volunteers or not, it is up to him, it is all the same to me; unless I stop work now, I shall be very tired.

Exercise 56

(a) Badala ya; karibu na; kabla ya; sawa na; peke yangu; mbali na; zaidi ya; sawasawa; pamoja na; habari ya; baada ya; wala . . . wala.

(b) Hawezi (wala) kusoma wala kuandika; umefanya sawa sawa; walikwenda peke yao; karibu na mti; baada ya saa tisa; zaidi ya kumi; mwambie habari ya mkutano; tulifika pamoja; kitabu hiki ni sawa na kile; nunua mkate kisha njoo/rudi nyumbani; mti huu na ule ni mbalimbali; anakaa mbali na mimi/nami; tuliona karibu (na) wanyama mia mbili (or tuliona wanyama karibu na mia mbili); usianze kabla ya saa nane; chukua kitabu hiki badala ya kile; anapenda chai tamu zaidi; tulikuja pamoja na watoto; jaribu peke yako bila msaade wo wote; hawezi kuja (wala) leo wala kesho; yeye atakwenda ama mimi nitakwenda.

(c) Gari langu limeharibika karibu na mto; hajui wala Kiingereza, wala Kiswahili; tukikaa, tusikae ni mamoja kwake; wamekuja/toka mbali peke yao bila msaada wo wote; tumenunua vitu mbalimbali vingi (kwa) sababu tunakaa mbali na mji ('kwa sababu' could be replaced by '(kwa) maana', 'kwa ajili' or 'kwa kuwa'); baada ya kuondoka Nairobi, tuliendelea zaida ya maili hamsini; hujasikia habari ya mtihani wangu?; kwa nini hukai kivulini badala ya kusimama katika jua kali?; njoo unione kabla hujaondoka; twende tuzungumze pamoja.

(d) The doctor lives near the town; he forgot to explain to me about that society/club; go further ahead; you can go either alone or with your servant; I did not know because he did not tell me; I have come instead of him/her; come to see me before you go/leave; don't go closer; he has neither relative nor friend; those two people live together.

Exercise 57

(a) Wao ambao walikuja; nguo ambazo zilifuliwa; mto ambao tuliuona; mwanamume ambaye anavaa kofia; wale ambao walichelewa; sisi ambao tumelipwa; kitabu ambacho nilikisoma; mlango ambao ulifunguliwa; chakula ambacho kililiwa; wadudu ambao walikula chakula; maji ambayo yaliletwa; wale ambao hawajui; bonde ambalo halionekani; mayai ambayo yanapatikana; mkuki ambao niliununua; wanyama ambao mkulima ana-wafuga; maziwa ambayo ng'ombe wanayatoa; mlima ambao niliupanda; yeye ambaye ni mpishi wangu; maua ambayo yanaota.

(b) Ukitafute kisu ambacho nilikipoteza jana; mbwa ambao wanakula nyama nyingi wana nguvu nyingi; kuna/pana (mtu) yeyote huku/hapa ambaye ana kalamu? (or) huku/hapa mwenye kalamu?; rafiki yako ambaye alikuja hapa juzi amerudi tena; maziwa ambayo niliyapata asubuhi hii yameharibika; barua ambayo niliiandika juzijuzi haijafika; watu ambao wanajua Kiingereza wasiseme (kitu) cho chote; barabara ambayo inakwe-nda Tanga imefungwa kwa sababu ya matope; mlima ambao tuliupanda unaitwa (mlima wa) Meru; mtoto ambaye alilivunja dirisha ambalo uliliona anakaa kule/pale.

(c) The car I bought; the children who are taught by that teacher; the examination which was difficult; the room which you have not yet cleaned; the guest who arrived yesterday; the clothes you are wearing; the leg which is broken; the mountains which are visible; the knife which is lost; that person who is called Hamisi; the telegram which I received yesterday; the examination we shall try; the old man who died; we who are strangers; the knives which are sharp; the tree which fell; the newspaper you read; the game the children will play; the rope which came apart; the medicine you ate.

Exercise 58

(a) Waliokuja; nguo zilizofuliwa; mto tuliouona; mwanamume anayevaa kofia; wale waliochelewa; sisi tunaolipwa; kitabu nilichokisoma; mlango uliofunguliwa; chakula kilicholiwa; wadudu waliokula chakula; maji yaliyoletwa; wale waliojua; bonde linaloonekana; mayai yanayopatikana; mkuki niliununua; wanyama mkulima anaowafuga; maziwa ng'ombe wanayoyatoa; mlima nilioupanda; yeye aliyekuwa mpishi wangu; maua yanayoota.

(b) Ng'ombe waliokuwa katika shamba lile wamekufa wote (or) ng'ombe ambao walikuwa katika shamba lile wamekufa wote; maji uliyoweka jikoni yamechemka (or . . . uliyoyaweka . . . .) maji ambayo uliweka jikoni yamechemka (or . . . uliyaweka . . . .); kalamu uliyonipa imevunjika (or) kalamu ambayo ulinipa imevunjika; mishahara inayolipwa ni ya mwezi huu (or) mishahara ambayo inalipwa ni ya mwezi huu; watoto unaowaona wanakaa katika kijiji kile (or) watoto ambao unawaona wanakaa katika kijiji kile; wale wanaotaka kwenda Nairobi ni nani? (or) wale ambao wanataka kwenda Nairobi ni nani?; kitambaa nilichonunua juzijuzi kilikuwa rahisi sana (or . . . nilichokinunua . .) (or) kitambaa ambacho nilinunua juzijuzi kilikuwa rahisi sana (or . . . nilikinunua . . .); mbegu ninazopanda zilinunuliwa katika duka lililofunguliwa mjini (or . . . ninazozipanda . . .) (or) mbegu ambazo ninapanda zilinunuliwa katika duka ambalo lilifunguliwa mjini (or . . . ninazipanda . . .); katika siku zilizopita watu walikaa katika nyumba unazoona kule (or . . . unazoziona kule) (or) katika siku ambazo zilipita watu walikaa katika nyumba ambazo unaona kule (or . . . unaziona kule); motokaa iliyonipita ilimwangusha mzee yule anayelala kando ya barabara (or) motokaa ambayo ilinipita ilimwangusha mzee yule ambaye analala kando ya barabara.

(c) The vehicle I bought; the children who were taught by this teacher; the examination which was difficult; the room you are cleaning; the visitor who is arriving today; the clothes you wore; the leg which broke; the mountains which were visible; the knife which was lost; that one who is called Hamisi; the telegram I am sending; the examination which they tried; the old man who died; we who were strangers; the knives which were sharp; the tree which fell; the newspaper you are reading; the game the children are playing; the rope which came apart; the medicine you are using now.

Exercise 59

(a) Mkutano utakaoanza; barua nitakayoiandika; mchezo utakaochezwa; wageni watakaofika; chakula kitakacholiwa; zawadi nitakazompa; msha-hara utakaolipwa; nyumba nitakayoinunua; kodi itakayolipwa; maji utakayokunywa; cheti utakachopewa; safari tutakayoifanya; karabai itakayochukuliwa; majani yatakayoota; watoto watakaocheza; vitu vita-kavyofaa; mtu atakayekuwa mpishi; moto utakaowaka; mizigo wata-kayoichukua; Mzungu atakayekuja.

(b) Mkutano utakaoanza kesho utakuwa mfupi (or) mkutano ambao utaanza kesho utakuwa mfupi; chakula nitakachokileta kitakuwa tayari mapema (or) chakula ambacho nitakileta kitakuwa tayari mapema; safari tutakayoifanya itaanza Alhamisi (or) safari ambayo tutaifanya itaanza Alhamisi; vitabu wanafunzi watakavyovinunua havijafika (or) vitabu ambavyo wanafunzi watavinunua havijafika; jina nitakalompa litakuwa John (or) jina ambalo nitampa litakuwa John; nitalirudia sanduku seremala atakalolimaliza kesho (or) nitalirudia sanduku ambalo seremala atalimaliza kesho; watoto watakaokwenda Dar es Salaam kesho lazima waje hapa kwanza (or) watoto ambao watakwenda Dar es Salaam kesho lazima waje hapa kwanza; muda itakaochukua utakuwa mfupi tu (or) muda ambao itachukua utakuwa mfupi tu; mganga atakayekuja leo atafika saa tisa mchana/alasiri (or) mganga ambaye atakuja leo atafika saa tisa mchana/alasiri; matunda mti huu utakayoyazaa yatauzwa sokoni (or) matunda ambayo mti huu utayazaa yatauzwa sokoni.

(c) Chakula alichokipika; kitabu ninachokisoma; kazi atakayoifanya; miji ambayo nimeiona; watu waliosahauliwa; misumari ambayo haikufaa; sisi ambao hatutakuwa pale/kule; mtihani nilioujaribu; wageni watakaokuja kesho; maua tuliyoyapanda; maziwa ambayo yameoza/yameharibika; mlango utakaokuwa wazi; nguo alizozipiga pasi; mtoto aliyeitwa Michael; lugha tuanayojifunza (NOTE *not* 'tunayo *i* jifunza', i.e. only one object infix)

(d) Water which will be sufficient; the milk you will bring; the door which will be opened; the letters I shall write; the loads which will be heavy; the parts you will clean today; the club/society we shall join/enter; the profit they will get; we who will drink coffee; the valley which will be seen/visible; I shall mount the vehicle which will arrive at noon/midnight; we shall use all the trees which will be felled; all people with the names which will be called are to come here; the guest who will come is my friend; the salary you will get will be 4 shillings daily; the food I shall take must be sufficient for three days; I am waiting for a guest who will arrive at any time; the knife I shall use is yours; the dog I shall get will be fierce; the work they will do will be hard/difficult.

Exercise 60

(a) Anayekuja nami ni nani? (or) yule/yeye ambaye anakuja nami ni nani?; watu waliofika jana ni nani? (or) watu ambao walifika jana ni nani?; watoto utakaowaona kesho ni nani? (or) watoto ambao utawaona kesho ni nani?; mbwa huyu ambaye hajala ni wa nani? (cannot use the relative within the verb for this tense); atakayesema katika mkutano wetu ni nani? (or) yule/yeye ambaye atasema katika mkutano wetu ni nani?; anayetaka kununua gari zuri ni nani? (or) yule/yeye ambaye anataka kununua gari zuri ni nani? yule/yeye ambaye hajasikia habari ni nani? (cannot use the relative within the verb for this tense); wanafunzi waliokosa kuja Jumamosi ni nani? (or) wanafunzi ambao walikosa kuja Jumamosi ni nani?; kitabu hiki cha nani? (no relative at all in this sentence); yule/yeye ambaye amekivunja kikombe ghali hiki ni nani? (cannot use the relative within the verb with this tense).

(b) He (that person) who will do this work is who? (who will do this work?); the old man who died is who? (who is the old man who died?); the child who broke this window is who? (who is the child who broke this window?); that stranger who is standing at the door is who? (who is that stranger who is standing at the door?); the labourers who have not yet been paid are who? (who are the labourers who have not yet been paid?); the members who did not go to the meeting are who? (who are the members who did not go to the meeting?); the one having a watch is who? (who has a watch?); that person (he) who gave you this present is who? (who gave you this present?); he who took my pencil is who? (who took my pencil?); she (that person [female]) who will be married is who? (who will be married? [or] who will be getting married?).

273

Exercise 61

(a) Wasiokuja/wale ambao hawakuja; tusiojua/sisi ambao hatujui; nisiyepa-nda/mimi ambaye sijapanda; nguo zisizofuliwa/nguo ambazo hazikufuliwa; chakula kisichopikwa/chakula ambacho hakikupikwa; mlango usiofu-ngwa/mlango ambao hautafungwa; usiyejaribu/wewe ambaye hukujaribu; tusioweza/sisi ambao hatuwezi; msiofanya kazi/ninyi ambao hamfanyi kazi; mizigo isiyoletwa/mizigo ambayo haikuletwa.

(b) Nao (mkate); nazo (barua); nalo (ua); nayo (maziwa); navyo (vitu); nayo (kalamu); nayo (mizigo); nacho (kitabu); nao (watoto); nayo (magari).

(c) Watu wasiovuta sigara wana nguvu nyingi (or) watu ambao hawavuti sigara wana nguvu nyingi; mwizi asiyekamatwa anakaa porini sasa (or) mwizi ambaye hakukamatwa anakaa porini sasa; watoto wasiokuja ni wale wasiojua kusoma (or) watoto ambao hawatakuja ni wale ambao hawajui kusoma; huyu ni Mwislamu asiyekula nyama ya ng'ombe (or) huyu ni Mwislamu ambaye hali nyama ya ng'ombe; kuna/pana gari lingine lisilofika (or) kuna/pana gari lingine ambalo halijafika; nitaharibu miti isiyozaa (or) nitaharibu miti ambayo haizai; kulikuwa/palikuwa na wanawake wachache wasioondoka (or) kulikuwa/palikuwa na wanawake wachache ambao hawakuondoka; sipendi maua yasiyonukia (or) sipendi maua ambayo hayanukii; waite vibarua wasionipa vyeti vyao (or) waite vibarua ambao hawajanipa vyeti vyao; sihitaji mtu asiyejaribu sana (or) sihitaji mtu ambaye hajaribu sana.

(d) We shall use the trees which were not felled another year; make the beds now which you did not make in the morning; I shall try again the examination which I did not succeed in January; those who did not go yesterday, may go today; the luggage which did not come yesterday will be brought later/afterwards; those who were not here yesterday should read this paper; one leg broke, but that one which did not break has a very bad sore; there is a meeting today for those who do not know reading and writing; the animal which did not eat its food is sick; we must speak Swahili on account of these people who cannot speak English.

(e) The letters (the mail) which were (was) written yesterday are (is) lost; the women who will arrive to-morrow are teachers; the plants which that farmer planted in March (the third month) will not be suitable (not do); the mountain which he has not yet climbed is Kilimanjaro; this water which was brought by Ali has become dirty; the flower which he/she brought me has a very nice smell (smells very nice); the society/club which opened yesterday is for men only; I am unable today (i.e. I feel under the weather) because the food which I ate yesterday was bad; the language which we are learning is not hard like English; all who did not go the day before yesterday to Dodoma, wait outside.

Exercise 62

(a) Ku-tangulia; ku-nyamaza; ku-zunguka; ku-vuka; ku-nyoa; ku-kwama; ku-changanya; ku-gawa; ku-ogopa; ku-tumaini; ku-tupa; ku-wahi; ku-vuna; ku-jenga; ku-chinja; ku-onyesha; ku-shona; ku-sukuma; ku-tapika; ku-tengeneza; ku-uma; ku-linda; ku-fahamu; ku-cheka; ku-zima; ku-vuja; ku-ng'oa; ku-sumbua; ku-ruka; ku-uma.

(b) Chinja kuku yule (mchinje kuku yule); usinisumbue; ukivuka daraja lile; uwahi kesho; mbwa yule alimwuma; usizime taa ile; mtangulie; mgonjwa yule amepona; nyamaza!; changanya dawa hii pamoja na chakula; tunasikitika sana; tupa hii nje; mguu huu unauma; anataka kung'oa jino hili; usisahau kukusanya karatasi zile; mbwa ametapika; gari langu lime-kwama katika matope yale; usukume motokaa yangu, tafadhali; saa yangu imetengenezwa; wanatumaini kwamba watajenga nyumba yao hapa.

(c) To send; to kill; to hold/catch; to collect; to put; to excavate; to understand; to fear; to harvest; to shut off/cork; to get better; to meet; to shave; to throw; to leak; to precede; to get stuck; to divide; to cross; to repair; to protect/guard; to jump/fly; to send; to be early; to extinguish; to uproot; to laugh; to sew; to bite/sting; to be sorry/grieve.

(d) We have dug this ditch because of this water; who threw this rubbish here? (that person who threw this rubbish here is who?); those visitors have gone round all this country; this debe (4-gallon can) does not leak; don't (pl.) be afraid to hold this thing; I am sorry, you cannot cross this river; if you burn this grass (these leaves) which was/were collected/heaped up, put the fire out before you leave; if I send a letter today, I hope to get a reply the day after tomorrow; if you meet him on the way, tell him to show you the tree which was uprooted; the vehicle which broke down/was damaged has already been repaired now.

Exercise 63

(a) Wale waogopao; sisi tujengao; mbwa watapikao; magari yakwamayo; mtu achekaye; debe livujalo; mguu uumao; chakula kichanganywacho; takataka ikusanywayo (or takataka zikusanywazo); barua zitumwazo; watu wanisumbuao; wanyama wachinjwao; mlango ufungwao; mwaka ujao; wiki ijayo; watu walao vibaya; mwezi ujao; mganga ajaye Jumanne; kitabu kisomwacho; vitanda vifaavyo.

(b) Niletee kisu kifaacho; vitu viuzwavyo katika duka lile ni rahisi sana; mlete rafiki yako aitwaye Hamisi; watu wakaao hapa ni Waamerika; nitamwoa mtu nimpendaye; atasaidia wale wajisaidiao (wenyewe); magari yasima-mayo hapa yote yanakwenda Nairobi; barabara izungukayo mlima ule si nzuri; hatupendi watu wachelewao; Wazungu wajao Tanzania wanasaidia kujenga taifa.

(c) Insects which bite; the days which come; crops which are planted here; clothes which are sewn well; children who keep quiet; a person who extracts (pulls out) teeth; next Sunday; water which boils (boiling water); patients who sleep/lie down; a youth called Juma (a youth who is called Juma); a flower which smells sweet; men who take wives (get married); we who read a lot; the bridge which crosses the river; people who smoke cigarettes; old men who are able to read; water which is obtainable here; local beer which is drunk in these parts; a knife which cuts badly; birds which fly very high.

Exercise 64

(a) Watoto walio wadogo; mizigo iliyo mizito; milima iliyo mirefu; vitu vilivyo ghali; mlango ulio wazi; kikapu kilicho kitupu; mgeni aliye hapa; mayai yaliyo rahisi; maji yaliyo safi; viatu vilivyo vyekundu; nguo zilizo chafu; habari iliyo nzuri; barua zilizo zako; kalamu iliyo yangu; kitabu kilicho cha Hamisi; moshi ulio mweusi; watu ambao wamechelewa; mgeni aliye Mdachi; mtu aliye wa mwisho; taifa lililo letu.

(b) Mtihani usio mgumu; kazi isiyo nzuri; mtu asiye Mzungu; vitabu visivyo vyangu; gari lisilo jipya; maji yasiyo (ya) moto; mshahara usio mkubwa; watu wasio wagonjwa; viti visivyofaa; vitu visivyo sawa; duka lisilo karibu; mashamba yasiyo yetu; bonde lisilo pana; vijana wasio Wamasai;

jua lisilo kali; kisima kisicho kirefu; mkate usio mweupe; watumishi wasio waminifu; majibu yasiyo tayari; sahani zisizo safi.

(c) Mlima ambao upo pale ni Kilimanjaro (or) mlima ulio kule/pale ni Kilimanjaro; lete mto ambao upo katika/juu ya kitanda changu (or) lete mto ulio katika/juu ya kitanda changu; umeuona moto ambao uko mlimani? (or) umeuona moto ulio mlimani?; mtu/mwanamume ambaye yumo katika nyumba ile ni mgeni (or) mtu/mwanamume aliye katika nyumba ile ni mgeni; ninahitaji maua ambayo ni mekundu tu (or) ninahitaji maua yaliyo mekundu tu; unipe karatasi ambayo ipo mezani (or) unipe karatasi iliyo mezani; nyumba ambazo ni mali ya Hamisi zimewaka zote (or) nyumba zilizo mali ya Hamisi zimewaka zote; miiba ambayo ipo katika mti ule ina sumu (or) miiba iliyo katika mti ule ina sumu; lazima unywe maji ambayo ni safi tu (or) lazima unywe maji yaliyo safi tu; kisima ambacho ni kirefu kina maji (ya) baridi (or) kisima kilicho kirefu kina maji (ya) baridi.

(d) Kila mmoja ila wale ambao si madereva waondoke (or) kila mmoja ila wale wasio madereva waondoke; usile chakula ambacho si kizuri (or) usile chakula kisicho kizuri; usinywe maji ambayo si safi (or) usinywe maji yasiyo safi; andika majina ya watu ambao hawapo hapa leo (or) andika majina ya watu wasio hapa leo; mpe mtoto yule mzigo ambao si mzito (or) mpe mtoto yule mzigo usio mzito; usitumie vitu ambavyo si vyako (or) usitumie vitu visivyo vyako; huwezi kutumia siagi ambayo si laini (or) huwezi kutumia siagi isiyo laini; kisu ambacho si kikali hakikati vizuri (or) kisu kisicho kikali hakikati vizuri; usiniletee barua ambazo si zangu (or) usiniletee barua zisizo zangu; hawezi kutoa majibu ambayo si rahisi (or) hawezi kutoa majibu yasiyo rahisi.

(e) Cloth/material which is not cheap; possessions which are ours; feet which are not clean; cups which are not dry; news which is true; a room which is small; a teacher who is good; the shop which is best/better; a rhino who is fierce; a carpet which is not clean; a knife which is not mine; a house which is theirs; a basket which is not empty; work which is useless; all (people) who are here; some (people) who are far away; a language which is easy; a matter which is secret; sea-fish (fish which are of the sea); cattle which are not theirs.

(f) I do not like food which is not cooked well; I shall not see the people who will be here tomorrow; he/she did not bring the things which were not ready; they used the vehicle which was over there; he/she took a book which was not his/hers; we sold cattle which were not that farmer's; the door which was open yesterday has been closed today; the piece which was used was useless; he/she had a car which was not very good; the dog with feet which were very dirty entered the room.

Exercise 65

(a) Wao walio na watoto; mguu ulio na kidonda; kikapu kilicho na viazi; mashamba yaliyo na mimea; vitanda vilivyo na mito; nyumba zilizo na vyumba vingi; jembe lililo na mpini mrefu; mimi niliyekuwa na shida nyingi; chama kitakachokuwa na wanachama wengi; siku zisizokuwa na mvua.

(b) Mimi ambaye nina mke nyumbani ninapata chakula kizuri (or) (mimi) niliye na mke nyumbani, ninapata chakula kizuri (or) mimi mwenye mke nyumbani, ninapata chakula kizuri; wale ambao walikuwa na barua jana, wainue mikono yao (or) wale waliokuwa na barua jana, wainue mikono yao (not suited to use of "-enye"); nyama ambayo haina chumvi si nzuri (or) nyama isiyo na chumvi si nzuri (or) nyama bila chumvi si nzuri; usinilete chakula ambacho hakina moto (or) usinilete chakula kisicho na moto (or) usinilete chakula bila moto; miti ambayo itakuwa na maua mengi, itakuwa na matunda mengi (or) miti itakayokuwa na maua mengi, . . . (not suited to use of "-enye"); duka ambalo lina mkate liko wapi? (or) duka lililo na mkate liko wapi? (or) duka lenye mkate liko wapi?; kazi ambayo haina faida ni bure (or) kazi isiyo na faida ni bure (or) kazi bila faida ni bure; watu ambao hawana nyumba watapewa msaada (or) watu wasio na nyumba watapewa msaada (or) watu bila nyumba watapewa msaada; wale ambao wana shida wangoje nje (or) wale walio na shida wangoje nje (or) wale wenye shida, wangoje nje; barabara ambazo zitakuwa na matope mengi hazifai (or) barabara zitakazokuwa na matope mengi, hazifai (not suited to use of "-enye").

(c) Work which had no profit; tea which has sugar; a vehicle which has a big load; fields which will have many crops; a person who has nothing at all; a letter which had much news; a Muslim who has two wives; a town which has few inhabitants; an old man who has no strength; rivers which have no abundance of water.

Exercise 66

(a) Nguo alizo nazo; mizizi mti uliyo nayo; mshahara niliokuwa nao; msaada watakaokuwa nao; jibu nililokuwa nalo; mpishi tuliye naye; faida tusiyokuwa nayo; ninaye mgeni; unacho kiberiti? Ninacho; mnayo ruhusa? Hatuna; chakula tulichokuwa nacho; barua tutakazokuwa nazo; wagonjwa mganga alio nao; ninalo gari jipya; unalo gari? Ninalo; unacho kitabu nilicho nacho pia? Nilikuwa nacho lakini sasa sina; kazi tulizo nazo; milima nchi hii iliyo nayo; mke wa kwanza aliyekuwa naye; majembe waliyo nayo ni bure.

(b) Mayai niliyokuwa nayo hayakuwa mazuri; koti hii niliyo nayo ilikuwa ghali sana; mpishi nitakayekuwa naye kesho atakuwa msaada mkubwa; nyumba ulizo nazo mji huu ni safi sana; niliiuza motokaa niliyokuwa nayo mwaka uliopita (or) nililiuza gari nililokuwa nalo mwaka uliopita; mizizi utakayokuwa nayo mti huu itakwenda chini sana; watumishi tulio nao ni waminifu sana; mbwa aliyekuwa naye Bwana Smith aliuawa kwa motokaa/gari; watu walio na mbwa, hawaibiwi; kazi aliyokuwa nayo haikumfaa.

(c) The tea which I have is cold now; the chair he has is not good; have you (pl.) children? We have; the problem/affair we had with him; the monies they will have; the conversation they had; the bread that shop has; have you a cook? I have one; the newspaper he has; the strength they have.

(d) Mwanamume aliye na kofia; watoto tulio nao; wakulima walio na mimea mizuri; watu ambao wamejaribu; duka lililo na mkate mzuri; mkate ulio mtamu; watumishi walio nao; Wazungu walio na watumishi; watu wasio na mali; wale ambao hawajaniona; (wao) walio na bahati; bahati waliyo nayo; yeye ambaye amekuwa mpishi; nyumba niliyo nayo; mganga aliye na nyumba kubwa.

Exercise 67

(a) Mti ulipoanguka; kama mti ulivyoanguka; jinsi ya kusoma; iinue kadiri unavyoweza; kama ujuavyo; kila anapokuja (or ajapo); mvua ilipoanza; unavyofikiri; sijui jinsi anavyofundisha; mgeni alipofika; mkutano utakapoanza; mkutano utaanza lini?; mbwa aliniamsha kila alipofika mzee; panda juu kadiri unavyoweza; utakapofika juu; usiifanye kama anavyoifanya; walipofungua mlango; anapokula; mzee atakapokufa, njoo hapa upesi kadiri utakavyoweza; tulipoipokea barua hii.

(b) Niite watakapofika vibarua (or vibarua watakapofika); kama ujuavyo/ unavyojua, lazima usimame mgeni aingiapo chumba (or) lazima usimame kila mgeni aingiapo chumba; hakumbuki (wala) alipofika, wala atakapoondoka; lazima ufanye kazi hii jinsi atakavyokuonyesha; mtoto yule atakuwa hodari sana atakapokuwa mkubwa; siwezi kukumbuka jinsi alivyoitwa; kila afikapo/ajapo anaacha mlango wazi; jaribu kadiri iwezekanavyo kuja mapema kila siku (or) jaribu kadiri iwezekanavyo kuwahi kila siku; atanipa pesa yangu/zangu atakaporudi; kama tulivyowaambieni, barabara/njia hii inafungwa mvua inapoanza/ianzapo.

(c) When they will leave; as they said; as they will think; how he did the work (how he worked); whenever he passes here; when I returned home; when the animals will eat; as they are lying now; when I entered, he was sitting as he is sitting now; when the vehicle arrived; when the work was finished; tell me when you will finish this programme; I don't know how he will answer me; that old man does not know how to write; he did not do as I showed him; when you will go to town, buy me a (news) paper; as you (pl.) know, when this society was started . . .; the plate broke when it fell; do as I say, not as I do; choose as you like yourself.

Exercise 68

(a) Umaskini; uzee; mbao; unene; Ulaya; ulimi; umande; uhuru; usafi; nywele; wakati; umeme; wino; ugomvi; uchafu; utoto; uzuri; Unguja; udongo; kuni.

(b) Ufunguo mwingine; kurasa nyingi; upepo mkali; urefu wake; uhodari wa watu; ndevu zangu; pande zote; udongo mzuri; nyuzi ndefu; wakati wo wote; umoja wa nchi hii; kuni kavu; uso ule; usingizi mzuri; funguo zile; wali huu; uchafu ule; kuta zile; ufa mbaya ule; usiku mweusi ule.

(c) Ubao uliokuwa hapa uko wapi?; wino niliokuwa nao umepotea; uwezo alio nao unafaa; mbao ambazo zimepasuka; udongo ulio huku ni mwekundu; ana ugonjwa wa ulimi wenyewe; ugali unapikwa uani; utamu chakula kilio nao; ukurasa wa kumi na moja wa kitabu hiki; wino mwekundu ule utatosha.

(d) Pana uchafu mwingi katika uso wako; lete ubao wenye urefu wa futi kumi na tano, na upana wa inchi sita; nywele zake zilikuwa nyeusi, lakini sasa ni nyeupe; niliona umande mwingi asubuhi hii; ukuta huu hauna nguvu, kwa sababu una ufa mkubwa; mgonjwa yule ana ugonjwa wa ulimi ulio mbaya sana; ninahitaji mtu mwenye uaminifu, siyo uvivu; sanduku hili halina uzito mkubwa; watu wa Usukuma wana udongo mzuri; tumesafiri katika pande zote za nchi hii.

(e) The Muslim religion; Germany; gruel; a razor (blade); cooked rice; plenty; honesty/trustworthiness; clan; quarrel; thread; fatness; wealth; love; a side; rottenness; Portugal; a fork; a crack; a face; ability; socialism.

(f) Difficulty/hardness of work; let those people eat their cooked rice; split/ saw all that firewood; where are the keys? Hamisi has them; a plank/board with a length of 7 feet; the heavy soil which is here is unsuitable; you have forgotten to put the forks on the table; wait until the dew goes; there is a scarcity of razor blades about here; he comes from a clan which has a strong unity.

(g) I need the key of the door which is in the courtyard; I have bought more firewood (other firewood) because this does not burn properly; I cannot shave my beard because razor blades are unobtainable; the teacher will be able to write with ease on this black board; the Bwana is asleep now, so come back in the evening period; England/Britain has given independence/freedom to this country now; what is that dirt, that which is on the wall?; those cattle have a disease which was brought by insects; if you want to grow nice flowers you must have soil having goodness; that wall has a length of 25 feet, a height of 4 feet, and a width of 1½ feet.

Exercise 69

(a) Aenda; wala; twakaa; navuta sigara; yafaa; kisu chakata vibaya; anywa pombe; mwafanya kazi vizuri; vikombe vyavunjika ukiviangusha; barua zafika saa tatu; umande watelemka wakati wa usiku; ng'ombe wafugwa huku; mkate wauzwa katika duka lile; wafundisha watoto wangu; nyumba zile zafaa; mishahara yalipwa Jumamosi; yeye ala nyama yo yote, lakini mimi sili kuku; ruhusa yapatikana katika afisi ile; miti hii yatoa kivuli kingi; duka lile lafungwa saa kumi na moja.

(b) Aamka saa kumi na mbili na nusu kila asubuhi; mzee yule aandika vizuri sana; watoto wacheza mpira Jumamosi; magari yaenda Dar es Salaam kila siku; kisu hiki chakata vibaya; maua yale yanukia sana; magari mazito yakwama matopeni; ninasikitika sana kusikia kwamba wakopa pesa/fedha; barabara hii yazunguka mlima ule; afurahi anaponiona/anionapo.

(c) The doctor comes here every Thursday; meetings start at one o'clock sharp; this road goes to Dar es Salaam; this soil is very suitable; those mountains are visible from here; this light is put off at the door; those labourers help a lot; these plants are planted in February; work starts at 7 o'clock (and) is finished at 3 o'clock; he summons me whenever he arrives.

Exercise 70

(a) Ku-achana; ku-fundishana; ku-pigana; ku-kubaliana; ku-andikiana; ku-cheza pamoja; ku-ngojana; ku-fuatana; ku-fahamiana; ku-kamatana; ku-shindana; ku-kumbukana; ku-pendana; ku-ulizana; ku-vutana; ku-rudiana; ku-peana; ku-onana; ku-saidiana; ku-itana.

(b) Waambie wangojane watakapopanda mlima; watoto walivutana juu ya mlima; wazuie watoto wale wasipigane; tutaonana tena kesho; wanyama hawa wafuatana misituni; tutangojana saa kumi na moja na robo jioni; watu wale hawapendani; walifundishana lugha zao; tutashindana nanyi katika mchezo ule; wanataka kukutana/kupatana kuzuia watu wale wasiuane.

(c) I met with him yesterday (I saw him yesterday); the children are fighting in the courtyard; we have told each other all the news; they have agreed with us; the animals followed each other; we saw each other in town; the members are meeting in the club; we and our companions helped one another; we took leave of one another at one o'clock; we do not agree with each other; all people must love one another; the children are competing for the silver cup; the thief fought with the shop owner; we shall see each other again tomorrow; all people are able to teach one another; the children are playing together; the days follow one another; it is a bad matter for people to kill one another; we shall wait for one another under the bridge; youths are tripping each other up.

Exercise 71

(a) (Mahali) pazuri; mahali pengine; karibu petu; nimetafuta pote; penye mti; pengine; pana peupe pale; walingojana katika mahali pawili mbalimbali;

279

(mahali) pengi pana ng'ombe; (mahali) pake nilipo(pa)ona jana; weka mzigo ule po pote; (mahali) panapofaa/pafaapo; mahali pa siri; chukua barua hii pako; pana (mahali) pachache penye maji; alitafuta mahali pengine; mahali penyewe palikuwa padogo sana; mgeni yupo hapa; (mahali) pale hapatafaa; mahali walipokaa.

(b) Ninapokwenda Moshi (niendapo Moshi), pengine ninakwenda mahali pake; ninapapenda sana ninapokaa; pana wanyama wengi pale peusi; (mahali) hapa hapafai kwa sababu ni padogo; hawakupapenda pale, kwa hiyo (basi) walikwenda pengine; alikwenda kukaa katika mahali pake pa kawaida; mahali penyewe palikuwa padogo lakini hapakuwa na uchafu; funguo zako zipo pale mezani; hapana kazi hapa; ngojeni wote (mahali) pamoja, si (siyo) katika mahali pengi.

(c) By the bridge; that place will have a few trees; there is no room here (this place has no room); don't stand anywhere here; go over there by that car; his place has many trees (at his place there are many trees); when I left; the place where we shall go; he found my knife where we did not look; there are many places with Europeans here.

Exercise 72

(a) Kuzuri; kwingine; karibu kwetu; nimetafuta kote; kwenye mbuyu ule; kuna kweupe kule; walingojana kule kwenye nyumba zile; kwingi kuna ng'ombe; kwake nilikoona jana; weka mzigo ule ko kote huku; kunakofaa/kufaako; barua hii imetoka kwetu; kuna kuchache kwenye maji; alitafuta kwingine; kwenyewe kulikuwa kudogo sana; mgeni yuko huku; kule hakutafaa; walikokaa; nimekwenda kote; sijui alikokwenda.

(b) Kule tulikokwenda kuwinda, kulikuwa na vilima vingi; chukua mizigo hii kule kwangu; wanyama hawa hawakupendi huku, basi lazima tuwatafutie kwingine; kuna milima kwenu?; zamani, kulikuwa na wadudu wengi kule; hakuna ruhusa kuvua samaki huku; habari ni nzuri kwetu. Kwenu, je?; utajiri wetu uko wapi? Ni kote; kulikuwa na moto kule kuliko kweusi; Bwana hayuko huku. Kule, je?

(c) Somewhere by the bridge; that area will have a few trees; there is no permission to smoke about here; don't go anywhere about there; go over there by those cars; their homeland was pure bush; the area where I went; the area where they will go; he found my pipe in the area where I did not look myself; we shall go in the area with animals tomorrow.

Exercise 73

(a) Mfukoni mwake; chumbani mle; mjini kule/pale; mabondeni kule; vikapuni mwao; sandukuni mwangu; nyumbani mwako; mfereji alimoanguka; mezani pake; chumba alimoingia.

(b) Mna samaki wengi mtoni mle; viweke (weka) viazi vile kikapuni mkubwa mle; usiweke sahani zile mezani pale; kuna wenyeji wengi vijijini kule; usiweke pesa/fedha zake mfukoni mwako; weka kitambaa hiki chumbani kwa mgeni/chumbani mwa mgeni; usianguke mferejini maji yalimoingia; nimeandika jina langu kitabuni mwangu; Serengeti ni kuzuri sana. Kuna wanyama wa pori wengi; bora (afadhali) usiweke mkono wako mle mwenye nyoka (or) mle mlimo na nyoka.

(c) He has added firewood to that fire; leave that letter on his table; when I arrived, he was working in his house; sometimes I go to his place, sometimes he comes to mine; where am I to put this knife? In the box will do; there will be no-one at all inside that house; he fears to enter into the forest where (at the place where) those animals went (in); have you read the news in this newspaper?; have you seen where Mohamed went? No, I did not see; when he comes, tell him where I live.

Exercise 74

(a) Mimi ni mrefu kuliko wewe; yeye ni tajiri kuliko sisi; sanduku hili ni dogo kushinda yote; chai hii ni tamu zaidi; wewe una nguvu kuliko mimi; nyumba hii ina vyumba vingi kushinda zote; kitambaa kile ni ghali kuliko hiki; mbwa wao ni mkali kuliko wetu; kwetu ni kudogo kuliko kwenu; sanduku lako ni refu kuliko lake, lakini lake ni pana zaidi.

(b) Wanapata mishahara mikubwa kuliko sisi; Kenya ni nchi kubwa kuliko Uganda, lakini Tanzania ni kubwa kushinda zote; Nairobi ina wenyeji wengi kuliko Mombasa; barabara/njia ile ni fupi kuliko hii; sahani ile ni kubwa, lakini hii ni kubwa zaidi; watoto wachukue mizigo myepesi. Sisi tutachukua mizigo iliyo mizito zaidi; ni haraka zaidi kwenda kwa motokaa kuliko kutembea (kwa miguu); lete gari kubwa kushinda yote unayoweza kupata; Kiswahili ni lugha rahisi kujifunza kuliko Kiingereza; inachukua muda mrefu kwenda New York kuliko kwenda London.

(c) This book is better than that one: this field gave out more crops than yours; this Baobab tree is the biggest of all; that medicine is suitable, but this one is better; I am running faster than you; his cook has greater ability than ours, but Mr. John's beats them all (for ability); they have done more work than you (pl.); that house will be bigger than this one; Hamisi lives further than Juma, but Ali lives furthest of all; he has become more efficient than you.

Exercise 75

(a) Kamwite mwalimu!; ukasafishe gari; (twende) tukale sasa!; wakawatafute watoto; mgeni alifika saa moja akala kwetu; NDEGE KAANGUKA; mkasome kitabu hiki; (nenda) kaninunulie sigara dukani; nilimwona mjini, nikamwambia habari, akaondoka asirudi; (twende) tukapumzike.

(b) (Uende) Ukaniletee maji, tafadhali; (nenda) kaone kama watakwenda Nairobi kesho; alikwenda kuvua samaki, akaanguka mtoni, asiweze kujitoa; walikwenda kuwinda, waka(mw)ua mnyama, wakamla; (nenda) ukampe jibu (ukamjibu); hatukuenda Nairobi, tulikaa nyumbani, tukasoma vitabu vingi; twende tukanywe kahawa sasa; wakaende kutuletea kuni nyingine; walikwenda kununua gari jipya, wakalileta nyumbani, wakalionyesha kwa kila mtu; usipojua (kama hujui), nenda kaulize.

(c) We arrived in this country by aeroplane. When we arrived in Nairobi, we saw that the town/city itself was enormous. After the luggage was attended to, we entered the town/city, and tried to get a room in an hotel and were unsuccessful. So we tried another hotel and succeeded in getting one small room. We wanted to stay in Nairobi for two days (for a period of two days) and then to continue on our journey. After buying many things in the town/city, we bought a new car, filled it with petrol and started on our long safari to go to Dar es Salaam. On the way, we saw an extremely high mountain which was white at the top. I asked my companion "What is that mountain?" and he replied "I think it is Mount Kilimanjaro, but let us go and ask that old man". When we asked him, he said that it was Kilimanjaro, and we went on our way.

Exercise 76

(a) Ungesoma; ungalipanda; mti usingalianguka; nyumba isingekuwa hapa; usingekuwa mwalimu; tungalikula; mzee asingalikufa; wangalijaribu; ungemsamehe; asingekuwa mgonjwa; mkono usingalivunjika; mlango huu ungalifungwa; barua zingeletwa; ningekuwa na ufunguo; daraja lisingalianguka; safari yetu ingalikuwa fupi zaidi; pangalikuwa na mkutano leo; maji yangechemka; mgeni asingalifika; asingalipoteza nafasi yake.

(b) Ungalikuja jana, ungaliweza kunisaidia; wangekwenda Moshi sasa, wangemwona; angekuwa mwalimu, angalikwenda mkutanoni; angaliletwa, tungeweza kumwuliza; asingalianguka, asingalikufa; nyumba hii isingekuwa kubwa, tusingekaa hapa; asingekuwa mgonjwa, mganga asingalikuja; mti usingalianguka, tusingekuwa na kuni hizi; wasingalikuja hapa, tungalikwenda kule/pale; ningemkamata mnyama yule asingekuwa na hatari.

(c) If you were not to smoke; if you were to ask me; if he were able to come to-day; if you had sent a letter; if the mountain were not visible; if the luggage had been brought here; if the vehicle had not turned over; if the house had been mine; if we had been paid salaries; if you were to make this bed; if I had not been told; if you had drunk that local beer; if he had not entered that room; if we had not had assistance; if the clock/watch had not been broken/out of order; if the cup was not dirty; if the inhabitants had not agreed; if we were to know Swahili; if the seeds were sown; if you had not failed to come/arrive.

(d) If you were to wear a raincoat, you would not feel cold; if he had planted those crops earlier, he would have got a big profit; if they were to make an effort today, they would be able to rest tomorrow; if you had come/arrived yesterday, you would have seen our Minister; if I had come yesterday, I would not have failed to get my salary; if you had told him your difficulties, he would have been able to help you; if you had told me a long time ago, I would not have gone to ask him; if it had not rained today, we would have gone to see him; if the knife were sharp, it would be able to cut this meat; if I were you, I would not wear that garment.

Exercise 77

(a) Hilo (duka); hicho (kitabu); hiyo (sabuni); hayo (maji); huo (usingizi); hizo (funguo); huyo (mtoto); huyo (mpishi); hao (wanawake); huo (mkate); hiyo (milima); hicho (kijiji); hiyo (dawa); huo (umande); hivyo (visu); hizo (tarehe); hizo (mbao); hao (wakulima); hiyo (miiba); huyo (mwanachama).

(b) Nilikwenda katika lile duka nikanunua hivi/hivyo vitu; ukimwona huyo mwanamume, niambie; umekisoma hicho kitabu kizuri? (or) umekisoma kitabu hicho kizuri?; hao Wazungu wametoka Udachi; huo mkate si mtamu. Siupendi; hao ng'ombe ni mali ya mkulima yule hodari; piga dawa kufukuza hao inzi (or) inzi hao; ile barua ilichukua muda wa miezi mitatu kufika; hizo nyumba zilinunuliwa na yule Mwafrika; majani ya ule mti ni mazuri kula.

(c) There is a new shop in town; this shop sells bread; this bread has sweetness; this sweetness is because of sugar which was put (in); this sugar is got from fields/farms of this country; these fields/farms must have adequate water; this water must not have any salt; this salt can destroy the crops; these crops are the property of farmers; these farmers are inhabitants of Tanzania.

Exercise 78

(a) Ndilo (jibu); ndivyo (vidonge); ndiyo (sehemu); ndio (mchezo); ndio (wanyama); ndiye (Mzungu); ndimi; ndiyo (maziwa); ndicho (kisima); ndio (sisi); ndicho (cheti); ndiwe; ndio (mmea); ndio (wao); ndio (uchafu); ndizo (kuni); ndicho (kitambaa); ndiye (dereva); ndicho (kivuli); ndiyo (maua).

(b) Ile ndiyo mizigo yangu; wale ndio watoto anaowafundisha; pale ndipo ninapokwenda; hapo ndipo mwisho; hizo ndizo pesa/fedha nilizopewa; ilikuwa ndiye aliyeniambia; hivyo ndivyo nilivyofikiri; ule ndio mshahara anaolipwa; zile ndizo funguo nilizozipoteza wiki iliyopita; hicho ndicho chakula ninachokipenda bora.

(c) This is indeed the knife I was given; this stranger is the very person whom I saw yesterday; this medicine is indeed very good; indeed as I said; seven o'clock is indeed when he arrived; this work is indeed very difficult; that cook is indeed efficient; these potatoes are the very ones I planted in March; this is the very river we were looking for; this is indeed the vehicle which turned over.

Exercise 79

(a) Mimi huenda; barua hufika kila siku; sisi hupumzika Jumapili; mikutano huanza saa moja; umande huja wakati wa usiku; yeye hufikiri; wao huja; wewe hula saa hii?; mimi husoma sana; yeye huchelewa.

(b) Wakulima hupanda mbegu zao mwezi huu; mishahara hulipwa kila mwisho wa mwezi; mimi heunda Nairobi mara mbili kwa mwezi; dawa hii huua wadudu hawa (dawa hii huwaua wadudu hawa); galoni mbili za mafuta ya taa hutosha kwa wiki mbili; mayai hupatikana sokoni; mbu huleta ugonjwa; Kilimanjaro huonekana toka hapa; hunyesha mvua mwezi wa Machi (mvua hunyesha mwezi wa Machi); wao huja Jumapili.

(c) Those mountains are generally visible; eggs are usually obtainable these days; this work is usually very popular/liked; the water usually enters the ditch; the doors are generally opened at 8 o'clock; a person who goes up/climbs up, generally comes down; insects generally die by means of this chemical; this chair is usually put here; clothes are generally washed on Mondays; cars need petrol.

Exercise 80

(a) Mkutano upi? mito ipi? mtumishi yupi? wanyama wepi? kitanda kipi? funguo zipi? uchafu upi? misumari ipi? duka lipi? majani yapi? kupi? visu vipi? taa ipi? alama zipi? maji yapi? mbegu zipi? shamba lipi? kikombe kipi? unataka nguo ipi? ulileta barua zipi?

(b) Which local court/verandah? which dog? which chair? which potatoes? which house? which fire? which thorns/thorn trees? which Europeans? which vessel? which bone? which days? which flag? which door? which box? which milk? which craftsmen? which youth? which river? which bananas? which year?

Exercise 81

(a) Walikuwa wamejaribu; hatukuwa tumeandika; maji yangekuwa yakiingia mfereji; barua zisingalikuwa zikija; angalikuwa akilala; hawakuwa wamemaliza kazi yao; nilipofika pale, walikuwa wamekwenda; watoto wasingalikuwa wakicheza wangaliambiwa; maji yasingalikuwa yakichemka usingaliwasha moto; isingekuwa ikinyesha mvua bondeni sasa.

283

(b) They had tried many times; you (pl.) would have been sleeping now if we had not arrived; the fire would be burning well if the firewood had been dry; if you were to have asked them they would not have been leaving now; we would not be going now if we had been told yesterday; I would have been climbing the mountain now if I had been given permission; they would be coming now if they had got the opportunity; those people had come last year; you would not have been staying here if another house had been obtainable; I would be working at home if I were not wanted here.

Exercise 82
The Moran and the Lion

One year when it absolutely did not rain and the Masai's cattle were in great difficulty, many cattle died and those which were left had no strength whatsoever, even when they were stabbed with an arrow, they did not give blood, but just watery stuff. The state of the people and animals was very bad and this problem continued for over two years.

But there was a large forest which was near the mountain which had plenty of grass and a few small rivers, and it was a journey of three days or more from the Masai's houses. Everyone feared to send their cattle down there, because there was a very ferocious lion about who had two fairly large cubs; this lion was extremely ferocious and even other animals feared to enter that forest.

One day, the Masai elders and Morans were having a conversation outside their compound (these are fortifications of thorns, hence the use of the word 'boma') making plans concerning their problem. In the end, one Moran, his name Ol Kidongoi, agreed to go and try to kill that lion.

On the second day that Moran made his journey and went as far as the forest area. In there he met that lion and after fighting with it for a long time, succeeded in killing it.

Exercise 83
Being bitten by Snakes

If a snake bites a person, it inserts poison by means of its teeth until it enters small blood vessels. In there, it passes quickly into larger blood vessels and spreads over the whole body. Therefore, first aid must be done extremely quickly right there where the person was bitten to prevent the poison from entering further in the body.

So if by luck you are there where the person has been bitten, do thus:—
1st step. Fasten on him a rope, string or cloth (handkerchief) very speedily, or whatsoever you have. Fasten it on the leg or arm which was bitten near the wound, but on the side of the heart. Thus you will prevent the poison from passing further inside the blood vessels.
2nd step. Lie the person down, so that he is not standing.
3rd step. Take a knife, cut him/her there on the wound until it bleeds. You must cut quite firmly so that blood comes out in quantity.
4th step. Use ingenuity to prevent the person from being afraid. Give him heart, also tell him that he will be helped to recover.
5th step. Tie up the wound with a cloth with salty water.
6th step. Send the patient to the hospital as quickly as possible.

If a person gets poison in the eye from a snake, clean his eye for him with either plenty of water or with milk. Then bandage his eye with a cloth soaked in cold water, then send him to hospital too.

Although snakes with poison are few in this country, it is better to follow these first aid steps than to leave a bitten person to die.

Exercise 84
Butterflies
The butterfly is indeed an insect which is the nicest of all in the world. There are many kinds of butterfly in this country, some large, and some small, but all have lovely colours. Any day, especially after rain, you will see them flying here and there by flowers.

If you look at the butterfly, you will see that his body is in three parts; the head, the thorax (chest) and the abdomen (stomach). His head has two eyes, one on each side. These eyes are of very great wonder (are extremely wonderful). If you were able to see them from very close, you would be able to see that each eye is not really one eye, like that of a person, but is really many small eyes, about one thousand seven hundred altogether. Therefore this insect is able to see forwards and backwards at one time. A person must turn his head if he wants to see behind him, but the butterfly can see on all sides without turning the head.

Many times he (the butterfly) is seen standing on a flower, and if you are able to stand and keep extremely quiet so that it cannot hear you, you will see its long tongue being inserted into that flower, the butterfly searching for honey (nectar). At the time of standing on the flower, you will see its wings open, with many colours. These colours help to hide the butterfly so that it is not seen by other insects or birds who would want to eat it.

Exercise 85
The Cave
When we arrived at the home/house of that owner of the field with the cave we just met his wife, the Bwana himself not being about. We asked his wife to give us permission to enter the cave and she refused, saying, 'My Bwana does not want anyone to enter this cave.' We continued to beg her until she agreed saying, 'As you (pl.) know, the Bwana is extremely strict and I don't want to be beaten on your account. If you want to go in, just go in. But if my Bwana returns before you have come out I shall tell him that you entered by force without my permission. If you agree thus, go in. If you do not agree be on your way, don't go on bothering me.'

We thanked her and went towards the cave. When we arrived at the cave, we found a very large stone/rock which had fallen in the entrance and which prevented us from being able to enter. I told my companion, 'I say, help me to remove this boulder so that we can go in.' So we tried together to remove that boulder and we succeeded with difficulty. When we entered my companion lit his pressure lamp and we went right inside.

Exercise 86
Maji
Katika nchi nyingine kuna sikuzote maji ya kutosha kwa hiyo watu na wanyama hawana hatari yo yote ya kufa kwa kiu. Katika nchi nyingine hunyesha mvua mara nyingi, kuna majani tele, visima na mito hujaa, na watu hawaendi mbali na nyumba zao ili wapate maji ya kunywa na kupikia. Lakini katika nchi nyingine, maji hayapatikani kwa wingi namna hii. Huko, kuna mvua kidogo sana kwa muda wa miezi mingi kidogo mwakani, majani hukauka mpaka yafe, visima hukauka, wingi wa maji mitoni hupungua, watu

lazima wachukue vyombo vyao vya maji mbali ili wapate maji ya kunywa na kupikia. Katika nchi zenye maji tele, watu hawaangalii maji yao, lakini katika nchi kavu, hawayatumii bila kufikiri, kwa sababu wajua kwamba wakiyatumia upesi zaidi, hayatabaki kwa matumizi yao wala ya ng'ombe zao na labda ama wao ama ng'ombe zao watakufa.

Exercise 87
Safari Yetu
Juzijuzi tulikwenda kumwona rafiki yangu aitwaye Hamisi, akaaye karibu na mto wa Ruvu. Tulipofika pale, tukaona kwamba alikuwa amekwenda Mombasa. Basi tukarudi nyumbani tena. Njiani, tukapita wanaume wawili waliokuwa wakipanda mbegu za mahindi. 'Kwa nini mnapanda sasa?' tukauliza, wakajibu 'Sisi hupanda mbegu zetu mwezi huu kwa ajili ya mvua ijayo mapema upande huu wa bonde.' Tukaendelea zetu. Baada ya kutembea kwa muda wa saa nne hivi, tukachoka sana tukakaa/keti chini ya mti kivulini mzuri (katika kivuli kizuri). Mwenzangu akaniambia, 'Nahitaji chakula. Unafikiri chakula cho chote kinapatikana huku?' 'Sijui,' nikamjibu 'Nenda ukamwulize mkulima yule pale kama anaweza kutuambia tutakapoweza kukipata'. Basi akaenda kumwuliza yule mkulima aliyemwambia kwamba palikuwa na duka kijijini lililofaa sana kwa chakula. Basi tukaendelea kutembea kijijini tulipoliona duka, tukashiba tukaenda zetu.

Exercise 88
Jinsi Nilivyofika Kenya
Baada ya kusikia kwamba nilikuwa nimepewa kazi hii, nikaenda kufunga mizigo yangu niwe tayari kuondoka wakati wo wote. Niliposikia tarehe ya safari yangu, iliyokuwa tarehe thelathini na moja ya mwezi wa nane (Agosti), niliwaambia rafika zangu wote kwamba ningekwenda katika nchi iitwayo Kenya. Siku hiyo ilipofika, nilichukua vitu vyangu vyote nikaenda katika kiwanja cha ndege nikangoja kupanda ndege.

Kwa bahati mbaya, ndege ikachelewa kidogo, lakini mwishoni ikaondoka saa kumi na mbili na nusu jioni. Ilikuwa ndege yenye nguvu nyingi iliyokwenda kwa mwendo mkali na juu sana pia. Lakini kwa sababu ilikuwa wakati wa usiku, sikuweza kuona cho chote mpaka alfajiri siku iliyofuata (kesho yake). Nilipoona Nairobi chini yetu, nikafurahi sana, na baada ya dakika chache ndege ikatelemka kufika Nairobi, iitwayo 'Mji juani' ('Mji wa juani'). Baada ya kuangaliwa mizigo yangu nikapewa ruhusa kutoka, nikapanda gari lililonipeleka mjini, na pale nikatembea kidogo halafu nikaenda kupumzika.

Exercise 89
Kupanda Kilimanjaro
Kila mgeni wa Tanzania hutaka kupanda mlima mkubwa na mzuri huu uitwao Kilimanjaro. Urefu wake ni futi elfu kumi na tisa, mia tatu, arobaini na moja juu ya bahari, pia ni mrefu kushinda milima yote Afrika. Wahitaji kama siku tano kuupanda mlima huo, yaani siku tatu kupanda, na siku mbili kutelemka. Ukichukua mizigo yako mingine safari haitakuwa ghali sana, labda shilingi mia moja au zaidi. Lakini ukiajiri wapagazi kuchukua mizigo yako yote, safari itakuwa ghali zaidi. Pia, lazima uajiri mwongozi (anayehitaji mpagazi vilevile) kwa sababu ungepoteza njia yako kwa urahisi bila mtu wa kukuonyesha njia yenyewe. Tena katika siku ya mwisho ya kupanda, watu huondoka kama saa sita au saba usiku ili wafike kileleni alfajiri. Kuna baridi

nyingi sana kule juu, kwa hiyo (basi) ni lazima kuvaa nguo za kufaa kuzuia baridi isiingie mwilini mwako. Ukifika kileleni, utakuta kitabu cha kuandikia jina lako kuonyesha kila mtu kwamba umefaulu kupanda huo mlima mkuu. Ufikapo sehemu ya chini tena, wapagazi wakupa taji ya maua yaotayo katika mitelemko ya mlima. Taji hiyo yaonyesha kwamba wewe ndiye (ndiwe) umeshinda mlima mrefu kushinda yote Afrika.

N.B. The English in these exercises has been deliberately kept to an approximate literal translation for easy understanding of the Swahili equivalent.

Vocabulary Swahili—English

An asterisk (*) denotes a word included in the text of this book.
N.B. Verbs are listed without their 'infinitive' 'Ku-'
N.B. The plurals shown in this vocabulary show the class of the noun. Although the plural may be given, not all nouns may necessarily have a plural.
It may be assumed that nouns listed without a plural being shown are N class nouns. Certain nouns do not fit permanently into either the N class or the MA-class, thus may be encountered in either.

* -a of
* acha to leave, abandon
* ada fee
  adabu manners
  adhabu punishment
* adhuhuri noon
  adui enemy
* afadhali preferable, better
  afisa(ma-) an officer
* afisi office
  afya health
  aga to take leave of
  Agano Jipya New Testament
  Agano la Kale Old Testament
  agiza to order
* Agosti August
  ahidi to promise
  aibu shame, disgrace
* AIDS ukimisi
  aina kind, species
  ajabu wonder
  ajali accident, fate
* ajili reason
      * kwa ajili ya on account of
  ajiri to employ
* -ake his, hers, its
* akiba store, reserve
* akili intelligence
  akina connections
  akina mama women-folk
* -ako your, yours (singular)
* alama mark, stain, sign
* alasiri afternoon
* alfajiri dawn
* Alhamisi Thursday
  almasi diamond
* ama either, or
  amani peace
* amba- who, which
* ambia to tell, inform
  amini to believe
* -aminifu honest, trustworthy
* amka to awake
* amkia to greet
  amri command, order
* andika to write
* angalia to pay attention, take care
* -angu my, mine
* anguka to fall
  anwani address (postal)
* anza to begin
* -ao their, theirs
* Aprili April

  ardhi earth, ground
* arobaini forty
  arusi wedding
  asali honey
* asante thanks
  asili origin
* askari soldier, policeman
  askofu(ma-) bishop
* asubuhi morning
* Ati! I say!
* au either, or
* aunsi ounce
  azima to borrow

* baada ya after
* baadaye afterwards
* baba father
* babu grandfather
* badala ya instead of
* badili to change
* bado not yet, still
* bahari sea, ocean
* bahasha envelope, bundle
* bahati luck, chance
* bahatisha to guess, take chance
  baisikeli bicycle
* baki to remain
  bakuli basin
  bandika to stick on
  bara continent, mainland
* barabara road, highway
* barafu ice, refrigerator
  baraka blessing
* baraza(ma-) verandah, local court
* baridi cold, coolness
  bariki to bless
* barua letter (pl. mail)
* basi well! That's all!
* basi? is that all?
  basi(ma-) bus
  bastola pistol, revolver
* bata(ma-) duck
* bati(ma-) corrugated iron, sheet iron
  batiza to baptize, christen
  bawa(ma-) wing
* -baya bad
  beba to carry on back
  bega(ma-) shoulder
* bei price
* bendera flag, banner
* bia bottled beer
  biashara trade, commerce
* bibi (ma-) grandmother, lady

Biblia Bible
-bichi unripe, damp, uncooked
bidhaa merchandise
*bidii effort, energy
*bila without
*bilauri tumbler, glass
bin son of
*binadamu human being (son of Adam)
*binamu cousin
*binti daughter
birika kettle, teapot, tank
-bivu ripe
blanketi(ma-) blanket
*boma(ma-) fortification, Government offices
bomoa to break down
*bonde(ma-) valley
*bora best, excellent
boriti(ma-) beam, thick pole
*-bovu rotten, worthless
budi alternative
buibui spider, cobweb
*bunduki gun, rifle
*bunge(ma-) parliament
buni coffee berries
burashi brush
*bure useless
  *-a bure free
bustani garden, nursery
*bwana(ma-) Mr., gentlemen, etc.
bwawa(ma-) swamp, bog

*-chache few, not many
*-chafu dirty
chafua to soil
chafya sneeze
  piga chafya to sneeze
*chagua to choose
*chai tea
chakaa to grow old, wear out
chaki chalk
*chakula(vy-) food
*chama(vy-) club, society, co-op.
chambua to sort out, grade
*chandalua(vy-) mosquito net, tarpaulin
*changanya to mix
*chapa brand, trademark
  piga chapa to print
*cheka to laugh
*chelewa to be late
chemchemi spring of water
*chemka to boil, bubble up
cheo(vy-) rank
cherehani sewing machine
*cheti(vy-) chit, certificate
*cheza to play
*chimba to excavate, dig
*chini down
*chini ya below, under
*chinja to slaughter
chipua to sprout
*chizi cheese
*choka to get tired
chokaa lime, whitewash
*choma to burn, pierce
*chombo(vy-) vessel, tool, container

*choo(vy-) lavatory, W. C., faeces
chora to draw, engrave
chota to take up bit by bit
chui leopard
*chukua to carry, take
*chuma(vy-) iron, steel
chuma to pluck, gather
*chumba(vy-) room
*chumvi salt
chunga to look after
-chungu bitter, acid
*chungwa(ma-) orange
chuo(vy-) school, college
*chupa bottle
chura(vy-) frog

*dada sister
daftari register
dafu(ma-) milky coconut
dai to claim
*daima constantly
*dakika minute (of time)
daktari doctor
*damu blood
danganya to deceive
*daraja(ma-) bridge, stairs
darasa(ma-) class, classroom
dau(ma-) native dhow
*dawa medicine, chemical, polish, etc.
*debe(ma-) 4-gallon tin
dengu grams, lentils
deni(ma-) debt
*dereva(ma-) driver
*Desemba December
desturi custom
dhahabu gold
dhambi sin
dhani to think
dharau to despise
dini religion
dira compass
*dirisha(ma-) window
dobi(ma-) laundry, laundryman
*-dogo small, little
dola government
*dudu(ma-) pest, large insect
*duka(ma-) shop
dume(ma-) male animals
dunia world, globe

*Ebu! I say!
*eka acre
*-ckundu red
*elea to be clear
elewa to understand
*eleza to explain
*elfu thousand
elimu knowledge
*-ema good (character)
*-embamba thin, narrow, slender
*embe(ma-) mango
*enda(kwenda) to go
*endelea to continue, progress
enea to spread about
*eneo(ma-) area (geometric)
*-enu your, yours(pl.)

*-enye having, with
*-enyewe -self
*-epesi light in weight, easy
*-erevu cunning, crafty
eropleni aeroplane
*-etu our, ours
*-eupe white, light coloured
*-eusi black, dark coloured
ezeka to thatch

*fa (kufa) to die
*faa to be suitable
*fagia to sweep
fagio(ma-) broom
*fahamu to know, understand
*faida profit
fanana(na) to resemble
*fanya to do, make
farasi horse
*faulu to succeed
*Februari February
*fedha silver, money
*ficha to hide
figo(ma-) kidney
*fika to arrive
*fikiri to think, consider
*filimbi whistle, pipe (flute)
fimbo walking stick
fisi hyena
fitina discord
*frasila 35 lb. measure
*fua nguo to wash clothes
*fuata to follow
*fuga to keep live-stock
*fukuza to drive off
*fulani someone/thing or other
*fundi(ma-) craftsman, skilled man
*fundisha to teach
fundo(ma-) knot
*funga to close, fasten, to fast
fungu(ma-) portion, heap
*fungua to open, undo
*funika to cover over
funza jigger, maggot
*-fupi short, low
*furaha joy, happiness
*furahi to be happy
*futa to wipe, obliterate
*futi foot measure
*fyeka to slash, cut down bush etc.

*galoni(ma-) gallon, gallon tin
ganda(ma-) shell, pod, fruit skin
*gani? what sort of?
*gari(ma-) vehicle
gauni(ma-) dress
*gawa to divide
*gazeti(ma-) newspaper etc.
*-geni strange
gereji(ma-) garage
*geuka to turn round
*ghafula suddenly
*ghali expensive
giza darkness
*gogo(ma-) log
goma to go on strike

gombana to quarrel
gonga to knock, strike
goti(ma-) knee
    piga magoti to kneel
*-gumu hard, difficult
gundi glue
gunia(ma-) sack
gurudumu(ma-) wheel
*gusa to touch

*habari news
*habari ya/za about, concerning
hadi until, up to
hadithi story
haja need
haki justice, right
*hakika certainty
*hakikisha to make sure
*halafu afterwards
*hali state, circumstance
    *U hali gani? How are you?
halmashauri committee
*hama to move away
*hamia to move to
*hamsini fifty
hanamu oblique, sloping
*hapa here
hapa hapa right here
*hapana no, there is not
*haraka haste
    kwa haraka quickly
*haribika to be destroyed
*haribu to destroy, spoil
harufu odour, smell
*hasa especially
*hasara loss
hasira anger
*hata even, not even, up to
*hatari danger
*hatua pace, step
*haya! right! O.K.
hekima wisdom
*hela money (old term)
*hema tent
    *piga hema pitch a tent
    hema to pant for breath
*heri happiness
    *Kwa heri! Goodbye!
herufi letter (alphabet)
hesabu addition, reckoning
hesabu to add, reckon
heshima honour, respect
hewa air
*hitaji to need
*hivi, hivyo thus
*hodari efficient, able
*hodi may I come in? etc.
hofu fear
hoi useless state
*homa fever
hotuba speech, sermon
hubiri to preach
huduma service, aid
*huku hereabouts
*huko down in, up in, etc.
husu to concern

*iba to steal
idara department (government)
*Ijumaa Friday
*ila except
*ili in order that
imani faith
*imba to sing
*inchi inch
ingawa although
*-ingi many, much
*ingia to enter into
*-ingine some, other(s), another
ini(ma-) liver
Injili Gospel
*inua to lift, raise
*inzi fly
*isha (kwisha) to be finished
*ishirini twenty
*ita to call, summon
*iva to get ripe, cooked

*ja (kuja) to come
*jaa to be filled
*jamaa family, relations
*jambo (mambo) matter, subject
*Jambo! (a greeting)
jamhuri republic
*jana yesterday
*jani(ma-) leaf (pl. grass)
-janja cunning
*Januari January
jaribio(ma-) experiment, trial
*jaribu to try, test
jasho sweat
*jaza to fill
*je? Well? How about?
*-je? how?
jela jail
*jembe(ma-) hoe
*jenga to build
jengo(ma-) building, building materials
jeraha(ma-) wound
jeshi(ma-) army
*jibu to answer, reply
*jibu(ma-) reply, answer
*jicho(macho) eye
*jifunza to learn
*jiko(meko) cooking place, kitchen
jimbo(ma-) province
*jina(ma-) name
*jino(meno) tooth
*jinsi how
*jioni late afternoon
*jipu(ma-) boil, abscess
jitahidi to make an effort
*jitolea to volunteer
*jitu(ma-) giant
*jiwe(mawe) stone, torch cell
jogoo cock
joto heat
*jua(ma-) sun
*jua to know
*Julai July
juma(ma-) week
*Jumamosi Saturday
*Jumanne Tuesday

*Jumapili Sunday
*Jumatano Wednesday
*Jumatatu Monday
*jumba(ma-) hall, large house
*Juni June
*juu up, above
*juu ya upon, concerning
*juzi day before yesterday
*juzijuzi the other day

*kaa to stay, live, sit
kaanga to fry
kabila(ma-) tribe
*kabisa completely, absolutely
*kabla(ya) before (of time)
kaburi(ma-) grave
kadhalika likewise
na kadhalika et cetera
n.k. etc.
*kadiri as far as
kagua to inspect
*kahawa coffee
*kaka elder brother
*kalamu pen, pencil
kale old times
-a kale old, ancient
*kalenda calendar
*-kali sharp, fierce, strict
*kama as; like, if, about
*kamata to seize
*kamba rope, cord, string
kambi camp
*kamili complete, exact
kamua to squeeze, milk
kamusi dictionary
*kando aside
*kando ya beside
*kanisa(ma-) church
kanuni rule, principle
kanzu man's garment
*kaptula shorts
*karabai pressure lamp
karanga groundnuts
*karani(ma-) clerk, typist
karata playing-cards
*karatasi paper (writing)
karibia to draw near
*karibu! Come in! Draw near!
*karibu na near, nearly
*kasa less by
*kasirika to get angry
kasisi(ma-) priest
kaskazini north
*kasoro less by, minus
*kata to cut, reduce
*kataa to refuse
katani sisal (fibre)
*kataza to forbid
*kati, katikati in the middle, centre
*kati ya between, among
*katika in, on, out of, to
*kauka to get dry
*-kavu dry
*kawaida custom, normal
*kaza to tighten, make fast
*kazi work, job

291

*-ke female
kelele(ma-) noise, uproar
*kesho tomorrow
*kesho kutwa day after tomorrow
*keti to sit
*kiasi(vi-) amount, quantity
*kiatu(vi-) shoe
*kiazi(vi-) potato
*kibaba(vi-) ½ litre measure
*kibanda(vi-) shed, hut
kibao(vi-) board, signpost
*kibarua(vi-) labourer
*kiberiti(vi-) matches, lighter
*kiboko(vi-) hippopotamus, whip
kibuyu calabash
*kichwa(vi-) head
*kidogo a little, fairly, quite, rather
*kidole(vi-) finger, toe
kidonda(vi-) sore, ulcer
*kidonge(vi-) pill, tablet
*kifaru(vi-) rhinoceros
kifo(vi-) death
kifua(vi-) chest, cold in chest
*kifupi shortly, briefly
    *-a kigeni unusual
*Kiingereza(vi-) English language
*kijana(vi-) youth, young person
*kijiji(vi-) village
*kijiko(vi-) spoon
kijiti(vi-) small stick, peg
*kikapu(vi-) basket
    *-a kike female
*kiko(vi-) pipe (smoker's)
*kikombe(vi-) cup
*kila every
*kilima(vi-) hill
*kilimo(vi-) agriculture
*kilo kilogramme
*kilometa kilometre
*kilugha(vi-) local language, dialect
*kimbia to run
kimya silence, quiet
kinanda(vi-) piano, etc.
kinu(vi-) mortar, mill
kinyozi(vi-) barber
*kioo(vi-) mirror, sheet of glass
*kipande(vi-) piece, portion
kipepeo(vi-) butterfly
*kipimo(vi-) measuring device
*kipini(vi-) small handle
*kipofu(vi-) blind person
*kiraka(vi-) patch
kiroboto(vi-) flea
*kisahani(vi-) saucer
    *-a kisasa modern
*kisha and then, afterwards
*kisima(vi-) well, water hole
*kisiwa(vi-) island
*kisu(vi-) knife
*Kiswahili(vi-) Swahili
*kitabu(vi-) book
*kitambaa(vi-) cloth, material
kitana(vi-) comb
*kitanda(vi-) bed
*kiti(vi-) chair, seat
    *-a kitoto childish

*kitu(vi-) thing, object
*kitunguu(vi-) onion
kiu(vi-) thirst
    *-a kiume male
kiungo(vi-) joint
*kivuli(vi-) shadow, shade
*kiwanda(vi-) workshop
*kiwanja(vi-) plot of ground
*kiwete(vi-) lame person, cripple
*kizibo(vi-) cork, stopper
*kiziwi(vi-) deaf person
kizunguzungu(vi-) dizziness
kobe(ma-) tortoise
*kodi to rent
kodi, kodisha to rent, let
kofi(ma-) open hand
    piga kofi to slap
    piga makofi to clap
*kofia hat, headwear
*kohoa to cough
kojoa to urinate
kokwa nut (fruit)
koleo(ma-) tongs, pliers, shovel
komaa to be ripe
konda to get thin
*kopa to borrow
*kopesha to lend
kopo(ma-) tin, can
koroga to stir
korosho(ma-) cashew nut
korti(ma-) court of law
kosa(ma-) mistake, fault
*kosa to be mistaken, to be without
*koti coat
*kubali to agree
*-kubwa big, large
kucha(ma-) claw, fingernail
kufuli padlock
*kuku chicken, hen
kulabu hook
*kule thereabouts
*kulia right (hand side)
*kuliko -er than (comparison)
*Kumbe! Fancy that!
*kumbuka to remember
*kumi ten
*kuni firewood (pl. agreements)
*kunja to fold
kupe cattle tick
kura lot, vote
    piga kura to vote
*kusanya to collect, heap up
*kushoto left (hand side)
kusini south
*kusudi(ma-) intention
    *kwa kusudi on purpose
*kuta to find, meet
kutu rust
*kutwa all day
    *kwa kutwa daily
*-kuu great, main
*kuwa to be, become
    *kwa kuwa because
*kuwa na to have
*kwa to, by, with, for, towards, by means
    of

*kwa heri good-bye
kwa hiyo therefore
*kwa kuwa because
*kwa nini? Why?
*kwa sababu because
*kwama to get stuck
*kwamba that (i.e. he said *that* . . . .)
kwani? why?
*kwanza first, at first
*kweli true, truth
  *kwa kweli truly, truthfully

*la! No!
*la (kula) to eat
*labda perhaps, maybe
*laini soft, smooth
*lainisha to soften, make smooth
laiti! if only!
*laki 100,000 unit
*lakini but, however
*lala to sleep, lie down
lami tar, bitumen
laza to make lie down
*lazima necessity, obligation
*lazimisha to compel
*legea to be loose, slack
lenga to take aim
*leo to-day
*leta to bring, fetch
*lewa to be intoxicated
*lia to make a sound, cry
*lima to cultivate, plough
*limau(ma-) lemon
*linda to guard, protect
*lini? when?
*lipa to pay
lipu plaster
*lugha language

maalum special
*maana meaning, reason
*maarifa knowledge, ingenuity
*Machi March
madaraka responsibility
maelezo explanation
maendeleo progress
*mafuta oil, fat, grease, etc.
  (NOT engine oil)
magharibi west
magugu weeds
*mahali place
maharagwe beans
*mahindi maize grain
*maili mile
maisha life
maiti corpse
majani grass, leaves
*maji water
*majivu ashes
maksai castrated animal
makuti thatching leaves
malale sleeping sickness
*mali property, wealth, possession
*malidadi fancy, smart
*maliza to finish
malkia queen
*mama mother

mamba crocodile
*mamoja all one, all the same
manjano yellow, turmeric
manyoya feathers
maombi petitions
mapatano agreement
mapato income
*mapema early, soon
*mara times (x)
*mara moja at once, once
maradhi sickness
*marahaba (answer to 'shikamuu')
  'Thanks'
*maridadi fancy, smart
marufuku prohibition, forbidden
*masalkheri good afternoon
mashariki east
mashindano contest, match
mashine machine, train
mashua boat
*maskini poor, miserable
matandiko bedding, furnishing
*matata trouble
mate saliva
matokeo outcome, result
maumivu pains
*mavi excrement, faeces
mavuno harvest
mazao produce, crops
*maziwa milk, breasts
*mazungumzo conversation
mbaazi pigeon-peas
*mbali (na) far (from)
*mbalimbali different
*mbao planks, boards
*mbegu seeds, planting material
*mbele (ya) in front of, before, beyond
mbinguni heaven
mbio running, speed
*mboga vegetables
mbogo buffalo
mbolea manure
*mbona? why? (astonishment)
*mbu mosquito
mbuga black cotton soil
mbung'o tsetse fly
mbuni ostrich
mbuni(mi-) coffee tree
*mbuyu(mi-) baobab tree
  adansonia digitata
mbuzi goat
*mbwa dog
mbweha jackal, fox
*mchana(mi-) daytime
mchanga sand
mchanganyiko(mi-) mixture
mchango(mi-) intestinal worm
mchawi witch doctor
mche(mi-) seedling
mchele(mi-) husked rice
*mchezo(mi-) a game, toy
*mchungaji(wa-) herdsman, pastor
mchungwa(mi-) orange tree
mchuzi(mi-) gravy, sauce
*mchwa termites ('white ants')
*Mdachi(wa-) a German
mdomo(mi-) lip, beak

* mdudu(wa-) insect
* Mei May
  meli ship
* Memsabu(ma-) Mistress (of household)
  menya to peel, shell
* meza table
  mfalme(wa-) king
  mfano(mi-) example
  mfanya(wa-) a doer
    mfanya(wa-) kazi worker
* mfereji(mi-) ditch, furrow
* mfuko(mi-) bag, pocket
  mfungwa(wa-) prisoner
* mfupa(mi-) bone
* mganga(wa-) doctor
* mgeni(wa-) stranger, visitor, new-comer, guest
* Mgiriki(wa-) a Greek
  mgomba(mi-) banana plant
* mgonjwa(wa-) patient, sick person
* mguu(mi-) leg, foot
  Mheshimiwa the Honourable
  Mhindi(wa-) an Indian
  mhuni(wa-) rogue
* mia hundred
  miayo yawn
    piga miayo to yawn
  mifugo livestock
  mihindi maize plants
* milele for ever, eternity
* milioni million
  mimba pregnancy
* mimi I, me
  miwani spectacles
  mizani weighing machine
  mjane(wa-) widow, widower
  mjanja(wa-) cunning person
* mji(mi-) town, city
  mjomba(wa-) uncle
  mkarafuu(mi-) clove tree
  mkasi(mi-) scissors (use singular)
* mkate(mi-) bread, loaf
* mke(wa-) wife
  mkebe(mi-) tin can
* mkia(mi-) tail
* mkoa(mi-) region, district
  mkojo(mi-) urine
  mkonge(mi-) sisal plant
* mkono(mi-) hand, arm
  mkorosho(mi-) cashew-nut tree
* Mkristo(wa-) a Christian
* mkuki(mi-) spear
* mkulima(wa-) farmer, cultivator
* mkutano(mi-) meeting
* mlango(mi-) door, opening
  mlevi(wa-) drunkard
* mlima(mi-) mountain
  mlimau(mi-) lemon tree
  mlingoti(mi-) mast, pole
  mlinzi(wa-) guard, watchman
  mlio(mi-) shout, sound, cry
* mmea(mi-) plant, vegetation
  mnada(mi-) auction
  mnara(mi-) tower
* mnazi(mi-) coconut palm
  mno exceedingly, very

* mnyama(wa-) animal
* mnyapara(wa-) foreman, overseer
  mnyororo(mi-) chain
* -moja one
  -moja -moja one by one
  moja kwa moja straight on
  mojawapo one of
* moshi(mi-) smoke
* mosi one (for date)
* moto(mi-) fire, heat
* motokaa car
* moyo(mi-) heart
  mpagazi(wa-) porter
* mpaka(mi-) boundary
* mpaka until, up to, as far as
* mpango(mi-) plan, arrangement
  mpapai(mi-) pawpaw tree
  mpenzi a lover, loved one, darling
* mpini(mi-) handle
* mpira(mi-) rubber, ball, hose, football game (anything rubber)
    * ku-cheza mpira to play football
* mpishi(wa-) cook
  mpunga(mi-) paddy, rice plant
* msaada(mi-) help, assistance
  msafiri(wa-) traveller
  msaidizi(wa-) helper
  msalaba(mi-) a cross
* mshahara(mi-) salary, wages
  mshale(mi-) arrow, matchstick
  mshipa(mi-) muscle, vein, etc.
  mshumaa(mi-) candle
  msichana(wa-) young girl
* msikiti(mi-) mosque
  msimamizi(wa-) foreman, overseer
  msingi(mi-) foundation
* msitu(mi-) forest, woodland
* mstari(mi-) line, row, queue
  msufi(mi-) kapok tree
* msumari(mi-) carpenter's nail
  msumeno(mi-) a saw
  mswaki(mi-) toothbrush
  mtaa(mi-) district
  mtama(mi-) sorghum
  mtambo(mi-) machine
  mtawala(wa-) ruler (political)
  mtego(mi-) trap
* mtelemko(mi-) slope
* mti(mi-) tree, post
* mtihani(mi-) examination (scholastic)
* mto(mi-) river, pillow
* mtoto(wa-) child
* mtu(wa-) person
* mtumishi(wa-) servant
* muda(mi-) period of time
  muhogo(mi-) cassava
  muhuri rubber stamp, seal
  mume(wa-) husband
  Mungu(mi-) God
  muwa(mi-) sugar cane
* mvua rain
  mvulana(wa-) young boy
  mvuvi(wa-) fisherman
* Mwafrika(wa-) an African
* mwaga to pour out, waste
* mwaka(mi-) year

*mwalimu(wa-) teacher
*Mwamerika(wa-) an American
*mwana(wa-) child, offspring
*mwanachama(wa-) member (of a club, etc.)
*mwanafunzi(wa-) a pupil, student
*mwanamke(wanawake) woman
*mwanamume (wanaume) man
*mwananchi(wa-) citizen, countryman
mwanzi(mi-) bamboo
Mwarabu(wa-) an Arab
mwaridi(mi-) rose tree
*mwashi(wa-) bricklayer, mason
*mwavuli(mi-) umbrella
*mwembe(mi-) mango tree
*mwendo(mi-) speed, journey
*mwenyewe(wa-) owner,-self
*mwenyeji(wa-) inhabitant
Mwenyezi Almighty
*mwenzi(wa-) companion
*mwenzangu(wa-) my companion
*mwezi(mi-) moon, month
*mwiba(mi-) thorn, thorn tree
*mwiko(mi-) wooden spoon
*mwili(mi-) living body
*mwindaji(wa-) hunter
*Mwingereza(wa-) an Englishman, Britisher
*mwisho(mi-) end, finish
*Mwislamu(wa-) a Muslim
*Mwitalia(wa-) an Italian
*mwitu(mi-) thick bush, forest
*mwizi(wezi) thief
mwongo(wa-) liar
mzazi(wa-) parent
*mzigo(mi-) load (pl. luggage)
mzinga(mi-) beehive, cannon
*mzizi(mi-) root
mzoga(mi-) carcass
*Mzungu(wa-) European, white person

*na and, with, by
*naam! I agree!
nafaka corn
*nafasi opportunity, space, spare-time, etc.
nafuu better, improvement
nakala copy
namba number
*nami with/and me
*namna sort, kind, like
*nanasi pineapple
*-nane eight
*nani? who?
*nanyi and/with you(pl.)
*nao and/with them
*nasi and/with us
nasibu chance
nauli fare
*nawa to wash hands and face
*nawe and/with you
*naye and/with him/her
nazi coconut
*ncha point, tip
*nchi country, land
ndama calf

*ndani (ya) inside (of)
*ndege bird, aeroplane
*ndevu beard (pl. agreements)
*ndi- indeed, the very . . .
*ndiyo indeed, it is so
*ndizi banana
ndoa marriage, wedding
ndoana fish-hook
*ndoo bucket
ndovu elephant
*ndugu brother, relative
ndui smallpox
*-nene fat, thick
nenepa to get fat (people)
neno(ma-) word
ng'aa to shine
*ng'ambo (ya) the other side (of)
*ngano wheat
ngao shield
*-ngapi? how many?
ngazi ladder
nge scorpion
*ng'oa pull up/out
*ngoja to wait
ngoma drum, traditional dance
*ng'ombe cow, ox, cattle
*nguo clothing, garment
nguruwe pig
*nguvu strength
nguzo pillar, strong pole
*ni is, are, am
nia intention
*nini? what?
*ninyi you (pl.)
njaa hunger, famine
*nje (ya) outside (of)
*njia way, path, road
njia panda crossroads
njiwa pigeon, dove
*-nne four
nona to get fat (animals)
-nono fat (animals)
*Novemba November
nta wax
*nuka to smell bad
*nukia to smell good
*nukta second, dot, point
*nunua to buy, purchase
*nusa to sniff, smell (at something)
*nusu half
*nyama meat, flesh
*nyamaza to be quiet
nyani baboon
nyanya tomato, grandmother
nyasi grass
nyati buffalo
*nyesha mvua to rain
*nyoa to shave
nyoka to be straight
*nyoka snake
nyosha to stretch out
nyota star
nyuki bee
*nyuma (ya) behind
*nyumba house
*nyumbani home, at home

295

nyumbu wildebeest, mule
nyundo hammer
nyunyiza to sprinkle
*nywa (kunywa) to drink
*nywele hair (pl. agreements)

*oa to marry (man)
*oga to bath, bathe
*ogopa to fear
*oili engine oil
oka to bake
okoa to save
*okota to come across, pick up
*Oktoba October
*olewa to be married (woman)
*omba to ask, beg, pray
*ona to see, feel, think
*ondoa to remove, take away
*ondoka to leave, set off
ongea to converse
*ongeza to add to, increase
*onyesha to show, point out
onyo warning
*orodha list
osha to wash
*ota to grow, dream, bask
*-ote all
*-o -ote any (at all)
ovyo useless, anyhow
*oza to rot, go bad
*oza to cause to marry (priest, parents)

*pa(kupa) to give
paa(ma-) side of roof
*painti pint
*paka cat
paka to smear on
paka rangi to paint
pakia to load
*pakua to unload, dish up
*pale there
pale pale right there
palilia to hoe (weeds)
pamba cotton
pamba to decorate
*pamoja (na) together (with)
*pana there is/are
*-pana wide, broad
*panda to climb, sow, plant
*panga matchet, bush-knife
*panga to arrange, hire
pango(ma-) cave
*pangusa to dust, wipe
panua to widen
panya rat, mouse
*papa shark
*papai(ma-) pawpaw
papasi tick (parasite)
Pasaka Easter
*pasi flat-iron
    *piga pasi to iron
*pasua to tear, saw, split
*pata to get, obtain
*paundi pound (£)
*peke y(angu) alone, (my)self
*pekee alone, -self

*peleka to send, take to
pembe horn, tusk, ivory, corner
*penda to love, like
*pengine sometimes, maybe
*pengine another place
*pesa money
pete ring (finger)
*-pi? which?
*pia also, too, as well
picha picture, photo
*piga to hit, beat, etc.
*pika to cook
pikipiki motorcycle
*pili (-a pili) second (2nd)
*pilipili pepper
*pima to measure, test
*pindua to turn upside down
pinga to obstruct
*pipa(ma-) barrel, oil drum
*pishi 2-litre measure
*pita to pass
plau plough
*poa to get cool
*pokea to receive
*pole! (condolence)
*polepole slow(ly)
polisi police
*pombe local beer
*pona to get well
popo bat (creature)
*pori(ma-) the bush, plain
posho rations
posta post, post office
*potea to get lost
pua nose
pumzi breath
*pumzika to rest, stop working
punda donkey
punda milia zebra
*pungua to reduce, grow less
pwani the coast
*-pya new

radi thunderclap
*rafiki friend
raha happiness, joy
*rahisi easy, cheap
raia citizen
Rais President
Ramadhani Muslim fasting month
ramani map, plan
*rangi colour, paint
*ratili pound (lb.)
*-refu long, tall, deep
reli railway
ripoti report
    piga ripoti to report
risasi lead, bullet
*robo quarter (¼)
robota (ma-) bundle, bale
*roho soul, spirit
*rudi to return
*ruhusa permission
*ruka to jump, fly
*ruksa permission

*saa clock, watch, hour, o'clock, time
*saba seven
Sabasaba TANU Day (7th July) (in Tanzania)
*sababu cause, reason
*kwa sababu because
*sabalkheri! good morning!
*sabini seventy
*sabuni soap
sadaka religious offering
sadiki to believe
*safari journey
*safi clean, pure
*safiri to travel
*safisha to clean
saga to grind
*sahani plate, dish, gramophone record
*sahau to forget
sahihi signature
*saidia to help, assist
sakafu concrete floor
sala prayer
*Salaam! Peace!
*salama peace, safety
sali to pray
salimu to greet
*samaki fish
sambaa to be scattered
*samehe to forgive
samli ghee
*sana very, a lot
*sanduku(ma-) box, suitcase, boot of car
*sasa now
sasa hivi at once
*sauti voice, sound
*kwa sauti loudly
*sawa (na) equal (to)
*sawasawa just so/right
*sawazisha to make equal
sebule entrance hall
*sehemu part, fraction, portion
*sekunde second (of time)
*sema to speak, say
seng'eng'e wire
sentensi sentence
*senti cent
*Septemba September
*seremala(ma-) carpenter, joiner
Serikali Government
shaba brass
shabaha target, aim
shaka doubt
*shamba(ma-) field, farm, plantation
*shangazi paternal aunt
*sharti(ma-) obligation
*shati shirt
*shauri(ma-) advice, affair, plan
*shemeji brother/sister in-law
-shenzi uncivilized
sheria law
*shiba to be satisfied with food
*shida difficulty, hardship
*shika to catch, hold
*shikamuu! (greeting to superior)
*shilingi shilling

shimo(ma-) pit
shina(ma-) trunk of tree
*shinda to conquer, excel, overcome
*shoka(ma-) axe
*shona to sew
shtaki to accuse
shugulika to be busy
shujaa hero
shuka(ma-) sheet, loincloth
shuka to drop, discharge
shukurani thanks, gratitude
shukuru to thank
shule school
*shusha to drop, lower
*si is/are not
siafu driver ants
*siagi butter
siasa politics
sifa praise
sifu to praise
*sifuri nought, zero
*sigara cigarette
siki vinegar
*sikia to hear, obey
*sikiliza to listen
sikio(ma-) ear
*sikitika to be sorry, grieve
*siku day
sikukuu festival, special day (birthday etc.)
*sikuzote always
silaha weapon
*simama to stand, halt
simba lion
*simu telegram/phone
simulia to narrate
sindano needle
sindikiza accompany part of way
*siri secret
*sisi us, we
sisimizi small ants
*sita six
*sitawi to flourish, prosper
*sitini sixty
sivyo not so
siyo not
sogea to move over
*soko(ma-) market
soksi sock
*soma to read, study
stadi expert, experienced
stakabadhi receipt
*starehe to be at ease
stimu electricity
sufuria handle-less saucepan
*sukari sugar
*sukuma to push
*sumbua to annoy, trouble
*sumni fifty cents
sumu poison
sungura hare, rabbit
sura face, appearance
sura chapter
*suruali trousers (use singular)
*suti suit
*swali(ma-) question

*taa lamp, light
taabu distress
taarifa report
tabia character, nature
*tafadhali! please!
tafsiri translation
tafuna to chew
*tafuta to look for, search
taga to lay eggs
tai neck-tie, vulture
*taifa(ma-) nation
taja to mention
taji crown
*tajiri(ma-) wealthy person, merchant,
  business man
*taka to want
*takataka rubbish, mess
tamaa desire
  kata tamaa to give up hope
tambarare plain, flat country
tambua to recognise
tamka to pronounce
*-tamu sweet
*tandika to spread out
tandiko(ma-) bedding
tangazo(ma-) notice, poster
tangi(ma-) tank
*tangu since, from (time only)
*tangulia to precede
*tani ton
*-tano five
*tapika to vomit
*tapuraita typewriter
taratibu order, method
*tarehe date (calendar)
*tarishi(ma-) messenger
*-tatu three
tawala to rule, govern
tawi(ma-) branch
*tayari ready
*tazama to gaze upon, look at
tega to trap
tegemea to depend upon
*tele plenty, abundance
*telemka to descend
*tembea to walk
tembo elephant
*tena again
tenda to act
*tengeneza to repair, put right
tetemeka to tremble, shake
thamani value
*thelathini thirty
*theluthi third ($^1/_3$)
*themanini eighty
*thumni fifty cents
*tia to put, place
*tisa nine
*tisini ninety
*toa to put out, offer, give out
toboa to bore a hole
tofali(ma-) a brick
tofauti difference
*toka to go out, come out
*toka from
tokeo(ma-) result, outcome

*tope(ma-) mud
toroka to run away
*tosha to be enough, sufficient
*tu only, just
*tuma to send
*tumaini to hope, to be of the opinion
  (that)
tumbako tobacco
tumbili monkey
tumbo(ma-) stomach, abdomen
*tumia to use
*tunda(ma-) fruit
*tundu hole
*tunza to take care of
tupa file, rasp
*tupa to throw
*-tupu empty, bare, pure
tuta(ma-) ridge (in field)
twiga giraffe

*u you are
*ua(ma-) flower
*ua(ny-) courtyard
*ua to kill
*uaminifu faithfulness
ubaguzi segregation
*ubao (mbao) plank, board
Ubatizo Baptism
ubavu (mbavu) rib
*ubaya badness, evil
*ubovu rottenness
*uchache scarcity
*uchafu dirt
uchawi sorcery, witchcraft
uchi nakedness
*Udachi Germany
*udongo soil
udongo ulaya cement
*ufa (nyufa) crack
ufagio (fagio) broom
*Ufaransa France
ufuko sea-shore
*ufunguo (funguo) key
*ufupi shortness
ufuta simsim (oilseed)
*ugali porridge
*Uganda Uganda
*ugeni strangeness
*ugomvi(ma-) quarrel
*ugonjwa(ma-) disease, illness
*ugumu hardness, difficulty
uhai life
uharibifu damage, destruction
*Uhindi India
*uhodari efficiency, ability
*uhuru freedom, independence
*Uingereza England, Britain
*Uislamu Muslim religion
*ujamaa brotherhood, socialism
*ujana youth
*uji gruel
ujuzi knowledge, experience
*ukali sharpness, severity, ferocity
*Ukimisi AIDS
*ukoo clan, kinship
*Ukristo Christian religion
*ukubwa size, bulk

298

ukucha (kucha) nail, claw
ukulima agriculture
*ukuni (kuni) stick of firewood (firewood in pl.)
*ukurasa (kurasa) page of book etc.
*ukuta (kuta) wall
*Ulaya Europe
*ulimi (ndimi) tongue
ulimwengu world
*uliza to ask, question
*uma to hurt, bite, sting
*uma (nyuma) fork
*umande dew
*umaskini poverty
*umeme lightning, electricity
*umoja unity
umri age
*unene fatness, thickness
unga flour, powder
unga to join
*Unguja Zanzibar
*upana width
*upande (pande) side, part of country
*upendo love
*upepo (pepo) wind
*upesi quickly
upinde bow (for arrows)
*urahisi ease
*urefu length, depth, height
*Ureno Portugal
*usafi cleanliness
usaha pus
*usiku (siku) night
*usingizi sleep
*uso (nyuso) face
*utajiri wealth
utambi (tambi) wick
*utamu sweetness
*utoto childhood
*uvivu laziness
*uwezo power, ability
*uza to sell
*uzee old age
*uzi(nyuzi) thread, string
*uzito weight, heaviness
*uzuri goodness

*vaa to wear, dress
*vibaya badly
vifaa equipment
*vigumu hard, difficult
*vilevile just the same, as well, also
vimba to swell
*vita war, battle
*-vivu lazy
*vizuri well, nicely, properly
*vua nguo to undress
*vua samaki to fish
*vuja to leak
*vuka to cross
*vuna to harvest
*vunja to break
*vunjika to be broken

vuruga to stir
*vuta to pull, drag
*vuta sigara to smoke (cigarettes)

*wa(kuwa) to be, become
*wa na (kuwa na) to have
*wahi to be early/on time
*waka to burn
*wakati (nyakati) period, time of year
*wala neither, nor (+negative tense)
*wali cooked rice
*wao they, them
*wapi? where?
*wapi! (expression of disbelief)
*watu people
wavu (nyavu) net
*wazi open
*waziri(ma-) minister (of state)
wazo(ma-) thought
*weka to put
*wembe (nyembe) razor, razor blade
*wewe you
*weza to be able
*wiki week
wilaya district
*-wili two
wima straight, upright
*winda to hunt
*wingi plenty, abundance
wingu(ma-) cloud
*wino ink
-wivu jealous
wizara Ministry (Government)

yaani that is to say
*yadi yard (3 feet)
*yafaa it is as well
*yai(ma-) egg
*yaya child's nurse
*yeye he, she, him, her,.
*yu he/she is

*zaa to bear offspring
zaburi psalm
*zaidi(ya) more (than)
*zaliwa to be born
zama to sink
*zamani a long time ago
*zamu turn, period of duty
*zawadi present, gift
*ziba to stop up, block
zidi to increase
zika to bury
*zima to extinguish
*-zima whole, complete
zimia to faint
*-zito heavy
*-ziwa(ma-) breast, lake (pl. also means 'milk')
*zoea to get used to
*zuia to prevent
*zulia(ma-) carpet
*zunguka to go round
*zungumza to converse
*-zuri good, nice, lovely, beautiful
zuru to visit

Vocabulary English —Swahili

*abandon ku-acha
abdomen tumbo(ma-)
*ability uwezo
*able hodari
    *be able ku-weza
*about (approx.) kama
*about (concerning) habari ya
*above juu (ya)
*abscess jipu(ma-)
*absolutely kabisa
*abundance wingi, tele
*accept ku-kubali, ku-pokea
accident ajali
accuse ku-shtaki
*accustomed (to be) ku-zoea
acid -chungu
*acre eka, ekari
act ku-tenda
*acute -kali
*add ku-ongeza, ku-hesabu
address (postal) anwani
address (sermon) hotuba
*adequate -a kutosha
adult mtu mzima
*advantage faida, heri
*advice shauri(ma-)
aerodrome kiwanja cha ndege
*aeroplane ndege, eropleni
*affair shauri
*afraid (to be) ku-ogopa
*African Mwafrika(wa-)
*after baada ya
*afternoon alasiri
*afterwards baadaye, halafu, kisha
*again tena
age umri
*old age uzee
*ago zamani
*agree to ku-kubali
*agriculture kilimo(vi-), ukulima
*ahead mbele
*aid msaada(mi-), ku-saidia
aim shabaha, nia
*air hewa
*alike sawa na
alive hai
*all -ote
    *not at all hata kidogo
allow ku-ruhusu
Almighty Mwenyezi
*almost karibu na
*alone peke y(angu) etc.
*alongside kando ya
*already kwisha
*also pia, vilevile, tena
*alter ku-badili
although ingawa
*always sikuzote
*am ni
*American (person) Mwamerika(wa-)

*amongst katikati ya, kati ya
*amount kiasi(vi-)
ancestry jadi
*and na
*angry (to be) ku-kasirika
*animal mnyama(wa-)
announce kut-tangaza
announcement tangazo(ma-)
*annoy ku-sumbua
*another -ingine
*answer jibu(ma-)
*answer ku-jibu
ant siafu, sisimizi, etc.
    white ant mchwa
ant hill kichuguu(vi-)
*any -o -ote
*anybody yeyote
*anything cho chote
*apart mbali
*appear ku-onekana
appertain ku-husu
*apply ku-tia
*approve ku-kubali
Arab Mwarabu(wa-)
*are ni
*area eneo(ma-)
*arm mkono(mi-)
army jeshi(ma-)
*arrange ku-panga
*arrangement mpango(mi-)
*arrive ku-fika
arrow mshale(mi-)
*as kama
*as well pia, vilevile
*ash majivu
*ask ku-uliza
*ask for ku-omba
*asleep (to be) ku-lala (usingizi)
*assist ku-saidia
*assistance msaada(mi-)
*association chama(vy-)
*attempt ku-jaribu
*attend to ku-angalia
attendant mwangalizi(wa-)
auction mnada(mi-)
*August Agosti
*aunt shangazi
author mtungaji(wa-)
*automobile motokaa
average wastani
*awake ku-amka
*axe shoka(ma-)

baboon nyani
back (person's) mgongo
*back(wards) nyuma
*bad -baya
    *go bad ku-oza, ku-haribika
*badness ubaya
*badly vibaya

300

*bag mfuko(mi-)
*baggage mizigo
bake ku-oka
balance (scales) mizani
bale robota(ma-)
*ball mpira(mi-)
bamboo mwanzi(mi-)
*ban ku-kataza
*banana ndizi
banana plant mgomba(mi-)
*banner bendera
*baobab tree mbuyu(mi-)
baptise mu-batiza
barber kinyozi(vi-)
*bare -tupu
*barrel pipa(ma-)
basin bakuli
*bask ku-ota
*basket kikapu(vi-)
*bathe ku-oga
*battery (torch) jiwe(ma-)
battery (car) betri
*battle vita
*be ku-wa
beach pwani, ufukoni
beads ushanga
beam boriti(ma-)
beans maharagwe
*bear (carry) ku-chukua
*beard ndevu(pl. agreements)
*beast mnyama(wa-)
*beautiful -zuri
*beauty uzuri
*because kwa sababu(ya)
*become ku-wa
*bed kitanda(vi-)
bedclothes matandiko
bee nyuki
bee-hive mzinga(mi-)
beef nyama ya ng'ombe
*beer (local) pombe
*beer (bottled) bia
*before kabla (ya), mbele (ya)
*beg ku-omba
*begin ku-anza
beginning mwanzo(mi-)
*behind nyuma (ya)
*behold ku-tazama
believe ku-amini, ku-sadiki
bell kengele
belly tumbo(ma-)
beloved mpenzi(wa-)
*below chini (ya)
belt ukanda
bend ku-pinda
*beneath chini (ya)
*benefit faida
*beside kando (ya)
*best bora
*better afadhali, bora
  *be better ku-pona
  get better ku-pata nafuu
*between kati ya
*beyond mbele (ya), ng'ambo (ya)
Bible Biblia
bicycle baisikeli

*big -kubwa
*bill hesabu (ya fedha)
*bin pipa(ma-)
*bird ndege
birth uzazi
biscuit biskuti
bishop askofu(ma-)
*bite ku-uma
bitter -chungu
bitterness uchungu
*black -eusi
blanket blanketi(ma-)
bleed ku-toka damu
bless ku-bariki
blessing baraka
*blind man kipofu(vi-)
*block ku-ziba
*blood damu
. blue kibluu
*board ubao (mbao)
*boat chombo(vy-), meli
*body mwili(mi-)
bog bwawa(ma-)
*boil ku-chemka, ku-chemsha
*boil (abscess) jipu (majibu)
*bone mfupa(mi-)
*book kitabu(vi-)
*boot kiatu(vi-)
*border mpaka(mi-)
*born (to be) ku-zaliwa
*borrow ku-azima, ku-kopa
*bottle chupa
*boundary mpaka(mi-)
bow (for arrows) upinde
*box sanduku(ma-)
*boy mvulana(wa-), mtoto wa kiume
brain ubongo, akili
branch tawi(ma-)
*brand chapa, aina
*bread mkate(mi-)
*breadth upana
*break ku-vunja
breathe ku-vuta pumzi
brick tofali(ma-)
*bricklayer mwashi(wa-)
*bridge daraja(ma-)
*brief -fupi
*briefly kwa kifupi
*bring ku-leta
*Britain Uingereza
*Britisher Mwingereza(wa-)
*broad -pana
brook kijito(vi-)
broom ufagio (fagio)
*brother (elder) kaka
*brother (younger) ndugu
*brotherhood ujamaa
brush burashi
*brush ku-fagia
*bubble up ku-chemka
*bucket ndoo
buffalo mbogo, nyati
*build ku-jenga
bullet risasi
bullock ng'ombe maksai
*bundle bahasha

*burden mzigo(mi-)
*burglar mwizi (wezi)
*burn ku-waka, ku-choma
bury ku-zika, ku-fukia
bus basi(ma-)
*businessman tajiri(ma-)
*but lakini
*butter siagi
butterfly kipepeo(vi-)
button kifungo(vi-)
*buy ku-nunua
*by kwa, na, karibu na

*calendar kalenda
calf ndama
*call ku-ita
camera kamera
camp kambi
can mkege(mi-), kopo(ma-)
*canal mfereji(mi-)
*cancel ku-futa
candle mshumaa(mi-)
canoe mtumbwi(mi-)
*cap kofia
*capable ku-weza
*capable hodari
*capture ku-kamata
*car motokaa
carcass mzoga(mi-)
cards (playing) karata
care uangalifu
  *take care ku-angalia, ku-tunza
*carefully polepole, taratibu
*carpenter seremala(ma-)
*carpet zulia(ma-)
*carry ku-chukua
*carry on ku-endelea
*cartridge risasi
*cat paka
*catch ku-shika, ku-kamata
catholic katoliki
*cattle ng'ombe
*cell (torch) jiwe (mawe)
*cent senti
*centre kati (ya), katikati (ya)
cereal nafaka
*certain(ty) hakika
*certainly bila shaka
*certificate cheti(vy-)
chain mnyororo(mi-)
*chair kiti(vi-)
chalk chaki
*chance nafasi, bahati
*change ku-badili, ku-geuza
*channel mfereji(mi-)
charcoal makaa
chart ramani
*cheap rahisi
cheese chizi
*chemical dawa
chest (human) kifua(vi-)
chew ku-tafuna
*chicken kuku
*child mtoto(wa-), mwana(wa-)
*childhood utoto
*childish -a kitoto

*chit cheti(vy-)
*choose ku-chagua
Christ Kristo
christen ku-batiza
*Christian Mkristo(wa-)
*Christian religion Ukristo
*church kanisa(ma-)
*cigarette sigara
*cinema sinema
*circle duara
*circumstance hali
*citizen raia, mwananchi(wa-)
*city mji(mi-) mkubwa(mi-)
*clan ukoo
clap ku-piga makofi
class, classroom darasa(ma-)
claw kucha(ma-)
clay towe, udongo mzito
*clean safi
*clean ku-safisha
*cleanliness usafi
*clear (to be) ku-elea
*clear bush ku-fyeka
*clerk karani(ma-)
*climb ku-panda
*clock saa
*close ku-funga
*close (by) karibu (na)
*cloth kitambaa(vi-)
*clothes nguo
cloud wingu(ma-)
cloves karafuu
*club, society chama(vy-)
coast pwani
*coat koti
cob (maize) gunzi(ma-)
cock jogoo(ma-)
cockroach mende
*coconut palm mnazi(mi-)
*coconut (milky) dafu(ma-)
coconut (hard) nazi
*coffee (drink) kahawa
*coffee bush mbuni(mi-)
*cold baridi, -a baridi
  *get cold ku-poa
*collapse ku-anguka
*collect ku-kusanya
*colour rangi
comb kitana(vi-), chanuo
*come ku-ja, ku-fika
*come across kut-kuta, ku-okota
*come back ku-rudi
come down ku-shuka, ku-telemka
*come from ku-toka
*come in ku-ingia, "karibu!"
*come out ku-toka
command amri
command ku-toa amri
commerce biashara
committee halmashauri
*common -a kawaida
*companion mwenzi(wa-)
compass dira
*compel ku-lazimisha
competition mashindano
*complete kamili

*completely kabisa
compose ku-tunga
*compressed air upepo
*compulsory -a lazima
*concerning habari ya
*conclusion mwisho(mi-)
*condition hali
*confidential -a siri
congratulations pongezi
*conquer ku-shinda
*consider ku-fikiri
*constantly daima
*container chombo(vy-)
*continue ku-endelea
*conversation mazungumzo
*converse ku-zungumza, ku-ongea
*cook mpishi(wa-)
*cook ku-pika
*cooked (to be) ku-iva
*cooker jiko (meko)
*cool -a baridi
*cool, to get ku-poa
*co-operative society chama(vy-)
copper shaba nyekundu
copy nakala
*cord kamba
*cork kizibo(vi-)
corn nafaka
corner pembe, kona
corpse maiti
*cost bei, gharama
cotton pamba
*cough ku-kohoa
council baraza, halmashauri
count ku-hesabu
*country (land) nchi
*countryman mwananchi(wa-)
*court baraza(ma-), korti
*courtyard ua(ny-)
*cousin binamu
*cover ku-funika
*cow ng'ombe
*crack ku-pasua
*crack ufa(ny-)
*craftsman fundi(ma-)
*crafty -erevu
*cripple kiwete(vi-)
*crop mmea(mi-), zao(ma-)
cross msalaba(mi-)
*cross ku-vuka
cross-roads njia panda
*cry ku-lia
*cultivate ku-lima
*cultivation kilimo(vi-), ukulima
*cunning -erevu
*cup kikombe(vi-)
cupboard kabati(ma-)
curry bizari
*curtain kitambaa(vi-)
*cushion mto(mi-)
*customarily kwa kawaida
*cut ku-kata
*cut with panga ku-fyeka

*daily kwa kutwa, kila siku
*damage ku-haribu

dance dansi, ngoma
*danger hatari
*dangerous -a hatari
*dark(ness) giza
*dark -eusi
*date (calendar) tarehe
*daughter binti
*dawn alfajiri
*day siku
*day after tomorrow kesho kutwa
*day before yesterday juzi
*daytime mchana(mi-)
*deaf person kiziwi(vi-)
death kifo(vi-)
debt deni(ma-)
deceive ku-danganya
*December Desemba
*decompose ku-oza
decorate ku-pamba
*deep -refu
*delete ku-futa
demonstration onyesho(ma-)
dentist mganga wa meno
*depart ku-ondoka
department idara
depend upon ku-tegemea
*depth urefu
*descend ku-telemka
desk meza, deski
despair ku-kata tamaa
despise ku-dharau
*destroy ku-haribu
*dew umande
*dialect kilugha(vi-)
diamond almasi
diarrhoea tumbo la ku-hara
dictionary kamusi
*die ku-fa, ku-fariki
*different mbali(na)
difference tofauti
*difficult -gumu, vigumu
*difficulty shida
*dig ku-chimba, ku-lima
*diminish ku-pungua
*direction upande
*dirt uchafu
*dirty -chafu
*disciple mwanafunzi(wa-)
*disease ugonjwa(ma-)
disgrace aibu
*dish sahani
*dish up ku-pakua chakula
dismiss (sack) ku-achisha
distance umbali, mwendo(mi-)
*district mkoa(mi-), mtaa(mi), wilaya
*ditch mfereji(mi-)
*divide ku-gawa
*do ku-fanya
*doctor mganga(wa-), daktari(ma-)
*dog mbwa
donkey punda
*door mlango(mi-)
*dot nukta
doubt shaka
*down(wards) chini
doze ku-sinzia

303

*drag ku-vuta
drawing picha
*dream ku-ota
*drink ku-nywa
*drive ku-endesha
*drive away ku-fukuza
*driver dereva(ma-)
*drop ku-shuka, ku-shusha
*drug dawa
*drum ngoma
*drum, oil pipa(ma-)
*drunk (to be) ku-lewa
drunkard mlevi(wa-)
*dry -kavu
*dry (to get) ka-kauka
duck bata
dung mavi, mbolea
dust vumbi
*dust ku-pangusa
*dustbin pipa (la takataka)
*duster kitambaa cha ku-pangusia
*dwell ku-kaa

*each kila
ear sikio(ma-)
*early mapema
*early (to be) ku-wahi
*earth (soil) ardhi
earth (world) dunia
*ease raha, urahisi
east mashariki
*easy rahisi, -epesi
Easter Pasaka
*eat ku-la
*edge (of) kando (ya)
*efficiency uhodari
*efficient hodari
*effort bidii
e.g. kwa mfano
*egg yai(ma-)
*eight -nane
*eighty themanini
*either ama, au
*elder mzee(wa-)
*electricity stimu, umeme, spaki
elephant ndovu, tembo
*elsewhere pengine
employ (hire) ku-ajiri
employee mfanya kazi (wafanya kazi)
*employer tajiri
*employment kazi
*empty -tupu
*encircle ku-zunguka
*end mwisho(mi-)
enemy adui
*energetic hodari
*energy nguvu, bidii
engine mashine, injini
*England Uingereza
*English (people) Mwingereza(wa-)
*English language Kiingereza
*enough! basi!
*enough (to be) ku-tosha
*ensure ku-hakikisha
*enter ku-ingia
*entire -zima, kamili, -ote

*entirely kabisa
*envelope bahasha
*epidemic magonjwa
*equal (with) sawa (na)
*equalize ku-sawazisha
*erect wima
*erect ku-simamisha
*err ku-kosa
*especially hasa
*et cetera (etc.) na kadhalika (n.k.)
*eternally milele
*Europe Ulaya
*European Mzungu(wa-)
*even hata
*evening jioni (before sunset)
*ever, for milele, sikuzote
*everlastingly milele
*every kila
*evil ubaya
*exact kamili
*examination (school) mtihani
  (mi-)
*examine ku-pima
  example mfano(mi-)
*excavate ku-chimba
  exceed ku-zidi
*excellent bora
*except ila
*excreta mavi, choo (vy-)
  expect ku-tazamia
*expensive ghali
  experience ujuzi
  experiment jaribio(ma-)
*explain ku-eleza
*extinguish ku-zima
*extra zaidi
*extremely kabisa
*eye jicho(ma-)

*face uso(ny-), sura
*faeces choo(vy-), mavi
*fail ku-kosa, ku-shindwa
  faint ku-zimia
*faintly kidogo
*fairly kidogo
  faith imani
*faithful -aminifu
*faithfulness uaminifu
*fall ku-anguka
*family jamaa
  famine njaa
*fancy maridadi, malidadi
*fancy that! kumbe!
*far (from) mbali (na)
*far side (of) ng'ambo (ya)
    *as far as kadiri
  fare nauli
*farewell kwa heri
*farm shamba(ma-)
*farmer mkulima(wa-)
*fast upesi
*fast ku-funga chakula
*fasten ku-funga, ku-kaza
*fat (oil) mafuta
*fat (people) -nene
  fat (animals) -nono

304

fat (to get) ku-nenepa, ku-nona
*father baba
*fatness unene
*fear ku-ogopa
feather nyoya(ma-)
*February Februari
fee ada
*feed ku-lisha
*feel ku-ona
*feel cold ku-sikia baridi
*female -a kike
*ferment ku-oza
*ferocity ukali
fertility (soil) rutuba
*festival sikukuu
*fetch ku-leta
*fever homa
*few -chache
*field shamba(ma-)
*fierce -kali
*fifty hamsini
file (metal) tupa
*fill ku-jaza
filter chujio
*filth uchafu
*filthy -chafu
*final -a mwisho
*find ku-okota, ku-kuta, ku-ona
*finger kidole(vi-)
*finish ku-maliza
*finished (to be) ku-isha (kwisha)
*fire moto(mi-)
*firewood kuni(pl. agreements)
*first -a kwanza
    *at first kwanza, mwanzoni
*fish samaki
fisherman mvuvi(wa-)
fish-hook ndoana
fishing uvuvi
*five -tano
*flag bendera
flagstaff mlingoti(mi-)
*flask chupa
*flask, vacuum chupa ya chai
*flat -pana
flea kiroboto(vi-)
*flesh nyama
float ku-elea
floor sakafu
flour unga
*flourish ku-sitawi
*flower ua(ma-)
*fly (insect) inzi
*fly ku-ruka
*fold ku-kunja
*follow ku-fuata
*food chakula(vy-)
*foot mguu(mi-)
*foot (ft.) futi
*football mpira(mi-)
*footstep hatua
*footwear viatu
*for kwa
*forbid ku-kataza
*forcibly kwa nguvu
*foreign -geni

*foreigner mgeni(wa-)
*foreman msimamizi(wa-),
    mnyapara(wa-)
*forest msitu(mi-)
*forget ku-sahau
*forgive ku-samehe
*fork uma(ny-)
*fort(ress) boma(ma-)
*fortune heri, bahati
*forty arobaini
*forward(s) mbele
*four -nne
*fowl kuku
*fraction sehemu
*France Ufaransa
*free -a bure
*freedom uhuru
fresh -bichi
*Friday Ijumaa
*friend rafiki
frock gauni(ma-)
frog chura(vy-)
*from toka, kutoka
*from (time) tangu
*front, in (of) mbele (ya)
*frontier mpaka(mi-)
*fruit tunda(ma-)
fry ku-kaanga
*fuel kuni, makaa, etc.
*full (to be) ku-jaa
*full with food ku-shiba
*fun furaha, raha
funeral maziko
funnel mrija(mi-)
*furniture vyombo (vya nyumbani)
*furrow mfereji(mi-)

*gain faida
*gallon galoni
*galvanised iron bati(ma-)
*game (to play) mchezo(mi-)
*gap nafasi
garden bustani, shamba(ma-)
*garment nguo
*gate mlango(mi-)
*gather ku-kusanya
*gaze upon ku-tazama
*gentleman bwana(ma-)
*gently polepole, taratibu
*German Mdachi(wa-) Mjermani(wa-)
*Germany Udachi
*get ku-pata
ghee samli
*giant jitu(ma-)
giddiness kizunguzungu
*gift zawadi
giraffe twiga
*girl mtoto wa kike, msichana(wa-)
*give ku-pa
*give birth ku-zaa
*give out ku-toa
*glass sheet kioo(vy-)
*glass, tumbler bilauri, glasi
glue gundi
*go ku-enda (kwenda)
*go ahead ku-tangulia

305

*go away ku-ondoka
   *have a go ku-jaribu
*go in ku-ingia
*go out ku-toka
 goat mbuzi
 God Mungu(mi-)
 gold dhahabu
*good -zuri
*good character -ema
*good-bye kwa heri
*goodness wema, uzuri
*good morning! sabalkheri!
 Gospel Injili
 government serikali
*government offices boma(ma-)
 grade cheo(vy-)
 grain nafaka
*grandfather babu
*grandmother bibi, nyanya
*grass majani, nyasi
 grasshopper panzi(ma-)
 gratuity bakshishi
 gravel changarawe
 graveyard makaburini
 gravy mchuzi(mi-)
*grease mafuta, grisi
*great -kuu
*Greek person Mgiriki(wa-)
 green kijani
*greet ku-salimu
*greetings salamu
 grey kijivu
*grieve ku-sikitika
 ground ardhi
 groundnuts karanga, njugu
 group kundi(ma-), kikundi(vi-)
*grow ku-ota, ku-otesha
*grow less ku-pungua
*grower mkulima(wa-)
*gruel uji
*guard mlinzi(wa-)
*guess ku-bahatisha
*guest mgeni(wa-)
 guide mwongozi(wa-)
 guinea-fowl kanga
 gum gundi
*gun bunduki

*hair nywele (pl. agreements)
*half nusu
*hall jumba(ma-)
*halt ku-simama
 hammer nyundo
*hand mkono(mi-)
*handle mpini(mi-), mkono (mi-), kipini
   (vi-)
 hang ku-tungika
 haphazard ovyo-ovyo
*happiness furaha, heri
*happy (to be) ku-furahi
*hard -gumu
*hardness ugumu
*hardship shida
 hare sungura
 harm ku-dhuru
*haste haraka

*hastily kwa haraka, upesi
*hat kofia
*have ku-wa na
*having -enye
*he yeye
*head kichwa(vi-)
 headache maumivu ya kichwa
 health afya
*hear ku-sikia
*heart moyo(mi-)
*heat moto(mi-), joto
 heaven mbinguni
*heavy -zito
*heaviness uzito
*height urefu (wa kwenda juu)
*hello! jambo!
*help msaada(mi-)
*help ku-saidia
*hen kuku
*her yeye, -ake, -m-
*herd ku-fuga, mifugo
*herdsman mchungaji(wa-)
*here hapa
*hereabouts huku
*herein humu
 hero shujaa(ma-)
*hide ku-ficha
 hide (skin) ngozi
*high -refu
*highroad barabara
 hike ku-safiri kwa miguu
*hill kilima(vi-)
*him yeye, -m-
*hippopotamus kiboko(vi-)
*hire (things) ku-panga
 hire (person) ku-ajiri
*his -ake
 history historia
*hit ku-piga
*hoe jembe(ma-)
*hoe ku-palilia, ku-palia
*hold ku-shika
*hole tundu, shimo(ma-)
 holy -takatifu
*home nyumbani, kwetu etc.
*honest -aminifu
 honey asali
 honour heshima
 hook kulabu
*hope ku-tumaini
 horn pembe
 horse farasi
*hose mpira (wa maji)
 hospital hospitali
*hot -a moto
 hotel hoteli
*hour saa
*house nyumba
*householder mwenyeji(wa-)
*how? -je?
*how jinsi
*how many? -ngapi?
*however lakini
*human being binadamu
 humorous -a kuchekesha
*hundred mia

306

hunger njaa
*hunt ku-winda
*hunter mwindaji(wa-)
*hurriedly upesi, kwa haraka
*hurry haraka, ku-fanya haraka
*hurt ku-uma, ku-dhuru
*husband mume(wa-)
*hut kibanda(vi-)
hyena fisi
hymn wimbo (nyimbo)

*I mimi, ni-
*ice barafu
idea mawazo
*idle -vivu
*idleness uvivu
i.e. yaani
*if kama
*ignite ku-washa
*ill (to be) ku-wa mgonjwa(wa-)
illicit marufuku
*illness ugonjwa
image mfano(mi-)
immaterial si kitu
imperfection ila
*implement chombo(vy-) (cha kazi)
*importance maana
important muhimu
*imprison ku-funga
*in katika, -ni, ndani ya
*inch inchi
*including pamoja na
income mapato
income tax kodi ya mapato
*increase ku-ongeza
*indeed ndi-
*India Uhindi
*infant mtoto(wa-)
    mdogo(wa-)/mchanga(wa-)
*inform ku-ambia
*information habari
*ingenuity akili, maarifa
*inhabit ku-kaa
*inhabitant mwenyeji(wa-)
inhale ku-vuta pumzi
injection dawa ya sindano
    give injection ku-piga sindano
injury jeraha(ma-)
*ink wino
inn hoteli
*inquire ku-uliza
inquiry swali(ma-)
insanity kichaa(vi-)
*insect mdudu(wa-)
*insecticide dawa ya wadudu
*insert ku-ingiza
*inside ndani ya, katika
inspect ku-kagua
instance mfano(mi-)
    for instance kwa mfano
instantly mara moja, sasa hivi
*instead badala ya
*instruct ku-fundisha
*instructor mwalimu(wa-)
*instrument chombo(vy-)
*intact kamili

*intelligence akili
*intention kusudi, nia
*intentionally kwa kusudi
interpret ku-tafsiri
*into ndani ya, katika
*intoxicated (to be) ku-lewa
*invalid mgonjwa(wa-)
*iron chuma(vy-)
*iron (for clothes) pasi
*iron ku-piga pasi
irrigate ku-leta maji shambani
*is ni
*island kisiwa(vi-)
*Italian(person) Mwitalia(wa-)
*item kitu(vi-)
*its -ake
*itself -enyewe
    *by itself peke yake

*jacket koti
jail jela
*January Januari
jealous -wivu
jerk ku-shtuka
Jew Myahudi(wa-)
jigger funza
*job kazi
joint kiungo(vi-)
*journal gazeti(ma-)
*journey safari, mwendo(mi-)
*joy furaha
judge hakimu, jaji
judgement hukumu
*July Julai
*jump ku-ruka
*June Juni
*junk takataka
*just (only) tu
justice haki

kapok (cotton) sufi
kapok tree msufi(mi-)
*keep livestock ku-fuga
*keep on ku-endelea
*kerosine mafuta ya taa
kettle birika(ma-)
*key ufunguo (funguo)
kidney figo(ma-)
*kill ku-ua
*kilogram kilo
kilometre kilometa
*kind (sort) namna
*kind (good) -ema
king mfalme(wa-)
*kinship ukoo
*kitchen jiko(ni)
knee goti(ma-)
kneel ku-piga magoti
*knife kisu(vi-)
knit ku-fuma
knock ku-gonga
knot fundo(ma-)
*know ku-jua, ku-fahamu
*knowledge maarifa
*known (to be) ku-julikana

*labour kazi

*labourer kibarua(vi-)
lad mvulana(wa-)
ladder ngazi
*ladle mwiko(mi-)
*lady bibi(ma-)
lake ziwa(ma-), zilwa(ma-)
*lame kiwete(vi-)
*lamp taa
*land (country) nchi
*language lugha
*large -kubwa
lass msichana(wa-)
*last -a mwisho
*last year mwaka uliopita
*late (to be) ku-chelewa
*lately siku hizi
*later baadaye, halafu
*latest -a kisasa
*latrine choo(vy-)
*laugh ku-cheka
*lavatory choo(vy-)
law sheria
law court korti, baraza
in-law shemeji
*lay ku-laza
*lay eggs ku-taga (mayai)
*lay table ku-panga meza
*laziness uvivu
*lazy -vivu
lead(metal) risasi
lead ku-ongoza
*leaf jani(ma-)
*leak ku-vuja
*leap ku-ruka
*learn ku-jifunza
*learner mwanafunzi(wa-)
*learning elimu
*least (not in the) hata kidogo
leather ngozi
*leave ku-acha, ku-ondoka
*leave ruhusa, livu, likizo
take leave of ku-aga
*left kushoto, -a kushoto
*leg mguu(mi-)
*lemon limau(ma-)
*lemon tree mlimau(mi-)
*lend ku-kopesha
*length urefu
*lengthy -refu
leopard chui
leprosy ukoma
*less kasa, kasoro
lesson somo(ma-)
*letter (mail) barua
letter (alphabet) herufi
lettuce saladi
*level sawasawa, usawa
*level ku-sawazisha
*liberty uhuru
lid kifuniko(vi-)
lie (untruth) uongo
*lie ku-lala
life uhai, maisha
lifetime maisha
*lift ku-inua
*light rahisi, -epesi

*light coloured -eupe
*light ku-washa
*lighter kiberiti(vi-)
lighting umeme
*like ku-penda
*like namna, kama
*limit mpaka(mi-)
*line mstari(mi-)
liner meli
lion simba
lip mdomo(mi-)
*list orodha
*listen ku-sikiliza
*litter takataka
*little -dogo
*a little kidogo
*live ku-kaa, ku-ishi
livestock mifugo
liver ini(ma-)
lizard mjuzi(mi-)
*load mzigo(mi-)
*loaf mkate(mi-)
loan mkopo(mi-)
lock kufuli, kitasa(vi-)
*lock ku-funga
locomotive gari la moshi
locomotive (small gauge) kiberenge(vi-)
locust nzige
*lodge ku-kaa
*log gogo(ma-)
loincloth shuka(ma-)
*long -refu
*long ago zamani
*look, look at ku-tazama
*look after ku-tunza
*look for ku-tafuta
look like ku-fanana na
*looking glass kioo(vi-)
*loose (to be) ku-legea
*loss hasara
*lost (to be) ku-potea
*loudly kwa sauti
*love upendo
*love ku-penda
*lovely -zuri
*low -fupi
*loyal -aminifu
*lubricant mafuta
*luck bahati
*luggage mizigo

machine mashine, mtambo(mi-)
*madam memsabu(ma-), bibi(ma-)
*magazine gazeti(ma-)
magician mchawi(wa-)
*mail barua (pl. agreements)
*main -kuu
mainland bara
*maize grain mahindi
maize plants mihindi
*make ku-fanya
*make a bed ku-tandika kitanda
*make equal ku-sawazisha
*make sure ku-hakikisha
*malady ugonjwa
malaria ugonjwa wa mbu, homa ya

mbu, melerya
*male -a kiume
*man mwanamume (wanaume)
*manage to ku-weza
manager meneja
*mango (fruit) embe(ma-)
*mango tree mwembe(mi-)
manioc muhogo(mi-)
manure mbolea
*many -ingi
map ramani
*March Machi
*mark alama, ku-tia alama
*market soko(ma-)
marriage ndoa, arusi
*marry (man) ku-oa
*marry (woman) ku-olewa
*marry (priest) ku-oza
marsh bwawa(ma-)
marvel ajabu
*mason mwashi(wa-)
mast mlingoti(mi-)
*master bwana(ma-), mwalimu(wa-)
mat jamvi(ma-), mkeka (mi-)
*matchbox kiberiti(vi-)
*material (cloth) kitambaa(vi-)
*matter jambo (mambo)
mattress godoro(ma-)
*May Mei
*maybe labda
*me mimi, -ni-
*meal chakula(vy-)
*meaning maana
*means uwezo
*measure (device) kipimo(vi-)
*measure ku-pima
*meat nyama
*medicine dawa
*meet ku-kutana na
*meeting mkutano(mi-)
*member (club) mwanachama(wa-)
*men wanaume
*mend ku-tengeneza
*merchant tajiri(ma-)
*messenger tarishi(ma-)
*metal chuma(vy-)
*metre (metric) meta
*mid, middle -a katikati
*midnight saa sita usiku
*mile maili
*milk maziwa
*million milioni
*mind akıli
*mind ku-angalia, ku-tunza
never mind haidhuru
*I don't mind ni mamoja kwangu
*mine -yangu
*minister (church) mchungaji(wa-)
*minister (state) waziri(ma-)
*minus kasa, kasoro
*minute (time) dakika
miracle ajabu
*mirror kioo(vi-)
*miserable maskini
misfortune bahati mbaya
*misgiving shaka(ma-)

*mislay ku-poteza
*mislaid (to be) ku-potea
*miss ku-kosa
mist ukungu
mistake kosa(ma-)
*mistaken (to be) ku-kosa
*mistress of house Memsabu(ma-)
*mix ku-changanya
mixture mchanganyiko(mi-)
*moderation kiasi(vi-)
*modern -a kisasa
moisture majimaji
*Monday Jumatatu
*money pesa, fedha, hela
monkey tumbili, etc.
*month mwezi(mi-)
*moon mwezi(mi-)
*more (than) zaidi (ya)
*morning asubuhi
*Moslem Mwislamu(wa-)
*mosque msikiti(mi-)
*mosquito mbu
*mosquito net chandalua(vy-)
*mother mama
motor mota, injini
*motorcar motokaa
motorcycle pikipiki
*mount ku-panda
*mount, mountain mlima(mi-)
mouse panya
mouth kinywa(vi-)
*move ku-hama, ku-sogea
*movement mwendo(mi-)
*Mr. Bwana(ma-)
*much -ingi
*mud tope(ma-)
*mug kikombe(vi-)
muscle mshipa(mi-)
music muziki
*Muslim Mwislamu(wa-)
*must lazima
*my -angu

*nail (carpenter's) msumari(mi-)
nail, claw kucha(ma-)
*name jina(ma-)
namely yaani
narrate ku-simulia
*narrow -embamba
*nation taifa(ma-)
*native mwananchi(wa-), mwenyeji(wa-)
*natural -a kawaida
naturally bila shaka
*naughty -baya
*near, nearly karibu na
*necessary lazima, -a lazima
*necessity lazima
neck shingo
necktie tai
*need ku-hitaji; haja
needle sindano
neighbour jirani
*neither wala(+negative)
net(ting) wavu (nyavu)
*mosquito net chandalua(vy-)
*nevertheless lakini

309

*new -pya
*newcomer mgeni(wa-)
New Testament Agano Jipya
*news habari
*newspaper gazeti(ma-)
*nice -zuri
*nicely vizuri
*night usiku (pl. siku)
  all night usiku kucha
*nine tisa
*ninety tisini
  noise kelele
*noon adhuhuri
*nor wala (+negative)
*normal -a kawaida
*normally kwa kawaida
  north kaskazini
  nose pua
*not si, siyo
*not so sivyo
*not yet bado
*note (written) cheti
  notice tangazo(ma-)
  notify ku-julisha, ku-ambia
*nought sifuri
*now sasa
*nowadays siku hizi
*November Novemba
*number namba, hesabu
*nurse (child's) yaya

  obey ku-tii
*object kitu(vi-)
  objective shabaha
*obligation sharti, lazima
*obtain ku-pata
    *be obtainable ku-patikana
*occasionally pengine, mara kwa mara
*o'clock saa
  odour harufu
*of -a
*off katika, mbali
  offend ku-chukiza
*offer ku-toa
*office afisi
*office (government) boma(ma-)
  officer afisa
*offspring mwana(wa-)
*often mara nyingi
*oil mafuta
*October Oktoba
*old -a zamani
*old age uzee
*old person mzee(wa-)
*on juu ya, katika
*once mara moja tu
    at once mara moja
    once upon a time zamani, -a kale
*one -moja
    one by one -moja -moja
*onion kitunguu(vi-)
*only tu
*open wazi
*open ku-fungua
*opening nafasi, mlango(mi-)
*opportunity nafasi

  oppose ku-pinga
  option hiari
*or au, ama
*orange chungwa(ma-)
  orange tree mchungwa(mi-)
  order (command) amri
    *in order that ili
  origin asili
*originally mwanzoni
  ornament pambo(ma-)
  ostrich mbuni
*other(s) -ingine
    *the other day juzijuzi
*ounce aunsi
*our(s) -etu
*out (of) nje (ya)
  outcome tokeo(ma-)
*outdo ku-shinda
  outnumber ku-zidi
*outside nje
*oven jiko
*over juu(ya), zaidi
*over again tena
    *be over ku-baki
*overcome ku-shinda
  overturn ku-pindua, ku-pinduka
  owe ku-wa na deni
*owing to kwa sababu ya
  owl bundi(ma-)
*owner mwenyewe(wa-)
*ox ng'ombe (maksai)

*pace hatua
*package, packet bahasha
  padlock kufuli
*page (of book) ukurasa (kurasa)
*pail ndoo
  pain maumivu
    *be painful ku-uma
*paint rangi
*pants (trousers) suruali
*paper karatasi
    *newspaper gazeti(ma-)
*paraffin mafuta ya taa
*parcel bahasha, paketi
  parent mzazi(wa-)
*parliament bunge(ma-)
*parson mchungaji(wa-)
*part sehemu, kipande(vi-)
*particularly hasa
*pass ku-pita
*past -a zamani
    *go past ku-pita
*pastor mchungaji(wa-)
*patch kiraka(vi-)
*path njia
*patient mgonjwa(wa-)
*pawpaw papai(ma-)
*pawpaw tree mpapai(mi-)
*pay mshahara(mi-)
*pay ku-lipa
  peace amani, salama
  peak kilele(vi-)
*peasant mkulima(wa-)
  peel ganda(ma-)
  peel ku-menya

*pen kalamu (ya wino)
penalty adhabu, malipo
*pencil kalamu (ya risasi)
*people watu
*pepper pilipili
*per kwa
perforate ku-toboa
*perhaps labda
*peril hatari
*period muda(mi-), wakati
*permission ruhusa, ruksa
permit cheti cha ruhusa
*perpetually daima
*person mtu(wa-)
perspiration jasho
*pest dudu(ma-)
petrol petroli
photograph picha
piano kinanda(vi-)
pick ku-chuma
pick (axe) sululu
*pick out ku-chagua
*pick up ku-okota
picture picha
*piece kipande(vi-)
*pierce ku-choma
pig nguruwe
pigeon njiwa
*pill kidonge(vi-)
pillar nguzo
*pillow mto(mi-)
pillow-case foronya
pin pini
*pineapple nanasi(ma-)
*pink -ekundu -eupe
*pint painti, kibaba(vi-)
*pipe (smoker's) kiko(vi-)
pipe (plumber's) bomba(ma-)
pistol bastola
pit shimo(ma-)
*pitch kiwanja(vi-)
*pitch a tent ku-piga hema
*place mahali
*place ku-weka, ku-tia
plain (topographical) tambarare
*plan ramani, shauri(ma-), mpango(mi-)
*plank ubao (mbao)
*plant mmea(mi-)
*plant ku-panda
*plantation shamba(ma-)
plaster lipu
*plate sahani
*play ku-cheza
player mchezaji(wa-)
*pleasant -tamu, -zuri
*pleasantness utamu, uzuri
*please tafadhali
*pleasure furaha, raha
*plenty wingi, tele
*plot (ground) kiwanja(vi-)
*plough ku-lima
*pocket mfuko(mi-)
pod ganda(ma-)
*point ncha
*point out ku-onyesha
poison sumu

*pole mti(mi-), nguzo, mlingoti(mi-)
police polisi
*policeman askari (polisi)
*polish dawa
politics siasa
polite -enye adabu
politeness adabu, heshima
*poor maskini
pork nyama ya nguruwe
*porridge ugali
porter mpagazi(wa-)
*portion sehemu, kipande(vi-)
*Portugal Ureno
*possess ku-wa na
*possession mali
*be possible ku-wezekana
*possibly labda
post (pillar) nguzo
post (G.P.O.) posta
postage ada ya posta
postmark chapa ya posta
poster tangazo(ma-)
*pot chombo(vy-), chungu
*potato kiazi(vi-)
*pouch mfuko(mi-)
*poultry kuku
*pound (lb.) ratili
*pound (£) paundi
pour ku-mimina
*pour away ku-mwaga
*poverty umaskini
powder unga
*power nguvu
powerful -enye nguvu
praise sifa, ku-sifu
*pray ku-omba
prayer sala
preach ku-hubiri
*precede ku-tangulia
*preferable afadhali, bora
pregnancy mimba
pregnant (to be) ku-wa na mimba
*present (gift) zawadi
president rais
*pressure lamp karabai
*pretty -zuri
*prevent ku-zuia
*price bei
*prick ku-choma
*prickle mwiba(mi-)
priest kasisi(ma-)
Prime Minister Waziri mkuu
*print chapa, ku-piga chapa
*prior to kabla ya
prison jela, gereza(ma-)
prisoner mfungwa(wa-)
*prize zawadi
*probably labda
*proceed ku-endelea
proclaim ku-tangaza
*procure ku-pata
proficient -stadi
*profit faida
progress maendeleo
*progress ku-endelea
promise ahadi, ku-ahidi

311

*properly vizuri, sawasawa
*property mali
*proportion sehemu
prosecute ku-shtaki
*prosper ku-sitawi
*protect ku-linda
*provisions vyakula
psalm zaburi
public, the watu
public house hoteli
*pull ku-vuta
*pull out ku-ng'oa
pump bomba(ma-)
pumpkin boga(ma-)
*punctual (to be) ku-wahi
punishment adhabu
*pupil mwanafunzi(wa-)
*purchase ku-nunua
*pure safi, -tupu
*purity usafi
*purpose kusudi
    *on purpose kwa kusudi
pus usaha
*push ku-sukuma
*put ku-weka, ku-tia
*put out ku-toa
*put out (extinguish) ku-zima
python chatu

*quantity kiasi(vi-)
*quarrel ugomvi
*quarter (¼) robo
queen malkia
*query ku-uliza
*question ku-uliza
*question swali(ma-)
*queue mstari(mi-)
*Quick! Upesi!
*quickly kwa haraka, upesi
*quiet (to be) ku-nyamaza
*quite kidogo

rabbit sungura
radio redio
rail reli
*rain mvua, ku-nyesha mvua
*raise ku-inua
rat panya
*rather kidogo
rations posho
raw -bichi
*razor wembe(ny-)
*read ku-soma
reading somo(ma-)
*ready tayari
*really kweli, hasa
*reap ku-vuna
*rear (back) nyuma
*reason sababu, maana
receipt stakabadhi
*receive ku-pokea, ku-pewa
recite ku-simulia
`recognize ku-tambua
recommend ku-sifu
*red -ekundu

*reduce ku-pungu(z)a
*reference cheti(vy-)
refresh ku-burudisha
*refrigerator barafu
*refuse ku-kataa
*refuse takataka
*region mkoa(mi-), wilaya
*regular -a kawaida
*reject ku-kataa
*rejoice ku-furahi
*relation jamaa, ndugu
religion dini
rely on ku-tegemea
*remain ku-baki, ku-kaa
*remember ku-kumbuka
*remove ku-ondoa
*rent ku-panga, ku-kodisha
*rent kodi
*repair ku-tengeneza
*reply ku-jibu, jibu(ma-)
republic jamhuri
*request ku-omba, ombi(ma-)
rescue ku-okoa
*reserve akiba
*rest ku-pumzika
restaurant hoteli
result matokeo
*retain ku-shika
*return ku-rudi
revolver bastola
*rhinoceros kifaru(vi-)
rib ubavu(mbavu)
rice (paddy) mpunga(mi-)
rice (husked) mchele(mi-)
*rice (cooked) wali
*rich person tajiri(ma-)
*riches utajiri, mali
*rifle bunduki
*right kulia, -a kulia
    *just right sawasawa
ring ku-piga kengele
*rip ku-pasua
ripe -bivu
*ripen ku-iva
*river mto(mi-)
*road barabara, njia
roast ku-oka, ku-choma
*robber mwizi(wezi)
roof mapaa
*room chumba(vy-)
*root mzizi(mi-)
*rope kamba
*rot ku-oza
*rotten -bovu
*rottenness ubovu
round duara, mviringo
    *go round ku-zunguka
*route njia
*row (line) mstari(mi-)
*rubber mpira(mi-)
*rubbish takataka
*rug zulia(ma-)
*ruler (political) mtawala(wa-)
ruler (foot-rule) rula
*run ku-kimbia
rust kutu

312

sack gunia(ma-)
*safe salama
safety usalama
saint mtakatifu(wa-)
salad saladi
*salary mshahara(mi-)
sale mnada(mi-)
saliva mate
*salt chumvi
salvation wokovu
*same, just the vilevile, sawa na
sample mfano(mi-)
sand mchanga(mi-)
Satan Shetani
*satisfactory -a kufaa
*satisfied with food ku-shiba
*Saturday Jumamosi
sauce mchuzi(mi-)
saucepan sufuria
*saucer kisahani(vi-)
save ku-okoa
saw msumeno(mi-)
*saw ku-pasua
*say ku-sema
scales (weighing) mizani
*scarcity uchache
school shule, skuli, chuo(vy-)
scissors mkasi(mi-) (use sing.)
scorpion nge
screw skrubu
*scrub floor ku-piga deki
*sea bahari
*search ku-tafuta
*season wakati
*seat kiti(vi-)
*second (time) nukta, sekondi
*second (2nd) -a pili
*secret siri, -a siri
*see ku-ona
*seed mbegu
seedling mche(mi-)
*seek ku-tafuta
*seize ku-kamata
*self -enjewe, -ji-, peke y-
*sell ku-uza
*send ku-peleka, ku-tuma
*send back ku-rudisha
*sense akili
*separate mbalimbali
*September Septemba
*servant mtumishi(wa-)
settlers masetla
*seven saba
*seventy sabini
*severe -kali
*sew ku-shona
*shade kivuli(vi-)
*shark papa
*sharp -kali
*sharpness ukali
sharpen (blade) ku-noa
sharpen (pencil) ku-chonga
*shave ku-nyoa
*she yeye, a-
shears mkasi mkubwa
*shed kibanda(vi-)

sheep kondoo
sheet shuka
*sheet (paper) karatasi
*shepherd mchungaji(wa-)
shield ngao
*shilling shilingi
shine ku-ng'aa
ship meli
*shirt shati
*shoe kiatu(vi-)
*shop duka(ma-)
*short -fupi
*shortness ufupi
*shorts kaptula (use in sing.)
shout ku-piga kelele
*show ku-onyesha
*shrink ku-rudi
*shut ku-funga
*shut off ku-ziba
*sick person mgonjwa(wa-)
*sick (to be) (vomit) ku-tapika
*sickness ugonjwa(ma-)
*side upande (pande)
*at side of kando ya
sieve chekecheke
*sign alama
*sign ku-tia sahihi
signature sahihi
*silver fedha
*similarly vilevile
sin dhambi
*since tangu
*sing ku-imba
*singly -moja -moja
*Sir Bwana(ma-)
sisal katani
sisal plant mkonge(mi-)
*sister dada
*sit ku-kaa, ku-keti
*six sita
*sixty sitini
*size ukubwa
skid ku-teleza
*skilled person fundi(ma-)
skin (animal) ngozi
skin (fruit, etc.) ganda(ma-)
sky mbingu
*slack (to be) ku-legea
slap ku-piga kofi
*slash ku-fyeka
*slaughter ku-chinja
*sleep ku-lala (usingizi)
*sleep usingizi
*slender -embamba
*slice kipande(vi-)
slide ku-teleza
*slightly kidogo
*slit ku-pasua
*slope mtelemko(mi-)
*slowly polepole
*small -dogo
smallpox ndui
smear ku-paka
*smell bad ku-nuka
*smell good ku-nukia
smell harufu (noun)

313

smell ku-sikia harufu, ku-nusa
smile ku-chekelea
*smoke moshi(mi-)
*smooth laini
*snake nyoka
sneeze ku-piga chafya
*sniff, smell at ku-nusa
snow theluji
*so hivi, kwa hiyo, basi
*so that ili
*soap sabuni
*socialism ujamaa
*society chama(vy-)
*soft laini
*soften ku-lainisha
*soil (earth) udongo, ardhi
*soldier askari
*some (part of whole) -ingine
*someone or other fulani
*something or other fulani
*sometimes pengine
*son mwana(wa-)
song wimbo (nyimbo)
*soon mapema, sasa hivi
*sore kidonda(vi-)
*sore (to be) ku-uma
*sorry (to be) ku-sikitika
*sort namna, aina
   *what sort? gani?
*soul roho
*sound (noise) sauti, kelele
*sound (whole) -zima
soup supu
sour -chungu
source asili
south kusini
*sow ku-panda
*space (room) nafasi
spanner spena, kolea
*spare time nafasi
*speak ku-sema
*spear mkuki(mi-)
species aina
specimen mfano(mi-)
spectacles miwani
speech usemi, hotuba
*speed mwendo(mi-)
*speedily kwa haraka
spider buibui
*spirit roho
spit ku-tema mate
*split ku-pasua
*spoil ku-haribu
*spoon kijiko(vi-)
*spray ku-piga dawa, ku-nyunyiza
spread about ku-enea
*spread out ku-tandika
spring (water) chemchemi
sprout ku-chipuka
*stab ku-choma
*stain alama
*staircase daraja(ma-)
*stand ku-simama
star nyota
*start ku-anza
starvation njaa

*state (circumstance) hali
station stesheni
*stay ku-kaa
*steal ku-iba
*steel chuma(vy-)
*steep -kali
*step hatua
*steps daraja(ma-)
*still (going on) bado, hata sasa
*still (but) lakini
*sting ku-uma
*stink ku-nuka
stir ku-koroga
stitch ku-shona
*stock akiba
stockings soksi ndefu
stomach tumbo(ma-)
*stone jiwe (mawe)
*stool kiti(vi-)
*stop (halt) ku-simama
*stop (leave off) ku-acha
*stop up ku-ziba
*stopper kizibo(vi-)
*store akiba
storm dhoruba
story hadithi
straighten ku-nyosha
*strange -geni
*strangeness ugeni
*stranger mgeni(wa-)
*strength nguvu
*strict -kali
*string uzi(ny-), kamba
*stuck (to get) ku-kwama
*student mwanafunzi(wa-)
*study ku-soma, ku-jifunza
*subject (thing) kitu(vi-)
*subordinate -a chini
subscription malipo
*subtract ku-toa, kasoro
*succeed ku-faulu
*sudden ghafula, -a ghafula
*suddenly kwa ghafula
sue ku-dai
*suffice ku-tosha (quantity)
*sufficient (to be) ku-tosha
*sugar sukari
sugar-cane muwa (miwa)
*suicide ku-jiua
*suit ku-faa
suit suti
*suitable -a kufaa
*suitcase sanduku(ma-)
sum jumla, hesabu
summit kilele(vi-)
*summon ku-ita
*sun jua(ma-)
*Sunday Jumapili
*sunshine jua(ma-)
*superior bora
supper chakula cha jioni
*sure (to make) ku-hakikisha
surname jina la ukoo
*Swahili Kiswahili
swamp bwawa(ma-)
sweat jasho, ku-toa jasho

*sweep ku-fagia
*sweet -tamu
*sweetness utamu
swell ku-vimba
*swift -epesi
switch swichi

*table meza
*tablet kidonge(vi-)
*tail mkia(mi-)
*take ku-chukua
*take away ku-ondoa
*take care ku-angalia
*take care of ku-tunza
take leave ku-aga
*take out ku-toa
*take to ku-peleka
*talk ku-ongea, ku-zungumza
*tall -refu
tar lami
*tarpaulin chandalua(vy-)
*tax kodi
*tea chai
teapot birika ya chai
*teach ku-fundisha
*teacher mwalimu(wa-)
*tear ku-pasua
*teaspoon kijiko(vi-)
*telegram simu
*telephone simu
*tell ku-ambia
*ten kumi
*tend ku-tunza
*tent hema
*termite mchwa
*test ku-jaribu, ku-pima
test jaribio(ma-)
thank ku-shukuru
thankfulness shukurani
*thanks, thank you! Asante!
*that -le
*that (he said that . . .) kwamba
thatch ku-ezeka
*their(s) -ao
*them wao, -wa-
*then kisha, halafu
*there pale
*thereabouts kule
*therefore kwa hiyo/kwa sababu hii
*therein mle
*these hawa, hizi, etc.
*they wao, wa-
*thick -nene
*thickness unene
*thief mwizi(wezi)
*thin -embamba
*thing kitu(vi-)
*think ku-fikiri, ku-dhani, ku-ona
*third -a tatu
*third (⅓) theluthi
thirst kiu(vi-)
*thirty thelathini
*this huyu, hii, etc.
*thorn mwiba(mi-)
*those wale, zile, etc.
though ingawa

thought wazo(ma-)
*thousand elfu
*thread uzi(ny-)
*three -tatu
*throw ku-tupa
*Thursday Alhamisi
*thus hivi, hivyo
tick kupe, papasi
ticket tikiti
tie (neck) tai
*tie ku-funga
*tighten ku-kaza
*till ku-lima
*till (until) mpaka, hata
*time saa, wakati, nafasi
*time (to be in) ku-wahi
*times mara
tin kopo, mkebe(mi-), bati(ma-)
*tin (4-gallon) debe(ma-)
tin-opener kifungua-kopo(vi-)
*tired (to be) ku-choka
*to kwa
toast tosti
*toast ku-choma
tobacco tumbako
*today leo
*toe kidole (cha mguu)
*together pamoja na
*toilet choo(vy-)
*tomato nyanya
tomb kaburi(ma-)
*tomorrow kesho
    *day after tomorrow kesho kutwa
*ton tani
*tongue ulimi (ndimi)
*too pia, vilevile
*tool chombo(vy-)
*tooth jino (meno)
toothbrush mswaki(mi-)
tortoise kobe(ma-)
total jumla
*touch ku-gusa
*tough -gumu
*tow ku-vuta
*towards kwenda kwa
*towel kitambaa(vi-)
tower mnara(mi-)
*town mji(mi-)
*toy mchezo(mi-)
tractor trekta(ma-)
trade biashara
*trade-mark chapa
train gari la moshi, mashine
transfer ku-hamisha
translate ku-tafsiri
transplant ku-pandikiza
trap mtego(mi-)
*trash takataka
*travel ku-safiiri
traveller msafiri(wa-)
tread ku-kanyaga
*tree mti(mi-)
tribe kabila(ma-)
*trouble shida, matata
*trouble ku-sumbua
*trousers surali (use singular)

315

*true kweli, -a kweli
*truly kwa kweli
*trustworthy -aminifu
*truth kweli
*truthfully kwa kweli
*try ku-jaribu
*try luck ku-bahatisha
tsetse fly mbung'o, ndorobo
*Tuesday Jumanne
*tumbler bilauri, glasi
*turn (bout) zamu
*turn ku-geuza, ku-geuka
*turn over ku-pindua
tusk pembe
*twenty ishirini
*two -wili, mbili
*typewriter tapuraita
tyre mpira wa gurudumu

*Uganda Uganda
*ulcer kidonda(vi-)
*umbrella mwavuli(mi-)
*under chini ya
*underneath chini ya
*understand ku-fahamu
*undo ku-fungua
*undress ku-vua nguo
*unfasten ku-fungua
*unity umoja
unless isipokuwa
*unload ku-pakua
*unpack ku-pakua
unripe -bichi
*untie ku-fungua
*until mpaka
*up, upon juu, juu ya
*uproot ku-ng'oa
*up to mpaka
*us sisi, -tu-
*use ku-tumia
*use, to be of ku-faa
*useless bure
*usual -a kawaida
*usually kwa kawaida
*utensil chombo(vy-)
*utter ku-lia

*vacant -tupu
*valley bonde(ma-)
value thamani
*vegetables mboga
*vegetation mimea
*vehicle gari(ma-)
vein mshipa wa damu
*verandah baraza(ma-)
vertical wima
*very sana
*vessel chombo(vy-)
*vexed (to be) ku-kasirika
*vile -baya
*village kijiji(vi-)
*visible ku-onekana
*visitor mgeni(wa-)
*voice sauti
*volunteer ku-jitolea
*vomit ku-tapika

*wage mshahara(mi-)
*wait ku-ngoja
*wake up ku-amka, ku-amsha
*walk ku-tembea
*wall ukuta (kuta)
*want ku-taka
*war(fare) vita
warn ku-onya
warning onyo(ma-)
wash ku-osha
*wash clothes ku-fua nguo
*wash hands ku-nawa
wash up ku-safisha vyombo
*waste ku-mwaga
*watch saa
*watch over ku-angalia
*water maji
*water-closet (W.C.) choo(vy-)
*water hole kisima(vi-)
wax nta
*way njia
  *to be on one's way kwenda z-
*we sisi, tu-
*wealth mali, utajiri
*wear clothes ku-vaa
wear out ku-chakaa
wedding arusi, ndoa
*Wednesday Jumatano
*week wiki, juma(ma-)
*weep ku-lia(machozi)
*weigh ku-pima (uzito)
*weight uzito
*well (water) kisima(vi-)
*well (good) -zima, vizuri
*Well! Basi!
*Well? Je?
  *get well ku-pona
west magharibi
wet majimaji
*what? nini?
*what for? kwa nini?
*what sort? gani?
*wheat ngano
*when? lini?
*when -po-
*where? wapi?
*whether kama
*which? -pi?
*whip kiboko(vi-)
*whistle filimbi
*white -eupe
white ants mchwa
*white person Mzungu(wa-)
whitewash chokaa
*who? nani?
*who, which amba-
*whole -zima, kamili
*why? kwa nini? mbona?
*wide -pana
widen ku-panua
*width upana
*wife mke(wa-)
*wild -a mwitu, -a porini
*wind upepo (pepo)
*window dirisha(ma-)
*wipe ku-futa, ku-pangusa

witchcraft uchawi
*with na, kwa, pamoja na, -enye
*within ndani ya, katika
*without bila
*without (to be) ku-kosa
*woman mwanamke (wanawake)
*wood mti(mi-), mbao, msitu(mi-)
word meno(ma-)
*work kazi, ku-fanya kazi
*work metal ku-fua chuma
*workshop kiwanda(vi-)
world ulimwengu, dunia
worm mchango(mi-)
wound (sore) jeraha
wring ku-kamua
*wrinkle ku-kunja
*write ku-andika
writer mwandishi(wa-)
*wrong ubaya
*wrong (to be) ku-kosa, ku-kosea
*wrong (to do) ku-kosa

*yard (3 ft.) yadi
*yard, courtyard ua(nyua)
*year mwaka(mi-)
*yes (see 'indeed')
  'I agree' naam!
*yesterday jana
*yet lakini
  *not yet bado
*you (sing.) wewe, u-, -ku-
*you (plur.) ninyi, m-, -wa-
  young -changa
*your (sing.) -ako
*your (plur.) -enu
*youth kijana(vi-)

*Zanzibar Unguja
*zeal bidii
  zebra punda milia
*zero sifuri